About the Author

John Lewis-Stempel is the father of two. He lives with his wife and children on a small-holding in Herefordshire. Under a pen name he has edited and written numerous previous anthologies and books.

FATHERHOOD
AN ANTHOLOGY

Edited and introduced by
John Lewis-Stempel

POCKET
BOOKS

LONDON · SYDNEY · NEW YORK · TOKYO · SINGAPORE · TORONTO

First published in Great Britain by Simon & Schuster UK Ltd, 2001
This edition first published by Pocket Books, 2002
An imprint of Simon & Schuster UK Ltd
A Viacom Company

1 3 5 7 9 10 8 6 4 2

Simon & Schuster UK Ltd
Africa House
64–78 Kingsway
London WC2B 6AH

www.simonsays.co.uk

Simon & Schuster Australia
Sydney

A CIP catalogue record for this book is available from the
British Library.

ISBN 0-7434-0871-3

Typeset by Palimpsest Book Production Limited,
Polmont, Stirlingshire
Printed and bound in Great Britain by
Bookmarque Ltd, Croydon, Surrey

For my wife and children, without whom I would
never have had the honour of being a father
And for my father, too
Thank you

Contents

Part 2

Fathers and Sons   41

Part 5

Experience   155

Part 6

Introduction

Fatherhood: ME . . . 1. The relation of a father to a child;
paternity. Also *fig.* +2.
Authority of or as of a father – 1690
The Oxford English Dictionary

I should declare an interest. Seven years ago I watched my son being born. He was, to borrow a phrase of Laurie Lee's, 'an ordinary miracle', but as I gazed in near-religious wonder at that blue-eyed boy I realised many brilliant things, not least that he wasn't the only thing born in that moment. I had become a Father. Out of the old me, fallen like a husk on the floor of the operating theatre, stepped a new me, a pater, a daddy, a Father, a man with awesome responsibility, the care – with my partner, soon to become my wife (we got married in church, very grown-uply) – of this tiny, precious parcel of humanity. For ever.

My head also filled with a grateful image of my own father, whose discarded Christmas-present underpants I was wearing as a lucky charm (no, really), for I had suddenly, in the pitiful music of an infant's cry, become what he had always been to me. Dad.

And so is the mantle of fatherhood passed down the ages.

The problems began when we got home from the hospital. For I hadn't the faintest idea of what being a father actually meant. Or, what a father was actually required to do. There was a vague thirtysomething notion of being emotionally more hands-on than my own father (though, in truth he was a good dad, and even raised me alone for a period of my early childhood) but not much else. It took me some time to realise that my personal bafflement was not really personal at all.

This was 1994 and society had long before lost the plot on fathers. Newspapers and government castigated 'deadbeat dads', 'new dads' were the advertisers' darlings, some dads had given up the rat race to become SAHDs (stay-at-home-dads, with their spouses earning the family mortgage), certain influential psychologists promoted androgynous parenting, while numerous radical feminists suggested that fathers were not only unnecessary but a total, utter hindrance to a child's development. And lurking under the mixed messages was a devastating social development: the nuclear family had fallen apart and fathers were lost in the wreckage. By 1994, divorce, and birth outside marriage, meant that nearly one in five British children was going to sleep at night without their biological father in the home.

Four years on, my own experience of fatherhood was only confirmed by the arrival of an unfeasibly lovely daughter (the wonder of it all never diminishes), while the whatistobedone-withdad? din outside only loudened. To someone who is a writer and anthologist by trade, an anthology of paternity in all its diversity seemed timely. But to be honest my motives were private. I believed that, if I could trawl through as many sources on fatherhood as I could find, from ancient Greek plays to Freudian psychology, from Russian literature to Bob Dylan, from poetry to *The Simpsons*, from newspaper reports to Groucho Marx, I myself might glean some clues as to my job as father. And then pass the clues on. Because I'm a believer in fatherhood. You might as well know that now.

So, what follows is a celebration of fatherhood, but also a revelation. It shows, I hope, what fatherhood is like and why it is like it is. It's a sort of literary toolkit for fathers and anybody who wants to understand the mystery of his or her own father (because everybody has a father, be he good or bad, close or never known). There's nothing new under the paternal sun; every fatherly deed, thought or doubt has been expressed by someone somewhere. It helps to know it and to read it, so as to understand it, even fix it. Dad – unwarrantedly chastised your so-small son? Then read Coventry Patmore's Victorian poem 'The Toys'. Feel like announcing the joyous news of your child's birth from the rooftops? Of course you do, just like Hector in Homer's *Iliad*. Realised that in becoming a father your ambition has dipped? Francis Bacon was writing about just that in 1601.

1601. Homer's Ancient Greece. The Victorian era. The past speaks clearly about fatherhood for anyone wishing to hear it. Paternal affection and care is not a modern invention; it's as old as man himself. One reason why is reported in *The Times* of 6 January 2000 (see page 11); on becoming fathers, men undergo a hormonal change (testosterone levels crash) which makes them protective and caring of their offspring. So do nearly all animals. If paternal affection is a transcendent natural truth, fatherhood is nonetheless largely socially conditioned. And until the 1800s, no one doubted that a man's place was in the family (childcare manuals of the 1700s – yes, they had them even then – were invariably addressed to the father), but then came the Industrial Revolution and its ravening factories. Work went out of the home, and with it went father. He couldn't be in two places at once. Separated from the family hearth, Dad became a more distant figure, and probably more disciplinarian. Unable to guide children by the example of living and working alongside them, he relied on coercion to assert his authority. The Victorian Sunday pater was born, depicted in all his spanking infamy in Samuel Butler's *The Way of All Flesh*. And yet it is clear from Patmore and a thousand Victorian fathers' letters that many Victorian men cherished their children and wished a more companionate relationship with them. The ebb of 'progress' was against them.

Father's lot has improved little since. He has, valiant individual efforts aside, been pushed to the margin of the magic family circle, assigned to the sole role of breadwinner. By the 1980s even that role had been denied him, lost to unemployment and the expansion of the female labour force. With no clear role in view, it is small wonder that many men, after kindly donating their sperm, fail to pick up the gauntlet of fatherhood. As the poet Les Murray puts it, 'Becoming a father, that is no/Achievement. Being one is, though.'

Because, let's face it, fatherhood is a challenge. It's the worst job in the world. There's no pay, no job description, no training, no medals, the hours are endless and you never, ever, retire. I still phone *my* father (75) for advice and worry him silly ('Drive carefully . . . ring us when you get home'). It is also, alongside motherhood, the best job in the world; the raising and care of another human being. And the most important. Here's why. Children with a father on hand are more likely to do well at school, be caring as an adult, be happier; they are less likely than the fatherless to be delinquent, to rape (if male), become pregnant as a teenager, be poor, go to prison, murder, have emotional problems, commit suicide. They are even less likely to smoke.

No, not all fathers are perfect. There are plenty of ogres in

'The Sins of the Father'. But in general the world is better for having fatherhood in it. (Those who wish to serve as fathers, incidentally, will find advice in this book from Jean-Jacques Rousseau, *Esquire* magazine, Bill Cosby, Shakespeare, the National Fatherhood Initiative, and scores more.)

And for those who do serve as fathers the pleasures are great. The smiling upturned face of your child . . . well, there's nothing to compare to that.

It's as good as it gets.

1

A Father is Born

Letter to Daniel

Fergal Keane, 1996

My dear son, it is six o'clock in the morning on the island of Hong Kong. You are asleep cradled in my left arm and I am learning the art of one-handed typing. Your mother, more tired yet more happy than I've ever known her, is sound asleep in the room next door and there is soft quiet in our apartment.

Since you arrived, days have melted into night and back again and we are learning a new grammar, a long sentence whose punctuation marks are feeding and winding and nappy changing and these occasional moments of quiet.

When you're older we'll tell you that you were born in Britain's last Asian colony in the lunar year of the pig and that when we brought you home, the staff of our apartment block gathered to wish you well. 'It's a boy, so lucky, so lucky. We Chinese love boys,' they told us. One man said you were the first baby to be born in the block in the year of the pig. This, he told us, was good Feng Shui, in other words a positive sign for the building and everyone who lived there.

Naturally your mother and I were only too happy to believe that. We had wanted you and waited for you, imagined you and dreamed about you and now that you are here no dream can do justice to you. Outside the window, below us on the harbour, the ferries are ploughing back and forth to Kowloon. Millions are already up and moving about and the sun is slanting through the tower blocks and out on to the flat silver waters of the South China Sea. I can see the contrail of a jet over Lamma Island and, somewhere out there, the last stars flickering towards the other side of the world.

We have called you Daniel Patrick but I've been told by my Chinese friends that you should have a Chinese name as well and this glorious dawn sky makes me think we'll call you Son of the Eastern Star. So that later, when you and I are far from Asia, perhaps standing on a beach some evening, I can point at the sky and tell you of the Orient and the times and the people we knew there in the last years of the twentieth century.

Your coming has turned me upside down and inside out. So much that seemed essential to me has, in the past few days, taken on a different colour. Like many foreign correspondents I know, I have lived a life that, on occasion, has veered close to the edge: war zones, natural disasters, darkness in all its shapes and forms.

In a world of insecurity and ambition and ego, it's easy to be drawn in, to take chances with our lives, to believe that what we do and what people say about us is reason enough to gamble with death. Now, looking at your sleeping face, inches away from me, listening to your occasional sigh and gurgle. I wonder how I could have ever thought glory and prizes and praise were sweeter than life.

And it's also true that I am pained, perhaps haunted is a better word, by the memory, suddenly so vivid now, of each suffering child I have come across on my journeys. To tell you the truth, it's nearly too much to bear at this moment to even think of children being hurt and abused and killed. And yet looking at you, the images come flooding back. Ten-year-old Andi Mikail dying from napalm burns on a hillside in Eritrea, how his voice cried out, growing ever more faint when the wind blew dust on to his wounds. The two brothers, Domingo and Juste, in Menongue, southern Angola. Juste, two years old and blind, dying from malnutrition, being carried on seven-year-old Domingo's back. And Domingo's words to me. 'He was nice before, but now he has the hunger.'

Last October, in Afghanistan, when you were growing inside your mother, I met Sharja, aged twelve. Motherless, fatherless, guiding me through the grey ruins of her home; everything was gone, she told me. And I knew that, for all her tender years, she had learned more about loss than I would likely understand in a lifetime.

There is one last memory. Of Rwanda, and the churchyard of the parish of Nyarabuye where, in a ransacked classroom, I found a mother and her three young children huddled together where they'd been beaten to death. The children had died holding on to their mother, that instinct we all learn from birth and in one way or another cling to until we die.

Daniel, these memories explain some of the fierce protectiveness

I feel for you, the tenderness and the occasional moments of blind terror when I imagine anything happening to you. But there is something more, a story from long ago that I will tell you face to face, father to son, when you are older. It's a very personal story but it's part of the picture. It has to do with the long lines of blood and family, about our lives and how we can get lost in them and, if we're lucky, find our way out again into the sunlight.

It begins thirty-five years ago in a big city on a January morning with snow on the ground and a woman walking to hospital to have her first baby. She is in her early twenties and the city is still strange to her, bigger and noisier than the easy streets and gentle hills of her distant home. She's walking because there is no money and everything of value has been pawned to pay for the alcohol to which her husband has become addicted.

On the way, a taxi driver notices her sitting, exhausted and cold, in the doorway of a shop and he takes her to hospital for free. Later that day, she gives birth to a baby boy and, just as you are to me, he is the best thing she has ever seen. Her husband comes that night and weeps with joy when he sees his son. He is truly happy. Hungover, broke, but in his own way happy, for they were both young and in love with each other and their son.

But, Daniel, time had some bad surprises in store for them. The cancer of alcoholism ate away at the man and he lost his family. This was not something he meant to do or wanted to do, it just was. When you are older, my son, you will learn about how complicated life becomes, how we can lose our way and how people get hurt inside and out. By the time his son had grown up, the man lived away from the family, on his own in a one-roomed flat, living and dying for the bottle.

He died on the fifth of January, one day before the anniversary of his son's birth, all those years before in that snowbound city. But his son was too far away to hear his last words, his final breath, and all the things they might have wished to say to one another were left unspoken.

Yet now, Daniel, I must tell you that when you let out your first powerful cry in the delivery room of the Adventist Hospital and I became a father, I thought of your grandfather and, foolish though it may seem, hoped that in some way he could hear, across the infinity between the living and the dead, your proud statement of arrival. For if he could hear, he would recognise the distinct voice

of family, the sound of hope and new beginnings that you and all
your innocence and freshness have brought to the world.

⁓

To Ianthe

Percy Bysshe Shelley, 1792–1822

> I love thee, Baby! For thine own sweet sake;
> Those azure eyes, that faintly dimpled cheek,
> Thy tender frame, so eloquently weak,
> Love in the sternest heart of hate might wake;
> But more when o'er thy fitful slumber bending
> Thy mother folds thee to her wakeful heart,
> Whilst love and pity, in her glances bending,
> All that thy passive eyes can feel impart:
> More, when some feeble lineaments of her,
> Who bore thy weight beneath her spotless bosom,
> As with deep love I read thy face, recur! –
> More dear art thou, O fair and fragile blossom;
> Dearest when most thy tender traits express
> The image of thy mother's loveliness.

⁓

'I think I was reasonably shaken'

From Laurie Lee, *The Firstborn*, 1964

She was born in the autumn and was a late fall in my life, and
lay purple and dented like a little bruised plum, as though she'd
been lightly trodden in the grass and forgotten.

Then the nurse lifted her up and she came suddenly alive, her
bent legs kicking crabwise, and her first living gesture was a thin
wringing of the hands accompanied by a far-out Hebridean
lament.

This moment of meeting seemed to be a birthtime for both of
us; her first and my second life. Nothing, I knew, would be the
same again, and I think I was reasonably shaken. I peered intently
at her, looking for familiar signs, but she was convulsed as an

Aztec idol. Was this really my daughter, this purple concentration of anguish, this blind and protesting dwarf?

Then they handed her to me, stiff and howling, and I held her for the first time and kissed her, and she went still and quiet as though by instinctive guile, and I was instantly enslaved by her flattery of my powers.

⌒

The biological programming of fatherhood

News article in *The Times*, 6 January 2000

Men are biologically programmed to become soppy after their children are born. A study shows that hormone changes put fathers through a similar emotional rollercoaster to that experienced by mothers.

Levels of testosterone, the male sex hormone, crash by an average of a third just after a baby is born. The lower it goes, the more a father dotes on the newborn. The effects, reported in *New Scientist*, are thought to be an evolutionary device to create an emotional bond with mother and child and make men less likely to stray.

Recent studies show that most male birds, rats and some primates are primed for their young in this way, but Anne Storey, a researcher at Memorial Hospital, in St John's, Newfoundland, is the first to find the effect in human beings. Dr Storey analysed blood samples from 34 couples. Hormone changes in fathers were triggered even by watching videos of newborn babies.

⌒

The smell of you

From Peter Carey's 'Letter to Our Son', 1995

Outside the penumbra of our consciousness trolleys were wheeled. Sterile bags were cut open. The contractions did not stop, of course.

The obstetrician had not arrived. She was in a car, driving fast towards the hospital.

I heard a midwife say: 'Who can deliver in this position?' (It was still unusual, as I learned at that instant, for women to deliver their babies on all fours.)

Someone left the room. Someone entered. Your mother was pressing the gas mask so hard against her face it was making deep indentations on her skin. Her eyes bulged huge.

Someone said: 'Well get her, otherwise I'll have to deliver it myself.'

The door opened. Bushfire came in.

Bushfire was aboriginal. She was about fifty years old. She was compact and taciturn like a farmer. She had a face that folded in on itself and let out its feelings slowly, selectively. It was a face to trust, and trust especially at this moment when I looked up to see Bushfire coming through the door in a green gown. She came in a rush, her hands out to have gloves put on.

There was another contraction. I heard the latex snap around Bushfire's wrists. She said: 'There it is. I can see your baby's head.' It was you. The tip of you, the top of you. You were a new country, a planet, a star seen for the first time. I was not looking at Bushfire. I was looking at your mother. She was all alight with love and pain.

'Push,' said Bushfire.

Your mother pushed. It was you she was pushing, you that put that look of luminous love on her face, you that made the veins on her forehead bulge and her skin go red.

Then – it seems such a short time later – Bushfire said: 'Your baby's head is born.'

And then, so quickly in retrospect, but one can no more recall it accurately than one can recall exactly how one made love on a bed when the jacaranda petals were lying like jewels on the grass outside. Soon. Soon we heard you. Soon you slipped out of your mother. Soon you came slithering out not having hurt her, not even having grazed her. You slipped out, as slippery as a little fish, and we heard you cry. Your cry was so much lighter and thinner than I might have expected. I do not mean that it was weak or frail, but that your first cry had a timbre unlike anything I had expected. The joy we felt. Your mother and I kissed again, at that moment.

'My little baby,' she said. We were crying with happiness. 'My little baby.'

I turned to look. I saw you. Skin. Blue-white, shiny-wet.

I said: 'It's a boy.'

'Look at me,' your mother said, meaning: stay with me, be with me, the pain is not over yet, do not leave me now. I turned to her. I kissed her. I was crying, just crying with happiness that you were there.

The room you were born in was quiet, not full of noise and clattering. This is how we wanted it for you. So you could come into the world gently and that you should – as you were now – be put on to your mother's stomach. They wrapped you up. I said: 'Couldn't he feel his mother's skin?' They unwrapped you so you could have your skin against hers.

And there you were. It was you. You had a face, the face we had never known. You were so calm. You did not cry or fret. You had big eyes like your mother's. And yet when I looked at you first I saw not your mother and me, but your two grandfathers, your mother's father, my father; and, as my father, whom I loved a great deal, had died the year before, I was moved to see that here, in you, he was alive.

Look at the photographs in the album that we took at this time. Look at your mother and how alive she is, how clear her eyes are, how all the red pain has just slipped off her face and left the unmistakable visage of a young woman in love.

We bathed you in warm water and you accepted this gravely, swimming instinctively.

I held you (I think this must be before), and you were warm and slippery. You had not been bathed when I held you. The obstetrician gave you to me so she could examine your mother. She said: 'Here.'

I held you against me. I knew then that your mother would not die. I thought: 'It's fine, it's all right.' I held you against my breast. You smelt of love-making.

Being there

From figures presented to the Fatherhood Research
Group by Anne Wollett, 1985, and the records of the
Royal College of Midwives, 2000

Fathers at Birth	1940s	1950s	1960s	1970s	1980s	1990s
Mother wanted father to be present:	14.3%	38.9%	50.0%	73.1%	–	–
Father was present	none	8.5%	32.2%	64.0%	76.0%	92.1%

Soul man

From *The Rainbow* by D. H. Lawrence, 1915

FROM the first, the baby stirred in the young father a deep, strong
emotion he dared scarcely acknowledge, it was so strong and
came out of the dark of him. When he heard the child cry, a
terror possessed him, because of the answering echo from the
unfathomed distances in himself. Must he know in himself such
distances, perilous and imminent?

He had the infant in his arms, he walked backwards and
forwards troubled by the crying of his own flesh and blood. This
was his own fiesh and blood crying! His soul rose against the
voice suddenly breaking out from him, from the distances in him.

Sometimes in the night, the child cried and cried, when the
night was heavy and sleep oppressed him. And half asleep, he
stretched out his hand to put it over the baby's face to stop the
crying. But something arrested his hand: the very inhumanness
of the intolerable, continuous crying arrested him. It was so impersonal, without cause or object. Yet he echoed to it directly, his
soul answered its madness. It filled him with terror, almost with
frenzy.

He learned to acquiesce to this, to submit to the awful, oblit-
erated sources which were the origin of his living tissue. He was
not what he conceived himself to be! Then he was what he was,
unknown, potent, dark.

He became accustomed to the child, he knew how to lift and

balance the little body. The baby had a beautiful, rounded head that moved him passionately. He would have fought to the last drop to defend that exquisite, perfect round head.

He learned to know the little hands and feet, the strange, unseeing, golden-brown eyes, the mouth that opened only to cry, or to suck, or to show a queer, toothless laugh. He could almost understand even the dangling legs, which at first had created in him a feeling of aversion. They could kick in their queer little way, they had their own softness.

One evening, suddenly, he saw the tiny, living thing rolling naked in the mother's lap, and he was sick, it was so utterly helpless and vulnerable and extraneous; in a world of hard surfaces and varying altitudes, it lay vulnerable and naked at every point. Yet it was quite blithe. And yet, in its blind, awful crying, was there not the blind, far-off terror of its own vulnerable nakedness, the terror of being so utterly delivered over, helpless at every point. He could not bear to hear it crying. His heart strained and stood on guard against the whole universe.

~

High anxiety

James Boswell, 1740–95

Diary: Monday, 9 October 1775

My wife having been seized with her pains in the night, I got up about three o'clock, and between four and five Dr Young came. He and I sat upstairs mostly till between three and four, when, after we had dined, her labour became violent. I was full of expectation, and meditated curiously on the thought that it was already certain of what sex the child was, but that I could not have the least guess on which side the probability was. Miss Preston attended my wife close. Lady Preston came several times to inquire, but did not go into the room. I did not feel so much anxiety about my wife now as on former occasions, being better used to an inlying. Yet the danger was as great now as ever. I was easier from the same deception which affects a soldier who has escaped in several battles. She was very ill. Between seven and eight I went into the room. She was just delivered. I heard her say, 'God be thanked for whatever he sends.' I supposed then the child was a daughter. But she herself had not then seen it. Miss Preston said, 'Is it a daughter?' 'No,' said Mrs Forrest, the nurse-keeper, 'it's a son.' When I had seen the little man I said that I should now be so anxious that probably I should never again have an easy hour. I said to Dr Young with great seriousness, 'Doctor, Doctor, let no man set his heart upon anything in this world but land or heritable bonds; for he has no security that anything else will last as long as himself.' My anxiety subdued a flutter of joy which was in my breast.

⌐⌐

Serenade

Thomas Hood, 1799–1845

'Lullaby, oh lullaby!'
Thus I heard a father cry,
'Lullaby, oh, lullaby!
The brat will never shut an eye;
Hither come, some power divine!
Close his lids, or open mine!' . . .
'Lullaby, oh, lullaby!
Two such nights, and I shall die!
Lullaby, oh, lullaby!
He'll be bruised, and so shall I.
How can I from bedpost keep,
When I'm walking in my sleep?'

⌐⌐

From IVF to paternity

From 'Trying Times' by Charles Spencer, 1997

IVF is hellishly expensive, about £2000 a time, and several hundred quid more if a cost-conscious GP refuses to prescribe fertility drugs on the NHS as they sometimes, cruelly, do. A few months ago there was a news story about a woman who stole £20,000 from her employer but was spared a prison sentence when the judge, an unusually enlightened one, heard she had used the money to pay for test-tube baby treatment (it worked, I'm delighted to report). We could afford our treatments, just about, but I can't put my hand on my heart and say Nicki and I wouldn't have resorted to dishonesty if we'd been broke and had found an illegal opportunity of getting our hands on the cash.

The desperation of infertility is, I think, truly appreciated only by those who have been through the whole heartbreaking business. What's more, I feel like something of an impostor writing all this, because there is little doubt that women suffer far more than their men when they try and repeatedly fail to have a baby.

As someone who enjoys a gamble, I found the best way of handling the whole bizarre and ruinously expensive business was to imagine that IVF treatment was a form of roulette: a minimum stake of £2000 with the big pay-off of a child if your number came up. Even now, nineteen years after the birth of the first test-tube baby, Louise Brown, the odds are lousy. The average live-birth rate for IVF treatments in Britain in 1994–95 was 14.5 per cent. Some clinics managed almost 25 per cent: the worst managed less than 5 per cent. During our treatment we always thought our hospital had one of the highest rates of success, but I see from recently published data that last year it actually achieved only 9 per cent. IVF is big business and it was apparently not unknown in the past for clinics to massage their figures to attract punters to their high-stakes game.

For my wife, it was far harder to regard IVF dispassionately as a gamble against the odds. The fertility drugs, which I have a horrible suspicion come from human corpses, play merry havoc with the emotions as well as the hormones, and Nicki had to go to the doctor's each day for an injection like some helpless junkie. There were also regular, invasive ultrasound scans.

On the big day itself, however, when the woman's eggs are removed under anaesthetic, the onus is all on the chap. You have to produce your sperm on the hospital premises and the thought of humiliating failure in such desperate circumstances doesn't exactly set the libido racing. After producing endless samples over the years of treatment, I felt I could masturbate for England by now, but there were nevertheless some exceptionally dodgy moments.

On arrival at the hospital, while the woman gets enjoyably spaced-out on the pre-med, the man is dispatched to what I came to know as the wanking room. At our swanky hospital, it was got up to look like an anonymous four-star hotel room, complete with sofa, inoffensive modern art prints and expensive table lamps. I half expected to find a courtesy bowl of fruit and a mini-bar, and the latter would certainly have been most welcome. On one of the occasional tables a pile of well-thumbed soft-porn magazines is coyly placed. In one hand you clutch your little plastic pot, in the other . . . well, you can guess the rest. Ridiculously, for a room entirely devoted to masturbation, there was no lock on the door. The memory of a nurse bursting in, without knocking, while I was in mid-wank, still brings me out in a hot flush of embarrassment.

Two days later, if the eggs have been satisfactorily fertilised by the sperm after being mixed together by white-coated technicians in the lab, the tiny four-cell embryos are placed in the womb. On the fourth treatment we saw them, three in number, projected on to a wall with a magnifying epidiascope. Our doctor thought one of them looked suspect, so only two were actually used: the thought that those two amoeba-like blobs might one day become babies was almost unbearably moving.

After the embryos have been put into the womb, the agonising wait begins. Feverish hope alternates with a morbid conviction of failure, hour by hour, sometimes minute by minute. When it becomes clear that a treatment has failed – either because the woman's period starts, or following a pregnancy test at the hospital – the sense of desolation is indescribable. The emotional roller-coaster is so gruelling that both Nicki and I decided that we would make the fourth attempt our last – whatever the result. We simply couldn't take the pressure any more.

Nicki became increasingly convinced that it would be yet another failure. Oddly enough, seeing those strange, alien creatures on the wall of the hospital made her feel even more despairing. So near and yet so far. She decided that she wanted to be alone when the result came through to give her a chance to howl in peace, so I was packed off to France for a few days with a friend. I too was convinced of failure and got blind and maudlin drunk on the ferry and continued drinking deep into the night. The following day, horribly hungover, fearful and trembling, I phoned her from a Normandy seaside resort. She was officially pregnant, though the pregnancy would be precarious for the first three months. The hangover disappeared, just like that, and I tucked into a giant celebratory plate of *fruits de mer*.

In the early hours of 16 April 1993, Edward was born by caesarean section and I held him in my arms for the first time. What had once seemed like sinister science fiction now felt like nothing less than a miracle.

╭╴╮

Echo, homo

From a letter by Lafcadio Hearn, 1850–1904

Last night my child was born – a very strong boy, with large black eyes. If you ever become a father, I think the strangest and strongest sensation of your life will be hearing for the first time the thin cry of your own child. For a moment you have the strange feeling of being double; but there is something more, quite impossible to analyse – perhaps the echo in a man's heart of all the sensations felt by all the fathers and mothers of his race at a similar instant in the past. It is a very tender, but also a very ghostly feeling.

╭╴╮

To *father* is to be *human*

From Margaret Mead, *Male and Female*, 1949

Somewhere at the dawn of human history, some social invention was made under which males started nurturing females and their young. We have no reason to believe that the nurturing males had any knowledge of physical paternity, although it is quite possible that being fed was a reward meted out to the female who was not too fickle with her sexual favours. In every known human society, everywhere in the world, the young male learns that when he grows up, one of the things which he must do in order to be a full member of society is to provide food for some female and her young. Even in very simple societies, a few men may shy away from the responsibility, become tramps or ne'er-do-wells or misanthropists who live in the woods by themselves. In complex societies, a large number of men may escape the burden of feeding females and young by entering monasteries – and feeding each other – or by entering some profession that their society will classify as giving them a right to be fed, like the Army and the Navy, or the Buddhist orders of Burma. But in spite of such exceptions, every known human society rests firmly on the learned nurturing behaviour of men.

Frost at Midnight

Samuel Taylor Coleridge, 1798

The Frost performs its secret ministry,
Unhelped by any wind. The owlet's cry
Came loud – and hark, again! loud as before.
The inmates of my cottage, all at rest,
Have left me to that solitude, which suits
Abstruser musings: save that at my side
My cradled infant slumbers peacefully.
'Tis calm indeed! so calm, that it disturbs
And vexes meditation with its strange
And extreme silentness. Sea, hill, and wood,
This populous village! Sea, and hill, and wood,

With all the numberless goings on of life,
Inaudible as dreams! the thin blue flame
Lies on my low burnt fire, and quivers not;
Only that film, which fluttered on the grate,
Still flutters there, the sole unquiet thing.
Methinks, its motion in this hush of nature
Gives it dim sympathies with me who live,
Making it a companionable form,
Whose puny flaps and freaks the idling Spirit
By its own moods interprets, every where
Echo or mirror seeking of itself,
And makes a toy of Thought.

                                    But O! how oft,
How oft, at school, with most believing mind,
Presageful, have I gazed upon the bars,
To watch that fluttering *stranger*! and as oft
With unclosed lids, already had I dreamt
Of my sweet birth-place, and the old church-tower,
Whose bells, the poor man's only music, rang
From morn to evening, all the hot Fair-day,
So sweetly, that they stirred and haunted me
With a wild pleasure, falling on mine ear
Most like articulate sounds of things to come!
So gazed I, till the soothing things I dreamt
Lulled me to sleep, and sleep prolonged my dreams!
And so I brooded all the following morn,
Awed by the stern preceptor's face, mine eye
Fixed with mock study on my swimming book:
Save if the door half opened, and I snatched
A hasty glance, and still my heart leaped up,
For still I hoped to see the *stranger's* face,
Townsman, or aunt, or sister more beloved,
My play-mate when we both were clothed alike!

Dear Babe, that sleepest cradled by my side,
Whose gentle breathings, heard in this deep calm,
Fill up the interspersed vacancies
And momentary pauses of the thought!
My babe so beautiful! it thrills my heart
With tender gladness, thus to look at thee,
And think that thou shalt learn far other lore,
And in far other scenes! For I was reared

In the great city, pent 'mid cloisters dim,
And saw nought lovely but the sky and stars.
But *thou*, my babe! shalt wander like a breeze
By lakes and sandy shores, beneath the crags
Of ancient mountain, and beneath the clouds,
Which image in their bulk both lakes and shores
And mountain crags: so shalt thou see and hear
The lovely shapes and sounds intelligible
Of that eternal language, which thy God
Utters, who from eternity doth teach
Himself in all, and all things in himself.
Great universal Teacher! he shall mould
Thy spirit, and by giving make it ask.

Therefore all seasons shall be sweet to thee,
Whether the summer clothe the general earth
With greenness, or the redbreast sit and sing
Betwixt the tufts of snow on the bare branch
Of mossy apple-tree, while the nigh thatch
Smokes in the sun-thaw; whether the eave-drops fall
Heard only in the trances of the blast,
Or if the secret ministry of frost
Shall hang them up in silent icicles,
Quietly shining to the quiet Moon.

The Birthnight: To F.

Walter de la Mare, 1873–1956, written for
his daughter Florence

Dearest, it was a night
That in its darkness rocked Orion's stars;
A sighing wind ran faintly white
Along the willows, and the cedar boughs
Laid their wide hands in stealthy peace across
The starry silence of their antique moss:
No sound save rushing air
Cold, yet all sweet with Spring,
And in thy mother's arms, crouched weeping there,
Thou, lovely thing.

Lie still with thy daddy

Anonymous lullaby, from *Songs from the Nursery*,
1805

> Hush thee, my babby,
> Lie still with thy daddy,
> Thy mammy has gone to the mill,
> To grind thee some wheat
> To make thee some meat,
> Oh, my dear babby, lie still.

An affair of the heart

From Honoré de Balzac, *Old Goriot*, 1834

Some day you will know that a father is much happier in his
children's happiness than in his own. I cannot explain it to you:
it is a feeling in your body that spreads gladness through you.
In short, I live three times over. Shall I tell you something
strange? Well, when I became a father I understood God. He
is there complete in everything because creation sprang from
Him. It is just like that with me and my daughters. Only I love
my daughters more than God loves the world, for the world is
not as beautiful as God is, and my daughters are more beautiful than I.

Clenched in it was my heart

Hugo Williams, from 'What Shall We Do Now That
We Have Done Everything?', 1992

It wasn't so long ago really, 1966, and yet I was given the impression by St Mary's, Paddington, that I was the first father ever to
attend the birth of his child. I had a letter from our GP saying
I could be present if I wanted to and I put on my tweediest suit

and daddyest tie to combat the hospital bureaucracy. I was a
knight errant on some ill-defined mission to save his lady, though
from what I had only the vaguest idea.

As a father barely out of my teens, I was intoxicated by self-
importance. I might not be the star, but I was aware of having
a plum part in this traditional drama: prestige without pain. I
thought it would be easy for me to turn in a convincing performance without getting too involved. Mine would be a cameo role
with a certain amount of glory attached to it by association. I
would drink a lot, go unshaved for a day or two, become 'stubbly
with goodness'.

For my wife there were no such options available. When a
nurse came to shave her there was nothing I could do to save
her from defilement. The razor-blade packet had a little blue bird
printed on it and we seized on this with relief. Did the NHS have
a contract, we asked, with this obscure brand of blunt razor
blade? The nurse didn't answer. The blue bird was put away for
the scrapbook.

A little while later, when the agony began, Hermine asked me
to find one of these inadequate weapons so she could commit
suicide. My eyes must have been popping out of my head as I
caught my first glimpse of what was really going on here.

'The worst thing was if a nurse came in during a contraction',
she wrote afterwards. 'They didn't seem to understand the mental
effort one was making. They would start talking inanely, asking
me questions, so that I had to blurt out, *"I am having a contraction!"* I didn't want to alienate them, but if I didn't get them to
stop they would go on shouting at me and touching my stomach,
which became intolerable.'

She had already had one injection, which was supposed to be
enough. The Natural Childbirth was supposed to take care of
the rest, but it wasn't working. I should have sat tight, but I
was still doing everything I was told by Hermine in those days.
I ran all over the hospital, looking for a sister who would sign
a chit authorising a nurse to open a cabinet and give my wife
another jab.

I think of all those wasted evenings practising natural childbirth, my wife and I breathing heavily in and out while raising
our right arm and left leg. The idea was to learn to relax your
muscles independently so they didn't get tangled up in the 'natural'

birth process. The exercises were so excruciatingly boring we invariably ended up asleep.

'The injection came and I remember no more, till half waking in a new room with a new, lesser pain, I thought vaguely that I was on the lavatory and I began crying because I had given birth unknowingly.'

After all the trouble she'd been to, this is what it came to: I was there and she wasn't; I had seen someone coming out of someone and she hadn't. Whether she blames me for this I don't know. I blame myself.

Our daughter, meanwhile, was fast asleep herself, one little hand showing above the bedclothes. Clenched in it was my heart.

To My Son

George Gordon, Lord Byron, written in 1807

Those flaxen locks, those eyes of blue,
Bright as thy mother's in their hue;
Those rosy lips, whose dimples play
And smile to steal the heart away,
Recall a scene of former joy,
And touch thy father's heart, my Boy!

And thou canst lisp a father's name –
Ah, William, were thine own the same, –
No self-reproach – but, let me cease –
My care for thee shall purchase peace;
Thy mother's shade shall smile in joy,
And pardon all the past, my Boy!

Her lowly grave the turf has prest,
And thou hast known a stranger's breast;
Derision sneers upon thy birth,
And yields thee scarce a name on earth:
Yet shall not these one hope destroy, –
A Father's heart is thine, my Boy!

Why, let the world unfeeling frown,
Must I fond Nature's claims disown?

Ah, no – though moralists reprove,
I hail thee, dearest child of love,
Fair cherub, pledge of youth and joy –
A Father guards thy birth, my Boy!

Oh, 'twill be sweet in thee to trace,
Ere age has wrinkled o'er my face,
Ere half my glass of life is run,
At once a brother and a son;
And all my want of years employ
In justice done to thee, my Boy!

Although so young thy heedless sire,
Youth will not damp parental fire;
And, wert thou still less dear to me,
While Helen's form revives in thee,
The breast which beat to former joy,
Will ne'er desert its pledge, my Boy!

Little Brown Baby

Paul Laurence Dunbar, African-American poet,
1872–1906

Little brown baby wif spa'klin' eyes,
Come to yo' pappy an' set on his knee.
What you been doin', suh – makin' san' pies?
Look at dat bib – you's ez du'ty ez me.
Look at dat mouf – dat's merlasses, I bet;
Come hyeah, Maria, an' wipe off his han's.
Bees gwine to ketch you an' eat you up yit,
Bein' so sticky an sweet – goodness lan's!

Little brown baby wif spaklin' eyes,
Who's pappy's darlin' an' who's pappy's chile?
Who is it all de day nevah once tries
Fu' to be cross, er once loses dat smile?
Whah did you git dem teef? My, you's a scamp!
Whah did dat dimple come f'om in yo' chin?
Pappy do' know you – I b'lieves you's a tramp;
Mammy, dis hyeah's some ol' straggler got in!

Let's th'ow him outen de do' in de san',
We do' want stragglers a-layin' roun' hyeah;
Let's gin him 'way to de big buggah-man;
I know he's hidin' erroun' hyeah right neah.
Buggah-man, buggah-man, come in de do',
Hyeah's a bad boy you kin have fu' to eat.
Mammy an' pappy do' want him no mo',
Swaller him down f'om his haid to his feet!

Dah, now, I t'ought dat you'd hug me up close.
Go back, ol' buggah, you sha'n't have dis boy.
He ain't no tramp, ner nor straggler, of co'se;
He's pappy's pa'dner an' playmate an' joy.
Come to you' pallet now – go to yo' res';
Wisht you could allus know ease an' cleah skies;
Wisht you could stay jes' a chile on my breas'—
Little brown baby wif spaklin' eyes!

Small men, big fathers

From Barry Hewlett's study *Intimate Fathers*, 1991

The Aka Pygmies of the African Congo perform more infant
care than any other fathers in known society.

The Aka data point to the importance of quantity time rather
than quality time. Aka fathers do provide some quality time,
but most (about 75 per cent) of their time with infants is spent
in basic caregiving (holding, watching, feeding). The Aka
father–child relationship is intimate not because of quality time
but because the father knows his child exceptionally well
through regular interaction. Aka fathers do not often play with
their infants because they can communicate their love and
concern in other ways. They know subtle means of interacting
with their children. They sleep with their infants and have
physical contact throughout the day. The Aka data suggest
that intimate parent–child relations contribute to emotional
security. I would suggest that the intimate parent–child relations

contribute substantially to the development of autonomy and self-assuredness. Aka children develop these characteristics at a very early age (five to six years old), while it may take a lifetime for many Americans. It is impossible for American parents today to spend as much time with their children as Aka parents do, but the Aka data do suggest that whenever possible it is important for American parents to hold or be near their children. This may mean sleeping with young children, taking children to adult activities, holding infants more often rather than letting them sit in infant carrying devices, or allowing children to play around grown-ups engaged in adult activities.

⌒

Exponential fatigue

Ogden Nash, 1902–71

As a father of two there is a respectful question which I wish to
     ask of fathers of five:
How do you happen to be still alive?

⌒

Birth wrong

From Sophocles, *Oedipus Rex*, *c.* 430 BC, translated
by Sir George Young, 1887

OEDIPUS: I am the son of Polybus of Corinth,
            And of a Dorian mother, Merope.
            And I was counted most preëminent
            Among the townsmen there; up to the time
            A circumstance befell me, of this fashion –
            Worthy of wonder, though of my concern
            Unworthy. At the board a drunken fellow
            Over his cups called me a changeling;
            And I, being indignant – all that day
            Hardly refrained – but on the morrow went
            And taxed my parents with it to their face;

Who took the scandal grievously, of him
Who launched the story. Well, with what they said
I was content; and yet the thing still galled me;
For it spread far. So without cognisance
Of sire or mother I set out to go
To Pytho. Phoebus sent me of my quest
Bootless away; but other terrible
And strange and lamentable things revealed,
Saying I should wed my mother, and produce
A race intolerable for men to see,
And be my natural father's murderer.
When I heard that, measuring where Corinth stands
Even thereafter by the stars alone,
Where I might never think to see fulfilled
The scandals of ill prophecies of me,
I fled, an exile. As I journeyed on,
I found myself upon the self-same spot
Where, you say, this king perished. In your ears,
Wife, I will tell the whole. When in my travels
I was come near this place where three roads meet,
There met me a herald, and a man that rode
In a colt-carriage, as you tell of him,
And from the track the leader, by main force,
And the old man himself, would thrust me. I,
Being enraged, strike him who jostled me –
The driver – and the old man, when he saw it,
Watching as I was passing, from the car
With his goad's fork smote me upon the head.
He paid, though! duly I say not; but in brief,
Smitten by the staff in this right hand of mine,
Out of the middle of the carriage straight
He rolls down headlong; and I slay them all!
But if there be a semblance to connect
This nameless man with Laius, who is now
More miserable than I am? Who on earth
Could have been born with more of hate from heaven?
Whom never citizen or stranger may
Receive into their dwellings, or accost,
But must thrust out of doors; and 'tis no other
Laid all these curses on myself, than I!

Yea, with embraces of the arms whereby
He perished, I pollute my victim's bed!
Am I not vile? Am I not all unclean?
If I must fly, and flying, never can
See my own folk, or on my native land
Set foot, or else must with my mother wed,
And slay my father Polybus, who begat
And bred me? Would he not speak truly of me
Who judged these things sent by some barbarous
    Power?
Never, you sacred majesties of Heaven,
Never may I behold that day; but pass
Out of men's sight, ere I shall see myself
Touched by the stain of such a destiny!

Artistic representations of Joseph the Father

From Adrienne Burgess,
Fatherhood Reclaimed, 1997

For a long time practical fatherly care [in art] was represented by Jesus' adoptive father St Joseph, and the development of his persona tells us a great deal about what was
considered right and proper for earthly fathers. In the
fifteenth century there are many illustrations of Joseph's
gentle domesticity. In pictures and engravings he is shown
drying the Baby Jesus' nappies and feeding him from a bowl
of milk. By the seventeenth century, childcare has ceased to
be his province (he is now shown protecting Mary and
working to keep her and the child), but in the occasional
painting or engraving he still holds the baby, who is softly
touching his face. As time passes Joseph's domestic involvement vanishes and, by the eighteenth century, he is portrayed
as a religious contemplative, praying or studying alone. So
it came about that fathers, in all their aspects, were rele-
gated to Heaven, elevated or reduced (depending on your
point of view) to one-dimensional lawgivers, in the image
of whom earthly fathers were to make themselves.

On the Birth of His Son

Su Tung-P'o, 1036–1101

Families, when a child is born,
Want it to be intelligent.
I, through intelligence,
Having wrecked my whole life,
Only hope the baby will prove
Ignorant and stupid.
Then he will crown a tranquil life
by becoming a Cabinet Minister.

Early Morning Feed

From Peter Redgrove, *Poems 1954–1987*

The father darts out on the stairs
To listen to that keening
In the upper room, for a change of note
That signifies distress, to scotch disaster,
The kettle humming in the room behind.

He thinks, on tiptoe, ears a-strain,
The cool dawn rising like the moon:
'Must not appear and pick him up;
He mustn't think he has me springing
To his beck and call,'
The kettle rattling behind the kitchen door.

He has him springing
A-quiver on the landing –
For a distress-note, a change of key,
To gallop up the stairs to him
To take him up, light as a violin,
And stroke his back until he smiles.
He sidles in the kitchen
And pours his tea . . .

And again stands hearkening
For milk cracking the lungs.
There's a little panting,
A cough: the thumb's in: he'll sleep,
The cup of tea cooling on the kitchen table.

Can he go in now to his chair and think
Of the miracle of breath, pick up a book,
Ready at all times to take it at a run
And intervene between him and disaster,
Sipping his cold tea as the sun comes up?

He returns to bed
And feels like something, with the door ajar,
Crouched in the bracken, alert, with big eyes
For the hunter, death, disaster.

My Baby

Song sung by Charlie Bakus at the San Francisco
Minstrels Opera House, *c.* 1880

I'm the father of an infant,
Baby mine, baby mine;
He won't let me rest an instant,
Baby mine, baby mine;
He won't do a thing he's bid,
How I wish that I was rid
Of that awful sassy kid,
Baby mine, baby mine,
Of that awful sassy kid,
Baby mine.

At my meals I have to hold him,
Baby mine, baby mine;
But I never dare to scold him,
Baby mine, baby mine;
My face he'll surely scratch,
And the tablecloth he'll snatch,
All my crockery goes smash,

Baby mine, baby mine,
All my crockery goes smash.
Baby mine, baby mine.

In my hair he often lingers,
Baby mine, baby mine;
With molasses on his fingers,
Baby mine, baby mine;
You ought to hear him roar,
While I have to walk the floor,
Oh, I'd like to break his jaw,
Baby mine, baby mine.
Yes, I'd like to break his jaw,
Baby mine.

⌐⌐

Forever Young

Bob Dylan, song written for his infant son,
Jacob, 1972

May God bless and keep you always. May your wishes
all come true.
May you always do for others, and let others do for you.

May you build a ladder to the stars and climb on every rung.
And, may you stay forever young.

May you grow up to be righteous. May you grow up to be true.
May you always know the truth and see the light
surrounding you.

May you always be courageous, stand upright and be strong.
And, may you stay forever young.

Forever young. Forever young. May you stay forever young.

May your hands always be busy. May your feet always be
swift.
May you have a strong foundation when the winds of
changes shift.

May your heart always be joyful. May your song always
  be sung.
And, may you stay forever young.

Forever young. Forever young. May you stay forever young.

~~

Long time coming; the history of Father's Day

From *The Modernisation of Fatherhood*,
Ralph LaRossa, 1997

Although neither Father's Day nor Mother's Day were immediately embraced, and while each had their opponents, when
the two were given their official sendoffs (in 1910 and 1908,
respectively), Mother's Day took off more like a rocket,
while Father's Day took off . . . well, more like a rock.

By 1911, three years after the West Virginia and
Pennsylvania celebrations, every state in the nation was
observing Mother's Day. Two years later, Congress voted to
make Mother's Day a national holiday. In 1914, Woodrow
Wilson issued a presidential proclamation 'legalising and
immortalising' the second Sunday in May for generations to
come.

No similar groundswell of support emerged for Father's
Day. As I said, President Wilson did participate, if only from
afar, in the Father's Day festivities that took place in
Spokane, Washington, in 1916. Also, President Coolidge did
encourage the states to organise their own Father's Day celebrations in 1924. But Coolidge (and Harding before him)
did not accede to Harry Meek's request that Father's Day
be made a federal holiday.

Congress also did not follow its 1913 resolution for
Mother's Day with an equivalent resolution for Father's Day
– at least not immediately. It was not until 1971 – fifty-eight
years after Mother's Day received its imprimatur – that
Congress finally saw fit to pass a bill in favour of Father's
Day. In response, President Richard Nixon issued, in 1972,
a proclamation ('In Witness Whereof . . .') asking everyone
in the country to make the third Sunday in June 'an occasion
for renewal of the love and gratitude we bear to our fathers'.

~~

The contrariness of early fatherhood

From Charles Jennings, *Father's Race*, 1999

The feeling of *being a father*, though: that was terrific. Away from any sort of social pressure or middle-class ritual – in fact, on my own, whenever possible, without even the distracting presence of the baby – it was a fantastic sensation. I had to restrain myself from grabbing passers-by in the street and shaking them and shouting in their faces, *I'm a father! Complete! Not firing blanks! My biological destiny fulfilled!* Obviously, part of this was relief that mother and child were okay and that the ordeal prefigured by Kitzinger and the others was over. But a lot of it was also late-developer exhilaration at having stepped beyond what I was before and into that real world of children and grown-ups and responsibility which I'd glimpsed a year earlier.

On the other hand, I got appalling mood swings – mood swings which every father of my acquaintance has suffered from, even though they haven't always chosen to use the phrase *mood swing* with its attendant static crackle of female unreliability: the way your feelings change from something moderated by the adult world to something ungovernable, unknowable, violently self-contradictory.

Nappies epitomise this contradictory state in the first year. Indeed, they provide a nice physical correlative for the whole new-baby period. There is a whole nappy culture out there. I know this because, working at home, there is no way I could escape the burden of nappy-changing. And the first time you deal with a nappy full of impacted crap (a bit like ten-week-old *tapenade*), it is a life-altering encounter. Your emotions when you come face to face with it are something you could never anticipate, unless you work in a hospital or on a pig farm. The whole thing is so powerfully real, so much in the present, that it borders on Zen. I can still remember the first time I changed a nappy. I was bubbling with a mixture of dread at what I might do to my newborn son by mistake and at what I might find inside the nappy when I undid it. The sun was shining and the room was overheated and there was an unfamiliar smell of medication from all the ointments and lotions we had lying around, just in case. Although I'd been acting out the caring man bit quite keenly up to now, I'd ruthlessly avoided nappies, using a system of weak excuses and outright refusals. So Susie had had to strong-arm me into it the first time, lots of threats and grievance. I held my breath, leaned forward and gripped the tabs. It can't have been anything but completely depressing for Alistair, trapped on the table with this scowling, grimacing face bearing down on him, one of his beloved parents looking as if he was peering into a road accident. And then I gripped a bit tighter. And I made one of those decisions which freeze time, in which you can hear the blood roar in your ears in the moment before you act. I thought – I don't know what I thought. I thought that something was going to explode across the ceiling and the walls. That I was going to be calcified in crap like one of those objects people leave in limestone stalactite caves to be turned into stone. I pulled. And then it turned out to be a false alarm – I mean, it was just pee rather than anything worse. God, I was relieved. 'Well *that's* all right!' I shouted at the little chap. '*That* I can deal with!' He must have thought I was mad.

Some of the images I keep with me from my nappy-changing years will live for ever in my mind, precisely because of the way they symbolise the contrariness of early fatherhood. You have, for instance, the unnatural loveliness of the baby's bottom, clagged up with the kind of stuff you normally wipe from the sole of your shoe, in a nexus of beauty and squalor; you have the desire to purify and care for your child, warring with an equal desire to forget the whole thing, or even wander away somewhere and puke; you have your paternal joy at seeing how fit and strong your kid is, fighting with your rage at the little bastard's refusal to lie still and *just get changed*.

⌒

A great nuisance

From Samuel Butler, *The Way of All Flesh*,
written 1873–4

The birth of his son opened Theobald's eyes to a good deal which he had but faintly realised hitherto. He had had no idea how great a nuisance a baby was. Babies come into the world so suddenly at the end, and upset everything so terribly when they do come: why cannot they steal in upon us with less of a shock to the domestic system? His wife, too, did not recover rapidly from her confinement; she remained an invalid for months; here was another nuisance and an expensive one, which interfered with the amount which Theobald liked to put by out of his income against, as he said, a rainy day, or to make provision for his family if he should have one. Now he was getting a family, so that it became all the more necessary to put money by, and here was the baby hindering him. Theorists may say what they like about a man's children being a continuation of his own identity, but it will generally be found that those who talk this way have no children of their own. Practical family men know better.

About twelve months after the birth of Ernest there came a second, also a boy, who was christened Joseph, and in less than twelve months afterwards, a girl, to whom was given the name of Charlotte. A few months before this girl was born Christina paid a visit to the John Pontifexes in London, and, knowing her condition, passed a good deal of time at the Royal Academy exhibition looking at the types of female beauty portrayed by the Academicians, for she had made up her mind that the child this time was to be a girl. Alethea warned her not to do this, but she persisted, and certainly the child turned out plain, but whether the pictures caused this or no I cannot say.

Theobald had never liked children. He had always got away from them as soon as he could, and so had they from him; oh, why, he was inclined to ask himself, could not children be born into the world grown-up? If Christina could have given birth to a few full-grown clergymen in priest's orders – of moderate views, but inclining rather to Evangelicalism, with comfortable livings and in all respects facsimiles of Theobald himself – why, there might have been more sense in it; or if people could buy ready-made children at a shop of whatever age and sex they liked, instead of always having to make them at home and to begin at the beginning with them – that might do better, but as it was he did not like it. He felt as he had felt when he had been required to come and be married to Christina – that he had been going on for a long time quite nicely, and would much rather continue things on their present footing. In the matter of getting married he had been obliged to pretend he liked it; but times were changed, and if he did not like a thing now, he could find a hundred unexceptionable ways of making his dislike apparent.

It might have been better if Theobald in his younger days had kicked more against his father: the fact that he had not done so encouraged him to expect the most implicit obedience from his own children. He could trust himself, he said (and so did Christina), to be more lenient than perhaps his father had been to himself; his danger, he said (and so again did Christina), would be rather in the direction of being too indulgent; he must be on his guard against this, for no duty could be more important than that of teaching a child to obey its parents in all things.

He had read not long since of an Eastern traveller, who, while exploring somewhere in the more remote parts of Arabia and Asia Minor, had come upon a remarkably hardy, sober, industrious little Christian community – all of them in the best of health – who had turned out to be the actual living descendants of Jonadab, the son of Rechab; and two men in European costume, indeed, but speaking English with a broken accent, and by their colour evidently Oriental, had come begging to Battersby soon afterwards, and represented themselves as belonging to this people; they had said they were collecting funds to promote the conversion of their fellow tribesmen to the English branch of the Christian religion. True, they turned out to be impostors, for when he gave them a pound and Christina five shillings from her private purse, they went and got drunk with it in the next village but one to Battersby; still, this did not invalidate the story of the Eastern traveller. Then there were the Romans – whose greatness was probably due to the wholesome authority exercised by the head of a family over all its members. Some Romans had even killed their children; this was going too far, but then the Romans were not Christians, and knew no better.

The practical outcome of the foregoing was a conviction in Theobald's mind, and if in his, then in Christina's, that it was their duty to begin training up their children in the way they should go, even from their earliest infancy. The first signs of self-will must be carefully looked for, and plucked up by the roots at once before they had time to grow. Theobald picked up this numb serpent of a metaphor and cherished it in his bosom.

Before Ernest could well crawl he was taught to kneel; before he could well speak he was taught to lisp the Lord's Prayer, and the general confession. How was it possible that these things could be taught too early? If his attention flagged or his memory failed him, here was an ill weed which would grow apace, unless it were plucked out immediately, and the only way to pluck it out was to whip him, or shut him up in a cupboard, or dock him of some of the small pleasures of childhood. Before he was three years old he could read and, after a fashion, write. Before he was four he was learning Latin, and could do rule of three sums.

Hector and son

From Homer, *The Iliad, c.* eighth century BC, translated by Alexander Pope

Thus having spoke, th'illustrious Chief of *Troy*
Stretch'd his fond Arms to clasp the lovely Boy.
The Babe clung crying to his Nurse's Breast,
Scar'd at the dazling Helm, and nodding Crest.
With secret Pleasure each fond Parent smil'd,
And *Hector* hasted to relieve his Child,
The glitt'ring Terrors from his Brows unbound,
And plac'd the beaming Helmet on the Ground.
Then kist the Child, and lifting high in Air,
Thus to the Gods prefer'd a Father's Pray'r.
    O Thou! whose Glory fills th' Ætherial Throne,
And all ye deathless Pow'rs! protect my Son!
Grant him, like me, to purchase just Renown,
To guard the *Trojans*, to defend the Crown,
Against his Country's Foes the War to wage,
And rise the *Hector* of the future Age!
So when triumphant from successful Toils,
Of Heroes slain he bears the reeking Spoils,
Whole Hosts may hail him with deserv'd Acclaim,
And say, This Chief transcends his Father's Fame:
While pleas'd amidst the gen'ral Shouts of *Troy*,
His Mother's conscious Heart o'erflows with Joy.
He spoke, and fondly gazing on her Charms
Restor'd the pleasing Burden to her Arms;

Rising late and playing with A-ts'ui, aged two

Po Chu-i, 772–846

All the morning I have lain perversely in bed;
Now at dusk I rise with many yawns.
My warm stove is quick to get ablaze;
At the cold mirror I am slow in doing my hair.
With melted snow I boil fragrant tea;
Seasoned with curds I cook a milk-pudding.
At my sloth and greed there is no one but me to laugh;
My cheerful vigour none but myself knows.
The taste of my wine is mild and works no poison;
The notes of my harp are soft and bring no sadness.
To the Three Joys in the book of Mencius
I have added the fourth of playing with my baby-boy.

Fatherhood, from the German

Les Murray, *Collected Poems*, 1998

Becoming a father, that is no
Achievement. Being one is, though.

2

Fathers and Sons

Little Boy Lost

William Blake, 1757–1827

Father! father! where are you going?
O do not walk so fast.
Speak, father, speak to your little boy,
Or else I shall be lost.

⌒

A Parental Ode to My Son, Aged Three Years and Five Months

Thomas Hood, 1837

Thou happy, happy elf!
(But stop – first let me kiss away that tear)
Thou tiny image of myself!
(My love, he's poking peas into his ear!)
Thou merry, laughing sprite!
With spirits feather-light.
Untouched by sorrow and unsoiled by sin –
(Good heavens, the child is swallowing a pin!)

Thou tricksy Puck!
With antic toys so funnily bestuck.
Light as the singing bird that wings the air –
(The door! the door! he'll tumble down the stair!)
Thou darling of thy sire!
(Why, Jane, he'll set his pinafore a-fire!)
Thou imp of mirth and joy!
In love's dear chain so strong and bright a link.
Thou idol of thy parents – (Drat the boy!
There goes my ink!)

Thou cherub! – but of earth:
Fit playfellow for Fays, by moonlight pale,

In harmless sport and mirth.
(That dog will bite him if he pulls its tail!)
Thou human humming-bee, extracting honey
From every blossom in the world that blows.
Singing in Youth's Elysium every sunny –
(Another tumble! – that's his precious nose!)

Thy father's pride and hope!
(He'll break the mirror with that skipping-rope!)
With pure heart newly stamped from Nature's mint
(Where *did* he learn that squint?)
Thou young domestic dove!
(He'll have that jug off, with another shove!)
Dear nursling of the hymeneal nest!
(Are those torn clothes his best?)
Little epitome of man!
(He'll climb upon the table, that's his plan!)
Touched with the beauteous tints of dawning life –
(He's got a knife!)

Thou enviable being!
No storms, no clouds, in thy blue sky foreseeing.
Play on, play on.
My elfin John!
Toss the light ball – bestride the stick –
(I knew so many cakes would make him sick!)
With fancies buoyant as the thistledown.
Prompting the face grotesque, and antic brisk.
With many a lamblike frisk –
(He's got the scissors, snipping at your gown!)

Thou pretty opening rose!
(Go to your mother, child, and wipe your nose!)
Balmy, and breathing music like the South.
(He really brings my heart into my mouth!)
Fresh as the morn, and brilliant as its star –
(I wish that window had an iron bar!)
Bold as the hawk, yet gentle as the dove –
(I tell you what, my love.
I cannot write, unless he's sent above!)

Nettles

From Vernon Scannell, *Collected Poems 1950–1993*

My son aged three fell in the nettle bed.
'Bed' seemed a curious name for those green spears,
That regiment of spite behind the shed:
It was no place for rest. With sobs and tears
The boy came seeking comfort and I saw
White blisters beaded on his tender skin.
We soothed him till his pain was not so raw.
At last he offered us a watery grin,
And then I took my billhook, honed the blade
And went outside and slashed in fury with it
Till not a nettle in that fierce parade
Stood upright any more. And then I lit
A funeral pyre to burn the fallen dead.
But in two weeks the busy sun and rain
Had called up tall recruits behind the shed:
My son would often feel sharp wounds again.

Teaching a son to walk

The Baal Shem Tov, 1698–1760

When a father sets out to teach his little son to walk, he stands in front of him and holds his two hands on either side of the child, so that he cannot fall, and the boy goes toward his father between his father's hands. But the moment he is close to his father, he moves away a little and holds his hands farther apart, and he does this over and over, so that the child may learn to walk.

Roughhousing rules ok

National Fatherhood Initiative, USA

New research suggests that little boys who are lucky enough to have fathers who roughhouse with them are actually better at controlling their aggression than those whose dads do no roughhouse with them. That's because if the little boy gets too rough and starts to hit or bite, Dad tells him to cool it. In this way, the little boy learns how to control – not act out – his aggressive impulses.

Play fellow

A letter from Richard Steele to his wife,
16 March 1717

Your Son at the present writing is mighty well employed in Tumbling on the Floor of the room and Sweeping the sand with a Feather. He grows a most delightfull Child, and very full of Play and Spiritt. He is also a very great Scholar. He can read His Primer, and I have brought down my Virgil. He makes most shrewd remarks upon the Pictures. We are very intimate Friends and Play fellows. He begins to be very ragged and I hope I shall be pardoned if I equip Him with new Cloaths and Frocks or what Mrs Evans and I shall think for His Service.

The main event

From Charles Jennings, *Father's Race*, 1999

The first time I found myself at a nursery-school sports day, I actually managed to butch it out and refused to have anything to do with the fathers' event. I stood my ground at the edge of the track, smirking uneasily. Fortunately, there were a couple of weaklings there with me (crippled by holiday accidents or squash games) so I got away with it. The second year, though, absolutely *every* father who'd turned up volunteered for the long-distance race, right round the perimeter of the borrowed cricket pitch on which the games were taking place. There was a lot of vicious joshing, a lot of evil-natured *How are you, David? You feeling UP TO IT?*, a certain amount of glancing spitefully in my direction. I had nowhere to hide. All the mums rounded on me (the deviant father, always around to collect his son) and jeered me up to the starting line. The other dads were already pulling off their shiny loafers and loosening their ties and smoothing back their hair and gazing down the grass track with a murderous fixity. Some of them had evidently been waiting for this moment for some time. I could tell that they had been practising. I tried to get into the mood by hitching up my socks and wiping my spectacles, but instead of fearsome competitiveness, nothing much entered my heart except dread. It was one of those calm, slightly sultry English summer days, a good day for lying on your back and staring thoughtfully at the sky. I thought I might be sick. The headmistress of the Montessori nursery said *Go* and immediately a pack of grunting men shot past me and ran off into the distance, their ties flying out behind them, their heels flashing in the sunshine.

I found myself right at the back, alongside a very old man – a late father, or possibly even a grandfather. His thinning grey hair flapped around on his crown. He looked into the distance with watery eyes. 'God,' he said, 'I must be mad.' We trudged round for a while, until it dawned on me that even he was moving slightly faster than I was. Another minute went by and the gap between us grew wider, and then he had deserted me and I was alone, stumbling along, the distance between me and the rest of them widening until they were two-thirds of a lap ahead of me, in a three-lap race. I struggled and sweated and groaned for air as I tried to close the margin between me and the old man (that affirming lard I had been carrying since Alistair was born coming back to haunt me), but he got further and further away, closer and closer to the rolling, jostling backs of the fit men, leagues away. Eventually, after they had all crossed the finish line, I was still yards off, lurching along, nearly in tears.

But then a wonderful thing happened. Alistair, who'd been watching with the rest of the children, coralled into a fairy ring next to the teachers, took pity on my state, ran up beside me and jogged along, making encouraging remarks. 'I thought I'd keep you company,' he said. And he did. I don't know whether I was more ashamed for myself for being a fat turd, or for Alistair for having to be seen with a father like me. But at the same time, and more than either, I loved him for being generous and companiable and brave. He saved that day from being one of those memories that cause me to yelp with uncontainable embarrassment in public whenever I suffer a flashback – and turned it instead into something bathed in a glow of fondness and hope. At last I staggered and wheezed over the line, to a smattering of sarcastic applause and ironical *well dones* from the nastier-minded teachers, while Alistair gave my hand a squeeze. I can't tell you how grateful I was to him for being there, and I still feel grateful to him, just thinking about it now. I hope his kids will do the same for him one day. It's typical of everything to do with children, that while some situations can – out of the blue – turn into disasters when emotions get out of control or when expectations get unmanageable, disasters such as this one can just as abruptly be filled with love and gratitude.

Nothing spared

From Ivan Turgenev, *Fathers and Sons*, 1862

'I ought to tell you, I . . . idolise my son . . .

'. . . And I don't only idolise him, Arkady Nikolaich, I am proud of him, and the height of my ambition is that some day there will be the following lines in his biography: "The son of a simple army-doctor, who was, however, capable of divining his greatness betimes, and spared nothing for his education . . ."' The old man's voice broke.

That's my pateras!

From Barry Strauss, *Fathers and Sons in Athens*,
1997

We find another example of paternal pride in Xenophon's
Symposium, a Socratic dialogue with the dramatic date of 421.
The guests of honour at the drinking party in the home of Kallias
in Piraeus are Lykon and his teenage son Autolykos. Father and
son recline next to each other on a couch at the symposium.
Famous for his good looks, Autolykos had just won the prize
in the pankration (a combination of boxing and wrestling) at
the Panathenaic games, and Kallias wanted to become his lover.
The conversation at the symposium turned to the question of
what possession or accomplishment each guest most prided
himself in having. When it was Lykon's turn to answer, he
responded, 'Don't you all know that it is my son?' (Xen. *Symp.*
3.12). One of the guests suggests snidely that what Autolykos
is proud of, on the other hand, is his prize. But Autolykos pipes
up with the reply that no, indeed, what he is proud of is his
father! Up to this point Autolykos had been sitting demurely
beside his father, while the other guests reclined; it was customary
for adult males alone to recline at an Athenian party. Now,
Autolykos underlines his respect by reclining beside his father
on the dining couch, a gesture perhaps even of affection and
ease, perhaps even a manly gesture: children were not expected
to speak at a symposium, but Autolykos' remark had delighted
the audience (3.12–13). As syrupy as the scene is, as 'goody-
two-shoes' as Autolykos is, the smitten Kallias is overcome, and
blurts out that Lykon is the richest man in the world; Lykon
agrees, naturally (Xen. *Symp.* 3.13).

A mystical estate

From *Ulysses* by James Joyce, 1922

Fatherhood, in the sense of conscious begetting, is unknown to man. It is a mystical estate, an apostolic succession, from only begetter to only begotten On that mystery and not on the madonna which the cunning Italian intellect flung to the mob of Europe the church is founded and founded irremovably because founded, like the world, macro and microcosm, upon the void. Upon incertitude, upon unlikelihood, *Amor matris*, subjective and objective genitive, may be the only true thing in life. Paternity may be a legal fiction. Who is the father of any son that any son should love him or he any son?

A Boy Named Sue

Song popularised by Johnny Cash, 1958

My daddy left home when I was three/ And he didn't leave much to ma and me/ Just this old guitar and an empty bottle of booze. Now, I don't blame him 'cause he run and hid/ But the meanest thing that he ever did/ Was before he left, he went and named me 'Sue'.

Well, he must o' thought that it was quite a joke/ And it got a lot of laughs from a' lots of folk/ It seems I had to fight my whole life through/ Some gal would giggle and I'd get red/ And some guy'd laugh and I'd bust his head/ I tell ya, life ain't easy for a boy named 'Sue'.

Well, I grew up quick and I grew up mean/ My fist got hard and my wits got keen/ I'd roam from town to town to hide my shame/ But I made me a vow to the moon and stars/ That I'd search the honky-tonks and bars/ And kill that man that give me that awful name.

Well, it was Gatlinburg in mid-July/ And I just hit town and my throat was dry/ I thought I'd stop and have myself a brew/ At an old saloon on a street of mud/ There at a table, dealing stud/ Sat the dirty, mangy dog that named me 'Sue'.

Well, I knew that snake was my own sweet dad from a worn-out picture that my mother'd had/ And I knew that scar on his cheek and his evil eye/ He was big and bent and gray and old/ And I looked at him and my blood ran cold/ And I said: 'My name is Sue! How do you do! Now you gonna die!!'

Well, I hit him hard right between the eyes/ And he went down but, to my surprise/ He come up with a knife and cut off a piece of my ear/ But I busted a chair right across his teeth/ And we crashed through the wall and into the street/ Kicking and a' gouging in the mud and the blood and the beer.

I tell ya, I've fought tougher men/ But I really can't remember when/ He kicked like a mule and he bit like a crocodile/ I heard him laugh and then I heard him cuss/ He went for his gun and I pulled mine first/ He stood there lookin' at me and I saw him smile.

And he said: 'Son, this world is rough/ And if a man's gonna make it, he's gotta be tough/ And I know I wouldn't be there to help ya along/ So I give ya that name and I said goodbye; I knew you'd have to get tough or die/ And it's that name that helped to make you strong.'

He said: 'Now you just fought one hell of a fight/ And I know you hate me, and you got the right/ To kill me now, and I wouldn't blame you if you do/ But ya ought to thank me, before I die, For the gravel in ya guts and the spit in ya eye/ Cause I'm the son-of-a-bitch that named you "Sue".'

I got all choked up and I threw down my gun/ And I called him my pa, and he called me his son/ And I come away with a different point of view/ And I think about him, now and then/ Every time I try and every time I win/ And if I ever have a son, I think I'm gonna name him Bill or George! Anything but Sue! I still hate that name!

What makes a father's love distinct?

From David Blankenhorn, *Fatherless America*, 1995

This conditional nature of paternal sponsorship – I am a good father if my children become good adults – often means that a father's love is qualitatively different from a mother's love. This difference takes us to the heart of the matter. Compared to a mother's love, a father's love is frequently more expectant, more instrumental, and significantly less unconditional.

For the child, from the beginning, the mother's love is an unquestioned source of comfort and the foundation of human attachment. But the father's love is almost always a bit farther away, more distant and contingent. Compared to the mother's love, the father's must frequently be sought after, deserved, earned through achievement. My mother loves me unconditionally because I am her child. My father loves me, but he tends to make me work for it. Lucky is the child who receives both varieties of parental love.

⌒

'This is a poem to my son Peter'

Peter Meinke, 1932–

this is a poem to my son Peter
whom I have hurt a thousand times
whose large and vulnerable eyes
have glazed in pain at my ragings
thin wrists and fingers hung
boneless in despair, pale freckled back
bent in defeat, pillow soaked
by my failure to understand.
I have scarred through weakness
and impatience your frail confidence forever
because when I needed to strike
you were there to be hurt and because
I thought you knew
you were beautiful and fair
your bright eyes and hair

but now I see that no one knows that
about himself, but must be told
and retold until it takes hold
because I think anything can be killed
after a while, especially beauty
so I write this for life, for love, for
you, my oldest son Peter, age 10,
going on 11.

⌒

Boy *tyrannus*

From Plutarch *c*. 46–*c*. 120, *Themistocles*

Themistocles used to say of his son (who bullied his mother and, through her, himself) that he was the most powerful person in Greece. The Athenians controlled the rest of Greece, he himself controlled the Athenians, the boy's mother controlled him, and the boy controlled his mother.

⌒

The Judgement

By Franz Kafka, written during the night of
22–23 September 1912

George was amazed at how dark his father's room was, even on that sunny morning. What a shadow it cast, that high wall beyond the narrow courtyard! His father was sitting by the window, in a corner of the room that was adorned with various mementoes of George's late mother; he was reading the newspaper, holding it up to his eyes at an angle in an attempt to compensate for some deficiency in his eyesight. On the table stood the remains of his breakfast, not much of which appeared to have been consumed.

'Ah, George!' his father said, coming across the room towards him. His heavy dressing-gown fell open as he walked, the flaps swirling about him – 'He's still a giant, my father,' George said to himself.

Then he said, 'It's intolerably dark in here.'

'It's dark, all right,' his father replied.

'And you have the window shut?'

'I prefer it that way.'

'It's really warm outside,' said George, as if following up his earlier remark. He took a seat.

His father cleared the breakfast things away and put them on top of a cupboard.

'I just wanted to tell you,' George went on, following the old man's movements with a forlorn look, 'that I've sent word of my engagement to Petersburg after all.' He pulled the letter out of his pocket a little way; then let it drop back.

'Why to Petersburg?' his father asked.

'To my friend, *you* know,' said George, looking his father in the eye. 'He's not at all like this in the office,' he was thinking, 'sitting there so four-square with his arms across his chest!'

'Quite. Your friend,' his father said with emphasis.

'But I told you, Father, how I didn't want to tell him of my engagement at first. Purely out of consideration, for no other reason. You know yourself how difficult he is. What I said to myself was, he may hear about my engagement from someone else, though it's hardly likely in view of the solitary life he leads – I can't help that – but he's not going to hear about it from me.'

'And now you've changed your mind, is that it?' his father inquired, putting his huge newspaper down on the window-sill, placing his spectacles on top of it, and covering the spectacles with his hand.

'Yes, now I've changed my mind. If he's a good friend of mine, I said to myself, then my being happily engaged will make him happy too. That's why I no longer had any hesitation in notifying him of the fact. But before I posted the letter I wanted to tell you what I'd done.'

'George,' his father said, pulling his toothless mouth into a broad slit, 'listen to me! You've come to me with this thing because you want to talk it over with me. That does you credit, no doubt about it. But it's no good, in fact it's less than no good, if you're not going to tell me the whole truth. I don't want to stir up things that have no place here. Since the death of your beloved mother certain not very nice things have been happening. Maybe there's a time for them too, and maybe that time comes sooner than we expect. A great deal escapes me in the office, though perhaps not because it's kept from me – the last thing I'm trying to suggest is that things are being kept from me – but I haven't the strength any more, my memory is beginning to go, and I no longer have an eye for all the little details. This is simply nature taking its course for one thing, and for another, Mummy's death hit me much harder than it did you. But as long as we're on the subject of this letter, promise me one thing, George: don't try to hood-wink me. It's a trifle, it's not worth bothering about, so don't try to hoodwink me. Do you really have this friend in Petersburg?'

George stood up in embarrassment. 'Never mind about my friends. A thousand friends could never take the place of my father. Do you know what I think? You don't look after yourself enough. Old age is demanding its due. I can't do without you in the office, you know that as well as I do, but if the business should ever start undermining your health I'd shut up shop for good tomorrow. I'm not having that. No, we're going to have to start a new regimen for you. Radically new, I mean. Here you are, sitting in the dark, when in the living-room it would be lovely and light for you. You peck at your breakfast instead of building yourself up properly. You sit around with the window shut when fresh air would do you so much good. No, Father, no! I'll get the doctor round and we'll do exactly what he says. We'll swap rooms: you move into the front room and I'll come in here. There'll be no difference as far as you're concerned because we'll move all your things over too. But there's time enough for all that. You go back to bed for a bit now; you've got to take things easy. Here, I'll help you get undressed. I can, you know. Or would you like to go in the front room now? You can have my bed for the time being. In fact that would be a very sensible arrangement.'

George was standing right beside his father, whose head of shaggy white hair had sunk to his breast.

'George,' his father said softly, not moving.

George immediately knelt down beside his father; he looked into his father's weary face and into the huge pupils staring out at him from the corners of his father's eyes.

'You have no friend in Petersburg. You've always liked to have your little joke, even with me. How should you have a friend there, of all places! I find that too much to believe.'

'Think back for a moment, Father,' George said, heaving the

old man out of his chair and, as he stood there in a really extremely weak condition, pulling off his dressing-gown. 'Nearly three years ago now my friend came here to see us. You didn't particularly like him, I remember. On at least two occasions I disowned him in conversation with you, although he was sitting in my room at the time. I could understand your dislike of him perfectly well; my friend has his peculiarities. But then there was that other time when you got on with him very well. I was really proud of the fact that you listened to him, nodded at what he said, and asked questions. Think back – you must remember. He was telling us those incredible stories about the Russian Revolution. About how for example on a business trip to Kiev he had become involved in a disturbance and seen a priest up on a balcony cut a large, bleeding cross in the flat of his hand, hold the hand in the air, and shout to the crowd. You've even recounted the story yourself on occasion.'

In the meantime George had managed to lower his father into his chair again, carefully remove the woollen trousers he wore over his linen pants, and pull off his socks. Seeing the not particularly clean state of his father's underwear, he reproached himself for having neglected to ensure that his father changed his clothes whenever necessary. He and his fiancée had not yet discussed in so many words how they were going to arrange his father's future; they had tacitly assumed that he would stay on in the old flat by himself. Now, however, George resolved on the spur of the moment to take his father with him when he set up house. In fact, on second thought, it looked as if the care and attention he planned to give his father there might almost come too late.

He picked his father up and carried him into bed. An awful feeling came over him as he became aware during the few steps to the bed that his father, curled up in his arms, was playing with the watch chain at his lapel. So firmly did his father grasp the watch chain that for a moment George was unable to put him to bed.

Once he was in bed, however, everything seemed to be fine. He arranged the bedclothes himself, pulling the quilt unusually high over his shoulders. He looked up at George in a not unfriendly fashion.

'You do remember him, don't you?' George asked, nodding encouragingly.

'Am I covered up now?' asked his father, as if he could not tell whether his feet were adequately covered.

'See, you like it in bed,' said George, tucking the quilt in around him.

'Am I covered up?' his father asked again. He seemed to be particularly interested in what the answer would be.

'Don't worry, you're well covered up.'

'No, I'm not!' his father shouted, slamming the answer down on the question, and he threw the quilt back with such force that for a moment it opened out completely in flight. He stood up in bed, one hand pressed lightly to the ceiling. 'You wanted to cover me up, you scoundrel, I know you did, but I'm not covered up yet. If it's my last ounce of strength it's enough for you – more than enough for you. I know your friend, all right. A son after my own heart, he'd have been. That's why you've been deceiving him all these years, isn't it? Why else? Do you think I haven't wept for him? That's why you shut yourself in your office – the boss is busy, no one's to disturb him – purely in order to write your lying notes to Russia. But luckily for your father he doesn't need anyone to teach him to see through his son. And now that you thought you'd got the better of him, so much so that you could plant your bottom down on him and he wouldn't move, what does my high and mighty son do but decide to get married!'

George looked up at this terrifying vision of his father. The friend in Petersburg, whom his father suddenly knew so well, affected him as never before. He thought of him, lost in the depths of Russia. He saw him at the door of his empty, looted shop against a background of smashed-up shelving, ransacked stock, and bent gas brackets, barely able to stand. Why had he had to go so far away?

'Look at me, will you!' his father shouted, and George almost distractedly ran over to the bed to take everything in but came to a halt halfway there.

'Because she hauled up her skirts,' his father began in a slimy falsetto, 'because she hauled up her skirts like this, the filthy bitch,' and by way of illustration he lifted the hem of his night-shirt so high that the war wound on his thigh was exposed, 'because she hauled up her skirts like this and like this and like this you had to have a go at her, and to make sure you can have your way with her undisturbed you defile your mother's memory, betray your friend, and stick your father in bed where he can't budge. Well, can he budge or can't he?'

And he stood without holding on at all and kicked his legs in the air. His eyes blazed with insight.

George was now standing in a corner, as far away from his father as possible. A long time ago he had made up his mind to keep a really close watch on everything lest he should ever, by some devious means, either from behind or from above, be caught by surprise. He recalled his long-forgotten resolution and promptly forgot it, like drawing a short thread through the eye of a needle.

'But the friend isn't betrayed after all!' his father shouted, and a wagging forefinger corroborated this. 'I was his locum tenens here.'

'Playactor!' George could not refrain from shouting; realising his mistake he immediately, though too late – there was a glazed look in his eyes – bit his tongue so hard that he doubled up in pain.

'Of course I've been playacting! Hah, that's just the word for it! What other consolation was left to your old widowed father? Tell me – and for the space of your answer be my living son still – what else was left to me in my little back room, persecuted by disloyal staff, an old man to the marrow of my bones? And my son went about rejoicing, clinching deals that I had set up, giddying himself with pleasure, and departing from his father's presence with the opaque face of a man of honour! Do you think I didn't love you – having fathered you?'

'Now he's going to lean forward,' George thought. 'If only he'd fall and smash to pieces!' The words went hissing through his head.

His father leant forward but did not fall. Since George did not approach as he had expected, he straightened up again.

'Stay where you are, I don't need you! You think you still have the strength to come over here and are just holding back because you want to. Well, don't delude yourself! I'm still the stronger by far. On my own I might have had to stand down, but Mother has left me her strength. I'm in business with your friend in a big way; I've got your customer right here in my pocket!'

'He's even got pockets in his nightshirt!' George said to himself, thinking that he could make him look ridiculous in the eyes of the whole world by this remark. He only thought it for a moment, because he always forgot everything.

'Just you take your fancy woman on your arm and come up

and see me! I'll swat her away from your side for you, you'll see if I don't!'

George made a face as if he did not believe it. His father simply nodded, driving home the truth of his words, in the direction of George's corner.

'You made me laugh today, coming to ask whether you should write to your friend about your engagement! He knows everything, stupid, he knows everything! I wrote to him myself, because you forgot to take my writing things away. That's why he hasn't been here for years. He knows everything a hundred times better than you do yourself. He screws your letter up unread in his left hand while holding up my letters to read in his right!'

He waved an arm about enthusiastically above his head. 'He knows everything a thousand times better!' he yelled.

'Ten thousand times!' George said to poke fun at his father, but even before the words had left his lips they had a deadly serious sound.

'For years I've been waiting for you to come along with that question! Do you think I care about anything else? Do you think I read the papers? Here!' And he threw George a sheet of newspaper that had somehow got carried into bed with him. An old newspaper with a name George did not begin to recognise.

'The time it's taken you to grow up! Your mother had to die, she was not to see the joyful day, your friend's going to rack and ruin in Russia, he looked as if he was on his last legs three years ago, and you can see for yourself the state I'm in! You've got eyes, haven't you?'

'So you've been trying to catch me out!' cried George.

Sympathetically his father observed, 'You wanted to say that before, probably. Now it's completely out of place.'

And in a louder voice: 'So now you know what else there was apart from you; up to now you only knew about yourself! You were an innocent child, to tell the truth – though to tell the whole truth you were the devil incarnate! Therefore know: I hereby sentence you to death by drowning!'

George felt himself thrust from the room, the thud with which his father fell on the bed behind him still echoing in his ears. On the stairs, which he took at a rush as if descending an inclined plane, he surprised his cleaning lady, who was going up to tidy the flat after the night. 'Jesus!' she cried, hiding her face in her apron, but he had already gone. Out of the door he shot, his momentum carrying him across the road to the water's edge. He clutched the railing as a hungry man will clutch at food.

He vaulted over it, expert gymnast that he had been in his boyhood days, much to his parents' pride. Still holding on with weakening grip, he glimpsed a bus through the bars, knew it would easily cover the noise of his fall, called softly, 'Dear parents, I did love you, always,' and let himself drop.

Crossing the bridge at that moment was a simply endless stream of traffic.

～

What will daddy say?

From Sophocles, *Ajax*, written *c.* 440 BC

AJAX: With what face shall I appear before my father
Telamon? How will he find heart to look
On me, stripped of my championship in war,
That mighty crown of fame that once was his?
No, that I dare not. Shall I then assault
Troy's fortress, and alone against them all
Achieve some glorious exploit and then die?
No, I might gratify the Atreidae thus.
That must not be. Some scheme let me devise
Which may prove to my aged sire that I,
His son, at least by nature am no coward.

～

Sons, what things you are

William Shakespeare, *Henry IV, Part 2*
(Act IV, Scene 5), *c.* 1597

KING HENRY: See, sons, what things you are!
How quickly nature falls into revolt
When gold becomes her object!
For this the foolish over-careful fathers

Have broke their sleep with thoughts, their
    brains with care,
Their bones with industry;
For this they have engrossed and pil'd up
The canker'd heaps of strange-achieved gold:
For this they have been thoughtful to invest
Their sons with arts and martial exercises:
When, like the bee, tolling from every flower
The virtuous sweets,
Our things with wax, our mouths with honey
    pack'd.
We bring it to the hive: and, like the bees,
Are murder'd for our pains. This bitter taste
Yield his engrossments to the ending father.

Repentance

Moliere [Jean-Baptiste Poquelin], 1622–73

How easily a father's tenderness is recalled and how quickly a
son's offences vanish at the slightest word of repentance.

Father's pride

From the memoir of a schoolboy, Mesopotamia,
c. 2000 BC

Arriving at school in the morning I recited my tablet, ate my
lunch, prepared my new tablet, wrote it, finished it, then they
assigned me my oral work . . . When school was dismissed, I
went home, entered the house, and found my father sitting there.
I told my father of my written work, then recited my tablet to
him, and my father was delighted.

The Toys

Coventry Patmore, 1823–96

My little Son, who looked from thoughtful eyes,
And moved and spoke in quiet grown-up wise,
Having my law the seventh time disobeyed,
I struck him, and dismissed
With hard words and unkissed,
– His Mother, who was patient, being dead.
Then, fearing lest his grief should hinder sleep,
I visited his bed,
But found him slumbering deep,
With darkened eyelids, and their lashes yet
From his late sobbing wet.
And I, with moan,
Kissing away his tears, left others of my own;
For on a table drawn beside his head,
He had put, within his reach,
A box of counters and a red-veined stone,
A piece of glass abraded by the beach,
And six or seven shells,
A bottle with bluebells,
And two French copper coins, ranged there with careful art,
To comfort his sad heart.
So when that night I prayed
To God, I wept, and said:
Ah, when at last we lie with trancéd breath,
Not vexing Thee in death,
And Thou rememberest of what toys
We made our joys,
How weakly understood
Thy great commanded good,
Then fatherly not less
Than I whom Thou has moulded from the clay,
Thou'lt leave Thy wrath, and say,
'I will be sorry for their childishness.'

All children should be equal in the eyes of the father

Advice from Jean-Jacques Rousseau's *Emile*, 1762

A father has no choice and ought to have no preferences in the family God gives him. All his children are equally his children; he owes to them all the same care and the same tenderness. Whether they are crippled or not, whether they are sickly or robust, each of them is a deposit of which he owes an account to the hand from which he receives it; and marriage is a contract made with nature as well as between the spouses.

A liberal allowance

From *Brief Lives* by John Aubrey, 1626–97

Sir William Platers, Knight, was a Cambridgeshire Gentleman . . . He was temperate and thriftie as to all other things. He had only one Sonne, who was handsome and ingeniose, and whome he cultivated with all imaginable care and Education, and knowing that he was flesh and blood, tooke care himselfe to provide sound and agreable females for him. He allowed his son liberally but enjoyned him still temperance, and to settdowne his expences, e.g. Item for a semel tetegit [single session] 20s [£1].

Older and wiser

Mark Twain, 1835–1910

When I was a boy of fourteen, my father was so ignorant I could hardly stand to have the old man around. But when I got to be twenty-one, I was astounded at how much the old man had learned in seven years.

My Son, My Executioner

Donald Hall, 1954

My son, my executioner.
I take you in my arms,
Quiet and small and just astir,
And whom my body warms.

Sweet death, small son, our instrument
Of immortality.
Your cries and hungers document
Our bodily decay.

We twenty-five and twenty-two,
Who seemed to live forever,
Observe enduring life in you
And start to die together.

⌒

On an Old Photograph of My Son

From Raymond Carver, *A New Path to
the Waterfall*, 1989

It's 1974 again, and he's back once more. Smirking,
a pair of coveralls over a white tee-shirt,
no shoes. His hair, long and blond, falls
to his shoulders like his mother's did
back then, and like one of those young Greek
heroes I was just reading about. But
there the resemblance ends. On his face
the contemptuous expression of the wise guy,
the petty tyrant. I'd know that look anywhere.
It burns in my memory like acid. It's
the look I never hoped I'd live to see
again. I want to forget that boy
in the picture – that jerk, that bully!

What's for supper, mother dear? Snap to!
Hey, old lady, jump, why don't you? Speak
when spoken to. I think I'll put you in

a headlock to see how you like it. I like
it. I want to keep you on
your toes. Dance for me now. Go ahead,
bag, dance. I'll show you a step or two.
Let me twist your arm. Beg me to stop, beg me
to be nice. Want a black eye? You got it!

Oh, son, in those days I wanted you dead
a hundred – no, a thousand – different times.
I thought all that was behind us. Who in hell
took this picture, and
why'd it turn up now,
just as I was beginning to forget?
I look at your picture and my stomach cramps.
I find myself clamping my jaws, teeth on edge, and
once more I'm filled with despair and anger.
Honestly, I feel like reaching for a drink.
That's a measure of your strength and power, the fear
and confusion you still inspire. That's
how mighty you once were. Hey, I hate this
photograph. I hate what became of us all.
I don't want this artefact in my house another hour!
Maybe I'll send it to your mother, assuming
she's still alive somewhere and the post can reach
her this side of the grave. If so, she'll have
a different reaction to it, I know. Your youth and
beauty, that's all she'll see and exclaim over.
My handsome son, she'll say. My boy wonder.
She'll study the picture, searching for her likeness
in the features, and mine. (She'll find them, too.)
Maybe she'll weep, if there are any tears left.
Maybe – who knows? – she'll even wish for those days
back again! Who knows anything anymore?

But wishes don't come true, and it's a good thing.
Still, she's bound to keep your picture out
on the table for a while and make over you
for a time. Then, soon, you'll go
into the big family album along with the other crazies –
herself, her daughter and me, her former husband. You'll be
safe in there, cheek to jowl with all your victims. But don't
worry, my boy – the pages turn, my son. We all
do better in the future.

The son of my father

From *Sherwood Anderson's Memoirs*, 1942

A boy wants something very special from his father. You are always hearing it said that fathers want their sons to be what they feel they cannot themselves be but I tell you it also works the other way. I know that, as a small boy, I wanted my father to be a certain thing he was not, could not be. I wanted him to be a proud silent dignified one. When I was with other small boys and he passed along the street, I wanted to feel in my breast the glow of pride.

'There he is. That is my father.'

But he wasn't such a one. He couldn't be. It seemed to me then that he was always showing off. Let's say someone in our town had got up a show. They were always doing it. At that time it would have been the GAR, the Grand Army of the Republic. They did it to raise some money to help pay the rent of their hall.

So they had a show, the druggist in it, the fellow who clerked in the shoe store. A certain horse doctor was always in such shows in our town and, to be sure, a lot of women and girls. They got as many in it as they could so that all of the relatives of the actors would come. It was to be, of course, a comedy.

And there was my father. He had managed to get the chief comedy part. It was, let's say, a Civil War play and he was a comic Irish soldier. He had to do the most absurd things. They thought he was funny, but I didn't think so.

I thought he was terrible. I didn't see how Mother could stand it. She even laughed with the others. It may be that I also would have laughed if it hadn't been my father.

Or there was a parade, say on the Fourth of July or on Decoration Day. He'd be in that too. He'd be right at the front of it. He had got himself appointed Grand Marshal or some such office, had got, to ride in the parade, a white horse hired from a livery stable.

He couldn't ride for shucks. He fell off the horse and everyone hooted with laughter but he did not care. He even seemed to like it. I remember one such occasion when he had done something ridiculous, and right out on the main street too, when I couldn't stand it. I was with some other boys and they were laughing and

shouting at him and he was shouting back to them and having
as good a time as they were. I ran away. There was an alleyway
back of the stores on Main Street and I ran down that. There
were some sheds, back of the Presbyterian church, where country
people stabled horses during church on Sundays and I went in
there. I had a good long cry.

And then there came a certain night. Mother was away from
home when Father came in and he was alone. He'd been
off somewhere for two or three weeks. He found me alone in
the house.

He came silently into the house and it was raining outside. It
may be there was church that night and that Mother had gone.
I was alone and was sitting in the kitchen. I had a book before
me and was sitting and reading by the kitchen table.

So in came my father. He had been walking in the rain and
was very wet. He sat and looked at me and I was startled for,
on that night, there was on his face the saddest look I have ever
seen on a human face. For a long time he sat looking at me, not
saying a word.

And then something happened to me.

There are times when a boy is so sad, he doesn't quite know
why, that he thinks he can hardly bear to go on living. He thinks
he'd rather die. The sadness comes mostly when it has been
raining or it comes in the fall when the leaves fall off the trees.
It isn't anything special. It is just sadness.

So there was Father on the rainy summer night. He was sad
and looking at him made me sad. He sat for a time, saying
nothing, his clothes dripping. He must have been walking a long
time in the rain. He got up out of his chair.

'You come on, you come with me,' he said.

I got up and went with him out of the house. I was filled
with wonder but, although he had suddenly become like a
stranger to me, I wasn't afraid. We went along a street. At that
time we lived in a little yellow frame house, quite far out at
the edge of our town. It was a house we hadn't lived in very
long. We had moved a lot. Once I heard my mother say to my
father, 'Well, I guess we'll have to be moving,' she said. She
said we were back three months on our rent and that there
wasn't any money to pay it with. She didn't scold. She even

laughed. She just took it as a fact that when the rent got far
behind we had to move.

I was walking with my father and we went out of the town.
We were on a dirt road. It was a road that led up a little hill,
past fields and strips of woodland, and went on over the hill and
down into a little valley, about a mile out of town, to where there
was a pond. We walked in silence. The man who was always
talking had stopped talking.

I didn't know what was up and had the queer feeling that I
was with a stranger. I don't know now whether or not my father
intended it so. I don't think he did.

The pond at the edge of the town was quite large. It was a
place where a creek had been dammed and was owned by a man
who sold ice in our town. We were there at the edge of the pond.
We had come in silence. It was still raining hard and there were
flashes of lightning followed by thunder. We were on a grassy
bank at the pond's edge, when my father spoke, and in the darkness and rain his voice sounded strange. It was the only time
during the evening that he did speak to me.

'Take off your clothes,' he said and, still filled with wonder, I
began to undress. There was a flash of lightning and I saw that
he was already naked.

And so naked we went into the pond. He did not speak or
explain. Taking my hand he led me down to the pond's edge and
pulled me in. It may be that I was too frightened, too full of a
feeling of strangeness to speak. Before that night my father had
never seemed to pay any attention to me.

'And what is he up to now?' I kept asking myself that question. It was as though the man, my father I had not wanted as
father, had got suddenly some kind of power over me.

I was afraid and then, right away, I wasn't afraid. We were in
the pond in darkness. It was a large pond and I did not swim
very well but he had put my hand on his shoulder. Still he did
not speak but struck out at once into the darkness.

He was a man with very big shoulders and was a powerful
swimmer. In the darkness I could feel the movement of his muscles.
The rain poured down on us and the wind blew and there were
the flashes of lightning followed by the peals of thunder.

And so we swam, I will never know for how long. It seemed
hours to me. We swam thus in the darkness to the far edge of the

pond and then back to where we had left our clothes. There was the rain on our faces. Sometimes my father turned and swam on his back and when he did he took my hand in his large powerful one and moved it over so that it rested always on his shoulder and sometimes as we swam thus I could look into his face. There would be a flash of lightning and I could see his face clearly.

It was as it was when he had come earlier into the kitchen where I sat reading the book. It was a face filled with sadness. There would be the momentary glimpse of his face and then again the darkness, the wind and the rain. In me there was a feeling I had never known before that night.

It was a feeling of closeness. It was something strange. It was as though there were only we two in the world. It was as though I had been jerked suddenly out of myself, out of a world of the schoolboy, out of a world in which I was ashamed of my father, out of a place where I had been judging my father.

He had become blood of my blood. I think I felt it. He the stronger swimmer and I the boy clinging to him in the darkness. We swam in silence and in silence we dressed, in our wet clothes, and went back along the road to the town and our house.

It had become a strange house to me. There was the little porch at the front where on so many nights my father had sat with the men. There was the tree by the spring and the shed at the back. There was a lamp lighted in the kitchen and when we came in, the water dripping from us, there was my mother. She was as she had always been. She smiled at us. I remember that she called us 'boys'. 'What have you boys been up to?' she asked, but my father did not answer. As he had begun the evening's experience with me in silence so he ended it. He turned and looked at me and then he went, I thought with a new and strange dignity, out of the room.

He went to his room to get out of his wet clothes and I climbed the stairs to my own room. I undressed in darkness and got into bed. I was still in the grip of the feeling of strangeness that had taken possession of me in the darkness in the pond. I couldn't sleep and did not want to sleep. For the first time I had come to know that I was the son of my father. He was a storyteller as I was to be. It may be that on the night of my childhood I even laughed a little softly there in the darkness in my bed in the room. If I did, I laughed knowing that, no matter how much as a storyteller I might be using him, I would never again be wanting another father.

⤚

So there!

A boy writes to his father, Greece, *c.* 300

Theon to his father Theon, greeting. Thank you for not taking me to town with you. If you won't take me with you to Alexandria I won't write you a letter or speak to you or say goodbye to you; and if you go to Alexandria I won't take your hand nor greet you again. That is what will happen if you won't take me. Mother said to Archelaos, 'He drives me crazy: take him.' Thank you for sending me presents . . . Send for me, *please*. If you don't I won't eat, I won't drink; there now!

⤚

The old chestnut

From Oliver Goldsmith, *The Good Natur'd Man*, 1768

LEONTINE: An only son, sir, might expect more indulgence
CROAKER: An only father, sir, might expect more obedience

⤚

The Father and the Son

David Citino, 1947–

I nick my chin while shaving;
my son bares his wrist,
searches for the rustiest blade,
sorrow pooling in his eyes.

I scold; he thrusts his hand
into ice, fire, calls himself
'Forever Second Best', climbs
the cross, singing 'It is finished.'

I grow comic; he invents love,
the erection, children.
He watches as I go ashen,
fall backwards into the casket.

We trade places; I bring flowers,
light memory's candles with
his last breath. We trade places.
This goes on forever and ever.

The prestige of the father

From Simone de Beauvoir, *The Second Sex*, 1949

The life of the father has a mysterious prestige: the hours
he spends at home, the room where he works, the objects
he has around him, his pursuits, his hobbies, have a sacred
character. He supports the family, and he is the responsible
head of the family. As a rule his work takes him outside,
and so it is through him that the family communicates with
the rest of the world: he incarnates that immense, difficult
and marvellous world of adventure; he personifies tran-
scendence, he is God.

'As long as my dad was there'

News report in *The Daily Telegraph*, August 2000

A boy was saved from drowning when a plaster cast on his fractured arm wedged him above the waterline after he fell down a
narrow outlet pipe.

Seven-year-old Sean Herman spent 40 minutes trapped inside
the shaft as the tidal waters began to rise around him.

He was freed when his father and a fireman managed to lasso a rope on to the wrist of his uninjured arm and pull him out.

Sean had broken his left arm when he fell while climbing a fence.

Wayne Herman, 28, his father, took him and his two-year-old sister Courtney fishing at Smith's Dock, North Shields, North Tyneside, on Sunday.

Sean disappeared when he stepped into some undergrowth behind him and fell 12ft down the concealed outlet pipe.

Rescuers believe his plaster cast prevented him falling a further 15ft down the pipe at the abandoned dry dock.

Mr Herman, a merchant seaman, said: 'If ever there was a lucky break it was this one. The cast was sticking out at a funny angle and added that extra vital inch that wedged him in the pipe.'

Another angler ran over and Mr Herman asked him to call the fire brigade as he grabbed a rope from a boat. He tied a slip knot which he lowered down to his son, who grabbed it in his teeth.

Mr Herman said: 'I told him to keep calm but that it was very important he got his good arm free . . . I managed to lasso his wrist and pulled the slip knot tight, so at least I had him secure . . . and held the rope and made sure he didn't slip below the waterline.

'It must have taken about 20 minutes for the fire brigade to arrive but it felt like an eternity. I could see his little face looking up at me and he was calling "Please get me out, Daddy."'

A fireman joined him and they were able gradually to hoist Sean up until he emerged from the pipe. Mr Herman said: 'We had to act quickly because of the tide but thankfully we managed to get him out before the water level rose any further.'

Sean, who suffered cuts and bruises, was taken to hospital for a check-up. He said: 'I was scared but I knew as long as my dad was there I would be all right.'

~

'Dads ought to have their whack sometimes'

From a letter by Edward Burne-Jones, 1861, shortly
after his marriage

I want my dad to come and live near me: business doesn't answer and he grows old [he was 59], and a little cottage twelve miles out of London seems a good idea. Next year I hope it can be managed – by then I shall be out of debt and getting on a bit. Dads ought to have their whack sometimes; it's very dull to be a dad and have a son cutting about and enjoying himself and still be working on drearily. I shall hate it when I'm a dad.

~

An aperitif for the world of men

From Kirk Douglas, *The Ragman's Son*, 1988

I loved my father but I hated him, too. He was a ragman who drove a horse and wagon and couldn't read or write. But to me he was big. He was strong. He was a man. I didn't know what I was. But I wanted to be accepted by him, to be given a pat on the back. I would walk past the saloon at night, its curtains raised high on the tall windows so that no young boy could peer over them. I'd hear my father's voice in there, in that roaring accent, regaling his drunken cronies with some story about things that had happened in Russia; I'd hear them all burst into laughter. It was the world of men. No women were allowed, and I wasn't allowed either. I kept waiting for my father to take me by the hand into the world of men.

Once he gave me just a taste of it, a tease. One hot summer day, Pa took me by the hand and led me into a saloon. I can see it so clearly, the streaks of brilliant sunlight streaming through the window and then the black shadows in contrast . . . just like the movie sets that I would later play in. No one was there but the bartender. My father bought me a glass of loganberry. Nectar of the gods! I was in the world of men for a brief moment, even though the men had not yet arrived. But I was in their habitat. Later on, I would be in those settings often with Burt Lancaster or John Wayne. It always made me smile, because it seemed to me that we were all still children pretending to be in the world of men.

~

Anecdote for Fathers

William Wordsworth, 1798

I have a boy of five years old;
His face is fair and fresh to see;
His limbs are cast in beauty's mould,
And dearly he loves me.

One morn we strolled on our dry walk,
Our quiet home all full in view,
And held such intermitted talk
As we are wont to do.

My thoughts on former pleasures ran;
I thought of Kilve's delightful shore,
Our pleasant home when spring began,
A long, long year before.

A day it was when I could bear
Some fond regrets to entertain;
With so much happiness to spare,
I could not feel a pain.

The green earth echoed to the feet
Of lambs that bounded through the glade,
From shade to sunshine, and as fleet
From sunshine back to shade.

Birds warbled round me – and each trace
Of inward sadness had its charm;
Kilve, thought I, was a favoured place,
And so is Liswyn farm.

My boy beside me tripped, so slim
And graceful in his rustic dress!
And, as we talked, I questioned him,
In very idleness.

'Now tell me, had you rather be,'
I said, and took him by the arm,
'On Kilve's smooth shore, by the green sea,
Or here at Liswyn farm?'

In careless mood he looked at me,
While still I held him by the arm,
And said, 'At Kilve I'd rather be
Than here at Liswyn farm.'

'Now, little Edward, say why so:
My little Edward, tell me why.' –
'I cannot tell, I do not know.' –
'Why, this is strange,' said I;

'For here are woods, hills smooth and warm:
There surely must some reason be
Why you would change sweet Liswyn farm
For Kilve by the green sea.'

At this my boy hung down his head,
He blushed with shame, nor made reply;
And three times to the child I said,
'Why, Edward, tell me why?'

His head he raised – there was in sight,
It caught his eye, he saw it plain –
Upon the house-top, glittering bright,
A broad and gilded vane.

Then did the boy his tongue unlock,
And eased his mind with this reply:
'At Kilve there was no weather-cock;
And that's the reason why.'

O dearest, dearest boy! my heart
For better lore would seldom yearn,
Could I but teach the hundredth part
Of what from thee I learn.

Boxing lesson

From *The Autobiography of Benvenuto Cellini*,
1558–62

When I was already about three years old my grandfather Andrea was still alive and over a hundred. One day they were changing a cistern pipe when a large scorpion which they had not noticed crawled out of it, slipped to the ground, and scuttled away under a bench. I caught sight of it, ran over, and picked the thing up. It was so big that when I had it in my little hand its tail hung out at one end and both its claws at the other. They say that laughing happily I ran up to my grandfather and said: 'Look, grandpapa, look at my lovely little crab.' He recognised what it was and almost dropped dead from shock and anxiety. Then he tried to coax me into giving it to him, but the more he did so the more I screamed tearfully, refusing to give it to anyone.

My father was also in the house and, hearing the noise, he ran in to see what it was all about. He was so terror-stricken that his mind refused to work and he could not think up any way of stopping the poisonous creature from killing me. Then his eyes fell on a pair of scissors and he managed to wheedle me into letting him snip off the scorpion's tail and claws. When the danger was past he regarded it as a good omen.

Another time, when I was about five, my father was sitting alone in one of our small rooms, singing and playing his viol. Some washing had just been done there and a good log fire was still burning. It was very cold, and he had drawn near the fire. Then, as he was looking at the flames, his eye fell on a little animal, like a lizard, that was running around merrily in the very hottest part of the fire. Suddenly realising what it was, he called my sister and myself and showed it to us. And then he gave me such a violent box on the ears that I screamed and burst into tears. At this he calmed me as kindly as he could and said: 'My dear little boy, I didn't hit you because you had done wrong. I only did it so that you will never forget that the lizard you saw in the fire is a salamander, and as far as we know for certain no one has ever seen one before.'

Then he kissed me and gave me a little money.

Rebel son without a pause

From the diary of Reverend Ralph Josselin

Oct. 9 [1669]:	A sad morning with John, his stout heart outwardly submitted(,) I forgave him and god I hope mee.
Nov. 29 [1669]:	John tooké his clothes and mony and in the morning unknown to any of us. or without a line to tell what he aimed at went away. Lord let him not outrun thy mercy. I will daily seeke to god to keepe him. to breake his heart and deliver him from his own evill mind, and save his soule. lord heare prayer. hasten an houre of love for him for Christs sake.
Feb. 4 [1670]:	faire and dry. John returned, but lord change his heart, make us wise to win him to thee, god good in his word, lord owne us for thine
Feb. 12:	A good day in my affectionate strivings to recover sinners out of Satans and their hearts snare, my soule yearned over John. oh Lord overcome his heart in obedience to thee.
Feb. 19:	A sad weeke with John, his carriage intolerable. uncertain what to resolve. Lord direct mee. a day of comfort in the word, though troubles in my house. 26. came home opportunely to save a cow cast. found John within, but as I dreamed high and proud so he was(,) cast him lord down as that cow that he may rise up again.
Mar. 12:	Sad with my sons as to their trades, and sadder nearer mee. the lord helpe mee, for I stand alone as to all helpe and comfort, but from thee. god carries on my outward affaires beyond expectations(.) a sweet raine
Mar. 19:	John rid away, carried some things with him. without taking his leave of mee.
Mar. 22:	god in mercy looke after him

Crime and punishment

Deuteronomy 21: 18–22

18 ¶ If a man have a stubborn and rebellious son, which will not obey the voice of his father, or the voice of his mother, and *that*, when they have chastened him, will not hearken unto them:

19 Then shall his father and his mother lay hold on him, and bring him out unto the elders of his city, and unto the gate of his place;

20 And they shall say unto the elders of his city. This our son *is* stubborn and rebellious, he will not obey our voice; *he is* a glutton, and a drunkard.

21 And all the men of his city shall stone him with stones, that he die: so shalt thou put evil away from among you; and all Israel shall hear, and fear.

Off with his hand

Code of Hammurabi, Babylon, eighteenth century BC

If a son has struck his father, they shall cut off his hand.

The elephant's tale

Dr Wade F. Horn, *The Washington Times*, 1999

Recently, the National Fatherhood Initiative released a television public service announcement recounting the true story of the consequence when a group of young male elephants was transported from one wild game preserve in Africa to another without also transporting older bull elephants with them.

Without the presence of older male elephants, this group of juvenile elephants began to do something elephants just don't do in the wild – they began marauding in bands, wantonly killing other animals. This pack of 'wilding' juvenile elephants especially liked to harass white rhinos – chasing them over great distances, throwing sticks at them and finally stomping them to death.

It was only after a group of adult male elephants was transported into the game preserve that this delinquent and violent behaviour stopped.

How did this happen? Did the older elephants bring the younger males together to express their feelings? No. They started to enforce the rules. In no uncertain terms, the older males began to discipline the younger elephants. Quickly, the younger males fell back into line. There hasn't been a report of a single murderous elephant since.

If we want to prevent future tragedies such as the Littleton school massacre, we have to take a lesson from the elephants. Little boys, like juvenile elephants, need the presence of adult males who monitor their behaviour and enforce the rules. And in doing so, we also have to give them opportunities to express their maleness and desire for meaning in ways that don't involve worshipping Adolf Hitler or Marilyn Manson.

Boys will be boys. Whether they grow up to be well-socialised, decent men is up to us.

~~

Father knows best (even when you're forty)

From Blake Morrison's *And When Did You Last See Your Father?*, 1985

He isn't drinking, isn't eating. He wears his trousers open at the waist, held up not by a belt but by pain and swelling. He looks like death, but he is not dead and won't be for another four weeks. He has driven down from Yorkshire to London. He has made it against the odds. He is still my father. He is still here.

'I've brought some plants for you.'

'Come and sit down first, Dad, you've been driving for hours.'

'No, best get them unloaded.'

It's like Birnam Wood coming to Dunsinane, black plastic bags and wooden boxes blooming in the back seat, the rear window, the boot: herbs, hypericum, escallonia, cotoneaster, ivies, potentillas. He directs me where to leave the different plants – which will need shade, which sun, which shelter. Like all my father's presents, they come with a pay-off. He will not leave until he has seen every one of them planted: 'I know you. And I don't want them drying up.'

We walk round the house, the expanse of rooms, so different from the old flat. 'It's wonderful to see you settled at last,' he says, and I resist telling him that I'm not settled, have never felt less settled in my life. I see his eyes taking in the little things to be done, the leaky taps, the cracked paint, the rotting window-frames.

'You'll need a new switch unit for the mirror light – the contact has gone, see.'

'Yes.'

'And a couple of two-inch Phillips screws will solve this.'

'I've got some. Let's have a drink now, eh?'

'What's the schedule for tomorrow?' he asks, as always, and I'm irritated, as always, at his need to parcel out the weekend into a series of tasks, as if without a plan of action it wouldn't be worth his coming, not even to see his son or grandchildren. 'I don't think I'll be much help to you,' he says, 'but I'll try.' By nine-thirty he is in bed and asleep.

I wake him next day at nine, unthinkably late, with a pint-mug of tea, unthinkably refused. After his breakfast of strawberry Complan he comes round the house with me, stooped and crouching over his swollen stomach. For once it's me who is going to have to do the hammering and screwing. We go down to the hardware shop in Greenwich, where he charms the socks off the black assistant, who gives me a shrug and a pat at the end, as if to say, 'Where'd you get a dad like this from?' Back home again, he decides that the job for him is to get the curtains moving freely on their rails. 'You know the best thing for it?' he says. 'Furniture polish. Get me a can of it and I'll sort it out for you.' He teeters on a wooden kitchen stool at each of the windows in the house, his trousers gaping open, and sprays polish on the rails and wipes it over with a dirty rag. His balance looks precarious, and I try to talk him down, but he is stubborn.

'No, it needs doing. And every time you pull the curtains from now on, you can think of me.'

I ask him about the operation: is he apprehensive?

'No point in being. They have to have a look. I expect it's an infarct, and they'll be able to cure that, but if not . . . well, I've had a good life and I've left everything in order for you.'

'I'd rather you than order.'

'Too true.'

I make sure there are only two light but time-consuming jobs for us. The first is to fix a curtain pole across the garden end of the kitchen, over the glazed door, and we spend the best part of two hours bickering about the best way to do this: there's a problem on the left-hand side because the kitchen cupboards finish close to the end wall, six inches or so, and you can't get an electric drill in easily to make the holes for the fixing bracket. The drill keeps sheering off, partly because I'm unnerved by him standing below, drawing something on the back of an envelope. I get down and he shows me his plan: a specially mounted shelf in the side wall to support the pole rather than a fixing bracket for it on the end. Sighing and cursing, I climb back up and follow his instructions in every detail – not just the size of screws and Rawlplugs needed, but how to clasp the hammer.

'Hold it at the end, you daft sod, not up near the top.'

'Christ, Dad, I'm forty-one years old.'

'And you still don't know how to hold a hammer properly – or a screwdriver.' Infuriatingly, his plan works – the shelf mounting, the pole, the curtain, all fine. I try not to give him the satisfaction of admitting it.

We bicker our way into the next room and the other job: to hang the chandelier he once gave me, inherited from Uncle Bert. At some point in the move, many of the glass pieces have become separated, and now, in the dim November light behind the tall sash-window, we spend the afternoon working out where they belong, reattaching them with bits of wire, and then strengthening the candelabra from which they dangle. 'This really needs soldering,' he says, meaning that he will find an alternative to soldering, since to solder would mean going out and spending money on a soldering iron when he has a perfectly good one at home. I watch him bowed over the glass diamonds, with pliers and fractured screw-threads and nuts and bits of wire: the improviser, the amateur inventor. I think of all the jobs he's done for me down the years, and how sooner or later I'll have to learn to do them for myself. The metal clasps joining glass ball to glass ball are like the clasps on his King Edward cigar boxes, and like those on his old student skeleton, Janet, whom we'd joined together once, bone to bone.

'I think that's it,' he says, attaching a last bauble. 'Three pieces missing, but no one will notice.' He stands at the foot of the stepladder, holding the heavy chandelier while I connect the two electrical wires to the ceiling rose, tighten the rose-cover and slip the ring-attachment over the dangling hook. He lets go tentatively – 'Gently does it' – unable to believe, since he has not done the fixing himself, that the chandelier will hold. It holds. We turn the light on, and the six candle-bulbs shimmer through the cage of glass, the prison of prisms. 'Let there be light,' my dad says, the only time I can ever remember him quoting anything. We stand there gawping upward for a moment, as if we had witnessed a miracle, or as if this were a grand ballroom, not a suburban dining-room, and the next dance, if we had the courage to take part in it, might be the beginning of a new life. Then he turns the switch off and it's dark again and he says: 'Excellent. What's the next job, then?'

The good father, he ain't heavy

From Maureen Green, *Goodbye Father*, 1976

Though a boy seems to need his father most in the years before five, the rest of his childhood also contributes to the man he ultimately becomes. And folk wisdom has always to some extent recognised this. Growing up alongside a father who talks to him, takes a constant interest in him, makes decisions that his son is aware of, sets some limits to what his son may or may not do, gets his son to work with him on jobs and play with him in sports, enriches and smooths the transition from young child to adolescent. If his father knows how to praise and encourage rather than criticise and undermine, he will learn all the faster. The 'heavy father', pompous and authoritarian, seems simply to put his son off.

Thoughtlessness

Harry Graham, the inventor of 'ruthless rhymes',
1874–1936

I never shall forget my shame
To find my son had forged my name.
If he'd had any thought for others
He might at least have forged his mother's.

～

The ungrateful son

From *Grimm's Fairy Tales*, 1812–22

A man and his wife were once sitting by the door of their house, and they had a roasted chicken set before them, and were about to eat it together. Then the man saw that his aged father was coming, and hastily took the chicken and hid it, for he would not permit him to have any of it. The old man came, took a drink, and went away. Now the son wanted to put the roasted chicken on the table again, but when he took it up, it had become a great toad, which jumped into his face and sat there and never went away again, and if any one wanted to take it off, it looked venomously at him as if it would jump in his face, so that no one would venture to touch it. And the ungrateful son was forced to feed the toad every day, or else it fed itself on his face; and thus he went about the world knowing no rest.

～

The prodigal son

The Gospel According to Saint Luke, 17: 11–32

11 ¶And he said, A certain man had two sons:
12 And the younger of them said to *his* father, Father, give me the portion of goods that falleth *to me*. And he divided unto them *his* living.

13 And not many days after the younger son gathered all together, and took his journey into a far country, and there wasted his substance with riotous living.

14 And when he had spent all, there arose a mighty famine in that land; and he began to be in want.

15 And he went and joined himself to a citizen of that country; and he sent him into his fields to feed swine.

16 And he would fain have filled his belly with the husks that the swine did eat: and no man gave unto him.

17 And when he came to himself, he said, How many hired servants of my father's have bread enough and to spare, and I perish with hunger!

18 I will arise and go to my father, and will say unto him, Father, I have sinned against heaven, and before thee,

19 And am no more worthy to be called thy son: make me as one of thy hired servants.

20 And he arose, and came to his father. But when he was yet a great way off, his father saw him, and had compassion, and ran, and fell on his neck, and kissed him.

21 And the son said unto him, Father, I have sinned against heaven, and in thy sight, and am no more worthy to be called thy son.

22 But the father said to his servants, Bring forth the best robe, and put *it* on him; and put a ring on his hand, and shoes on *his* feet:

23 And bring hither the fatted calf, and kill *it*; and let us eat, and be merry:

24 For this my son was dead, and is alive again; he was lost, and is found. And they began to be merry.

25 Now his elder son was in the field: and as he came and drew nigh to the house, he heard musick and dancing.

26 And he called one of the servants, and asked what these things meant.

27 And he said unto him. Thy brother is come; and thy father hath killed the fatted calf, because he hath received him safe and sound.

28 And he was angry, and would not go in: therefore came his father out, and entreated him.

29 And he answering said to *his* father, Lo, these many years do I serve thee, neither transgressed I at any time thy command-

ment: and yet thou never gavest me a kid, that I might make merry with my friends:

30 But as soon as this thy son was come, which hath devoured thy living with harlots, thou hast killed for him the fatted calf.

31 And he said unto him, Son, thou art ever with me, and all that I have is thine.

32 It was meet that we should make merry, and be glad: for this thy brother was dead, and is alive again; and was lost, and is found.

⌐

The toughest thing in the world

William Carlos Williams writes to his son Bill, in July 1942 and July 1944

That relationship between father and son is one of the toughest things in the world to break down. It seems so natural and it is natural – in fact it's inevitable – but it separates as much as it joins. A man wants to protect his son, wants to teach him the things he, the father, has learned or thinks he has learned. But it's exactly that which a child resents. He wants to know but he wants to know on his own – and the longer the paternal influence lasts the harder it is to break down and the more two individuals who should have much in common are pushed apart. Only a sudden enforced break can get through that one.

But I've sweated over wanting to do and say the right thing concerning you boys. Certain things stick in my mind – I just didn't do the right thing and I suffered for it. Once when you were a little kid some question of veracity came up between you and Elsie, that goofy girl we had here. I should have known that you were just a baby but I lost my temper, insisting one of you was lying when I should have known, if I had thought for a moment, that it wasn't you. Or if it was, then what the hell anyway? It might have been from fear – no doubt of me. Then one day at the close of Watty's camp in Maine you were in some sort of a canoe race and were about to win when someone quite unfairly cut you out and you cried. I like a God-damned fool laughed at you. Why? Just to hide my own embarrassment. You looked at me and said, 'It was my only chance to win anything!' I tell you that hurt. I've never forgotten it. Such are a father's inner regrets. Stupid enough. And what in the hell is a parent to do when an older child is tormented by a younger child, finally smears his younger tormentor and then comes up for punishment? I've never solved that one. I've done many more seriously stupid things than those mentioned – but I wanted so hard to give you the best.

On the other hand, when you say you've got so much more in the bank than some of the men you have to deal with, I feel that what we did for you wasn't too bad. The same for what you say about the kitten and the spiders. That you can get the good out of such trivia is a tribute to your mind which I have always respected and which I'm glad to see maintaining itself with distinction in the situation in which you are placed. I don't know what kind of a father I was but in things like that at least something 'took' of what I intended and that it wasn't all beside the point.

You say you'd like to see my book of poems. What the hell? Let 'em go. They are things I wrote because to maintain myself in a world much of which I didn't love I had to fight to keep myself as I wanted to be. The poems are me, in much of the faulty perspective in which I have existed in my own sight – and nothing to copy, not for anyone even so much as to admire. I have wanted to link myself up with a traditional art, to feel that I was developing individually it might be, but along with that, developing still in the true evolving tradition of the art. I wonder how much I have succeeded there. I haven't been recognised and I doubt that my technical influence is good or even adequate.

However, this is just one more instance of the benefits to be gained by breaking entirely with the father–son hook-up. It was logical for you not to have looked at my poems – or only casually to look at them. You had me in my own person too strongly before you to need that added emphasis. You did the right thing and I never cared a damn. Now, separated from me by distance and circumstance, it may after all be permissible for you to look at the poems. Not to do anything more than to enjoy them, man to man, if you can get any enjoyment out of them, I'll send them. I have a gold-edged copy reserved for you, one of the de luxe copies, but I'll not send that. Look, if you care to, at whatever

I have done as if you had never known me. That's the only way for a father and son to behave toward each other after the son's majority has been reached. Then, if you still find something to cherish, it will be something worthwhile.

*

Proud of you, Bill, real proud of you. A father follows the course of his son's life and notes many things of which he has not the privilege to speak. He sees, of course, his own past life unfolding – with many variations, naturally. Sees moments when he'd like to speak a word of warning or commendation – places where he himself went wrong or made a difficult decision that was profitable later. And all the time he can't say much.

He can't say anything largely because he realises that in the present case, the case of his son's life, a new and radically different individual is facing life, that the life he faces is different from the life the older man knew when he was young. But mostly he can't speak because – he can't. It would do no good. Likewise he can't praise, much as he'd like to.

My Papa's Waltz

Theodore Roethke, *Selected Poems*, 1969

> The whiskey on your breath
> Could make a small boy dizzy;
> But I hung on like death:
> Such waltzing was not easy.
>
> We romped until the pans
> Slid from the kitchen shelf;
> My mother's countenance
> Could not unfrown itself.
>
> The hand that held my wrist
> Was battered on one knuckle;
> At every step you missed
> My right ear scraped a buckle.

You beat time on my head
With a palm caked hard by dirt,
Then waltzed me off to bed
Still clinging to your shirt.

∽

Fatherwards

From *Iron John*, Robert Bly, 1993

It takes a while for a son to overcome these early negative
views of the father. The psyche holds on tenaciously to these
early perceptions. Idealisation of the mother or obsession with
her, liking her or hating her, may last until the son is thirty,
or thirty-five, forty. Somewhere around forty or forty-five a
movement toward the father takes place naturally – a desire
to see him more clearly and to draw closer to him. This
happens unexplainably, almost as if on a biological timetable.

A friend told me how that movement took place in his
life. At about thirty-five, he began to wonder who his father
really was. He hadn't seen his father in about ten years. He
flew out to Seattle, where his father was living, knocked on
the door, and when his father opened the door, said, 'I want
you to understand one thing. I don't accept my mother's
view of you any longer.'

'What happened?' I asked.

'My father broke into tears, and said, "Now I can die."'
Fathers wait. What else can they do?

∽

The ghost of Achilles seeks news of his son and father

From Homer's *The Odyssey*, Book II, in which Odysseus enters 'the infernal regions' Translated by William Cowper, 1792

But come – speak to me of my noble boy;
Proceeds he, as he promis'd, brave in arms,

Or shuns he war? Say also, hast thou heard
Of royal Peleus? shares he still respect
Among his num'rous Myrmidons, or scorn
In Hellas and in Phthia, for that age
Predominates in his enfeebled limbs?
For help is none in me; the glorious sun
No longer sees me such, as when in aid
Of the Achaians I o'erspread the field
Of spacious Troy with all their bravest slain.
Oh might I, vigorous as then, repair
For one short moment to my father's house,
They all should tremble; I would shew an arm,
Such as should daunt the fiercest who presumes
To injure *him*, or to despise his age.

Achilles spake, to whom I thus replied.
Of noble Peleus have I nothing heard;
But I will tell thee, as thou bidd'st, the truth
Unfeign'd of Neoptolemus thy son;
For him, myself, on board my hollow bark
From Scyros to Achaia's host convey'd.
Oft as in council under Ilium's walls
We met, he ever foremost was in speech,
Nor spake erroneous; Nestor and myself
Except, no Grecian could with him compare.
Oft, too, as we with battle hemm'd around
Troy's bulwarks, from among the mingled crowd
Thy son sprang foremost into martial act,
Inferior in heroic worth to none.
Beneath him num'rous fell the sons of Troy
In dreadful fight, nor have I pow'r to name
Distinctly all, who by his glorious arm
Exerted in the cause of Greece, expired.
Yet will I name Eurypylus, the son
Of Telephus, an Hero whom his sword
Of life bereav'd, and all around him strew'd
The plain with his Cetean warriors, won
To Ilium's side by bribes to women giv'n.
Save noble Memnon only, I beheld
No Chief at Ilium beautiful as he.
Again, when we within the horse of wood
Framed by Epeüs sat, an ambush chos'n
Of all the bravest Greeks, and I in trust

Was placed to open or to keep fast-closed
The hollow fraud; then, ev'ry Chieftain there
And Senator of Greece wiped from his cheeks
The tears, and tremors felt in ev'ry limb;
But never saw I changed to terror's hue
His ruddy cheek, no tears wiped *he* away,
But oft he press'd me to go forth, his suit
With pray'rs enforcing, griping hard his hilt
And his brass-burthen'd spear, and dire revenge
Denouncing, ardent, on the race of Troy.
At length, when we had sack'd the lofty town
Of Priam, laden with abundant spoils
He safe embark'd, neither by spear or shaft
Aught hurt, or in close fight by faulchion's edge,
As oft in war befalls, where wounds are dealt
Promiscuous at the will of fiery Mars.
So I; then striding large, the spirit thence
Withdrew of swift Æacides, along
The hoary mead pacing, with joy elate
That I had blazon'd bright his son's renown.

3

Daddy's Girl

Beattie is Three

Adrian Mitchell, *Heart on the Left: Poems 1953–84*

At the top of the stairs
I ask for her hand. OK.
She gives it to me.
How her fist fits my palm.
A bunch of consolation.
We take our time
Down the steep carpetway
As I wish silently
That the stairs were endless.

Devotion

From Honoré de Balzac, *Old Goriot*, 1834

Goriot's unreflecting devotion and touchy, easily alarmed, protective love for his daughters was so well known that one day one of his competitors, who wanted to make him leave the Exchange in order to have the field to himself, told him that Delphine had just been knocked down by a cab. The vermicelli-maker, his face ghastly pale, left the Exchange at once. He was ill for several days as a result of the shock of this false alarm and the reaction from it. If he did not make this man feel the weight of his murderous fist he yet drove him from the Corn Exchange, forcing him into bankruptcy at a crisis in his affairs.

Naturally his two daughters were spoiled: their education was not subject to the dictates of common sense. Goriot was worth more than sixty thousand francs a year and spent barely twelve hundred on himself; his sole pleasure was to gratify his daughters' whims. The best masters were engaged to endow them with the accomplishments which are the hallmark of a good education; they had a chaperon – luckily for them she was a woman of intelligence and good taste; they rode; they kept their carriage; they lived like the mistresses of a rich old lord; they had only to express a wish for something, however costly, to see their father rush to give it to them, and he asked nothing in return but a kiss. Goriot raised his daughters to the rank of angels, and so of necessity above himself. Poor man! He even loved them for the pain they caused him.

To My Daughter

Stephen Spender, 1909–95

Bright clasp of her whole hand around my finger,
My daughter, as we walk together now.
All my life I'll feel a ring invisibly
Circle this bone with shining: when she is grown
Far from today as her eyes are already.

Foster father

From *Silas Marner*, 1861, by George Eliot

Silas Marner's determination to keep the 'tramp's child' was matter of hardly less surprising and iterated talk in the village than the robbery of his money. That softening of feeling towards him which dated from his misfortune, that merging of suspicion and dislike in a rather contemptuous pity for him as lone and crazy, was now accompanied with a more active sympathy, especially amongst the women. Notable mothers, who knew what it was to keep children 'whole and sweet'; lazy mothers, who knew what it was to be interrupted in folding their arms and scratching their elbows by the mischievous propensities of children just firm on their legs, were equally interested in conjecturing how a lone man would manage with a two-year-old child on his hands, and were equally ready with their suggestions: the notable chiefly telling him what he had better do, and the lazy ones being emphatic in telling him what he would never be able to do.

Among the notable mothers, Dolly Winthrop was the one whose neighbourly offices were the most acceptable to Marner, for they were rendered without any show of bustling instruction. Silas had asked her what he should do about getting some clothes for the child.

'Eh, Master Marner,' said Dolly, 'there's no call to buy, no more nor a pair o' shoes; for I've got the little petticoats as Aaron wore five years ago, and it's ill spending the money on them baby-clothes, for the child 'ull grow like grass i' May, bless it – that it will.'

And the same day Dolly brought her bundle, and displayed to Marner, one by one, the tiny garments in their due order of succession, most of them patched and darned, but clean and neat as fresh-sprung herbs. This was the introduction to a great ceremony with soap and water, from which baby came out in new beauty, and sat on Dolly's knee, handling her toes and chuckling and patting her palms together with an air of having made several discoveries about herself, which she communicated by alternate sounds of 'gug-gug-gug', and 'mammy'. The 'mammy' was not a cry of need or uneasiness: Baby had been used to utter it without expecting either sound or touch to follow.

'Anybody 'ud think the angils in heaven couldn't be prettier,' said Dolly, rubbing the golden curls and kissing them. 'And to think of its being covered wi' them dirty rags; but there's Them as took care of it, and brought it to your door, Master Marner. The door was open, and it walked in over the snow, like as if it had been a little starved robin. Didn't you say the door was open?'

'Yes,' said Silas, meditatively. 'Yes – the door was open. The money's gone I don't know where, and this is come from I don't know where.'

'I think you're in the right on it to keep the little un, Master Marner, seeing as it's been sent to you, though there's folks as thinks different. You'll happen be a bit moithered with it while it's so little; but I'll come, and welcome, and see to it for you. I've a bit o' time to spare most days, for when one gets up betimes i' the morning, the clock seems to stan' still tow'rt ten, afore it's time to go about the victual. So, as I say, I'll come to see to the child for you, and welcome.'

'Thank you . . . kindly,' said Silas, hesitating a little, 'I'll be
glad if you'll tell me things. But,' he added, uneasily, leaning
forward to look at Baby with some jealousy, as she was resting
her head backward against Dolly's arm, and eyeing him content-
edly from a distance – 'But I want to do things for it myself, else
it may get fond o' somebody else, and not fond o' me. I've been
used to fending for myself in the house – I can learn, I can learn.'

'Eh, to be sure, I've seen men as are wonderful handy with
children. You see this goes first, next the skin,' proceeded Dolly,
taking up the little shirt, and putting it on.

'Yes,' said Marner, docilely, bringing his eyes very close that
they might be initiated in the mysteries; whereupon Baby seized
his head with both her small arms, and put her lips against his
face with purring noises.

'See there,' said Dolly, with a woman's tender tact, 'she's fondest
o' you. She wants to go o' your lap, I'll be bound. Go, then: take
her, Master Marner; you can put the things on, and then you can
say as you've done for her from the first of her coming to you.'

Marner took her on his lap, trembling with an emotion mysterious to himself, at something unknown dawning on his life.
Thought and feeling were so confused within him, that if he had
tried to give them utterance, he could only have said that the child
was come instead of the gold – that the gold had turned into the
child. He took the garments from Dolly, and put them on under
her teaching; interrupted, of course, by Baby's gymnastics.

'There, then! why, you take to it quite easy, Master Marner,'
said Dolly; 'but what shall you do when you're forced to sit in
your loom? For she'll get busier and mischievouser every day – she
will, bless her. It's lucky as you've got that high hearth i'stead of
a grate, for that keeps the fire more out of her reach; but if you've
got anything as can be spilt or broke, or as is fit to cut her fingers
off, she'll be at it – and it is but right you should know.'

Silas meditated a little while in some perplexity. 'I'll tie her to
the leg o' the loom,' he said at last – 'tie her with a good long
strip o' something.'

'Well, mayhap that'll do, as it's a little gell, for they're easier
persuaded to sit i' one place nor the lads. I know what the lads
are; for I've had four – four I've had, God knows – and if you was
to take and tie 'em up, they'd make a fighting and a crying as if
you was ringing pigs. But I'll bring you my little chair, and some

bits o' red rag and things for her to play wi'; an' she'll sit and chatter to 'em as if they was alive. Eh, if it wasn't a sin to the lads to wish 'em made different, bless 'em, I should ha' been glad for one of 'em to be a little gell; and to think as I could ha' taught her to scour, and mend, and the knitting, and everything. But I can teach 'em this little un, Master Marner, when she gets old enough.'

'But she'll be *my* little un,' said Marner, rather hastily. 'She'll be nobody else's.'

~

Cocooned in her father's shirt

From a letter by Thomas Meauty, 1632

Now I pray, give me leave to ask you a question, and that is, How you like my little girl . . . ? I must tell you that she hath been lapt in the skirts of her father's shirt, for she is beloved where she comes, and I love her very well, and so doth she me; and yet sometimes I can whip [smack] her and love her too. You must excuse me for using this language, for when I cannot see my children it does me good to talk of them.

~

My girl

From Laurie Lee, *Two Women*, 1983

As she grew and changed, I was increasingly wondering what this new girl could be, with her ecstatic adorations and rages. The beaming knife-keen awakening, cracking the dawn like an egg, her furies at the small frets of living, the long fat slumbers, almost continental in their reaches, the bedtimes of chuckles, private jokes and languors.

And who was I to her? The rough dark shadow of pummelling games and shouts, the cosy frightener, the tossing and swinging arms, lifting the body to the highest point of hysteria before lowering it back again to the safe male smell.

But she was my girl now, the second force in my life, and with her puffed, knowing eyes, forever moving with colour and light, she was well aware of it.

⌒

A *nineteenth-century father writes from a business trip*

Thomas Hood to his daughter, 23 October 1837

MY DEAR FANNY,

I hope you are as good still as when I went away – a comfort to your good mother and a kind playfellow to your little brother. Mind you tell him my horse eats bread out of my hand, and walks up to the officers who are eating, and pokes his nose into the women's baskets. I wish I could give you both a ride. I hope you liked your paints; pray keep them out of Tom's way, as they are poisonous. I shall have rare stories to tell you when I come home; but mind, you must be good till then, or I shall be as mute as a stockfish. Your mama will show you on the map where I was when I wrote this [Halle]; and when she writes will let you put in a word.

Now God bless you, my dear little girl, my pet, and think of your

Loving Father,
THOMAS HOOD.

⌒

Listen up

From the diary of Cotton Mather, America, 1698, when his daughter was four

I took my little daughter Katy into my Study and then I told my child I am to dye Shortly and shee must, when I am Dead, remember Everything I now said unto her. I set before her the sinful Condition of her Nature, and I charged her to pray in Secret Places every Day. That God for the sake of Jesus Christ would give her a New Heart. I gave her to understand that when I am taken from her she must look to meet with more humbling Afflictions than she does now she has a Tender Father to provide for her.

⌒

Like father, like daughter

The author William Godwin writes to his author
daughter, Mary Shelley

Tuesday, 18 February [1823]
Do not, I entreat you, be cast down about your worldly circumstances. You certainly contain within yourself the means of your
subsistence. Your talents are truly extraordinary. *Frankenstein* is
universally known, and though it can never be a book for vulgar
reading, is everywhere respected. It is the most wonderful work
to have been written at twenty years of age that I ever heard of.
You are now five and twenty, and, most fortunately, you have
pursued a course of reading, and cultivated your mind, in a
manner the most admirably adapted to make you a great and
successful author. If you cannot be independent, who should be?

Your talents, as far as I can at present discern, are turned for
the writing of fictitious adventures.

If it shall ever happen to you to be placed in sudden and urgent
want of a small sum, I entreat you to let me know immediately;
we must see what I can do. We must help one another.

Your affectionate Father,
William Godwin

⌁

A runaway daughter

From *The Vicar of Wakefield*, Oliver Goldsmith,
1776

The next morning we missed our wretched child at breakfast, where
she used to give life and cheerfulness to us all. My wife . . .
attempted to ease her heart by reproaches. 'Never,' cried she, 'shall
that vilest stain of our family again darken these harmless doors.
I will never call her daughter more. No, let the strumpet live with
her vile seducer: she may bring us to shame, but she shall never
more deceive us.'

'Wife,' said I, 'do not talk thus hardly: my detestation of her
guilt is as great as yours; but ever shall this house and this heart

be open to a poor returning repentant sinner. The sooner she returns from her transgressions, the more welcome shall she be to me. For the first time the very best may err; art may persuade, and novelty spread out its charm. The first fault is the child of simplicity, but every other the offspring of guilt. Yes, the wretched creature shall be welcome to this heart and this house, though stained with ten thousand vices. I will again hearken to the music of her voice, again will I hang fondly on her bosom, if I find but repentance there. My son, bring hither my Bible and my staff: I will pursue her, wherever she is; and though I cannot save her from shame, I may prevent the continuance of iniquity.'

Affection but not seduction

From Majorie Leonard, 'Fathers and Daughters',
International Journal of Psychoanalysis, 1981

A father can be not there enough, which leads a girl to idealise her father and men, or to endow them with immensely sadistic or punitive characteristics – or can be there too much (be too possessive, seductive, or identified with their daughter), requiring her to develop defensive measures against involvement with him and with men. Fathers . . . must be able to make themselves available as a heterosexual love object and to offer affection without being seduced by their daughters' fantasies or seducing them with their own.

Freudian electricity

From 'Sugar Daddy' by Angela Carter, 1983

He is still capable of surprising me. He recently prepared an electric bed for my boyfriend, which is the sort of thing a doting father in a Scots ballad might have done had the technology been available at the time. We knew he'd put us in separate rooms – my father is a Victorian, by birth – but not that he'd plug the metal base of Mark's bed into the electric-light fitment. Mark noticed how the bed throbbed when he put his hand on it and disconnected every plug in sight. We ate breakfast, next morning, as if nothing untoward had happened, and I should say, in the context of my father's house, it had not. He is an enthusiastic handyman, with a special fascination with electricity, whose work my mother once described as combining the theory of Heath Robinson with the practice of Mr Pooter.

All the same, the Freudian overtones are inescapable. However unconsciously, as if *that* were an excuse, he'd prepared a potentially lethal bed for his daughter's lover. But let me not dot the i's and cross the t's. His final act of low, emotional cunning (another Highland characteristic) is to have lived so long that everything is forgiven, even his habit of referring to the present incumbent by my first husband's name, enough to give anybody a temporary feeling.

~

'That you are my daughter shouldn't do you any harm, either'

Sigmund Freud to his daughter Mathilde,
19 March 1908

I think you probably associate the present minor complaint with an old worry about which I should very much like to talk to you for once. I have guessed for a long time that in spite of all your common sense you fret because you think you are not good-looking enough and therefore might not attract a man. I have watched this with a smile, first of all because you seem quite attractive enough to me, and secondly because I know that in reality it is no longer physical beauty which decides the fate of a girl, but the impression of her whole personality. Your mirror will inform you that there is nothing common or repellent in your features, and your memory will confirm the fact that you have managed to inspire respect and sympathy in any circle of human beings. And as a result I have felt perfectly reassured about your future so far as it depends on you, and you have every reason to feel the same. That you are my daughter shouldn't do you any harm, either. I know that finding a respected name and a warm atmosphere in her home was decisive in my choice of a wife, and there are certain to be others who think as I did when I was young.

～

More reveals his daughters' goods

From John Aubrey's *Brief Lives*, written *c.* 1690

Sir Thomas More, Lord Chancellour:
Memorandum that in his *Utopia*, his lawe is that the young people are to see each other stark-naked before marriage. Sir [William] Roper, of . . . ('tis by Eltham in Kent), came one morning pretty early to my Lord, with a proposall to marry one of [his] daughters. My Lord's daughters were then both together a bed in a truckle-bed in their father's chamber asleep. He carries Sir [William] into the chamber, and takes the sheet by the corner and suddenly whippes it off. They lay on their backs, and their smocks up as high as their arme pitts; this awakened them, and immediately they turned on their bellies. Quoth Sir William Roper, 'I have seen both sides', and so gave a patt on her buttock, he made choice of, sayeing, 'Thou art mine.'
Here was all the trouble of the wooeing.

～

Independent fortune

From *The Journal of Eliza Weeton*, 1824

My father was for some time captain of a merchantman in the African slave trade, but the American war breaking out, he was next commissioned . . . to command a vessel carrying a Letter of Marque [i.e., orders to attack enemy vessels and win prize money]. In this vessel he sailed, and in the course of his voyage took many prizes. He returned, and was loaded with congratulations for his successful bravery. During this period, my mother had brought him three children; Edward, the eldest, who died at 3½ years old; next myself, born on Christmas Day, 1776, and christened by the name of Nelly. My father being out on a voyage when I was born, my mother was at a loss what name to give me; but knowing that the ship Nelly in which he was sailing, was a great favourite of his, she thought to win his affection for me by naming me after it, as she had heard him say that he could wish his children to be all boys. When he returned, and she told him this, he expressed himself as very sorry that she should have been hurt by what he said; declaring that he loved me as much as Edward (who was only 11 months older than I); but, he said, unless a father can provide independent fortunes for his daughters, they must either be mop squeezers, or mantua makers, whereas sons can easily make their way in the world.

~~

A father suckled by his daughter

E. Cobham Brewer, *Dictionary of Phrase and Fable*, 1870

Euphra'sia, the Grecian daughter, so [by suckling him] preserved the life of Evander, her aged father.

Xantip'pe so preserved the life of her father Cimo'nos in prison. The guard, marvelling the old man held out so long, set a watch and discovered the fact. Byron alludes to these stories in his *Childe Harold*.

> 'There is a dungeon, in whose dim, drear light
> What do I gaze on? . . .
> An old man, and a female young and fair,
> Fresh as a nursing mother, in whose vein
> The blood is nectar . . .
> Here youth offers to old age the food,
> The milk of his own gift: – it is her sire
> To whom she renders back the debt of blood . . .
> Drink, drink and live, old ma! heaven's realm holds no such
>   tide.'

Byron: *Childe Harold*, iv: 148, 150

~~

The fall

From a 'Short Digest of a Long Novel'
by Budd Schulberg, 1953

It was just before Christmas and she was sitting on her little chair, her lips pressed together in concentration, writing a last-minute letter to Santa Claus. The words were written in some language of her own invention but she obligingly translated as she went along.

> Dear Santa, I am a very good girl and everybody likes me. So please don't forget to bring me a set of dishes, a doll that goes to sleep and wakes up again, and a washing machine. I need the washing machine because Raggedy Ann's dress is so dirty.

After she had finished her letter, folded it, and asked him to address it, he tossed her up in the air, caught her and tossed her again, to hear her giggle. 'Higher, Daddy, higher,' she instructed. His mind embraced her sentimentally: she is a virgin island in a lewd world. She is a winged seed of innocence blown through the wasteland. If only she could root somewhere. If only she could grow like this.

'Let me down, Daddy,' she said when she decided that she had indulged him long enough, 'I have to mail my letter to Santa.'

'But didn't you see him this afternoon?' he asked. 'Didn't you ask for everything you wanted? Mommy said she took you up to meet him and you sat on his lap.'

'I just wanted to remind him,' she said. 'There were so many other children.'

He fought down the impulse to laugh, because she was not something to laugh at. And he was obsessed with the idea that to hurt her feelings with laughter was to nick her, to blemish the perfection.

'Daddy can't catch me-ee,' she sang out, and the old chase was on, following the pattern that had become so familiar to them, the same wild shrieks and the same scream of pretended anguish at the inevitable result. Two laps around the dining-room table was the established course before he caught her in the kitchen. He swung her up from the floor and set her down on the kitchen table. She stood on the edge, poised confidently for another of their games. But this was no panting, giggling game like tag or hide-and-seek. This game was ceremonial. The table was several feet higher than she was. 'Jump, jump, and Daddy will catch you,' he would challenge. They would count together, *one, two* and on *three* she would leap out into the air. He would not even hold out his arms to her until the last possible moment. But he would always catch her. They had played the game for more than a year and the experience never failed to exhilarate them. You see, I am always here to catch you when you are falling, it said to them, and each time she jumped, her confidence increased and their bond deepened.

They were going through the ceremony when the woman next door came in with her five-year-old son, Billy. 'Hello, Mr Steevers,' she said. 'Would you mind if I left Bill with you for an hour while I go do my marketing?'

'No, of course not, glad to have him,' he said and he mussed Billy's hair playfully. 'How's the boy, Billy?'

But his heart wasn't in it. This was his only afternoon of the week with her and he resented the intrusion. And then too, he was convinced that Billy was going to grow up into the type of man for whom he had a particular resentment. A sturdy, good-looking boy, big for his age, aggressively unchildlike, a malicious, arrogant, insensitive extrovert. I can just see him drunk and red-faced and pulling up girls' dresses at Legion Conventions, Mr Steevers would think. And the worst of it was, his daughter seemed blind to Billy's faults. The moment she saw him she forgot about their game.

'Hello, Billy-Boy,' she called and ran over to hug him.

'I want a cookie,' said Billy.

'Oh, yes, a cookie; some animal crackers, Daddy.'

She had her hostess face on and as he went into the pantry, he could hear the treble of her musical laughter against the premature baritone of Billy's guffaws.

He swung open the pantry door with the animal crackers in his hand just in time to see it. She was poised on the edge of the table. Billy was standing below her, as he had seen her father do. 'Jump and I'll catch you,' he was saying.

Smiling, confident and unblemished, she jumped. But no hands reached out to break her flight. With a cynical grin on his face, Billy stepped back and watched her fall.

Watching from the doorway, her father felt the horror that possessed him the time he saw a parachutist smashed like a bug on a windshield when his chute failed to open. She was lying there, crying, not so much in pain as in disillusionment. He ran forward to pick her up and he would never forget the expression on her face, the *new* expression, unchildlike, unvirginal, embittered.

'I hate you, I hate you,' she was screaming at Billy through hysterical sobs.

Well, now she knows, thought her father, the facts of life. Now she's one of us. Now she knows treachery and fear. Now she must learn to replace innocence with courage.

She was still bawling. He knew these tears were as natural and as necessary as those she shed at birth, but that could not overcome entirely the heavy sadness that enveloped him. Finally, when he spoke, he said, a little more harshly than he had intended, 'Now, now, stop crying. Stand up and act like a big girl. A little fall like that can't hurt you.'

‿‿

Alice in the White House

Theodore Roosevelt, 1858–1919, 26th President
of the USA

I can do one of two things. I can be president of the United States or I can control Alice. I cannot possibly do both.

‿‿

Golden Bells

Po Chu-i, 772–846

When I was almost forty
I had a daughter whose name was Golden Bells.
Now it is just a year since she was born;
She is learning to sit and cannot yet talk.

Ashamed, – to find that I have not a sage's heart:
I cannot resist vulgar thoughts and feelings.
Henceforward I am tied to things outside myself:
My only reward, – the pleasure I am getting now.
If I am spared the grief of her dying young,
Then I shall have the trouble of getting her married.
My plan for retiring and going back to the hills
Must now be postponed for fifteen years!

Fathers and daughters in Ancient Greece

From *The Supplicants* by Euripides, *c.* 422 BC

For naught is there more sweet to an aged sire
Than a daughter's love; our sons are made of sterner
Stuff, but less winning are their caresses.

Mary be good

Lyric by Irving Berlin, 1888–1989

Mary Ellin, Mary Ellin
Is her Daddy's girl.
It must be understood
Only when she is good
Is Mary Ellin, Mary Ellin
Her Daddy's girl.

The earth father

From D. H. Lawrence, *The Rainbow*, 1915

At Eastertime one year, she helped him to set potatoes. It was
the first time she had ever helped him. The occasion remained
as a picture, one of her earliest memories. They had gone out

soon after dawn. A cold wind was blowing. He had his old
trousers tucked into his boots, he wore no coat nor waistcoat,
his shirt-sleeves fluttered in the wind, his face was ruddy and
intent, in a kind of sleep. When he was at work he neither
heard nor saw. A long, thin man, looking still a youth, with a
line of black moustache above his thick mouth, and his fine
hair blown on his forehead, he worked away at the earth in
the grey first light, alone. His solitariness drew the child like a
spell.

The wind came chill over the dark-green fields. Ursula ran up
and watched him push the setting-peg in at one side of his ready
earth, stride across, and push it in the other side, pulling the line
taut and clear upon the clods intervening. Then with a sharp
cutting noise the bright spade came towards her, cutting a grip
into the new, soft earth.

He struck his spade upright and straightened himself.

'Do you want to help me?' he said.

She looked up at him from out of her little woollen bonnet.

'Ay,' he said, 'you can put some taters in for me. Look – like
that – these little sprits standing up – so much apart, you see.'

And stooping down he quickly, surely placed the spritted potatoes in the soft grip, where they rested separate and pathetic
on the heavy cold earth.

He gave her a little basket of potatoes, and strode himself to
the other end of the line. She saw him stooping, working towards
her. She was excited, and unused. She put in one potato, then
rearranged it, to make it sit nicely. Some of the sprits were
broken, and she was afraid. The responsibility excited her like
a string tying her up. She could not help looking with dread
at the string buried under the heaped-back soil. Her father
was working nearer, stooping, working nearer. She was overcome by her responsibility. She put potatoes quickly into the
cold earth.

He came near.

'Not so close,' he said, stooping over her potatoes, taking some
out and rearranging the others. She stood by with the painful
terrified helplessness of childhood. He was so unseeing and confident, she wanted to do the thing and yet she could not. She stood
by looking on, her little blue overall fluttering in the wind, the
red woollen ends of her shawl blowing gustily. Then he went

down the row, relentlessly, turning the potatoes in with his sharp spade-cuts. He took no notice of her, only worked on. He had another world from hers.

She stood helplessly stranded on his world. He continued his work. She knew she could not help him. A little bit forlorn, at last she turned away, and ran down the garden, away from him, as fast as she could go away from him, to forget him and his work.

He missed her presence, her face in her red woollen bonnet, her blue overall fluttering. She ran to where a little water ran trickling between grass and stones. That she loved.

When he came by he said to her:

'You didn't help me much.'

The child looked at him dumbly. Already her heart was heavy because of her own disappointment. Her mouth was dumb and pathetic. But he did not notice, he went his way.

∼

By Duty Divided

William Shakespeare, *Othello* (Act I, Scene 3),
c. 1604

DESDEMONA: My noble father,
I do perceive here a divided duty:
To you I am bound for life and education;
My life and education both do learn me
How to respect you; you are lord of all my duty,
I am hitherto your daughter: but here's my husband:
And so much duty as my mother show'd
To you, preferring you before her father,
So much I challenge, that I may profess
Due to the Moor my lord.

BRABANTIO: God bu'y, I ha' done:
Please it your grace, on to the state affairs;
I had rather to adopt a child than get it.
Come hither, Moor:
I here do give thee that with all my heart,
Which, but thou hast already, with all my heart

I would keep from thee. For your sake, jewel,
I am glad at soul I have no other child,
For thy escape would teach me tyranny,
To hang clogs on 'em. I have done, my lord.

～

The Grief of Lear

From *History of the Kings of Britain*
by Geoffrey of Monmouth, *c.* 1120

Some long time after, when Lear began to wax more sluggish by reason of age, the aforesaid dukes, with whom and his two daughters he had divided Britain, rebelled against him and took away from him the realm and the kingly power which up to that time he had held right manfully and gloriously. Howbeit, concord was restored, and one of his sons-in-law, Maglaunus, duke of Albany, agreed to maintain him with threescore knights, so that he should not be without some semblance of state. But after that he had sojourned with his son-in-law two years, his daughter Goneril began to wax indignant at the number of his knights, who flung gibes at her servants for that their rations were not more plentiful. Whereupon, after speaking to her husband, she ordered her father to be content with a service of thirty knights and to dismiss the other thirty that he had. The king, taking his in dudgeon, left Maglaunus, and betook him to Henvin, duke of Cornwall, unto whom he had married his other daughter. Here, at first, he was received with honour, but a year had not passed before discord again rose betwixt those of the king's household and those of the duke's, insomuch as that Regan, waxing indignant, ordered her father to dismiss all his company save five knights only to do him service. Her father, beyond measure aggrieved thereat, returned once more to his eldest daughter, thinking to move her to pity and to persuade her to maintain himself and his retinue. Howbeit, she had never renounced her first indignation, but swore by all the gods of Heaven that never should he take up his abode with her save he contented himself with the service of a single knight and were quit of all the rest. Moreover, she upbraided the old man for that, having nothing of his own to give away, he should be minded to go about with such a retinue; so that finding she would not give way to his wishes one single tittle, he at last obeyed and remained content with one knight only, leaving the rest to go their way. But when the remembrance of his former dignity came back unto him, bearing witness to the misery of the estate to which he was now reduced, he began to bethink him of going to his youngest daughter oversea. Howbeit, he sore misdoubted that she would do nought for him, seeing that he had held her, as I have said, in such scanty honour in the matter of her marriage. Natheless, disdaining any longer to endure so mean a life, he betook him across the Channel into Gaul. But when he found that two other princes were making the passage at the same time, and that he himself had been assigned but the third place, he brake forth into tears and sobbing, and cried aloud: 'Ye destinies that do pursue your wonted way marked out by irrevocable decree, wherefore was it your will ever to uplift me to happiness so fleeting? For a keener grief it is to call to mind that lost happiness than to suffer the presence of the unhappiness that cometh after. For the memory of the days when in the midst of hundreds of thousands of warriors I went to batter down the walls of cities and to lay waste the provinces of mine enemies is more grievous unto me than the calamity that hath overtaken me in the meanness of mine estate, which hath incited them that but now were grovelling under my feet to desert my feebleness. O angry fortune! will the day ever come wherein I may requite the evil turn that hath thus driven forth the length of my days and my poverty? O Cordelia, my daughter, how true were the words wherein thou didst make answer unto me, when I did ask of thee how much thou didst love me! For thou saidst: "So much as thou hast, so much art thou worth, and so much do I love thee." So long, therefore, as I had that which was mine own to give, so long seemed I of worth unto them that were the lovers, not of myself but of my gifts. They loved me at times, but better loved they the presents I made unto them. Now that the presents are no longer forthcoming, they too have gone their ways. But with what face, O thou dearest of my children, shall I dare appear before thee? I who, wroth with thee for these thy words, was minded to marry thee less honourably than thy sisters, who, after all the kindnesses I have conferred upon them have allowed me to become an outcast and a beggar?'

Landing at last, his mind filled with these reflections and others of a like kind, he came to Karitia, where his daughter lived, and waiting without the city, sent a messenger to tell her into what indigence he had fallen, and to beseech his daughter's compassion inasmuch as he had neither food nor clothing. On hearing the tidings, Cordelia was much moved and wept bitterly. When she made inquiry how many armed men he had with him, the messenger told her that he had none save a single knight, who was waiting with him without the city. Then took she as much gold and silver as was needful and gave it unto the messenger, bidding him take her father to another city, where he should bathe him, clothe him, and nurse him, feigning that he was a sick man. She commanded also that he should have a retinue of forty knights well appointed and armed, and that then he should duly announce his arrival to Aganippus and herself. The messenger accordingly forthwith attended King Lear into another city, and hid him there in secret until that he had fully accomplished all that Cordelia had borne him on hand to do.

⌒

To Her Father

Mehetabel Wright, 1697–1750

In vain, mistaken Sir, you boast
Your Frown can give me lasting Pain;
Your Rigour, when you threaten most,
Attempts to wound my Peace in vain.

With transient Grief you may oppress
A Mind that greater Griefs can bear.
To make Unkindness past Redress,
Your child must *love*, as well as *fear*!

If your kind Hand had fixt me sure
From Want and Shame's impending Harms
Or lodg'd my ripen'd Bloom, secure,
Within some worthy Husband's Arms:

Or when you saw me circled round
With ills that vex and shorten Life,
Had once your dear Condolence found
My sufferings when a wretched Wife;

Altho' *I* was not worth your *Love*,
Had *you* a Parent's *Care* exprest;
Or by one tender Action strove
To make the Life you gave me blest;

How should I mourn had this been so!
How ill your Rage I should endure!
But *gentler Hands* must give the Blow,
Which *rankles*, and *admits no Cure*.

If any Hand a Stroke could send
To vanquish and undo me quite;
'Tis where the *Guardian, Father, Friend*,
And ev'ry kinder name unite.

From such a Sire, rever'd an Age,
A *Look*, perchance, or *Word unkind*,
Might wound beyond your utmost Rage,
With ev'ry faithless Friend combin'd.

The shocks that must on Life attend,
We firmly bear, or shun their Pow'r:
But hard Reproaches from a Friend
Will *torture* to our *latest Hour*.

Refrain your needless Rages then:
Your Anger touches me no more
Than *needless wounds* on dying Men,
Who felt the *mortal pang* before.

As Caesar, bay'd by cruel Foes,
Dauntless, awhile defers his Fate:
He bears, or wards, repeated Blows;
Nor deigns to sink beneath their Weight,

Till, wounded in the tend'rest Part,
He finds his Life not worth his Care:

His hand disdains to guard his Heart,
And ev'ry Stab is welcome there.

⌒

Daddy

Sylvia Plath, 1932–63

You do not do, you do not do
Any more, black shoe
In which I have lived like a foot
For thirty years, poor and white,
Barely daring to breathe or Achoo.

Daddy, I have had to kill you.
You died before I had time –
Marble-heavy, a bag full of God,
Ghastly statue with one grey toe
Big as a Frisco seal

And a head in the freakish Atlantic
Where it pours bean green over blue
In the waters off beautiful Nauset.
I used to pray to recover you.
Ach, du.

In the German tongue, in the Polish town
Scraped flat by the roller
Of wars, wars, wars.
But the name of the town is common.
My Polack friend

Says there are a dozen or two.
So I never could tell where you
Put your foot, your root,
I never could talk to you.
The tongue stuck in my jaw.

It stuck in a barb wire snare.
Ich, ich, ich, ich,
I could hardly speak.

I thought every German was you.
And the language obscene

An engine, an engine
Chuffing me off like a Jew.
A Jew to Dachau, Auschwitz, Belsen.
I began to talk like a Jew.
I think I may well be a Jew.

The snows of the Tyrol, the clear beer of Vienna
Are not very pure or true.
With my gypsy ancestress and my weird luck
And my Taroc pack and my Taroc pack
I may be a bit of a Jew.

I have always been scared of *you*,
With your Luftwaffe, your gobbledygoo.
And your neat moustache
And your Aryan eye, bright blue.
Panzer-man, panzer-man, O You –

Bit my pretty red heart in two.
I was ten when they buried you.
At twenty I tried to die
And get back, back, back to you.
I thought even the bones would do.

But they pulled me out of the sack,
And they stuck me together with glue,
And then I knew what to do.
I made a model of you,
A man in black with a Meinkampf look

And a love of the rack and the screw.
And I said I do, I do.
So daddy, I'm finally through.
The black telephone's off at the root,
The voices just can't worm through.

If I've killed one man, I've killed two –
The vampire who said he was you
And drank my blood for a year,
Seven years, if you want to know.
Daddy, you can lie back now.

There's a stake in your fat black heart
And the villagers never liked you.
They are dancing and stamping on you.
They always *knew* it was you.
Daddy, daddy, you bastard, I'm through.

⌐

Charmed

From the diary of James Boswell

4 January 1776:
. . . In the afternoon I was quite charmed with Veronica [his daughter]. She could now sing a number of tunes: Carrickfergus, O'er the Water to Charlie, Johnnie McGill, Wee Willy Gray, Nancy Dawson, Paddy Wake, Ploughman Laddie, Brose and Butter, O'er the Hills and Far Away. It was really extraordinary that a child not three years old should have such a musical memory, and she sung with a sweet voice and fine ear (if that expression be just). She could speak a great many words, but in an imperfect manner: 'Etti me see u picture' (Let me see your picture.) She could not pronounce 'f'. 'I heed.' (I'm feared. English, I'm afraid.) She rubbed my sprained ankle this afternoon with rum, with care and tenderness. With eager affection I cried, 'God bless you, my dearest little creature.' She answered, 'Od bess u, Papa.' Yet she loved her mother more than me, I suppose because her behaviour to her was more uniform.

⌐

The pillar tumbles

From *The Sibling Society* by John Bly, 1996

During our eighteenth century, the American father was thought of as the stone and roof-pillar of the family. The Puritan household in 1750 was set up so that it paralleled the Puritan State. Older men ran both. The service involved, for many fathers, more power than love; and it would be wrong to be sentimental or nostalgic about those families.

We are talking not of the wisdom of father-power but merely of the extent of it. If we look at a family in, say, Salem, Massachusetts, in 1750, the father was the Navigator in social waters; he was the Moral Teacher and Spiritual Comforter; he was the Earner, who brought in the income and kept the family alive; he was the Hearer of Distress as well; cares were brought to the mother and then to him. People imagined the family as a Hebraic unit, as if the children were all children of God, and the house a tiny house of Abraham.

But this arrangement soon faltered. When the West opened up, fathers and prospective fathers headed there. Many factories opened in New England. The father's eyes turned outward toward opportunity, factories, and long days; and the mother became the sole confidant of the children.

~~

The value of a daughter

From William Faulkner, *Absalom, Absalom!*, 1936

Son. Intrinsic val . . . Emotional val. plus 100% times nil plus val. crop. Emotional val. 100% times increase yearly for each child plus intrinsic val. plus liquid assets plus working acquired credit . . . Daughter and you could maybe even have seen the question mark after it and the other words even: *daughter? daughter? daughter?* trailing off not because thinking trailed off, but on the contrary, thinking stopping right still then, backing up a little and spreading like when you lay a stick across a trickle of water, spreading and rising slow around him in whatever place it was that he could lock the door to and sit quiet . . .

~~

The four ways in which fatherhood makes children richer

From David Blankenhorn, *Fatherless America*, 1995

Fatherhood is a social role that obligates men to their biological offspring. For two reasons, it is society's most important role for men. First, fatherhood, more than any other male activity, helps men to become good men: more likely to obey the law, to be good citizens, and to think about the needs of others. Put more abstractly, fatherhood bends maleness – in particular, male aggression – toward prosocial purposes. Second, fatherhood privileges children. In this respect, fatherhood is a social invention designed to supplement maternal investment in children with paternal investment in children.

Paternal investment enriches children in four ways. First, it provides them with a father's physical protection. Second, it provides them with a father's money and other material resources. Third, and probably most important, it provides them with what might be termed paternal cultural transmission: a father's distinctive capacity to contribute to the identity, character, and competence of his children. Fourth, and most obviously, paternal investment provides children with the day-to-day nurturing – feeding them, playing with them, telling them a story – that they want and need from both of their parents. In virtually all human societies, children's well-being depends decisively upon a relatively high level of paternal investment.

Indeed, many anthropologists view the rise of fatherhood as the key to the emergence of the human family and, ultimately, of human civilisation.

'Fathers imprint girls for sexual adequacy'

From Alex Comfort, *The Listener*, 1973

The greater a woman's conviction that love objects are not dependable, and must be held onto, the poorer her capacity for full response. This may come about through loss of a father, or childhood deprivation of the father's role. Some degree of parental seduction at the unconscious level seems to be necessary for human females to establish full function. Deprived of a stable father-figure, the non-orgasmic seem to be unable to face the blurring of personal boundaries which goes with full physiological orgasm. It looks as though sexual response in women is based on pre-sexual learning, and of a specific kind . . . This very important finding about the attitudinal basis of sexual contentment ought to be a salutary check on the idea of fatherless upbringing as a contribution to Women's Lib, an idea which no primatologist would regard with favour. Fathers are there to imprint girls for sexual adequacy.

⌒

A Prayer for My Daughter

W. B. Yeats, June 1919

Once more the storm is howling, and half hid
Under this cradle-hood and coverlid
My child sleeps on. There is no obstacle
But Gregory's wood and one bare hill
Whereby the haystack and roof-levelling wind,
Bred on the Atlantic, can be stayed;
And for an hour I have walked and prayed
Because of the great gloom that is in my mind.

I have walked and prayed for this young child an hour
And heard the sea-wind scream upon the tower,
And under the arches of the bridge, and scream
In the elms above the flooded stream;
Imagining in excited reverie
That the future years had come,

Dancing to a frenzied drum,
Out of the murderous innocence of the sea.

May she be granted beauty and yet not
Beauty to make a stranger's eye distraught,
Or hers before a looking-glass, for such,
Being made beautiful overmuch,
Consider beauty a sufficient end,
Lose natural kindness and maybe
The heart-revealing intimacy
That chooses right, and never find a friend.

Helen being chosen found life flat and dull
And later had much trouble from a fool,
While that great Queen, that rose out of the spray,
Being fatherless could have her way
Yet chose a bandy-leggèd smith for man.
It's certain that fine women eat
A crazy salad with their meat
Whereby the Horn of Plenty is undone.

In courtesy I'd have her chiefly learned;
Hearts are not had as a gift but hearts are earned
By those that are not entirely beautiful;
Yet many, that have played the fool
For beauty's very self, has charm made wise,
And many a poor man that has roved,
Loved and thought himself beloved,
From a glad kindness cannot take his eyes.

May she become a flourishing hidden tree
That all her thoughts may like the linnet be,
And have no business but dispensing round
Their magnanimities of sound,
Nor but in merriment begin a chase,
Nor but in merriment a quarrel.
O may she live like some green laurel
Rooted in one dear perpetual place.

My mind, because the minds that I have loved,
The sort of beauty that I have approved,
Prosper but little, has dried up of late,
Yet knows that to be choked with hate

May well be of all evil chances chief.
If there's no hatred in a mind
Assault and battery of the wind
Can never tear the linnet from the leaf.

An intellectual hatred is the worst,
So let her think opinions are accursed.
Have I not seen the loveliest woman born
Out of the mouth of Plenty's horn,
Because of her opinionated mind
Barter that horn and every good
By quiet natures understood
For an old bellows full of angry wind?

Considering that, all hatred driven hence,
The soul recovers radical innocence
And learns at last that it is self-delighting,
Self-appeasing, self-affrighting,
And that its own sweet will is Heaven's will;
She can, though every face should scowl
And every windy quarter howl
Or every bellows burst, be happy still.

And may her bridegroom bring her to a house
Where all's accustomed, ceremonious;
For arrogance and hatred are the wares
Peddled in the thoroughfares.
How but in custom and in ceremony
Are innocence and beauty born?
Ceremony's a name for the rich horn,
And custom for the spreading laurel tree.

〜

And never lose it

Amos Bronson Alcott to his daughter Anna, 1839

This is your birthday. You have now lived eight years with your
father and mother, six years with your loving sister Louisa, and
almost four years with your sweet little sister Elizabeth. Your
father knows how much you love him. . . . He wants to see his

little girl kind and gentle, and sweet-tempered, as fragrant as the flowers in springtime, and as beautiful as they are when the dew glitters on them in the morning dew.

Do you want to know how you can be so beautiful and sweet? It is easy. Only try, with all your resolution, to mind what that silent teacher in your breast says to you: that is all.

A birthday is a good time to begin anew: throwing away the old habits, as you would old clothes, and never putting them on again. Begin, my daughter, today, and when your next birthday shall come, how glad you will be that you made the resolution. Resolution makes all things new. . . .

When you were a few weeks old, you smiled on us. I sometimes see the same look and the same smile on your face, and feel that my daughter is yet good and pure. O keep it there, my daughter, and never lose it.

⌣

Thank heaven for a little girl

From *Angela's Ashes*, Frank McCourt, 1996

When Dad comes home from looking for a job he holds Margaret and sings to her:

> *In a shady nook one moonlit night*
> *A leprechaun I spied.*
> *With scarlet cap and coat of green*
> *A cruiskeen by his side.*
> *'Twas tick tock tick his hammer went*
> *Upon a tiny shoe.*
> *Oh, I laugh to think he was caught at last,*
> *But the fairy was laughing, too.*

He walks around the kitchen with her and talks to her. He tells her how lovely she is with her curly black hair and the blue eyes of her mother. He tells her he'll take her to Ireland and they'll walk the Glens of Antrim and swim in Lough Neagh. He'll get a job soon, so he will, and she'll have dresses of silk and shoes with silver buckles.

The more Dad sings to Margaret the less she cries and as the days pass she even begins to laugh. Mam says, Look at him trying to dance with that child in his arms, him with his two left feet. She laughs and we all laugh.

The twins cried when they were small and Dad and Mam would say Whisht and Hush and feed them and they'd go back to sleep. But when Margaret cries there's a high lonely feeling in the air and Dad is out of bed in a second, holding her to him, doing a slow dance around the table, singing to her, making sounds like a mother. When he passes the window where the streetlight shines in you can see tears on his cheeks and that's strange because he never cries for anyone unless he has the drink taken and he sings the Kevin Barry song and the Roddy McCorley song. Now he cries over Margaret and he has no smell of drink on him.

Mam tells Minnie MacAdorey, He's in heaven over that child. He hasn't touched a drop since she was born. I should've had a little girl a long time ago.

Och, they're lovely, aren't they? says Minnie. The little boys are grand, too, but you need a little girl for yourself.

My mother laughs, For myself? Lord above, if I didn't nurse her I wouldn't be able to get near her the way he wants to be holding her day, and night.

Minnie says it's lovely, all the same, to see a man so charmed with his little girl for isn't everyone charmed with her?

Everyone.

⌒

Papa Love Baby

Stevie Smith, 1902–71

My mother was a romantic girl
So she had to marry a man with his hair in curl
Who subsequently became my unrespected papa,
But that was a long time ago now.

What folly is it that daughters are always supposed to be
In love with papa. It wasn't the case with me

I couldn't take to him at all
But he took to me
What a sad fate to befall
A child of three.

I sat upright in my baby carriage
And wished mama hadn't made such a foolish marriage.
I tried to hide it, but it showed in my eyes unfortunately
And a fortnight later papa ran away to sea.

He used to come home on leave
It was always the same
I could not grieve
But I think I was somewhat to blame.

∿

Lap girl

From Naomi Mitchison, *Small Talk: Memories of an
Edwardian Childhood*, 1973

Of course there were areas of safety; nothing could get at me
if I curled up on my father's lap, holding on to his ear with
one thumb tucked into it. He had a big brown moustache and
a wide Haldane nose with a small lump on it which I liked.
When he kissed me it was rough and tickly. Across his front
was a gold watch chain with a big tick-tock watch on the end.
In my own children's time it also had a chocolate tree which
flowered into silver-paper-covered chocolates. All about him
was safe.

∿

Poem for Jane

Vernon Scannell, *Selected Poems*, 1971

So many catalogues have been
Compiled by poets, good and bad,
Of qualities that they would wish

To see their infant daughters wear;
Or lacking children they have clad
Others' daughters in the bright
Imagined garments of the flesh,
Prayed for jet or golden hair
Or for the inconspicuous
Homespun of the character
That no one ever whistles after.

Dear Jane, whatever I may say
I'm sure approving whistles will
Send you like an admiral on
Ships of welcome in a bay
Of tender waters where the fish
Will surface longing to be meshed
Among the treasure of your hair.
And as for other qualities
There's only one I really wish
To see you amply manifest
And that's a deep capacity
For loving; and I long for this
Not for any lucky one
Who chances under your love's sun
But because, without it, you
Would never know completely joy
As I know joy through loving you.

First Lesson

Philip Booth, 1922–

Lie back, daughter, let your head
be tipped back in the cup of my hand.
Gently, and I will hold you. Spread
your arms wide, lie out on the stream
and look high at the gulls. A dead-
man's float is face down. You will dive
and swim soon enough where this tidewater
ebbs to the sea. Daughter, believe
me, when you tire on the long thrash

to your island, lie up, and survive.
As you float now, where I held you
and let go, remember when fear
cramps your heart what I told you:
lie gently and wide to the light-year
stars, lie back, and the sea will hold you.

4

The Sins of the Father

Study of a figure in a landscape

From Paul Durcan, *Daddy, Daddy*, 1990

– Did your bowels move today?
– Yes, Daddy.
– At what time did your bowels move today?
– At eight o'clock, Daddy.
– Are you sure?
– Yes, Daddy.
– Are you sure that your bowels moved today?
– I am, Daddy.
– Were you sitting down in the long grass?
– I was, Daddy.
– Are you telling me the truth?
– I am, Daddy.
– Are you sure you are not telling me a lie?
– I am, Daddy.
– You are sure that your bowels moved today?
– I am, Daddy, but please don't beat me, Daddy.
Don't be vexed with me, Daddy.
I am not absolutely sure, Daddy.
– Why are you not absolutely sure?
– I don't know, Daddy.
– What do you mean you don't know?
– I don't know what bowels are, Daddy.
– What do you think bowels are?
– I think bowels are wheels, Daddy.
Black wheels under my tummy, Daddy,
– Did your black wheels move today?
– They did, Daddy.
– Then your bowels definitely did move today.
– Yes, Daddy.
– You should be proud of yourself.
– Yes, Daddy.
– Are you proud of yourself?
– Yes, Daddy.
– Constipation is the curse of Cain.

– Yes, Daddy.
– You will cut and reap the corn today.
– Yes, Daddy.
– Every day be sure that your bowels move.
– Yes, Daddy.
– If your bowels do not move, you are doomed.
– Yes, Daddy.
– Are you all right?
– No, Daddy.
– What in the name of the Mother of God
And the dead generations is the matter with you?
– I want to go to the toilet, Daddy.
– Don't just stand there, run for it.
– Yes, Daddy.
– Are you in your starting blocks?
– Yes, Daddy.
– When I count to three, leap from your starting blocks.
– I can't, Daddy.
– Can't can't.
– Don't, Daddy, don't, Daddy, don't, Daddy, don't.

A bad temper on a Sunday evening

From Samuel Butler, *The Way of all Flesh*, 1903

I was there on a Sunday, and observed the rigour with which the young people were taught to observe the Sabbath: they might not cut out things, nor use their paint box on a Sunday, and this they thought rather hard because their cousins the John Pontifexes might do these things. Their cousins might play with their toy train on Sunday, but though they had promised that they would run none but Sunday trains, all traffic had been prohibited. One treat only was allowed them – on Sunday evenings they might choose their own hymns.

In the course of the evening they came into the drawing-room and as an especial treat were to sing some of their hymns to me instead of saying them, so that I might hear how nicely they sang. Ernest was to choose the first hymn and he chose one about some people who were to come to the sunset tree. I am no botanist, and do not know what kind of a tree a sunset tree is, but the words began, 'Come, come, come: come to the sunset tree for the day is past and gone.' The tune was rather pretty and had taken Ernest's fancy, for he was unusually fond of music and had a sweet little child's voice which he liked using. He was, however, very late in being about to sound a hard C or K, and instead of saying 'Come,' he said 'tum, tum, tum'.

'Ernest,' said Theobald from the armchair in front of the fire where he was sitting with his hands folded before him, 'don't you think it would be very nice if you were to say "come" like other people, instead of "tum"?'

'I do say tum,' replied Ernest, meaning that he had said 'come'.

Theobald was always in a bad temper on Sunday evening. Whether it is that they are as much bored with their day as their neighbour, or whether they are tired, or whatever the cause may be, clergymen are seldom at their best on Sunday evening: I had already seen signs that evening that my host was cross, and was a little nervous at hearing Ernest say so promptly, 'I do say tum,' when his papa had said he did not say it as he should.

Theobald noticed the fact that he was being contradicted in a moment. He had been sitting in an armchair in front of the fire with his hands folded, doing nothing, but he got up at once and went to the piano.

'No Ernest, you don't,' he said: 'you say nothing of the kind, you say "tum" not "come". Now say "come" after me, as I do.'

'Tum,' said Ernest at once. 'Is that better?' I have no doubt he thought it was, but it was not.

'Now Ernest, you are not taking pains: you are not trying as you ought to do. It is high time you learned to say "come": why Joey can say "come", can't you, Joey?'

'Yeth I can,' replied Joey promptly, and he said something which was not far off 'come'.

'There, Ernest, do you hear that? There's no difficulty about it now, no shadow of difficulty. Now take your own time; think about it and say "come" after me.'

The boy remained silent for a few seconds and then said 'tum' again.

I laughed, but Theobald turned to me impatiently and said, 'Please do not laugh Overton, it will make the boy think it does not matter, and it matters a great deal'; then turning to Ernest he said, 'Now Ernest, I will give you one more chance, and if you don't say "come" I shall know that you are self-willed and naughty.'

He looked very angry and a shade came over Ernest's face, like that which comes upon the face of a puppy when it is being scolded without understanding why. The child saw well what was coming now, was frightened, and of course said 'tum' once more.

'Very well Ernest,' said his father, catching him angrily by the shoulder. 'I have done my best to save you but if you will have it so you will,' and he lugged the little wretch out of the room crying by anticipation. A few minutes more and we could hear screams coming from the dining-room across the hall which separated the drawing-room from the dining-room, and knew that poor Ernest was being beaten. 'I have sent him to bed,' said Theobald, as he returned to the drawing-room, 'and now, Christina, I think we will have the servants in to prayers,' and he rang the bell for them, red-handed as he was.

~

The philosophy of punishment

Aristophanes, *The Clouds, c.* 450 BC

PHIDIPPIDES: I will begin where you did interrupt me,
                 And first will ask, did you not beat me as a
                    child?
STREPSIADES: But that was out of love.
PHIDIPPIDES: 'Tis very right, tell men then, ought not I
                 To recompence your love with equall love;
                 If to be beaten be to be belov'd,
                 Why should I suffer stripes, and you have
                    none?

~

The no-praise man

From *The Journals of Anaïs Nin*, 1966–83
Nin writes about her childhood relationship
with her father

The child expected protectiveness, loyalty, comfort, attention, help, teaching, guidance, companionship. His failure to be re-assuring, present even, accessible, approving, companionable, dictated the judgement. If I had known him as a playmate with whom roughhousing and games might be treacherous, dangerous even, and a matter of pitting one's energy and skills, or sharing adventures, he would have been my companion in dangerous experiences. Instead he became the awesome figure of the no-praise man, creating in me such a need of approval,

'Most fathers prefer DIY to their kids'

The Daily Telegraph, 1998

Most fathers prefer watching television or doing sport, hobbies and gardening to spending time with their children, claims a report published yesterday.

More than half of fathers surveyed spent less than five minutes a day one-to-one with their child. Fifteen per cent spent no time at all with their child on a weekday.

Fathers who did want closer relationships with their children blamed lack of time and work pressures as the most common barriers.

The NOP poll among 2,000 adults was commissioned by the charity Care for the Family in a study of attitudes to fatherhood.

Nearly half of all fathers would have liked to have changed the way they brought up their children.

The survey also found that fathers were more likely to spend time with a son than a daughter. Mr Rob Parsons, executive director of the charity, an off-shoot of Christian Action Research and Education – CARE – said: 'What I find staggering is that fathers prefer sports and hobbies, gardening, DIY, television, and then time with kids comes way down.

'I'm as sad for the fathers as I am for the kids. I think they will regret it.'

～

You shall not go to the ball

From H. G. Wells, *Ann Veronica*, 1909

'There are plenty of things a girl can find to do at home.'

'Until someone takes pity on me and marries me?'

He raised his eyebrows in mild appeal. His foot tapped impatiently, and he took up the papers.

'Look here, father,' she said, with a change in her voice, 'suppose I won't stand it?'

He regarded her as though this was a new idea.

'Suppose, for example, I go to this dance?'

'You won't.'

'Well' – her breath failed her for a moment. 'How would you prevent it?' she asked.

'But I have forbidden it!' he said, raising his voice.

'Yes, I know. But suppose I go?'

'Now, Veronica! No, no. This won't do. Understand me! I forbid it. I do not want to hear from you even the threat of disobedience.' He spoke loudly. 'The thing is forbidden!'

'I am ready to give up anything that you show to be wrong.'

'You will give up anything I wish you to give up.'

～

The Stern Parent

From Harry Graham, *Ruthless Rhymes*, 1899

Father heard his Children scream,
So he threw them in the stream,
Saying, as he drowned the third,
'Children should be seen, *not* heard!

Lost fathers

From Jonathan Bradshaw *et al.*, *Absent Fathers*, 1999

It is difficult to produce reasonable estimates of the number of non-resident fathers in Britain. Certainly there are over two million and there could be as many as five million. Perhaps the best way to think about the scale of the experience of non-resident fathering is to note the fact that it is estimated that between a third and half of all children will experience a period of not living with both natural parents during their childhood. Each one of those children will have a non-resident parent and in most cases it will be the father.

⌒

Bygones

From *Fredi, Shirl & The Kids: The Autobiography in Fable of Richard M. Elman*, 1972

People are always saying: WEREN'T YOU JUST A LITTLE AFRAID OF FREDI & SHIRL?
OF MY FATHER . . . ?
YES.
MY LOVED ONES?
YES.
THOSE WHO WERE NEAR AND DEAR TO ME?
THEM TOO . . .
OF COURSE NOT. I WAS SCARED TO DEATH.

RICHARD WHY ARE YOU ALWAYS FLINCHING? ARE YOU AFRAID OF US?
I'M AFRAID NOT.
DON'T BE AFRAID RICHARD. WE DON'T WANT TO HURT YOU . . .
BUT YOU ALWAYS DO . . .
THAT'S JUST AN ACCIDENT.
WELL MAYBE YOU OUGHT TO BE MORE CAREFUL . . .
Fredi says, LOOK AT BIG SHOT RICHARD GIVING ADVICE. LISTEN TO HIM . . .

AFRAID SO.

RICHALEH, says Shirl, CAN'T WE JUST LET BYGONES BE BYGONES. IT'S NOT AS IF WE DIDN'T LOVE YOU.

I think about that one a minute. To Shirl letting bygones be bygones means I am not to remember all the times she gave me enemas and poured perfume on me and Fredi beat me with Mr Strap because, after all, I must have provoked them somehow, and it's not as if they didn't love me. On the other hand, it seems to me it's not as if they ever did . . .

AFTER ALL WE'VE DONE FOR YOU, Shirl says.

I TOLD YOU RIGHT FROM THE START SHIRL THAT KID WAS NO GOOD . . .

YOU SEE, I tell her, SEE WHAT I MEAN ABOUT HIM.

RICHALEH PLEASE BEHAVE.

YOU TOO!

I'LL KILL HIM. I'LL KILL HIM SHIRL FOR TALKING TO US LIKE THAT . . .

NOW DO YOU SEE WHAT YOU'VE DONE, Shirl says. YOU'VE MADE YOUR FATHER LOSE HIS TEMPER AND IT'S ALL YOUR FAULT.

The thing about growing up in an enlightened twentieth-century household like mine: if I was ever afraid of Fredi & Shirl I usually had good reasons.

⌒

Cuckolding thy own sonne

From 'The Father Hath Beguil'd the Sonne'
English ballad registered in 1629

> 4 For once on a day
>   The young man did say:
>   vnto his wise and aged dad,
>   That twas his intent
>   (Worse things to preuent)
>   with marriage to make him glad:
>   Me thinkes first quoth he,
>   Your wife I might see,
>   why will you hastily run:
>   On such brittle ware?

Yet for all his care,
(old fox) he beguil'd his owne sonne.

5 The sonne told his father,
   How that he had rather:
   to haue in the same his consent,
   So to haue a view
   Of his Louer true,
   the sonne with his father went:
   And when they came there
   The Lasse did appeare,
   so faire and so louely a one,
   That the old doting churle,
   Fell in loue with the girle
   and sought to beguile his owne sonne.

6 With such pleasant words
   As to loue accords,
   they all did depart for that season,
   The honest young Lad,
   Was ioyfull and glad:
   his sweet-hart had shew'd him good reasōn,
   The loue-sicke old man,
   Did looke pale and wan,
   and could to no pleasure be wonne,
   By night and by day,
   Still musing hee lay,
   how he might beguile his owne sonne.

7 Yet none did mistrust,
   A thing so vniust:
   for he was neere threescore yeeres old:
   Which yeeres one would thinke,
   Should make a man shrinke,
   when his vitall spirits are cold:
   But now to be briefe,
   That was all his griefe,
   from loue all this mischiefe begun:
   And nothing could serue,
   His life to preserue,
   but that vvhich must kill his owne sonne.

8 So once on a day,
   When his sonne to make hay:

was gone a good mile from the house,
Away the old man,
Is gone to see *Nan*,
as briske as a body louse:
And with a bold face,
He told her his case,
and into what care he was runne,
Unless that she,
Would kindly agree,
to take him in stead of his sonne.

The second part, To the same tune.

9 She mused in mind,
Such greeting to find,
and thus vnto him shee said,
Can such an old knaue,
With one foot in the graue:
set loue on a young tender maid,
That hardly sixteene
Cold winters had seene,
sure such thing cannot be done:
Nay more then all this
You know what past is,
tvvixt me and your onely sonne.

10 Sweet *Nan* quoth hee,
Ne're dally with me,
I loue thee as well as may be,
And though I am old
I haue siluer and gold
to keepe thee as braue as a Lady,
All my whole estate
Upon thee shall wait,
and whatsoere thou wouldst haue done,
With gold in thy hand
Thou shalt it command,
if thou wilt take me instead of my sonne.

11 If me thou doe shun,
In hope of my sonne
then take him and ift be thy minde,
But into the bargaine

Looke not for one farthing,
then be not with folly let blind,
For it lies in my power,
At this instant houre
(if thou say no it shall be done)
To giue all I haue,
Away from the knaue,
then take me and leaue off my sonne.

12 When she heard these words,
To him shee accords
vpon the same condition,
That of all his pelfe,
He should his owne selfe,
her set in full possession,
To which he agreed,
And gaue her a deed,
by which the poore Lad was vndone,
Unnaturally
To please his fancy,
he did dis-inherit his sonne.

13 These things being [said,]
And they both contriued,
by witnesse [conspires] so the Lad,
The old man home went
With hearty content,
reioycing at his courses bad,
And thus the next day,
He carryed away
the Lasse which with wealth he had won.
He maried was,
Twelue miles from the place,
thus the father beguil'd his own sonne.

14 The young-man with griefe,
Heard of this mischiefe
and blaming this monstrous part,
Before both their faces,
Unto their disgraces,
he stab'd himselfe to the heart:
The vnnaturall dad,
Ran presently mad:

repenting of what he had done,
He runs vp and downe,
From towne vnto towne,
and hourely calles on his sonne.

15 The faithlesse young wife,
Weary of her life,
(to thinke what folly befell)
Ran straight in all hast,
And headlong shee cast
herselfe in a deepe draw-well.
And there shee was found,
Next morning quite drown'd
these things for certaine were done,
Some sixe weekes agoe,
As many men know,
that knew both father and sonne.

16 Let euery good father
A warning here gather,
by this old mans punishment:
And let euery young Lasse,
(As in a glasse,)
looke on this disastrous euent;
For both were to blame,
And both suffer'd shame,
the old man yet liuing doth run
In mad franticke wise
And alwayes he cryes,
for casting away his owne sonne.

Finis.

∽

'Father jailed for chaining up son'

A report in *The Daily Telegraph*, 1996

A father who chained his 15-year-old son to the wall of a garage after reaching 'the end of his tether' following years of unruly behaviour was jailed for three years yesterday.

A judge told the father, who cannot be named for legal reasons, that his action had been 'brutal and sadistic'.

The boy's mother was jailed for 15 months, suspended for two years, after the couple admitted child cruelty. Nottingham Crown Court was told that the father, aged 37, forced his son to eat two cigarettes in an attempt to stop him smoking.

Suspecting him of arson, he splashed paint-thinner on the boy and then chained his right wrist to a hook, leaving a cigarette lighter nearby.

The boy was freed by police who had been called by some of his friends to the lock-up garage in Warsop, Notts, which was padlocked and had a Rottweiler outside.

~

We have no bananas

From *Will This Do?*, Auberon Waugh, 1991

On one occasion, just after the war, the first consignment of bananas reached Britain. Neither I, my sister Teresa nor my sister Margaret had ever eaten a banana throughout the war, when they were unprocurable, but we had heard all about them as the most delicious taste in the world. When this first consignment arrived, the socialist government decided that every child in the country should be allowed one banana. An army of civil servants issued a library of special banana coupons, and the great day arrived when my mother came home with three bananas. All three were put on my father's plate, and before the anguished eyes of his children, he poured on cream, which was almost unprocurable, and sugar, which was heavily rationed, and ate all three. A child's sense of justice may be defective in many respects, and egocentric at the best of times, but it is no less intense for either. By any standards, he had done wrong. It would be absurd to say that I never forgave him, but he was permanently marked down in my estimation from that moment, in ways which no amount of sexual transgression would have achieved . . . From that moment, I never treated anything he had to say on faith or morals very seriously.

~

Take that, you little whelp!

From James Joyce, 'Counterparts', *Dubliners*, 1914

His tram let him down at Shelbourne Road and he steered his great body along in the shadow of the wall of the barracks. He loathed returning to his home. When he went in by the side-door he found the kitchen empty and the kitchen fire nearly out. He bawled upstairs:

'Ada! Ada!'

His wife was a little sharp-faced woman who bullied her husband when he was sober and was bullied by him when he was drunk. They had five children. A little boy came running down the stairs.

'Who is that?' said the man, peering through the darkness.

'Me, pa.'

'Who are you? Charlie?'

'No, pa. Tom.'

'Where's your mother?'

'She's out at the chapel.'

'That's right . . . Did she think of leaving any dinner for me?'

'Yes, pa. I—'

'Light the lamp. What do you mean by having the place in darkness? Are the other children in bed?'

The man sat down heavily on one of the chairs while the little boy lit the lamp. He began to mimic his son's flat accent, saying half to himself: '*At the chapel. At the chapel, if you please!*' When the lamp was lit he banged his fist on the table and shouted:

'What's for my dinner?'

'I'm going . . . to cook it, pa,' said the little boy.

The man jumped up furiously and pointed to the fire.

'On that fire! You let the fire out! By God, I'll teach you to do that again!'

He took a step to the door and seized the walking-stick which was standing behind it.

'I'll teach you to let the fire out!' he said, rolling up his sleeve in order to give his arm free play.

The little boy cried '*O, pa!*' and ran whimpering round the table, but the man followed him and caught him by the coat.

The little boy looked about him wildly but, seeing no way of escape, fell upon his knees.

'Now, you'll let the fire out the next time!' said the man, striking at him vigorously with the stick. 'Take that, you little whelp!'

The boy uttered a squeal of pain as the stick cut his thigh. He clasped his hands together in the air and his voice shook with fright.

'O, pa!' he cried. 'Don't beat me, pa! And I'll . . . I'll say a *Hail Mary* for you . . . I'll say a *Hail Mary* for you, pa, if you don't beat me . . . I'll say a *Hail Mary* . . .'

I'll take you down a peg . . .

From Mark Twain, *The Adventures of Huckleberry Finn*, 1884

I had shut the door to. Then I turned around, and there he was. I used to be scared of him all the time, he tanned me so much. I reckoned I was scared now, too; but in a minute I see I was mistaken – that is, after the first jolt, as you may say, when my breath sort of hitched, he being so unexpected; but right away after I see I warn't scared of him worth bothering about.

He was most fifty, and he looked it. His hair was long and tangled and greasy, and hung down, and you could see his eyes shining through like he was behind vines. It was all black, no grey; so was his long, mixed-up whiskers. There warn't no colour in his face, where his face showed; it was white; not like another man's white, but a white to make a body sick, a white to make a body's flesh crawl – a tree-toad white, a fish-belly white. As for his clothes – just rags, that was all. He had one ankle resting on t'other knee; the boot on that foot was busted, and two of his toes stuck through, and he worked them now and then. His hat was laying on the floor – an old black slouch with the top caved in, like a lid.

I stood a-looking at him; he set there a-looking at me, with his chair tilted back a little. I set the candle down. I noticed the window was up; so he had clumb in by the shed. He kept a-looking me all over. By and by he says:

'Starchy clothes – very. You think you're a good deal of a big-bug, *don't* you?'

'Maybe I am, maybe I ain't,' I says.

'Don't you give me none o' your lip,' says he. 'You've put on considerable many frills since I been away. I'll take you down a peg before I get done with you. You're educated, too, they say – can read and write. You think you're better'n your father, now, don't you, because he can't? *I'll* take it out of you. Who told you you might meddle with such hifalut'n foolishness, hey? – who told you you could?'

'The widow. She told me.'

'The widow, hey? – and who told the widow she could put in her shovel about a thing that ain't none of her business?'

'Nobody never told her.'

'Well, I'll learn her how to meddle. And looky here – you drop that school, you hear? I'll learn people to bring up a boy to put on airs over his own father and let on to be better'n what *he* is. You lemme catch you fooling around that school again, you hear? Your mother couldn't read, and she couldn't write, nuther, before she died. None of the family couldn't before *they* died. *I* can't; and here you're a-swelling yourself up like this. I ain't the man to stand it – you hear? Say, lemme hear you read.'

I took up a book and begun something about General Washington and the wars. When I'd read about a half a minute, he fetched the book a whack with his hand and knocked it across the house. He says:

'It's so. You can do it. I had my doubts when you told me. Now looky here; you stop that putting on frills. I won't have it. I'll lay for you, my smarty; and if I catch you about that school I'll tan you good. First you know you'll get religion, too. I never see such a son.'

He took up a little blue and yaller picture of some cows and a boy, and says:

'What's this?'

'It's something they give me for learning my lessons good.'

He tore it up, and says:

'I'll give you something better – I'll give you a cowhide.'

He sat there a-mumbling and a-growling a minute, and then he says:

'*Ain't* you a sweet-scented dandy, though? A bed; and

bedclothes; and a look'n' glass; and a piece of carpet on the floor – and your own father got to sleep with the hogs in the tanyard. I never see such a son. I bet I'll take some o' these frills out o' you before I'm done with you. Why, there ain't no end to your airs – they say you're rich. Hey? – how's that?'

'They lie – that's how.'

'Looky here – mind how you talk to me; I'm a-standing about all I can stand now – so don't gimme no sass. I've been in town two days, and I hain't heard nothing but about you bein' rich. I heard about it away down the river, too. That's why I come. You git me that money tomorrow – I want it.'

'I hain't got no money.'

'It's a lie. Judge Thatcher's got it. You git it. I want it.'

'I hain't got no money, I tell you. You ask Judge Thatcher; he'll tell you the same.'

'All right. I'll ask him; and I'll make him pungle, too, or I'll know the reason why. Say, how much you got in your pocket? I want it.'

'I hain't got only a dollar, and I want that to—'

'It don't make no difference what you want it for – you just shell it out.'

He took it and bit it to see if it was good, and then he said he was going downtown to get some whisky; said he hadn't had a drink all day. When he had got out on the shed he put his head in again, and cussed me for putting on frills and trying to be better than him; and when I reckoned he was gone he came back and put his head in again, and told me to mind about that school, because he was going to lay for me and lick me if I didn't drop that.

Next day he was drunk, and he went to Judge Thatcher's and bullyragged him, and tried to make him give up the money; but he couldn't, and then he swore he'd make the law force him.

The judge and the widow went to law to get the court to take me away from him and let one of them be my guardian; but it was a new judge that had just come, and he didn't know the old man; so he said courts mustn't interfere and separate families if they could help it; said he'd druther not take a child away from its father. So Judge Thatcher and the widow had to quit on the business.

That pleased the old man till he couldn't rest. He said he'd cowhide me till I was black and blue if I didn't raise some money for him. I borrowed three dollars from Judge Thatcher, and pap took it and got drunk, and went a-blowing around and cussing and whooping and carrying on; and he kept it up all over town, with a tin pan, till most midnight; then they jailed him, and the next day they had him before court, and jailed him again for a week. But he said *he* was satisfied; said he was boss of his son, and he'd make it warm for *him*.

When he got out the new judge said he was a-going to make a man of him. So he took him to his own house, and dressed him up clean and nice, and had him to breakfast and dinner and supper with the family, and was just old pie to him, so to speak. And after supper he talked to him about temperance and such things till the old man cried, and said he'd been a fool, and fooled away his life; but now he was a-going to turn over a new leaf and be a man nobody wouldn't be ashamed of, and he hoped the judge would help him and not look down on him. The judge said he could hug him for them words; so *he* cried, and his wife she cried again; pap said he'd been a man that had always been misunderstood before, and the judge said he believed it. The old man said that what a man wanted that was down was sympathy, and the judge said it was so; so they cried again. And when it was bedtime the old man rose up and held out his hand, and says:

'Look at it, gentlemen and ladies all; take a-hold of it; shake it. There's a hand that was the hand of a hog, but it ain't so no more; it's the hand of a man that's started in on a new life, and'll die before he'll go back. You mark them words – don't forget I said them. It's a clean hand now; shake it – don't be afeard.'

So they shook it, one after the other, all around, and cried. The judge's wife she kissed it. Then the old man he signed a pledge – made his mark. The judge said it was the holiest time on record, or something like that. Then they tucked the old man into a beautiful room, which was the spare room, and in the night some time he got powerful thirsty and clumb out on to the porch-roof and slid down a stanchion and traded his new coat for a jug of forty-rod, and clumb back again and had a good old time; and toward daylight he crawled out again, drunk as a fiddler, and rolled off the porch and broke his left arm in two places, and was most froze to death when somebody found him after sunup. And when they come to look at that spare room they had to take soundings before they could navigate it.

The judge he felt kind of sore. He said he reckoned a body could reform the old man with a shot-gun, maybe, but he didn't know no other way.

⌒

Pour encourager les autres

King George V, 1865–1935

My father was frightened of his father, I was frightened of my father, and I am damned well going to see to it that my children are frightened of me.

⌒

What inconveniences do happen by the negligence of fathers?

From Plutarch, *The Morals*, c. AD 90, translated by Sir Thomas Eliot, 1535

Often times I have thought much occasion of ill and corrupted manners to be in such, which having children of their own, during their infancy and tender youth commit them to good masters and tutors, and as soon as they do enter into man's age, they abandon them, and suffer them to live at their pleasure, wherein contrariwise in that entre and jeoperdous time more heed ought to be taken of them, than when they were children. For men know well that the defaults of children be of light importance, and lightly redressed: as perchance it may hap, by negligence of tutors, and lack of obedience. But the offences of them which be common to perfect years be more grievous oftentimes and full of danger, as riotous living consuming substance and inheritance, inordinate and chargeable gaming, ingurgitations and surfeits, defloration of maids, corrupting good women. These inconveniences ought in time and speedily to be repressed. For the delicate flower of youth uneth may be preserved from the violence of bodily lust, unless he be bridelled, wherefore they which withstand not youth in their children: little foresee what liberty of imagination they give unto them to commit vice, wherefore wise fathers, having children, at that estate, and years will have to them a vigilante eye, that they may the rather induce them in to temperance, sometimes exhorting, another time menacing, other whiles desiring, in like wise counselling, efsoones promising, or other whiles alluring; sometimes declaring to them, what dangers and troubles themselves in youth have sustained: or how by virtue and sufferance they have attained both land and honour. For the two principal occasions of virtue be fear of pain and hope of reward: the one disposes a man to acts of honesty, the other maketh him slow to do ill . . .

Insensitivity

From Anny Thackeray, *Chapters from Some Memoirs*, 1894

I suppose the outer circuit of my own very limited wanderings must have been reached at the age of thirteen or thereabouts, when my father took me and my little sister for the grand tour of Europe. We had, of course, lived in Paris and spent our summers in quiet country places abroad with our grandparents, but this was to be something different from anything we had ever known before at St Germains or Montmorenci among the donkeys; Switzerland, and Venice, and Vienna, Germany and the Rhine! Our young souls thrilled with expectation. And yet those early feasts of life are not unlike the miracle of the loaves and the fishes; the twelve basketfuls that remain in after years are certainly even more precious than the feast itself.

We started one sleety summer morning. My father was pleased to be off, and we were enchanted. He had brought a grey wide-awake hat for the journey, and he had a new sketch book in his pocket, besides two smaller ones for us, which he produced as the steamer was starting. We sailed from London Bridge, and the decks were all wet and slippery as we came on board. We were scatter-brained little girls, although we looked demure enough in our mushroom hats and waterproofs. We also had prepared a travelling trousseau . . . which consisted I remember of a draught board, a large wooden work-box, a good many books, paint boxes, and other odds and ends: but I felt that whatever else might be deficient our *new bonnets* would bring us triumphantly out of every crisis. They were alike, but with a difference of blue and pink wreaths of acacia, and brilliant in ribbons to match, at a time when people affected less dazzling colours than they do now. Alas! for human expectations! When the happy moment came at last, and we had reached foreign parts and issued out of the hotel dressed and wreathed and triumphantly splendid, my father said 'My dear children go back and put those bonnets away in your box, and don't ever wear them any more!' How the sun shone as he spoke; how my heart sank under the acacia trees. My sister was eleven years old, and didn't care a bit; but at thirteen and fourteen one's clothes begin to strike root. I felt disgraced, beheaded of my lovely bonnet, utterly crushed, and I turned away to hide my tears.

～

'Now I don't like being touched in any way'

From *Behind Closed Doors* by Janine Turner, 1988

Dear Jan,

From an early age I remember my father touching me and hurting me. I thought that I had buried these memories until I had to sleep with Dave, my husband.

Now I'm married with two children, Mark who is 2½, and Miranda who is nearly 10 months. But ever since I got married three years ago, I don't like any kind of relationship, from holding hands to sleeping with Dave. When he touches me it's like my father all over again when he forced me to sleep with him.

I feel so dirty. I hate Dave even looking at me, and will think up any excuse to sleep in the babies' room. I remember my father when he was drunk, beating and hurting me, touching me where I didn't like him to be, and I'm ashamed to be a woman.

I try losing weight to reduce my body so I don't look like a woman. The nightmares are all about Dad hurting me, and they upset me greatly. I've also produced a boy which I resent very much. Each time I see him, the anger inside me seems to boil to the surface. I don't like holding Mark. I get Dave to bath and change him when I can.

I'm finding it hard to overcome this anger as I find I'm now projecting the anger which was for my father onto Mark and Dave.

When my father died, I thought that it was all over. But the memories are with me as if it were happening now. Today. And while this is going on, I haven't been able to say goodbye to my father. I'm very confused. On the one hand I'm supposed to love my dad. But he hurt me. Now I don't like being touched in any way. I don't enjoy skin contact with my little boy or girl.

My life is so empty and I'm making it so unhappy for my husband and children. Please help me.

Sandra

───

A stricture against deadbeat dads, eighteenth-century version

From *Emile* by Jean-Jacques Rousseau, 1762

A father, when he engenders and feeds children, does with that only a third of his task. He owes to his species men; he owes to society sociable men; he owes to the state citizens. Every man who can pay this triple debt and does not do so is culpable, and more culpable perhaps when he pays it halfway. He who cannot fulfil the duties of a father has no right to become one. Neither poverty nor labours nor concern for public opinion exempts him from feeding his children and from raising them himself. Readers, you can believe me. I predict to whoever has vitals and neglects such holy duties that he will long shed bitter tears for his offence and will never find consolation for it.

Too late to play the role

From Kirk Douglas, *The Ragman's Son*, 1988

It took a minute for my eyes to adjust to the dimness of Boggi's and find him sitting at the bar. He was drinking his usual boilermaker, a shot of raw whiskey followed by a swallow of beer. The bartender recognised me and with great solicitude walked away, leaving me with my father.

'Hi, Pa.'

'Hullo.' He got up, kissed me on the mouth, Russian style. I was shocked to find I was taller than he. He always seemed such a huge man.

'How are you, Pa?'

A grunt.

I studied my father's face. He seemed a lot older. His moustache was gone. So was one of his front teeth, those that he had never brushed ('brushing made teeth loose,' he always said), those teeth that could take the cap off a bottle or chew glass. He used to gnash his teeth, grind them together and make a terrible sound. As I looked at him, I thought I'd hate to put those teeth to that test now. He still had all his hair, but it was completely grey. And he needed a shave, which was unlike him.

I never saw my father shave himself. We were poor, but he went to a barber to get shaved. Years later, I was in New York, at the barber's. I thought, My God, I'm a rich man. 'Give me a shave.' It was luxurious; I liked it. I can afford it. But that was the only time I did it.

After a long pause, 'I made a new movie, Pa.'

'Yeah?'

'*Champion.*'

'Yeah.'

Another long pause. 'Did you see it, Pa?'

'Yeah.'

'Did you like it?'

'Yeah.'

That was a pretty long conversation with Pa. He ordered another boilermaker. I gave him some money and left. I got in my waiting limousine, told the driver to take me to Albany.

Years later, I was told that my father went to see *Champion* with one of his drinking buddies. When I was being slaughtered by my opponent in the ring, my father covered his face with both hands. At the end of the fight, when I was finally winning, Pa got up and yelled in broken English, 'Issur, give it to him! Issur, give it to him!'

If only Pa could have said, 'Issur, give it to him,' when I was a kid. Pa covered his eyes when Kirk Douglas was bleeding make-up in a movie. But when Issur was being carried home, head bleeding for real, Pa was on the other side of the street, grumbling, 'That's what you get for playing.' He should have covered his eyes *then*. Years later, many people told me how Pa would brag about me. But it was too late to get that pat on the back when Pa was dead.

⌒

Too far

From Mikal Gilmore's *Shot in the Heart: One Family's History of Murder*, 1994

Though I would later see indelible signs of my father's violence, I never experienced it in the unrestricted way that my brothers did. In fact, I remember being hit by my father on only one occasion. The cause of the spanking is vague – which only goes to support Frank's belief that all you truly carry away from such an incident is the bitterness of the punishment. I think I probably did something like drawing on a wall with a crayon or sassing my mother, and my father deemed that the act called for a whipping. I remember that he undressed me and stood me in front of him as he unbuckled his belt – a wide, black leather belt with a gleaming silver buckle – and pulled it from around his waist. This whole time he was telling me what my whipping was going to be like, how badly it was going to hurt. I remember I felt absolute terror in those moments – nobody had ever hit me before for any reason, and the dread of what was about to happen felt as fearful as the idea of death itself. My father was going to *hit* me, and it was going to hurt. It seemed horribly threatening – like the sort of thing I might not live through – and it also seemed horribly unjust.

My father doubled his belt over and held it in his hand. Then he sat down on his chair, reached out and took me by the arm and laid me across his lap. The next part is the only part I don't recall. I know I got whipped and that I cried out, but I can't remember a thing about the blows or the pain, or whether it was even truly bad. All I remember is that a few moments later I was standing in front of him again, this time held in my mother's embrace. 'That's enough, Frank,' she said. 'You've gone too far. You're not going to do to *this* one what you did to the others.' I stood there, looking at my father, rubbing my naked, sore butt, crying. I remember that what had really hurt me was that I felt I had lost my father's love, that the man I trusted most had hurt me in a way I had never expected. My father was smiling back at me – a smile that was meant to let me know that he was proud with what he had just done, that he enjoyed the power and the virtue of this moment. I looked back at him and I said: 'I hate you.'

I know it is the only time I ever said that to him in my life, and I cannot forget what those words did to his face. His smile fell – indeed, his whole face seemed to fall into a painful fear or sense of loss. He laid his belt on his desk and sat studying the floor, with a weary look of sadness.

My mother led me out of the room and dressed my nakedness.

～

Provoke not

From the Epistle of Paul the Apostle to the Colossians, 3: 21

Fathers, provoke not your children to anger, lest they be discouraged

～

Ten tips for fathers

Fatherhood USA, 1999

- **Be there.**
  Children want and need your physical presence, from infancy onward.
- **Listen.**
  Being there means more than being present physically.
- **Support your partner.**
  Work together on behalf of your child, even if you're not living together.
- **Learn to disagree appropriately with your partner.**
  Disagreement is a normal part of parenthood. It is how you resolve those differences that matters.
- **Get to know and be known to the people in your child's world.**
  Teachers, caregivers, doctors – all of them are an important part.
- **Get to know and be known to your children's friends and their parents.**
  If you have concerns about who your child is hanging out with, be sure to discuss this with your child.
- **Play with your children.**
  One of the best ways to learn about and develop a lasting connection with your children is to play with them – to enter their world.
- **Teach by example.**
  Children follow what you do more than what you say.
- **Discipline with love.**
  To discipline means to guide or lead out the best in your child, and that is best done with love.
- **Keep your sense of humour.**
  Nobody said fatherhood would be easy. If you can survive fatherhood, you can survive anything!

5

Experience

Things a Man Should Know about Fatherhood

Esquire magazine, 1999

Don't worry, your dad didn't know what he was doing, either.

No, no – not that Spock!

Second thought, maybe you should worry.

Never tell anybody that you and your wife are 'trying'.

We really don't need the visual, that's why.

Never tell anybody where your child was conceived, how long it took, or what song was playing.

Do not name your baby after cities, geographical points of interest, features of the solar system, seasons, plants, animals or current television stars.

Your child, at birth, already has a deeply complicated relationship with his mother, and, for the first year, you are only a curiosity.

For a couple of years after that, an amusement-park ride.

Then, a referee.

And finally, a bank.

If you want to subject your son to the unkindest cut, insist on a local anaesthetic, since many pediatricians don't bother to use one.

The anaesthetic is for the kid.

Baby gas is lessened with a good nipple connection during feeding, which decreases air intake.

Assuring that his lower lip is flipped out, not pursed, helps.

There is nothing wrong with thumb-sucking, which helps ease the pain of teething.

None the less, it probably ought to stop by kindergarten.

Diaper-rash remedy: expose baby's hydraulics to the air until dry. Soak baby's bottom in tepid water with a half-cup baking soda. Then Balmex. Or Lotrimin. Re-diaper.

You know how they say you'll get used to diapers? You won't.

Unless you wear them a lot . . .

The start of crawling: usually begins between six months and twelve months.

Standing: usually between nine and twelve months.

Walking: between twelve and fifteen months.

The onset of the above, as with all developmental skills, is hugely variable among individual children.

Avoid walkers, not only because they can be dangerous around stairs but because they don't require a child to balance and thus retard his walking progress.

Reason boys are better: they cannot get pregnant.

Reason girls are better: they're less likely to get arrested.

The threat of an unknown punishment is always more effective than a stated one.

Annals of great punishments: hang dolly from a noose!

That was a joke, Dad, a joke.

Annals of great punishments, for real: making him wash the car, clean the bathroom, and watch *The McLaughlin Group*.

You see, all great punishments should reduce the number of disagreeable tasks you would otherwise have to perform . . .

Your kids can develop an independent sense of good taste only if they're allowed to make their own mistakes in judgment.

Relax: lots of little boys want a Barbie and a dollhouse.

The first time you change your son's diaper and he pees all over you is not an accident. It's foreshadowing.

Children of too-strict parents are more likely to develop tics.

Let them take reasonable risks: a few scrapes in the long run are nothing compared with the scars left by hovering parents. Or tics.

In preparation for risks: a Red Cross first-aid course.

The most common cause of fatal injury among kids between five and nine involves cars, which is to say, hold their hands. And buckle them in.

Try to tuck them in every night, too . . .

Reason boys are better: they cost less, especially their clothes.

Reason girls are better: they're less likely to burn, slash or chew the clothes they have . . .

Dropping food on the floor is a new and delightful skill to a one-year-old, not a deliberate attempt to annoy you.

However small he or she might be, never underestimate an infant's ability to project chewed food over great distances.

The single most important thing a father can possess: Wet-Naps.

Now, more than ever, don't move into a place without laundry facilities.

Children's hobbies to nip quickly in the bud: drums, archery, matchbook collecting.

Beware your child's uncles, who will teach your kid dirty words, introduce him to liquor, and give him gifts of drums, archery sets and possibly matches.

It is, of course, your natural right to exert the above negative influences on your siblings' offspring.

You are under no obligation to tell children the truth.

Lying to children is, in fact, half the fun: 'Oh, that tree? That's a yellow-spotted spickle-gruber, of course.'

On the other hand, they do remember everything . . .

Your bedroom door gets a lock. Your teenage son's does not.

Lock or no, please knock before entering, as the disruption of a youth who is spanking his monkey will be twice as traumatic for you as it is for him.

Other doors to lock: those on the liquor cabinet.

There is only one reason for a teenager to burn incense, and we think you remember what it is . . .

Unfortunately, those books that say motherhood makes women desire more sex are referring to women who are not your wife.

No matter how wealthy you are, don't buy your kid a car – offer to match him.

Ditto for other adolescent big-ticket items; teach the little bastard some responsibility!

DNA tests are 99.9 per cent accurate, but check the ears to be absolutely sure.

Reason boys are better: boys start talking later than girls.

Reason girls are better: boys toilet-train later than girls.

The twos aren't always terrible.

Even if they are, take heart, as kids aged three to six generally believe their parents are the most amazing beings alive and wish to be exactly like them.

How scary is that?

Establishing savings accounts for your kids and requiring them to make regular monthly deposits teaches them how to eventually become J. R. Morgan.

The above could prove useful in your dotage . . .

Acceptable reading material: *Dr Seuss, Where the Wild Things Are, Harold and the Purple Crayon, Curious George* and any of the following by Roald Dahl – *James and the Giant Peach, Charlie and the Chocolate Factory* and *Danny the Champion of the World*.

Neither of the following by Roald Dahl: *Kiss Kiss* or *Switch Bitch* . . .

Some parents walk around naked in front of their children.

These parents should stop it.

Nearly all psychological problems result from feelings of worthlessness, which is to say, every now and then make sure that you tell your kid he's pretty great.

And never raise a hand to him. But being a good guy, you probably knew that.

The harder they play, the earlier they sleep.

Never turn down an invitation to play.

No toys that require batteries . . .

All in all, fatherhood is pretty terrific – filled with joy and triumph, promise and miracles – particularly other people's fatherhood.

You might think you know a lot about fatherhood, but not as much as you will when you're a grandfather.

If you're thinking that fatherhood means the end of life as you've known it, you, sir, are, of course, absolutely correct.

⌒

The nighttime father-jitters

From Laurie Lee, *The Firstborn*, 1964

Here she is then, my daughter, here, alive, the one I must possess and guard. A year ago this space was empty, not even a hope of her was in it. Now she's here, brand new, with our name upon her: and no one will call in the night to reclaim her.

She is here for good, her life stretching before us, twenty-odd years wrapped up in that bundle; she will grow, learn to totter, to run in the garden, run back, and call this place home.

Or will she? Looking at those weaving hands and complicated ears, the fit of the skin round that delicate body, I can't indulge in the neurosis of imagining all this to be merely a receptacle for Strontium 90. The forces within her seem much too powerful to submit to a blanket death of that kind.

But she could, even so, be a victim of chance; all those quick lively tendrils seem so vulnerable to their own recklessness – surely she'll fall on the fire, or roll down some crevice, or kick herself out of the window?

I realise I'm succumbing to the occupational disease, the father-jitters or new-parenthood-shakes, expressed in: 'Hark, the child's screaming, she must be dying.' Or, 'She's so quiet, d'you think she's dead?'

As it is, my daughter is so new to me still that I can't yet leave her alone. I have to keep on digging her out of her sleep to make sure that she's really alive.

The pram-pusher's knack

From Vladimir Nabokov on bringing up baby in
Nazi Germany, from *Speak Memory: An
Autobiography Revisited*, 1964

You know, I still feel in my wrists certain echoes of the pram-pusher's knack, such as, for example, the glib downward pressure one applied to the handle in order to have the carriage tip up and climb the curb. First came an elaborate mouse-grey vehicle of Belgian make, with fat autoid tyres and luxurious springs, so large that it could not enter our puny elevator. It rolled on sidewalks in slow stately mystery, with the trapped baby inside lying supine, well covered with down, silk, and fur; only his eyes moved, warily, and sometimes they turned upward with one swift sweep of their showy lashes to follow the receding of branch-patterned blueness that flowed away from the edge of the half-cocked hood of the carriage, and presently he would dart a suspicious glance at my face to see if the teasing trees and sky did not belong, perhaps, to the same order of things as did rattles and parental humour. There followed a lighter carriage, and in this, as he spun

along, he would tend to rise, straining at his straps; clutching at
the edges; standing there less like the groggy passenger of a
pleasure boat than like an entranced scientist in a spaceship;
surveying the speckled skeins of a live, warm world; eyeing with
philosophic interest the pillow he had managed to throw over-
board; falling out himself when a strap burst one day. Still later
he rode in one of those small contraptions called strollers; from
initial springy and secure heights the child came lower and lower,
until, when he was about one and a half, he touched ground in
front of the moving stroller by slipping forward out of his seat
and beating the sidewalk with his heels in anticipation of being
set loose in some public garden. A new wave of evolution started
to swell, gradually lifting him again from the ground, when, for
his second birthday, he received a four-foot-long, silver-painted
Mercedes racing car operated by inside pedals, like an organ, and
in this he used to drive with a pumping, clanking noise up and
down the sidewalk of the Kurfürstendamm while from open
windows came the multiplied roar of a dictator still pounding
his chest in the Neander valley we had left far behind.

⌒

Henry Miller changes diapers

From *My Life and Times* by Henry Miller, 1971

My two children were a blessing. They weren't born at home –
we had no conveniences. There was no doctor in Big Sur, not
even a telephone nearby. From the time they were born, I was a
very happy man.

When my children were very small I used to get up at night
to feed them. And much more. I changed their diapers too. In
those days, I didn't have a car; I would take the dirty diapers in
a bag, a big laundry bag, and walk six miles to the hot springs
(now taken over by Esalen) and wash them in that hot spring
water, then carry them home! Six miles! That's *one* thing I
remember about babies. For a time, after my wife left me, I was
there with the children alone. That's the hardest thing to ask a
man to do – take care of tots from three to five years of age,
bouncing with energy, and shut up with them in one room,

especially during the rains. In the winter when the rains came we were marooned. I fed them, changed their clothes, washed them, told them stories. I didn't do any writing. I couldn't. By noon every day I was exhausted! I'd say, 'Let's take a nap.' We'd get into bed, the three of us, and then they'd begin scrambling, screaming, fighting with each other. Finally I had to ask my wife to take them. As much as I loved them I couldn't handle the situation. It was something I'll never forget. That experience increased my respect for women, I guess. I realised what a tremendous job women have, married women, cooking meals, doing the laundry, cleaning house, taking care of children, and all that. This is something no man can understand or cope with no matter how hard his work may be.

The kids were fairly close together in age, two and a half years' difference. They fought all the time, like sworn enemies. Today, of course they're good friends.

When Val was able to toddle beside me, when she was about three years old, I took her into the forest every day for a long walk beside a narrow stream. I pointed out birds, trees, leaves, rocks, and told her stories. Then I'd pick her up and carry her on my shoulders. I'll never forget the first song I taught her. It was 'Yankee Doodle Dandy'. What joy, walking and whistling with this kid on my back. Anyone who hasn't had children doesn't know what life is. Yes, they were a great blessing.

⌒

'Restrain your mirth till you have children of your own'

Two scenes from Ancient Greece, as related in
The Percy Anecdotes, 1821

The warlike Agesilaus was, within the walls of his own house, one of the most tender and playful of men. He used to join with his children in all their innocent gambols, and was once discovered by a friend, showing them how to ride upon a hobby-horse. When his friend expressed some surprise at beholding the great Agesilaus so employed, 'Wait,' said the hero, 'till you are yourself a father, and if you then blame me, I give you liberty to proclaim this act of mine to all the world.'

The grave Socrates was once surprised in nearly a similar situation by Alcibiades, and made nearly the same answer to the scoffs of that gay patrician. 'You have not,' said he, 'such reason as you imagine to laugh so, at a father playing with his child. You know nothing of that affection which parents have to their children; restrain your mirth till you have children of your own, when you will, perhaps, be found as ridiculous as I now seem to you to be.'

~

A *wider arc*

From *A Man Called Daddy* by Hugh O'Neill, 1996

Since I have been a father, the pendulum of my life swings through a wider arc. Before Josh and Rebecca, I rarely whispered and I rarely yelled. Now I do both all the time. Before Josh and Rebecca, I merely strode through the world like a man. Now I crawl, hunker, scramble, hop on one foot, often see the world from my hands and knees. Before Josh and Rebecca, I knew nothing about water slides. Now I hold several American records in the over-thirty-five division. Before Josh and Rebecca, I heard only the sound of my own voice. Now I sometimes hear the principal, asking to see me at my 'earliest possible convenience'. Now I always carry two small voices in my soul. Before Josh and Rebecca the world was plain. Now it's fancy, full of portents and omens, solemnity and awe.

~

Kitchen sink drama

From Fraser Harrison's *A Father's Diary*, 1985

Tonight Jack asked if he could 'help' me wash up, but the thought of water swilling all over the floor and having to rewash everything after he had finished seemed unbearable, so I curtly told him to play somewhere else. This was brutal and quite unnecessary: he would have been quite happy with two or three plastic cups and he is much better about spilling the water than he used to be. In any case, it is the work of a moment to clear up after him and I had nothing else to do.

'I won't make a mess,' he whined.

'That's not the point,' I shouted back at him. 'I just don't want you near the sink. Find something else to do.'

Stubbornly, he dragged over a chair and climbed up to the sink.

Get down, Jack,' I shouted again, in my most furious voice. He took no notice. I picked him up and thrust him, very forcefully, on to the floor.

He clutched his foot and howled, 'You've hurt me.'

Tilly came in to see what was happening.

'Daddy's being 'orrible to me,' he told her.

He got up and hit my legs as hard as he could with his clenched fist, swinging his arm in a mighty arc. I pushed him away. Snivelling, he joined Tilly in their playroom.

Five minutes later, perhaps even less, he ran in to show me how fast one of his cars could go: there was nothing in his manner, not the faintest hint or echo, to suggest that I had just been his mortal enemy.

I hate myself for these incidents. What they ask for is always so simple and small, so easily given. And by the same token, my reasons for refusing are so trivial, so mean. Usually, my reason simply amounts to not wanting to inconvenience myself or disrupt some pettifogging system I have set up. Not that I ever admit as much to them.

I hate the thought of slamming doors in their faces, closing down their world before they know how to explore it, instead of showing them new excitements, new marvels, which at their age can be done with next to no effort. They are of course splendidly resilient and shrug off my rebuffs to find some other amusement that does not require my permission or help. They accommodate, without much complaint, to whatever position they are faced with, no matter how unreasonable. None the less, we are all impoverished by my small-mindedness.

Growing Pain

Vernon Scannell, 1922–

The boy was barely five years old.
We sent him to the little school
And left him there to learn the names
Of flowers in jam jars on the sill
And learn to do as he was told.
He seemed quite happy there until
Three weeks afterwards, at night,
The darkness whimpered in his room.
I went upstairs, switched on his light,
And found him wide awake, distraught,
Sheets mangled and his eiderdown
Untidy carpet on the floor.
I said, 'Why can't you sleep? A pain?'
He snuffled, gave a little moan,
And then he spoke a single word:
'Jessica.' The sound was blurred.
'Jessica? What do you mean?'
'A girl at school called Jessica,
She hurts –' he touched himself between
The heart and stomach '– she has been
Aching here and I can see her.'
Nothing I had read or heard
Instructed me in what to do.
I covered him and stroked his head.
'The pain will go, in time,' I said.

~

Real men do childcare

Extracts from William Cobbett's *Advice to a Father*,
1830

249. It is, however, of the part which the husband has to act in
participating in these cares and toils that I am now to speak. Let
no man imagine that the world will despise him for helping to
take care of his own child: thoughtless fools may attempt to
ridicule; the unfeeling few may join in the attempt; but all whose

good opinion is worth having will applaud his conduct, and will, in many cases, be disposed to repose confidence in him on that very account. To say of a man that he is fond of his family is, of itself, to say that, in private life at least, he is a good and trustworthy man; aye, and in public life, too, pretty much; for it is no easy matter to separate the two characters; and it is naturally concluded that he who has been flagrantly wanting in feeling for his own flesh and blood will not be very sensitive towards the rest of mankind. There is nothing more amiable, nothing more delightful to behold, than a young man especially taking part in the work of nursing the children; and how often have I admired this in the labouring men in Hampshire! It is, indeed, generally the same all over England; and as to America, it would be deemed brutal for a man not to take his full share of these cares and labours.

250. The man who is to gain a living by his labour must be drawn away from home, or at least from the cradle-side, in order to perform that labour; but this will not, if he be made of good stuff, prevent him from doing his share of the duty due to his children. There are still many hours in the twenty-four that he will have to spare for this duty; and there ought to be no toils, no watchings, no breaking of rest imposed by this duty, of which he ought not to perform his full share, and that, too, without grudging. This is strictly due from him in payment for the pleasures of the married state. What right has he to the sole possession of a woman's person; what right to a husband's vast authority; what right to the honourable title and the boundless power of father: what right has he to all, or any of these, unless he can found his claim on the faithful performance of all the duties which these titles imply?

251. One great source of the unhappiness amongst mankind arises, however, from a neglect of these duties; but, as if by way of compensation for their privations, they are much more duly performed by the poor than by the rich. The fashion of the labouring people is this: the husband, when free from his toil in the fields, takes his share in the nursing, which he manifestly looks upon as a sort of reward for his labour. However distant from his cottage, his heart is always at that home towards which he is carried at night by limbs that feel not their weariness, being urged on by a heart anticipating the welcome of those who attend

him there. Those who have, as I so many hundreds of times have, seen the labourers in the woodland parts of Hampshire and Sussex coming at nightfall towards their cottage wickets laden with fuel for a day or two; whoever has seen three or four little creatures looking out for the father's approach, running in to announce the glad tidings, and then scampering out to meet him, clinging round his knees or hanging on his skirts; whoever has witnessed scenes like this, to witness which has formed one of the greatest delights of my life, will hesitate long before he prefer a life of ease to a life of labour; before he prefer a communication with children intercepted by servants and teachers to that communication which is here direct, and which admits not of any division of affection.

⌒

A Nottingham father's place is . . . ?

From John and Elizabeth Newson, *Patterns of Infant Care in an Urban Community*, 1965

Not unexpectedly, we found that some of the activities of child care were more popular than others with the fathers (see Table). Whereas 80 per cent were prepared to get the baby to sleep, for instance, only 57 per cent ever changed a nappy, and still fewer (39 per cent) ever gave him his bath.

The total of 68 per cent who, at least sometimes, take the baby out without the mother is perhaps surprising in view of the traditional reluctance of the Englishman to be seen pushing a pram; and this percentage does not include fathers who 'wouldn't mind doing it, but we always go out as a family'. Many fathers took all the young children out of the mother's way on a Saturday or Sunday morning, while she cleared up; and a large number, especially those living on new housing estates, regularly took the baby without its mother on a visit to the paternal grandmother in the older part of the city. One father, who lived on the new council estate outside the city, cycled the seven miles to his mother's terrace house every Saturday afternoon with the baby sitting on the cross-bar.

Proportions of fathers undertaking various activities in the care of one-year-olds.

	Feed him %	Change nappy %	Play with him %	Bath him %	Get to sleep %	Attend in the night %	Take out alone %
Often	34	20	83	15	31	18	29
Sometimes	44	37	16	24	49	32	39
Never	22	43	1	61	20	50	32

Mr Ross, a highly participant father, was paid this tribute by his wife:

'Oh, he'll do anything for either of them – he always has – bath, change, feed, wash for them. They're all their daddy. There's a scream when he goes and a howl when he comes back in case he's going again. We always have a tantrum when daddy goes. Oh, they delight in their daddy.'

A moderately participant father is one who in general is prepared to help with the children *if he is asked* or in an emergency, but who doesn't do a great deal as a matter of course. Sometimes the father makes a principle of doing certain jobs only if the mother is quite unavailable, and in general he tends to pick and choose as to what he will do and what he won't.

House-painter's wife:

'No, he'll not change a nappy if he can help it. If I'm out he will. But if I ask him, he won't. It isn't his place to change a nappy. He'll give her a bottle though, and fuss her up a bit.'

Mrs Matthew, a non-participant father's wife, found life a continual battle with two high-spirited under-threes to cope with; her husband did not expect, and was not expected, to do anything at all in the house – not even to brush his own shoes.

'He never does anything for either of them – except he might perhaps give Julian a bottle if I was getting his supper ready. That's all he'd do.'

(Would he give Julian his dinner – feed him with a spoon?)

'Oh no – he'd say that was my job – I don't think he'd know how to, anyway.'

(Mr Matthew spends all his time at home lying on the sofa with the paper; his wife does not grumble at this, but thinks it fair and right.)

'He does just look after them on Saturday afternoon – that's when I do my shopping. Well – look after them – he just lies on the sofa and turns away from them, and I think he hopes they won't notice him – anyway, he lets them do whatever they like, just lets them get on with it. I *suppose* he'd stop them falling in the fire. Oh – you should have seen it when I got in last week! They'd got a packet of cornflakes and a packet of sugar out of the cupboard, and they'd emptied them out here all over the mat, and they were digging in it. And he just lay there!'

⌒

Even educated fish do it

From Konrad Lorenz's zoological study,
King Solomon's Ring, 1952

I came, late one evening, into the laboratory. It was already dusk and I wished hurriedly to feed a few fishes which had not received anything to eat that day; amongst them was a pair of jewel fishes who were tending their young. As I approached the container, I saw that most of the young were already in the nesting hollow, over which the mother was hovering. She refused to come for the food when I threw pieces of earthworm into the tank. The father, however, who, in great excitement, was dashing backwards and forwards searching for truants, allowed himself to be diverted from his duty by a nice hind-end of earthworm (for some unknown reason this end is preferred by all worm-eaters to the front one). He swam up and seized the worm, but, owing to its size, was unable to swallow it. As he was in the act of chewing this mouthful, he saw a baby fish swimming by itself across the tank; he started as though stung, raced after the baby and took it into his already filled mouth. It was a thrilling moment. The fish had in its mouth two different things, of which one must go into the stomach and the other into the nest. What would he do? I must confess that, at that moment, I would not have given twopence for the life of that tiny jewel fish. But wonderful what really happened! The fish stood stock still with full cheeks, but did not chew. If ever I have seen a fish think, it was in that moment! What a truly remarkable thing that a fish can find itself in a genuine conflicting situation and, in this case, behave exactly as a human being would; that is to say, it stops, blocked in all directions, and can go neither forward nor backward. For many seconds the father jewel fish stood riveted, and one could almost see how his feelings were working. Then he solved the conflict in a way for which one was bound to feel admiration: he spat out the whole contents of his mouth: the worm fell to the bottom, and the little jewel fish, becoming heavy in the way described above, did the same. Then the father turned resolutely to the worm and ate it up, without haste but all the time with one eye on the child which 'obediently' lay on the bottom beneath him. When he had finished, he inhaled the baby and carried it home to its mother.

Some students, who had witnessed the whole scene, started as one man to applaud.

~

Dad's department

Sam Harper, *National Fatherhood Initiative* website,
1999

Last Saturday morning I was about to tap in a birdie putt on the eighteenth green at the Dreamland Country Club, a luxury afforded by the miracle that my kids were also sleeping in, when a series of REM-piercing screams jangled my back-swing. I bolted awake, jumped out of bed, and raced down the hall toward the hubbub.

I found my wife standing on a chair in the kitchen, hyper-ventilating. Between palpitations she explained that she was flipping pancakes when she heard little paw-steps ticking against linoleum behind her. She turned around. Waddling toward her, following the pancake-scent, was an opossum the size of a cocker spaniel. That's when she screamed. The opossum skritched furiously into the living room and squeezed under a couch. 'Please get that thing out of this house,' she said with an it's-so-icky-I-can't-say-its-name shiver.

Let me point out here that I respect my wife. Deeply. I love her. Deeply. She represents her gender with intelligence, strength, grace and humour. She's a firm, responsible, loving mother and a communicative, thoughtful and giving wife. She can sink back-to-back free throws, carve turns on a snowboard, and where I would simply throw the phone against the wall, she demands to speak to a supervisor. In short, she meets challenges, doesn't shrink from them. So when I saw her standing on the chair, I blinked. It was an odd sight, anachronistic, like a scene from a '60s sitcom; Harriet sees a mouse, squeals, leaps on a chair and is stuck there until Ozzie returns home, summons his faded Boy Scout skills and comically vanquishes the creature.

At the risk of sounding like a chauvinist swine who's making gross generalisations based on sexual stereotypes, I'd like to make some gross generalisations based on sexual stereotypes and suggest that for all the glorious progress men and women have made in achieving parity in the home and workplace, there are still a few domestic chores that are categorised according to gender.

You know what I'm talking about. There's 'Dad's Department' and there's 'Mom's Department'. These departments are era-resistant, defined not by the times, but by an obscure and ageless code of suburban domestic duty that's been handed down from generation to generation. While Mom's Department includes every chore that involves fabric, tableaux and wainscoting, Dad's Department includes the following:

1. Rodents of Unusual Size. When was the last time your wife said, 'Gee, honey, you made the dinner and put the kids to bed last night, why don't I kill that pesky rat today.' Ridding the house of rodents, particularly rodents that resemble dogs, has always been and always will be Dad's department.

2. Noise Patrol. Was that noise a squirrel raiding the bird feeder or a half-dozen crack-crazed, AK-47-toting teenagers ransacking your living room? It doesn't matter. As Dad, you must defend the home, even if you don't have a nasty weapon in your bedside table. So grab your shoehorn and go kick some butt.

3. Zap. Gurgle. BOOM! All problems relating to utilities – electricity, plumbing and gas (also see 'Funky Smells') – are handled out of Dad's department. If you're one of those guys who doesn't know how to operate a hammer, just pretend you know what you're doing. You're good at that.

4. Sharp Things That Move. Jobs that include hedge clippers, lawn mowers, roto-tillers, Bush Hogs or any tool that has a

whirring blade are generally Dad's department. However, as Loraina Bobbit illustrated, there are exceptions.

5. Funky Smells. Gas vapours, septic tank miasma, crawlspace musk, or plain old death in the basement, it's Dad's job to pull that turtleneck collar over his nose and find the source of the offending odour, unless he can convince the dog to do it.

So basically you could say that if the job includes the possibility of bodily injury, it's Dad's department. And there's nothing wrong with that, as far as I'm concerned. I like the idea of being the hero. My wife, after all, is permanently, irrevocably, a hero for having given birth to our children. And if wrestling with an 80-pound rodent will help me achieve parity in the hero department, let's rumble!

So I pulled out my shoehorn and stealthily approached the living-room couch. I lifted the fabric thing that hangs off the bottom of a couch (ask your wife what it's called, that's her department) and looked under. Ooo. It was a big ol' possum. Long snout. Saliva dripping off its sharp teeth.

Did I mention that calling a professional exterminator is a chore that Dad can enjoy, too?

A *classically* good father

A portrait of Cato as *pater*, from *Vitae Parallae* by
Plutarch (*c.* 46–*c.* 120), translated by
Bernadotte Perrin, 1914

He . . . was also a good father, a considerate husband, and a household manager of no mean talent, nor did he give only a fitful attention to this, as a matter of little or no importance. Therefore I think I ought to give suitable instances of his conduct in these relations. He married a wife who was of gentler birth than she was rich, thinking that, although the rich and the high-born may be alike given to pride, still, women of high birth have such a horror of what is disgraceful that they are more obedient to their husbands in all that is honourable. He used to say that the man who struck his wife or child laid violent hands on the holiest of holy things. Also that he thought it more praiseworthy to be a good husband than a great senator, nay, there was nothing else to admire in Socrates of old except that he was always kind and gentle in his intercourse with a shrewish wife and stupid sons. After the birth of his son, no business could be so urgent, unless it had a public character, as to prevent him from being present when his wife bathed and swaddled the babe. For the mother nursed it herself, and often gave suck also to the infants of her slaves, that so they might come to cherish a brotherly affection for her son. As soon as the boy showed signs of understanding, his father took him under his own charge and taught him to read, although he had an accomplished slave, Chilo by name, who was a school-teacher, and taught many boys. Still, Cato thought it not right, as he tells us himself, that his son should be scolded by a slave, or have his ears tweaked when he was slow to learn, still less that he should be indebted to his slave for such a priceless thing as education. He was therefore himself not only the boy's reading-teacher, but his tutor in law, and his athletic trainer, and he taught his son not merely to hurl the javelin and fight in armour and ride the horse, but also to box, to endure heat and cold, and to swim lustily through the eddies and billows of the Tiber. His history of Rome, as he tells us himself, he wrote out with his own hand and in large characters, that his son might have in his own home an aid to acquaintance with his country's ancient traditions. He declares that his son's presence put him on his guard against indecencies of speech as much as that of the so-called Vestal Virgins, and that he never bathed with him.

꒰

The father's job

From *Sorrell and Son*, Warwick Deeping, 1925

Sorrell has taken a lowly post as hotel porter to
support his son.

Christopher never asked questions, awkward and embarrassing questions. He accepted his father's job, and he understood the significance of it far more subtly than Sorrell knew. It reacted on the boy, and deepened his sensitive seriousness.

At school he was very careful of his clothes. He did not say much about the school. It was all right. Better than London.

What did he do in the evenings? Oh, – went for walks, mostly. There were woods outside the town, and the river.

Those few minutes were very precious to Sorrell, but they tantalised him. His boy was so apart from him all through the day, and whenever they met he would look eagerly at that frankly radiant face for the shadow of any possible blemish.

He felt so responsible, greedily responsible. The boy's clean eyes made the life at the Angel possible.

On one occasion when he had walked a little way along the footpath with Christopher he became aware of a face at a window. The woman was watching them. He caught her bold, considering eyes fixed on the boy.

He went back rather hurriedly into the passage, and met her there.

'That your kid, Stephen?'

'Yes, madam.'

'He's not a bit like you. The mother's dead, I suppose?'

'I divorced her,' said Sorrell, pale and stiff about the lips.

Usually, it was about eleven at night when he went slowly up the narrow staircase to the top landing where the staff slept. He carried a candle. Sometimes he would hear giggling and chattering in one of the girls' rooms, but he always went straight to his own, shut the door, put the candlestick on the chair, sat down on the bed and turned out his pockets. At this hour he did his precious calculations. His little black notebook was a model of neatness, with credit and debit entries.

						Christopher – Board	£1	0	0
July	7:	Wages	£1	10	0	Christopher – Board	£1	0	0
July	7:	Tips		4	6	Tobacco		2	0
July	8:	Tips		3	0	Toothbrush		1	0
July	9:	Tips		0		Christopher – Boots	1	0	0
July	10:	Tips		7	0				
July	11:	Tips		5	6				
July	12:	Tips		1	0				
July	13:	Tips		9	0				

He found that his tips averaged about twenty-five shillings a week. He paid Mrs Barter a pound a week for Christopher's keep. He spent a few odd shillings on himself. He was contriving to save about a pound a week. £52 a year? If his health held out?

Already he had a plan for his boy, an objective that showed like a distant light through the fog of the days' confusion.

'It's my business to do my job thoroughly,' he thought, 'in order to get Kit a better one. I'll save every damned penny.'

⌒

My Thoughts

Victor Hugo, written 1837

My thoughts?
Far from the roof
sheltering you, my thoughts
are of you, my children, and the hopes
that lie in you. My summer days
have ripened and the sun
has started its decline. Each year
the shadow of your branches
creeps further up my wall
yet some furled petals still retain
the secret dazzle of your dawn.

I think of the two younger ones
laughing as they cry.
The threshold must be green
where they babble mingling
games with quarrels both with charm –
two flowers occasionally
rub against each other as they sway.

All fathers worry and I think
about the two older ones
already further from the shore
among deeper waves. They lean
their heads to one side now, the boy
all curiosity, the girl all thought.

Alone here, sad, I think these things
while sailors sing beneath the cliff.
The sea at evening
seems to breathe and sigh
when waves advance, recede.
The wind blends salt into the air

that stirs with strange
echoes of land and water.

I think of you, my children, seeing
a table surrounded with laughter,
a fireplace crackling.
all the piety and care
your mother and her father shed
in tenderness.
Here at my feet the clear sea spreads
set with sails and mirroring the stars.
Boatmen casually
glance from the unending
sea to the unending
sky and I think of you, my children,
trying to sound
the depth of love I have for you,
its gentleness, its power –
and in comparison how small the sea!

⌒

The tie that binds

Sir Thomas More writes to his children, Margaret,
Elizabeth, Cecilia and John, probably 1517

It is not so strange that I love you with my whole heart, for being
a father is not a tie which can be ignored. Nature in her wisdom
has attached the parent to the child and bound them spiritually
together with a Herculean knot. This tie is the source of my
consideration for your immature minds, a consideration which
causes me to take you often into my arms. This tie is the reason
why I regularly fed you cake and gave you ripe apples and pears.
This tie is the reason why I used to dress you in silken garments
and why I never could endure to hear you cry. You know, for
example, how often I kissed you, how seldom I whipped you.
My whip was invariably a peacock's tail. Even this I wielded hesitantly and gently so that sorry welts might not disfigure your
tender seats. Brutal and unworthy to be called father is he who
does not weep himself at the tears of his child. How other fathers

act I do not know, but you know well how gentle and devoted is my manner towards you, for I have always profoundly loved my own children and I have always been an indulgent parent – as every father ought to be. But at this moment my love has increased so much that it seems to me I used not to love you at all. This feeling of mine is produced by your adult manners, adult despite your tender years; by your instincts, trained in noble principles which must be learned; by your pleasant way of speaking, fashioned for clarity; and by your very careful weighing of every word. These characteristics of yours so strangely tug at my heart, so closely bind me to you, my children, that my being your father (the only reason for many a father's love) is hardly a reason at all for my love of you. Therefore, most dearly beloved children all, continue to endear yourselves to your father and, by those same accomplishments which make me think that I had not loved you before, make me think hereafter (for you can do it) that I do not love you now.

Missing figures

Statistics extracted from *Fathers and Fatherhood in Britain*, The Family Policy Studies Centre, 1997

- One-third of all fathers had their first child before they were 25 years old; of those fathers who had a second child, over two-thirds did so between 25 and 34.
- Fathers were more likely to be married than were men who were not fathers. Nine out of ten children were born to married fathers.
- Fatherhood was less common for young men than motherhood was for young women. Just 1 per cent of teenage men were fathers, while 5 per cent of teenage women were mothers.
- A majority of fathers – six in ten – reached their thirties before having their first child.
- More than eight in ten fathers of dependent children lived with all their own biological children and more than seven in ten were doing so within their first family.

- Of the 84 per cent of fathers of dependent children living with all of their own biological children, 6 per cent were in a relationship subsequent to their first relationships, and 5 per cent were lone fathers.
- One in six fathers lived apart from some or all of his own biological children. But these fathers were no more likely to be living apart from their daughters than their sons.

◡

No striker

From the diary of Reverend Henry Newcombe

22 February 1662

. . . a night of much dreameinge. Esp[ecially] how in ye way a lad had angered mee. & I had stricken him with a little sticke in my hand. But I was after much troubled at it, & yt of ye ap[?] came in upon mee. Ye servant of God must not strive. No striker. I was ashamed much at it, but glad w[he]n in it was but a dreame. But I desire to take warning hereby.

◡

Eppie was reared without punishment

From George Eliot, *Silas Marner*, 1861

By the time Eppie was three years old, she developed a fine capacity for mischief, and for devising ingenious ways of being troublesome, which found much exercise, not only for Silas's patience, but for his watchfulness and penetration. Sorely was poor Silas puzzled on such occasions by the incompatible demands of love. Dolly Winthrop told him punishment was good for Eppie, and that, as for rearing a child without making it tingle a little in soft and safe places now and then, it was not to be done.

'To be sure, there's another thing you might do, Master Marner,' added Dolly, meditatively: 'you might shut her up once i' the coal-hole. That was what I did wi' Aaron; for I was that silly wi' the youngest lad, as I could never bear to smack him. Not as I could find i' my heart to let him stay i' the coal-hole more nor a minute, but it was enough to colly him all over, so as he must be new washed and dressed, and it was as good as a rod to him – that was. But I put it upon your conscience, Master Marner, as there's one of 'em you must choose – ayther smacking or the coal-hole – else she'll get so masterful, there'll be no holding her.'

Silas was impressed with the melancholy truth of this last remark; but his force of mind failed before the only two penal methods open to him, not only because it was painful to him to hurt Eppie, but because he trembled at a moment's contention with her, lest she should love him the less for it. It was clear that Eppie, with her short toddling steps, must lead father Silas a pretty dance on any fine morning when circumstances favoured mischief.

For example. He had wisely chosen a broad strip of linen as a means of fastening her to his loom when he was busy: it made a broad belt round her waist, and was long enough to allow of her reaching the truckle-bed and sitting down on it, but not long enough for her to attempt any dangerous climbing. One bright summer's morning Silas had been more engrossed than usual in 'setting up' a new piece of work, an occasion on which his scissors were in requisition. These scissors, owing to an especial warning of Dolly's, had been kept carefully out of Eppie's reach; but the click of them had had a peculiar attraction for her ear. Silas had seated himself in his loom, and the noise of weaving had begun; but he had left his scissors on a ledge which Eppie's arm was long enough to reach; and now, like a small mouse, watching her opportunity, she stole quietly from her corner, secured the scissors, and toddled to the bed again, setting up her back as a mode of concealing the fact. She had a distinct intention as to the use of the scissors; and having cut the linen strip in a jagged but effectual manner, in two moments she had run out at the open door where the sunshine was inviting her, while poor Silas believed her to be a better child than usual. It was not until he happened to need his scissors that the terrible fact burst upon him: Eppie had run out by herself – had perhaps fallen into the Stone-pit. Silas, shaken by the worst fear that could have befallen him, rushed out, calling 'Eppie!' and ran eagerly about the unenclosed space, exploring the dry cavities into which she might have fallen, and then gazing with questioning dread at the smooth red surface of the water. The cold drops stood on his brow. How long had she been out? There was one hope – that she had crept through the stile and got into the fields where he habitually took her to stroll. The meadow was searched in vain; and he got over the stile into the next field, looking with dying hope towards a small pond which was now reduced to its summer shallowness, so as to leave a wide margin of good adhesive mud. Here, however, sat Eppie, discoursing cheerfully to her own small boot, which she was using as a bucket to convey the water into a deep hoof-mark, while her little naked foot was planted comfortably on a cushion of olive-green mud. A red-headed calf was observing her with alarmed doubt through the opposite hedge.

It was not until he had carried her home, and had begun to think of the necessary washing, that he recollected the need that he should punish Eppie, and 'make her remember'. The idea that she might run away again and come to harm, gave him unusual resolution, and for the first time he determined to try the coal-hole – a small closet near the hearth.

'Naughty, naughty Eppie,' he suddenly began, holding her on his knee, and pointing to her muddy feet and clothes – 'naughty to cut with the scissors, and run away. Eppie must go into the coal-hole for being naughty. Daddy must put her in the coal-hole.'

He half expected that this would be shock enough, and that Eppie would begin to cry. But instead of that, she began to shake herself on his knee, as if the proposition opened a pleasing novelty. Seeing that he must proceed to extremities, he put her into the coal-hole, and held the door closed, with a trembling sense that he was using a strong measure. For a moment there was silence, but then came a little cry, 'Opy, opy!' and Silas let her out again, saying, 'Now Eppie 'ull never be naughty again, else she must go in the coal-hole – a black naughty place.'

The weaving must stand still a long while this morning, for now Eppie must be washed and have clean clothes on; but it was to be hoped that this punishment would have a lasting effect, and save time in future – though, perhaps, it would have been better if Eppie had cried more.

In half an hour she was clean again, and Silas having turned his back to see what he could do with the linen band, threw it down again, with the reflection that Eppie would be good without fastening for the rest of the morning. He turned round again, and was going to place her in her little chair near the loom, when she peeped out at him with black face and hands again, and said, 'Eppie in de toal-hole!'

This total failure of the coal-hole discipline shook Silas's belief in the efficacy of punishment. 'She'd take it all for fun,' he observed to Dolly, 'if I didn't hurt her, and that I can't do, Mrs Winthrop. If she makes me a bit o' trouble, I can bear it. And she's got no tricks but what she'll grow out of.'

'Well, that's partly true, Master Marner,' said Dolly, sympathetically; 'and if you can't bring your mind to frighten her off touching things, you must do what you can to keep 'em out of her way. That's what I do wi' the pups as the lads are allays a-rearing. They *will* worry and gnaw – worry and gnaw they will, if it was one's Sunday cap as hung anywhere so as they could drag it. They know no difference, God help 'em: it's the pushing o' the teeth as sets them on, that's what it is.'

So Eppie was reared without punishment.

⌒

Batter up

From Bill Cosby, *Fatherhood*, 1986

A few days later, I called from Las Vegas and learned from my wife that this law of the house [obeying parental commands] had been broken. I was hardly taken by surprise to learn that the outlaw was my son.

'Why didn't you do what you were told?' I said to him on the phone. 'This is the second time I've had to tell you, and your mother's very upset. The school also says you're not coming in with the work.'

'Well, I just don't feel like doing it,' he said.

'Very well. How does this idea strike you? When I come home on Thursday, I'm going to kick your butt.'

Now I know that many distinguished psychologists feel that

kicking butt is a reversion to the Stone Age. But kids may have paid more attention in the Stone Age. When a father said, 'No shrinking heads this week,' his boy may have listened.

On Thursday, I came home, but I couldn't find the boy. He didn't make an appearance at dinner, and when I awoke the next morning, he still wasn't there. So I assembled my staff and solemnly said, 'Ladies, where is my son?'

'He's around here *somewhere*,' one of my daughters said. They were the French underground hiding one of their heroes from the Nazis.

At last, just before dinner, he entered the house, tired of wandering in the wilderness.

'Young man,' I said, 'I told you that when I came home, I would kick your behind.'

'Yes, Dad,' he replied.

'And you know why, don't you?'

'Yes, Dad.'

'Then let's go over to the barn.'

He may have been slow in his studies, but by now he must have suspected that I wasn't planning a lesson in animal husbandry. When we reached the barn, I said, 'Son, we are now going to have a little talk about breaking the law and lying.'

As the boy watched me roll up my sleeves, his usual cool gave way to fear, even though I was a father with absolutely no batting average: I had never before hit him or any of the other children. Was I making a mistake now? If so, it would just be mistake number nine thousand, seven hundred, and sixty-three.

'Dad, I know I was wrong,' he said, 'and I'm really sorry for what I did. I'll never do it again.'

'I appreciate your saying that,' I said, 'and I love you; but I made a promise to you and you wouldn't respect me if I broke it.'

'Oh, Dad, *I'd* respect you – I'd respect you like crazy!'

'Son, it's too late.'

'It's *never* too late!'

He was reaching heights of legal eloquence, which didn't help him because I've often wanted to hit lawyers, too.

'Just turn around,' I said. 'I want you to know that this is a form of punishment I truly do not believe in.'

'I hate to see you go against your *principles*, Dad.'

'I can make an exception. I also won't say that this will hurt

me more than it will hurt you. That would be true only if I
turned around and let you hit *me*. This is simply a barbaric
form of punishment, but it happens to match your barbaric
behaviour.'

And then I hit him. He rose up on his toes in the point position and the tears began.

'Now do you understand my point about never lying again?'
I said.

'Oh *yes*, Dad!' he said. 'I've never understood it better.'

'Fine. Now you can go.'

He turned around to leave and I hit him again. When he turned
back to me with a look of having been betrayed, I said, 'I'm
sorry; I lied. Do you ever want me to lie to you again?'

'No, Dad,' he said.

And to this day, he has not lied again to me or my wife.
Moreover, we received a letter from his school taking credit for
having done a wonderful job on our son. I'm glad I had been
able to supplement this work by the school with my own
parent–student conference in the barn.

Could I have done anything else to put him on the road to
righteousness? My wife and I spent long hours pondering this
question. The problem was that the reservoir was empty: we had
tried all the civilised ways to redirect him, but he kept feeling he
could wait us out and get away with anything. And we loved
him too much to let him go on thinking that.

The week after our trip to the barn, a friend of mine, Dr Eddie
Newman, said something that clicked with the boy.

'My boy is having his problems being a serious student,' I told
Eddie.

'Well, your studying is very important,' Eddie said, while the
boy sat smiling a smile that said: an old person is about to hand
out some Wisdom. Could this please be over fast? 'You know, a
jet plane burns its greatest energy taking off; but once it reaches
its cruising altitude, it burns less fuel. Just like studying. If you're
constantly taking off and landing, you're going to burn more fuel
as opposed to taking off and staying up there and maintaining
that altitude.'

A few days later, I ran into my son in the house. (He was
around a lot more now that he knew the designated hitter had
retired.)

'How's school?' I said.

Without a word, he raised his arm and laid his palm down and flat like a plane that had levelled off. He suddenly knew it was the only way to fly.

There are many good moments in fathering, but few better than that.

⌒

Distress of sperm donor children

Article in *The Times*, 31 August 2000

Children conceived by anonymous sperm donation often experience deep shock, feelings of abandonment and betrayal when they discover their origins, new research shows.

Their distress is further heightened when they discover they have no rights to find out the identity of their genetic father and must accept that they will never know who he is.

The study, conducted by psychologists at the University of Surrey and published in the scientific journal *Human Reproduction*, raises important questions about how much information should be made available to people born as a result of assisted reproduction techniques.

Until now, the debate on donor-assisted pregnancies has focused largely on the needs of the adults involved, with relatively little attention being given to the interests of the resulting children and their 'right to know' about their origins.

In Britain, more than 10,000 children have been born using donor insemination since 1991.

⌒

Generations

Evan Jones, *Two Centuries of Australian Poetry*,
1988

I go to see my parents
we chew the rag a bit,

I turn the telly on
and sit and look at it . . .

I go to see my son,
I'm like a Santa Claus;
he couldn't like me more;
mad about him, of course.

Still years before he learns
to judge, condemn, dismiss.
I stand against the light
and bleed for both of us.

The cat's in the cradle

Hit song by Harry and Sandra Chapin, 1974

My child arrived just the other day
He came to the world in the usual way
But there were planes to catch and bills to pay
He learned to walk while I was away
And he was talkin' 'fore I knew it
And as he grew, he'd say.
'I'm gonna be like you, Dad
You know I'm gonna be like you'

And the cat's in the cradle and the silver spoon
Little boy blue and the man in the moon
When you comin' home, Dad?
I don't know when, but we'll get together then
You know we'll have a good time then

My son turned ten just the other day
He said, 'Thanks for the ball, Dad, c'mon, let's play
Can you teach me to throw?' I said, 'Not today
I got a lot to do,' he said, 'That's OK'
And he walked away but his smile never dimmed
It said, 'I'm gonna be like him, yeah
You know I'm gonna be like him'

I've long since retired, my son's moved away
I called him up just the other day
I said, 'I'd like to see you if you don't mind'
He said, 'I'd love to, Dad, if I can find the time
You see, my new job's a hassle and the kids have the flu
But it's sure nice talkin' to you, Dad
It's been sure nice talkin' to you'
And as I hung up the phone, it occurred to me
He'd grown up just like me
My boy was just like me

⸺

The big event

From William Saroyan's autobiography, *Here Comes, There Goes, You Know Who*, 1961

My kids came out to California from New York that summer, and mainly we had a lot of fun, but one thing happened that was no fun.

We drove up to San Francisco to spend a couple of weeks at my sister's home, and then we drove back to Malibu, by way of Fresno, and as we were driving around among the vineyards near Malaga my son asked me to stop, so we could pick some grapes. So we could *steal* some, if you like. I stopped, and ran out into the vineyard and began picking the grapes, only to notice that my son was just standing there looking at them. I told him to start picking, but he just went right on looking.

'I don't think they're ripe,' he said.

'Even so,' I said, 'pick a couple of bunches.'

I ran back to the car. He came back, taking his time, but he didn't have a single bunch of grapes with him.

This bothered me.

He had asked me to stop, and I had stopped, and then he hadn't done anything to make the stop worth anything.

I bawled him out about this, and about his boredom all during the drive, and then I bawled out my daughter, too. My sister said something, and I bawled her out too, and then for an hour or more nobody spoke.

By that time I felt foolish, but at the same time I couldn't understand my son, so I asked him if he had had a bowel movement in the morning.

He hadn't. And he'd had a headache all day.

I told him about myself when I had been his age. I had had nothing, but I had always been interested, fascinated even, by everything. On and on.

I knew it at the time, I know it now, and I suppose he knew it too: I was being angry at his mother.

It was stupid, but I couldn't help it, that's all.

I stopped somewhere for an aspirin for him, but he said he believed a Coke would do him more good, so he had a Coke, as everybody did, but whatever had been going on went right on going on.

My past was kicking me around, and with it I was kicking my son around, and every now and then my daughter, a little, too.

I tried to get out of it, to get myself out of being so mad at their mother, and at them, too, but it didn't work, and so I blamed my son.

Why wasn't he livelier, more comic, more alert, so that I would be driven out of the madness?

He didn't know. All he knew, but didn't say, was that he hated me, and I couldn't blame him, but I hated being hated.

I said that my trouble had been that I had loved them too much, had tried to do too much for them, had paid too much attention to every wish they had ever had, and of course they knew I meant their mother hadn't, which I believed to be true. From now on I would be different, I said. I would be like other fathers. I would give them orders. The other fathers were right, I was mistaken. I had looked upon them from the beginning as equals, or even superiors, and now I could see the folly of that.

I talked for hours and miles, and nobody replied, nobody dared, or cared, or needed to.

Now, I must point out that such talking is traditional in my family. It is invariably loud, intense, righteous, and critical of all others.

All families probably have their own procedure for the achievement of psychiatric therapy or the restoration of balance, and the better part of this procedure is based upon talk, although it frequently moves along to shouting and fighting.

Six or seven times during the long recitation I tried to get out of the whole thing by laughing at myself, by making known that I knew I was being a fool, by saying things I believed were both true and amusing, but nobody laughed.

It was a very hot day in July, and from the beginning it had been a bad day.

In the back of the old Cadillac my daughter sat beside my sister, and beside me sat my son, drawn away on the car seat, the old Saroyan scowl all over his face.

At last the car began to climb the hills of Pacific Palisades, and soon we would be home.

I was still going strong when suddenly my son said in a tone of voice that still hurts me, and has twice come to me in my sleep: 'Papa, Papa, will you stop the car, please?'

I stopped the car, he leaped out, and in the very leap began to buckle and vomit, trying to hide behind a tree whose trunk was too narrow for hiding. The sound of his sickness sickened me. Once, twice, three times, four times, five times. Silence. His face was drained of colour and covered with sweat.

Immediately after he had jumped out of the car my daughter jumped out, saying, 'Aram, what's the matter? What's the matter, Aram?'

My sister said in Armenian, 'You've made the poor boy sick. He isn't like you. He's like himself.'

We got home, and I got him into the shower, and then into a robe, and at the table for some hot chocolate and toast and boiled eggs, and then I had them both go to bed, even though it was only beginning to be dark, and their old friends in the neighbourhood were coming to the door to ask them out for games.

That's the thing that bothered me in 1958, and will go right on bothering me the rest of my life.

I only hope it isn't the last thing I remember.

He told me the next day that it hadn't been my hollering at him that had made him sick, it had been other things.

I thanked him, but I didn't believe him, because I couldn't.

And my sister had been right in saying that he wasn't like me, only she'll never know how like him I was, but never vomited, because if I had, I might not be able to stop.

And I was sorry he wasn't like me, in that, because it is better not to get sick, it is better to find out how not to, it is better to insist on it, even, until it's almost impossible to get that sick, because getting sick doesn't get it, doesn't do it, at all.

But he hurt me, he hurt me deeper even than the failure and death of friends, and I loved him more than ever, and despised myself for never having been able to get sick that way, and for having made him sick that way, making him vomit for me forty years ago.

I went home one night from the winter streets of Fresno, possessed. Something had taken possession of me, hushed me, estranged me, put me aside from myself, and I wanted to get rid of it. The house was dark and empty when I got there, and cold, and I didn't know what to do. In the dining room was a bench my mother had made by placing planks over two apple-boxes and putting a coarse woven covering over the planks: red and black checks made out of some kind of sacking, made in Bitlis by somebody in the family. I couldn't sit and I couldn't lie down, so I kneeled on this bench and then put my head down, as Muslims do in praying, and I began to rock back and forth slowly because by doing that the thing that had taken possession of me, the sickness, the uselessness, whatever it was, seemed to go away. I half-slept, I half-prayed, and I thought, What *is* this, for God's sake? What's the matter? Why is my head like a damned rock?

At last I heard somebody at the door and quickly sat in the corner of the room, on the bench. My mother turned on a light, came in, and looked at me. I got up and fetched sawdust from the barn, so she could get the fire going, and in that way she wasn't able to notice that I was possessed, I was sick, I was useless, my head was a rock. Nobody would know.

The big event of 1958 was my son's sickness, known.

∽

And the son's-eye view

Aram Saroyan on his father, William Saroyan,
quoted in Jon Winokur's *Fathers*, 1994

My father never liked me or my sister, and he never liked our mother either, after an initial infatuation, and in fact, he never liked anyone at all after an hour or two, no, no one except a stooge, someone he could depend on to be a lackey, a nitwit he could make fun of behind his back, someone he could control completely by whatever means he could make work – fear, intimidation, or, because he was a famous and admired man, blind worshipfulness.

And he wanted me and Lucy and my mother to die.

⌒

Keeping Mum about Dad

Television review by Joe Joseph, *The Times*,
June 2000

It used to be thought that, in these days of easy promiscuity and high divorce rates, the most that a child could expect is that its father be present at the conception. But it seems that fathers may have been painted more blackly than they deserve. TV scientists now estimate that one in 20 people in this country – and maybe one in ten in America – don't have the father they think they have. Well, that should take some of the shine off this Sunday's Father's Day, unless you're planning to send your pop a DNA-testing kit instead of cufflinks.

But the evidence seems to suggest that it's promiscuous women who are fuelling the paternity crisis. Time and again, in *Family Secrets: Who's Your Father?* (Channel 4), it was blameless men who'd been duped into accepting another man's child as their own.

Women may like to blame Nature for this, and to cite research that shows that because women are biologically programmed to seek the best genes for their children, they are not only more likely to have sex with their lovers during their fertile times than with their regular sexual partners, but that they also retain more semen from their lovers. (Who exactly dreamt of measuring these things in the first place, let alone volunteered to do it?) It has also been found that young women in discos dress more provocatively when they're ovulating.

Imagine how many men would get away with offering biological excuses like that ('Darling, it was out of my control. When that provocatively dressed, ovulating woman at the party dragged me into a bedroom the laws of Nature took over. It was all as erotic as a physics lesson').

Who's Your Father was a documentary which made you wonder about the blessings of modern science. For every mother, or father, or child, that was relieved to have resolved nagging doubts about a child's paternity by means of DNA-testing, there seemed to be dozens more whose lives had shattered, like a dropped glass, on hearing the truth. If a father loves a child, how easy is it to love it in quite the same way once he has found out that it isn't his? As tricky as adoring your Picasso in quite the same way, once it's been identified as a fake?

Each case study in this film seemed to be more tragic than the last: a father finding out that three of his four children bore about as much matching DNA to him as would a cheese sandwich: another divorced father discovering that the daughter he dotes on is not actually his, jeopardising the future of her weekend visits to him on shared-custody agreements with his former wife. And there was Bryan Good who, for 43 years, had carried in his wallet a black-and-white photo of a baby girl. It was sent to him by the girl's mother who had refused to marry him and instead sent 'their daughter' for adoption. When Good finally traced the girl in the snap, both father and daughter were ecstatic until a DNA test proved he was not her father at all. A central pillar of Good's life for 43 years crumpled like a cigarette ash.

As Professor John Burn, head of Human Genetics at Newcastle University, points out to anyone thinking of undergoing DNA-testing: 'If you have a test and discover that you are not the father of a child you thought you were the father of, you can't unlearn that. And that's why it's really critical for people to think before they act.'

⌒

Don't Call Me Mr Mom! Or, what not to say to a Stay-at-home Dad

Buzz McClain, *slowlane.com* web page, 1999

Men who choose to stay at home to raise their children while the mothers commute to work experience things most fathers do not. Not the least of which are the insensitive comments by people who can't comprehend the concept.

It's the price at-home dads pay for being both daring and non-traditional. After all, it's not every day you encounter an at-home dad. Then again, maybe you do, and you just don't realise it. An at-home father looks like an ordinary father, except he has slightly more spit-up on his shoulders. So you can't be blamed for saying the wrong thing, right? Well, we're here to help. Here are a few things that make at-home fathers cringe, according the members of the North Texas At-home Dads Network, who have heard it all.

1. 'What are you going to do when you go back to work in the real world?'

   Oh, how at-home dads hate this. It implies raising children isn't real, and it isn't work. It is lots of both.

2. 'Wouldn't it be better for the kids if the mother stayed at home?'

   No offence, but no. Studies show that working mothers are more involved in their children's lives when the father stays at home than when they are given over to professional day care. And because of the circumstances, the fathers are more involved with the children than dads who see their children only briefly after work and on weekends. The kids get two parents with strong influences.

3. 'What do you do with all your spare time?'

   No matter what the ages and number of kids, this statement is baloney. There is no spare time. Besides seeing to the children's feeding, clothing, bedding, amusement and education, at-home dads typically assume command of household chores – from laundry to kitchen duty to lawn care. And you can't punch a clock after eight hours and go home. You are home.

4. 'Who wears the pants in the family?'

   This implies staying at home with the children makes you less masculine. True, at-home dads are likely to wash more dishes, fold more laundry and go to the tot lot more than the father who commutes. But when mom's home, dads play and watch just as many sports, ogle just as many women and perform just as many testosterone-driven activities as other fathers. And they do it with more gusto because getting out of the house means more to them.

5. 'Oh, so you're a Mr Mom.'
Don't call us 'Mr Mom'. The kids already have a mother. At-home fathers do not replace mothers; they simply assume duties traditionally performed by them. If you must call at-home dads something, try 'Mr Dad'.

6. 'That's a nice Mommy Wagon you drive.'
Ahem. It is not a Mommy Wagon. It's a marvellously functional all-purpose utility vehicle that happens to have enough room for more than half the Stingers Little League soccer team.

7. 'What does your wife think about you not working?'
Ordinarily a fair question, but often asked to see how the woman is handling the pressure of being the primary breadwinner. Get real: the empowerment is a heady sensation, one most women don't get to experience, and they love it. As a bonus, she goes to the office each day knowing her baby is in good hands. Real men deal with the role change very well, thank you.

8. 'How can you stand to change diapers all the time?'
Usually asked by the 'traditional man', the kind who will overhaul an engine but can't wipe a baby's butt. I know of one such man who, when confronted with a messy diaper, put the baby in the bathtub until the mother came home. Diapers are easy, pal. (Plum-and-sweet potato spit-up is another thing altogether.)

9. 'Do you miss the security of having a job?'
Maybe at first, but who isn't disillusioned by the general lack of loyalty companies express these days? Mergers, takeovers, lay-offs, forced relocations and a slavish devotion by corporations to the bottom line are enough to rattle anyone's sense of security. An at-home dad has the job of a lifetime – you can't be fired or transferred to a lesser position.

10. 'What do you mean, you didn't get a chance to finish the laundry?'
Most often asked by frazzled wives coming home from work. Well, honey, things got really fun at the tot lot with the playgroup, and we stayed a few hours longer than we expected.

Mothers ruin

From James Joyce, 'Ivy Day in the Committee
Room', *Dubliners*, 1914

Mr O'Connor tore a strip off the card and, lighting it, lit his cigarette. As he did so the flame lit up a leaf of dark glossy ivy in the lapel of his coat. The old man watched him attentively and then, taking up the piece of cardboard again, began to fan the fire slowly while his companion smoked.

'Ah, yes,' he said, continuing, 'it's hard to know what way to bring up children. Now who'd think he'd turn out like that! I sent him to the Christian Brothers and I done what I could for him, and there he goes boozing about. I tried to make him somewhat decent.'

He replaced the cardboard wearily.

'Only I'm an old man now I'd change his tune for him. I'd take the stick to his back and beat him while I could stand over him – as I done many a time before. The mother you know, she cocks him up with this and that . . .'

'That's what ruins children,' said Mr O'Connor.

'To be sure it is,' said the old man. 'And little thanks you get for it, only impudence. He takes th'upper hand of me whenever he sees I've a sup taken. What's the world coming to when sons speaks that way to their fathers?'

'What age is he?' said Mr O'Connor.

'Nineteen,' said the old man.

'Why don't you put him to something?'

'Sure, amn't I never done at the drunken bowsy ever since he left school? "I won't keep you," I says. "You must get a job for yourself." But, sure it's worse whenever he gets a job; he drinks it all.'

Mr O'Connor shook his head in sympathy, and the old man fell silent, gazing into the fire.

The devil is in the definition

Ambrose Bierce, *The Devil's Dictionary*, 1911

Father, *n.* A quartermaster and commissary of subsistence provided by nature for our maintenance in the period before we have learned to live by prey.

⌒

Tugging at the purse strings

Letter from Robert Louis Stevenson,
aged sixteen, 1866

Respected Paternal Relative,
    I write to make a request of the most moderate nature. Every year I have cost you an enormous – nay, elephantine – sum of money for drugs and physician's fees, and the most expensive time of the twelve months was March.
    But this year the biting Oriental blasts, the howling tempests, and the general ailments of the human race have been successfully braved by yours truly.
    Does not this deserve remuneration?
    I appeal to your charity, I appeal to your generosity, I appeal to your justice, I appeal to your accounts, I appeal, in fine, to your purse.
    My sense of generosity forbids the receipt of more – my sense of justice forbids the receipt of less – than half-a-crown. Greeting from, Sir, your most affectionate and needy son,
    R. Stevenson

⌒

Artful fellow

Dalton Trumbo writes to his son, November 1958

I have at hand your most recent letter addressed, I believe, both to your mother and to me. That portion which I assume was designed to capture my attention has. I refer to your addled account of an exchange between you and Mike [Butler] relative to mensal checks from home. You may be sure I shall give it much thought.

You also inform us you haven't made holiday travel reservations because you haven't the money to pay for them. Artful fellow! Do you truly think me so stupid as to send the fare directly to you, who'd only squander it in high living and end up stranded on Christmas Eve begging poorman's pudding in some snow-swept Bowery breadline?

The procedure is this: go at once to an airline office and make round-trip reservations (not de luxe, not a milk-run either). Do it immediately, for the seasonal rush is already at hand. Notify me of the airline, flight number, date and hour of arrival, and within twenty-four hours a cheque made out to the airline will be delivered into your greedy fist. Take it to the seller and the deal is consummated without laying you open to temptation.

⌒

To *the poorhouse with a smile*

From Bill Cosby, *Fatherhood*, 1986

It doesn't make any difference how much money a father earns, his name is always Dad-Can-I; and he always wonders whether these little people were born to beg. I bought each of my five children everything up to a Rainbow Brite Jacuzzi and still I kept hearing 'Dad, can I get . . . Dad, can I go . . . Dad, can I buy . . .'

Like all other children, my five have one great talent: they are gifted beggars. Not one of them ever ran into the room, looked up at me, and said, 'I'm really happy that you're my father, and as a tangible token of my appreciation, here's a dollar.' If one of them had ever done this, I would have taken his temperature.

A parent quickly learns that no matter how much money you have, you will never be able to buy your kids everything they want. You can take a second mortgage on your house and buy what you think is the entire Snoopy line: Snoopy pyjamas, Snoopy underpants, Snoopy linen, Snoopy shoelaces, Snoopy cologne and Snoopy soap, but you will never have it all. And if Snoopy doesn't send you to the poorhouse, Calvin Klein will direct the trip. Calvin is the slick operator who sells your kids things for eighty-five dollars that cost seven at Sears. He has created millions of tiny snobs, children who look disdainfully at you and say, 'Nothing from Sears.' However, Dad-Can-I fought back: I got some Calvin Klein labels and sewed them into Sears undershorts for my high fashion junkies.

Sometimes, at three or four in the morning, I open the door to one of the children's bedrooms and watch the light softly fall across their little faces. And then I quietly kneel beside one of the beds and just look at the girl lying there because she is so beautiful. And because she is not begging. Kneeling there, I listen reverently to the sounds of her breathing.

And then she wakes up and says, 'Dad, can I . . .'

⌒

The fathering class of the 1950s re-examined

From David Blankenhorn, *Fatherless America*, 1995

In much of our current cultural discourse, of course, the 1950s are portrayed as a paternal wasteland: workaholic commuter Dads in grey flannel suits; violence-prone tyrants who lorded it over women and children; materialists who thought father-hood meant paying bills; and cold, emotionally remote Old Fathers who wounded their children through distance.

Doubtless there were such fathers in the 1950s. We know they existed in part because so many of their highly educated children have written books saying so. But as a group, the fathers of the 1950s did rather well by their children, at least compared to the fathers who preceded and followed them. They got and stayed married. They earned a lot of money, much of which went to their children. Many of them worked in physically demanding jobs, wearing blue collars and washing their hands with Lava soap. If these fathers sometimes fell asleep after dinner while reading the paper or watching TV, they did so partly because their work made them tired.

They spent more time with their children than their own fathers had with them, and also more than their sons, living in a divorce culture, would later spend with *their* children. They coached Little League, installed Sears swing sets in the backyard, took countless photos of the kids, attended games, practices, and school plays, interviewed boys who wanted to date their daughters, washed the car, pottered in the yard, took the garbage out, came home every night for dinner. They stayed around.

⌒

They don't make them like that any more

From Tony Parsons, *Man and Boy*, 1999

'Hello, Harry. Happy birthday, son. Have you met our guests?'

At his feet were two youths, belly down on the carpet with their hands tied behind their backs.

At first I thought I recognised them – they had exactly the same washed-out menace that I had seen on the face of Sally's boyfriend over at Glenn's place, although they didn't look quite so menacing now – but I only recognised the type. Expensive trainers, designer denim, hair so slick with gel that it looked as sticky and brittle as the skin of a toffee apple. My dad had trussed them up with the pair of silk ties I had bought him last Christmas.

'Saw them out on the street a bit earlier. Skylarking around, they were. But it turned out to be a bit more than skylarking.'

Sometimes it felt like my old man was the curator of the English language. As well as his love for outmoded hipster jive, another peculiarity of his speech was his use of expressions from his youth that everyone else had thrown out with their ration books.

He was always using words like skylarking – his arcane expression for mischief, fooling around and generally just mucking about – words that had gone out of fashion around the same time as the British Empire.

'They came in through the French windows, bold as brass. Thought nobody was home. Your mother was doing the shopping for your birthday – she's got a lovely roast – and I was upstairs getting spruced up.'

Getting spruced up. That was another one he was preserving for the archives.

'They were trying to unplug the video when I walked in. One of them had the cheek to come at me.' He lightly prodded the thinnest, meanest looking youth with a carpet slipper. 'Didn't you, old chum?'

'My fucking brother's going to fucking kill you,' the boy muttered, his voice as harsh in this room where I had been a child as a fart in church. There was a yellow and purple bruise coming up on one of his pimply cheekbones. 'He'll kill you, old man. He's a gangster.'

My dad chuckled with genuine amusement.

'Had to stick one on him.' My father threw a beefy right hook into the air. 'Caught him good. Went out like a bloody light. The other one tried to make a run for it, but I just got him by the scruff of the neck.'

The muscles on my father's tattooed arms rippled under his short-sleeved shirt as he demonstrated his technique for getting a teenage burglar by the throat. He had my mother's name in a heart inscribed on one arm, the winged dagger of the Commandos on the other. Both tattoos were blurred with the ages.

'Got him on the floor. Lucky I was deciding which tie to wear when they appeared. Came in handy, those ties you gave me.'

'Jesus Christ, Dad, they could have had knives!' I exploded. 'The papers are full of have-a-go heroes who get killed for tackling criminals. Why didn't you just call the law?'

My dad laughed good-naturedly. This wasn't going to be one of our arguments. He was enjoying himself too much for that.

'No time, Harry. Came downstairs and there they were. Large as life, in my home. That's a bit naughty, that is.'

I was angry with him for taking on the two little goons, although I knew he was more than capable of handling them. I also felt the furious relief that comes when you finally find a child who has gone missing. But there was also something else. I was jealous.

What would I have done if I had found these two yobs – or any of the million like them – in my home? Would I have had the sheer guts and the bloody-minded stupidity to take them on? Or would I have run a mile?

Whatever I would have done, I knew I wouldn't have done it with the manly certainty of my father. I couldn't have protected my home and my family in quite the same way that he had protected his home and family. I wasn't like him. But with all my heart, I wanted to be.

～

Teacher man

Seventeenth-century English proverb

One father is worth more than a hundred schoolmasters.

～

Paternity and posterity

From Sir Francis Bacon, *Essayes or Counsels*, 1601

The joys of parents are secret: and so are their griefs and fears. They cannot utter the one, nor they will not utter the other. Children sweeten labours, but they make misfortunes more bitter. They increase the cares of life, but they mitigate the remembrance of death. The perpetuity by generation is common to beasts, but memory, merit, and noble works are proper to men. And surely a man shall see the noblest works and foundations have proceeded from childless men, which have sought to express the images of their minds, where those of their bodies have failed. So the care of posterity is most in them that have no posterity. They that are the first raisers of their houses are most indulgent towards their children, beholding them as the continuance not only of their kind but of their work; and so both children and creatures.

～

Power and paternity

From *The Father*, August Strindberg, 1887

LAURA.   You can't be sure that you are Bertha's father.
CAPTAIN.   I – can't be sure – !
LAURA.   No. No one can be sure, so you can't.

CAPTAIN.	Are you trying to be funny?
LAURA.	I'm only repeating what you've taught me. Anyway, how do you know I haven't been unfaithful to you?
CAPTAIN.	I could believe almost anything of you, but not that. Besides, if it were true you wouldn't talk about it.
LAURA.	Suppose I were prepared for anything – anything – to be driven out, despised, anything – rather than lose my child? Suppose I am telling you the truth now, when I say to you: 'Bertha is my child, but not yours!' Suppose—!
CAPTAIN.	Stop!
LAURA.	Just suppose. Your power over her would be ended.
CAPTAIN.	If you could prove I was not the father.
LAURA.	That wouldn't be difficult. Would you like me to?
CAPTAIN.	Stop it! At once!
LAURA.	I'd only need to name the true father, and tell you the time and place. For instance – when was Bertha born? Three years after our marriage—
CAPTAIN.	Stop it, or—!
LAURA.	Or what? All right, I'll stop. But think carefully before you take any decision. And, above all, don't make yourself ridiculous.
CAPTAIN.	God – I could almost weep – !
LAURA.	Then you *will* be ridiculous.
CAPTAIN.	But not you!
LAURA.	No. Things have been arranged more wisely for us.
CAPTAIN.	That is why one cannot fight with you.
LAURA.	Why try to fight with an enemy who is so much stronger?
CAPTAIN.	Stronger?
LAURA.	Yes. It's strange, but I've never been able to look at a man without feeling that I am stronger than him.

CAPTAIN. Well, for once you're going to meet your match
And I'll see you never forget it.
LAURA. That'll be interesting.
NURSE (*enters*). Dinner's ready. Will you come and eat?
LAURA. Thank you.

⟋⟍

Paternal ballast

From Jean-Paul Sartre, *The Words*, 1964, translated
by Bernard Frechtman

A father would have weighted me with a certain stable obstinacy. Making his moods my principles, his ignorance my knowledge, his disappointments my pride, his quirks my law, he would have inhabited me. That respectable tenant would have given me self-respect, and on that respect I would have based my right to live. My begetter would have determined my future. As a born graduate of the Ecole Polytechnique, I would have felt reassured for ever. But if Jean-Baptiste Sartre had ever known my destination, he had taken the secret with him. My mother remembered only his saying, 'My son won't go into the Navy.' For want of more precise information, nobody, beginning with me, knew why the hell I had been born. Had he left me property, my childhood would have been changed. I would not be writing, since I would be someone else. House and field reflect back to the young heir a stable image of himself. He touches himself on *his* gravel, on the diamond-shaped panes of *his* veranda, and makes of their inertia the deathless substance of his soul. A few days ago, in a restaurant, the owner's son, a little seven-year-old, cried out to the cashier, 'When my father's not here, *I'm* the boss!' There's a man for you! At his age, I was nobody's master and nothing belonged to me. In my rare moments of lavishness, my mother would whisper to me, 'Be careful! We're not in our own home!' We were never in our own home, neither on the Rue le Goff nor later, when my mother remarried. This caused me no suffering since everything was loaned to me, but I remained abstract. Worldly possessions reflect to their owner what he is; they taught me what I was not. *I was not* substantial or permanent, *I was not* the future continuer of my father's work, *I was not* necessary to the production of steel. In short, I had no soul.

◆

My father thought it bloody queer

Simon Armitage, 1963–

My father thought it bloody queer,
the day I rolled home with a ring of silver in my ear
half hidden by a mop of hair. 'You've lost your head.
If that's how easily you're led
you should've had it through your nose instead.'

And even then I hadn't had the nerve to numb
the lobe with ice, then drive a needle through the skin,
then wear a safety-pin. It took a jeweller's gun
to pierce the flesh, and then a friend
to thread a sleeper in, and where it slept
the hole became a sore, became a wound, and wept.

At twenty-nine, it comes as no surprise to hear
my own voice breaking like a tear, released like water,
cried from way back in the spiral of the ear. *If I were you,*
I'd take it out and leave it out next year.

◆

Disgusted of Albemarle Street

The Marquess of Queensberry writes to his son,
Alfred Douglas, concerning the latter's homosexual
relationship with Oscar Wilde

Carter's Hotel,
Albemarle Street,
1 April 1894

Alfred,
    It is extremely painful for me to have to write to you in the strain I must; but please understand that I decline to receive any

answers from you in writing in return. After your recent hysterical impertinent ones I refuse to be annoyed with such, and I decline to read any more letters. If you have anything to say do come here and say it in person. Firstly, am I to understand that, having left Oxford as you did, with discredit to yourself, the reasons of which were fully explained to me by your tutor, you now intend to leaf and loll about and do nothing. All the time you were wasting at Oxford I was put off with the assurance that you were eventually to go into the Civil Service or to the Foreign Office, and then I was put off with an assurance that you were going to the Bar. It appears to me that you intend to do nothing. I utterly decline, however, to just supply you with sufficient funds to enable you to leaf about. You are preparing a wretched future for yourself, and it would be most cruel and wrong for me to encourage you in this. Secondly, I come to the more painful part of this letter – your intimacy with this man Wilde. It must either cease or I will disown you and stop all money supplies. I am not going to try and analyse this intimacy, and I make no charge; but to my mind to pose as a thing is as bad as to be it. With my own eyes I saw you both in the most loathsome and disgusting relationship as expressed by your manner and expression. Never in my experience have I ever seen such a sight as that in your horrible features. No wonder people are talking as they are. Also I now hear on good authority, but this may be false, that his wife is petitioning to divorce him for sodomy and other crimes. Is this true, or do you know of it? If I thought the actual thing was true, and it became public property, I should be quite justified in shooting him at sight. These Christian English cowards and men, as they call themselves, want waking up.

Your disgusted so-called father,
Queensberry

⌒

The children are revolting

Phil Hogan, *The Observer* magazine, 18 June 2000

I can't quite work it out, but there has to be some reason why our fun-loving eleven-year-old turns into a monosyllabic

sociopath the minute I collect him from school. Hay fever?
Lack of essential vitamins and minerals? Bad day's Pokémon
trading?

'Good day today?' I ask.

'Nnnn.'

'Excellent. Better tie those laces, you'll be tripping over them.'

He ignores me.

'Laces, please.'

'Dad, don't bother, OK?'

Don't bother. What does that mean?

'Look,' I say, 'either you fasten those shoelaces or you don't
get in the car.'

He shrugs. 'I don't care.'

I lean towards him. 'You *will* care in a minute,' I hiss, which
is his cue to recoil dramatically, as if I'm about to beat him with
a golf club, a ploy he has picked up from *Grange Hill* as the one
best calculated to trigger a show of synchronised turning heads
from teachers and other parents.

I manage an indulgent smile while he takes all day tucking his
laces in.

'So. Where's your lunchbox?' I ask briskly, chivvying in tone
but not without warmth, cleverly changing the subject with a
question he might be able to answer without spitting at me. He
sighs. 'Duh, how about . . . in my *bag*?' he says, adopting his
bug-eyed home lobotomy kit expression.

I ignore him now. 'So – everyone else all right?' I say, turning
to the neglected other two, who of course don't care what mood
their big brother is in so long as he's not giving them grief about
breathing too loud when he's trying to watch *Buffy the Vampire
Slayer*, or why they insist on having such sad hair when they
could have it glued down with an upturned skateboard run at
the front like any normal kids who know the first thing about
being fashionable.

I march Mr Impossible to the car. 'In the car,' I bark. 'Hurry
up.' Soon we are roaring away on two wheels as if there's a helicopter gunship from the battlestar Unintuitive Parent Minor on
our tail as we make our escape from the powerful forcefield of
what his schoolmates think of him.

'Can we have the tape on, Dad?' he says with sudden brightness, clearly having decided to miraculously change back into

Doctor Jekyll for the purposes of getting home with musical accompaniment.

I drive on, tight-lipped.

'Daaad?'

The thing is, am I now supposed to lighten up and pretend nothing has happened or does the punishment of my own now uncommunicative, sullen bearing fit the crime of his? Do two wrongs make a right? Am I being Edwardian? I tut heavily and switch it on.

'Love you, Dad!' he says, as though we have spent the last fifteen minutes healthily bonding. What is his problem?

'Love you,' I say, even though my memory is longer than his.

When we get back, my wife is busy pressing karate outfits. 'He's probably just embarrassed at being picked up from school,' she says. 'It's probably hormones.'

Maybe she's right. He has been spending a lot of time in the bathroom recently spraying himself indiscriminately with Lynx body spray specially formulated for 18–30 holidays. And, come to think of it, what was it I heard on Radio 4 recently about scientists discovering that pubescent children start growing more brain cells than they know what to do with, causing untold consternation in the prefrontal cortex as they are confronted by a bewilderment of moral choices before the survival of the most sensible synaptic connections prevails in a frenzy of neural Darwinism, by which time the erstwhile deviants have settled safely into careers as civil engineers and assume habits no more objectionable than a spot of karaoke?

'He's growing up,' my wife says.

He dashes breathless into the house wearing only mud and a pair of Day-Glo shorts, beside himself with excitement because our three-year-old has urinated into a cup and thrown the contents all over him. Perhaps they have a future as performance artists.

'Er . . . have you thought about washing your hands,' I say.

'Don't bother, Dad,' he says, standing at the fridge door guzzling a pint of milk before charging out again. OK, I won't.

Did I really break my daughter's tooth?

From Hugo Williams, 'What Shall We Do Now That
We Have Done Everything?', 1992

When I think about fatherhood, a single memorable day comes back to haunt me, cutting me off for ever from any comfortable feelings I might have on the subject.

My daughter (fourteen) and I (thirty-seven) were drawing up our troops on the battlefield of the lunch table. There followed an explosion and an exit. I ran after her and, with a solicitude that was really anger, asked what was the matter. She flew at me with fists flying and I slapped her round the top of her head. I wore my watch on my right wrist in those days and as I lashed out the bracelet expanded and the watch hit her in the mouth. Blood began to flow. Moments of horror followed as I realised it was not just her lip that was broken: I had chipped one of her precious front teeth. It occurred to me that one ought to be able to decide against anything so grotesque, in the way that one decides not to poke a pen in one's eye. But no. There it was in my hand, a piece of my daughter's body that would not grow back again.

The horror increased as the three of us sat in a taxi on our way to University College Hospital. There was a bus strike that day and like the blood in our veins the traffic was frozen solid. For one terrible hour we sat murmuring and bleeding into hand-kerchiefs in the back of that taxi, which seemed to be trans-porting us gradually to hell.

Does one grow up suddenly at such times, or down? I remember wanting to turn away into the darkness, yet knowing that I had to fumble forward, pretending there was light up ahead, pretending I was still me.

Looking back, the wilderness of our joint adolescence stretches as far as the eye can see, while behind it, obscured by it, the much longer period of childhood seems to have concertinaed inexplicably with only one or two ecstatic moments sticking up from the gathered folds. My daughter's head hovering just behind my own as she perches on my back, head and shoulders above the world, reaching out to touch people's hair at some gallery opening. Her tangled blond hair flowing in the wind as she races down Parliament Hill on one of her birthday party picnics, ice-cream all over her face.

For a brief period, she spoke poetry. Quickly grasping the new game, she would stand beside my desk, dictating them as fast as I could write. If I look up now, I'll see her outside on the pavement, standing on a chair, selling them to passers-by for 10p each. If I listen, I can hear her on her walkie-talkie, playing 'Star Trek to the Planet of the Apes', which is in the attic with the dressing-up clothes. One person has to stay on base, while the other moves around the house saying, 'Beam me up, Scotty.' I remember having to rush back home from somewhere to find the LSD which I'd left lying around, visions of our little darling pinned to the wall by dinosaurs, never again to recognise her dad, who'd be in prison anyway.

All sense of time passing is lost in the glow of those golden days that I didn't know were golden. Did she have growing pains once, or many times? Did I rub her legs for her, or did I give her an aspirin and tell her to go back to sleep? I know what I'd do now, of course, but it is too late. All that is gone and doesn't bear thinking of.

Why do I feel such a helter-skelter of joy and remorse looking back on my family life? When I look at photographs of us then, photo-booth snaps on the way to Paris, off to Brighton, going back to school, I feel a split second of shame at some mysterious deficiency lurking almost visibly in my expression, before pride wells up to mask it. I look again and it is gone. Surely I can't have been faking it all those years?

Fatherhood is a mirror in which we catch glimpses of ourselves as we really are. It seems to me now that I skimped on my daughter's childhood in order to have my own life. You can do that if you only have one child: the parents outnumber it two to one, so the child has to grow up fast and join their gang. Better than no gang at all, I suppose, but it isn't the same as running wild in the country.

If children provide a glimmer of self-knowledge for their parents, does this knowledge include a true perception of their children? What a joke! That clarity is reserved for their perception of us – from their infantile fascination with our absurd noses, to their teenage contempt for our absurd values. Ashamed of my cheapskate life on the dole and grant, my daughter told her friends

I was manager of the Waterman's pen factory. I felt no qualms about letting her sleep with her boyfriend in the house, but perhaps she wished I had.

I remember so well opening the front door on her first short sticking-up bleached blond hairdo, the look of interested defiance on her face as I travelled the million miles from dismay to acceptance, from father to friend.

– What do you think?
– I like it.
– Really?
– Yeah.

And I did like it. I loved it. Or rather I liked something about it, its dandified contempt for what was given. Even as I smothered my sadness for the chestnut mane that had gone, I loved its mad bravado, its air of taking on the world. I looked at her with shocked, admiring eyes, and yet I experienced a sinking feeling, as if a great ship were getting under way, its thousands of streamers lifting and breaking finally as it pulled away from the quay.

Writing about fatherhood I have the impression I am cutting up sentimentality into smaller and smaller parcels in order to disguise its true nature: the dangerous illusion of flesh and blood, that it is part of us. When I saw her new hair, I found myself wanting to say, 'You're just so brilliant you can do anything,' as if I were talking to myself. I had to stop myself, having no way of proving it. In the past, my wishful compliments and reassurances have sometimes overshot the world's opinions and been returned to me with a disappointed look, as if she would rather have found out for herself that she couldn't draw very well, or play darts.

The fact remains that from the moment I first saw her, lying quietly in her first clothes, having a nap after her ordeal, I was convinced of her superior beauty and intelligence. I presume this is the mechanism which tries to persuade us to put our children's needs before our own, which tortures us if we fail to do so, and which finally persuades the child to agree with us and leave home.

Our daughter is grown up now, with a past of her own – as I write she is somewhere in Asia – while we two imagine we are still young, with a future ahead of us. What shall we do next, I wonder, now that we have done everything? I would like to look forward, but it is hard, with the weight of such experience dragging one back. Did these things really happen? Did I really once break my own daughter's front tooth?

I'm afraid so, but there's a happy ending to the story. At the end of a seemingly endless journey across London, the traffic would part, the taxi we were huddled in would reach University College Hospital and a man would stick a little false piece on to my daughter's tooth. Colour would seep back into the world, words would be tried out like very thin ice, we would buy a teddy bear and a duvet in the Reject Shop and by some twist of irony my daughter would thank me. I remember we went to see some terrifying film about violence in a post-holocaust wilderness. Magically, she enjoyed herself. A smile was attempted. A mirror was looked in without undue horror. Tea was made.

~

Detained by the boss

From 'Forty-five a Month' R. K. Narayan, 1906–

Venkat Rao, Shanta's father, was about to start for his office that morning when a *jutka* passed along the street distributing cinema handbills. Shanta dashed to the street and picked up a handbill. She held it up and asked, 'Father, will you take me to the cinema today?' He felt unhappy at the question. Here was the child growing up without having any of the amenities and the simple pleasures of life. He had hardly taken her twice to the cinema. He had no time for the child. While children of her age in other houses had all the dolls, dresses and outings that they wanted, this child was growing up all alone and like a barbarian more or less. He felt furious with his office. For forty rupees a month they seemed to have purchased him outright.

He reproached himself for neglecting his wife and child – even the wife could have her own circle of friends and so on: she was after all a grown-up, but what about the child? What a drab, colourless existence was hers! Every day they kept him at the office till seven or eight in the evening, and when he came home the child was asleep. Even on Sundays they wanted him at the office. Why did they think he had no personal life, a life of his own? They gave him hardly any time to take the child to the park or the pictures. He was going to show them that they weren't to toy with him. Yes, he was prepared even to quarrel with his manager if necessary.

He said with resolve, 'I will take you to the cinema this evening. Be ready at five.'

'Really! Mother!' Shanta shouted. Mother came out of the kitchen.

'Father is taking me to a cinema in the evening.'

Shanta's mother smiled cynically. 'Don't make false promises to the child –' Venkat Rao glared at her. 'Don't talk nonsense. You think you are the only person who keeps promises –'

He told Shanta, 'Be ready at five, and I will come and take you positively. If you are not ready, I will be very angry with you.'

He walked to his office full of resolve. He would do his normal work and get out at five. If they started any old tricks of theirs, he was going to tell the boss, 'Here is my resignation. My child's happiness is more important to me than these horrible papers of yours.'

All day the usual stream of papers flowed onto his table and off it. He scrutinised, signed and drafted. He was corrected, admonished and insulted. He had a break of only five minutes in the afternoon for his coffee.

When the office clock struck five and the other clerks were leaving, he went to the manager and said, 'May I go, sir?' The manager looked up from his paper. 'You!' It was unthinkable that the cash and account section should be closing at five. 'How can you go?'

'I have some urgent private business, sir,' he said, smothering the lines he had been rehearsing since the morning. 'Herewith my resignation.' He visualised Shanta standing at the door, dressed and palpitating with eagerness.

'There shouldn't be anything more urgent than the office work; go back to your seat. You know how many hours I work?' asked the manager. The manager came to the office three hours before opening time and stayed nearly three hours after closing, even on Sundays. The clerks commented among themselves, 'His wife must be whipping him whenever he is seen at home; that is why the old owl seems so fond of his office.'

'Did you trace the source of that ten–eight difference?' asked the manager.

'I shall have to examine two hundred vouchers. I thought we might do it tomorrow.'

'No, no, this won't do. You must rectify it immediately.'

Venkat Rao mumbled, 'Yes, sir,' and slunk back to his seat.

The clock showed 5:30. Now it meant two hours of excruciating search among vouchers. All the rest of the office had gone. Only he and another clerk in his section were working, and of course, the manager was there. Venkat Rao was furious. His mind was made up. He wasn't a slave who had sold himself for forty rupees outright. He could make that money easily; and if he couldn't, it would be more honourable to die of starvation.

He took a sheet of paper and wrote: 'Herewith my resignation. If you people think you have bought me body and soul for forty rupees, you are mistaken. I think it would be far better for me and my family to die of starvation than slave for this petty forty rupees on which you have kept me for years and years. I suppose you have not the slightest notion of giving me an increment. You give yourselves heavy slices frequently, and I don't see why you shouldn't think of us occasionally. In any case it doesn't interest me now, since this is my resignation. If I and my family perish of starvation, may our ghosts come and haunt you all your life –' He folded the letter, put it in an envelope, sealed the flap and addressed it to the manager. He left his seat and stood before the manager. The manager mechanically received the letter and put it on his pad.

'Venkat Rao,' said the manager, 'I'm sure you will be glad to hear this news. Our officer discussed the question of increments today, and I've recommended you for an increment of five rupees. Orders are not yet passed, so keep this to yourself for the present.' Venkat Rao put out his hand, snatched the envelope from the pad and hastily slipped it in his pocket.

'What is that letter?'

'I have applied for a little casual leave, sir, but I think . . .'

'You can't get any leave for at least a fortnight to come.'

'Yes, sir. I realise that. That is why I am withdrawing my application, sir.'

'Very well. Have you traced that mistake?'

'I'm scrutinising the vouchers, sir. I will find it out within an hour . . .'

It was nine o'clock when he went home. Shanta was already asleep. Her mother said, 'She wouldn't even change her frock, thinking that any moment you might be coming and taking her out. She hardly ate any food; and wouldn't lie down for fear of crumpling her dress . . .'

Venkat Rao's heart bled when he saw his child sleeping in her pink frock, hair combed and face powdered, dressed and ready to be taken out. 'Why should I not take her to the night show?' He shook her gently and called, 'Shanta, Shanta.' Shanta kicked her legs and cried, irritated at being disturbed. Mother whispered, 'Don't wake her,' and patted her back to sleep.

Venkat Rao watched the child for a moment. 'I don't know if it is going to be possible for me to take her out at all – you see, they are giving me an increment –' he wailed.

Tips for working fathers

From James A. Levine and Todd L. Pittinsky,
*Working Fathers: New Strategies for Balancing
Work and Family*, 1997

- Turn down extra work by showing why it would not be good for the business, or propose an alternative such as: 'I'll be able to take on this assignment if I give up some of the other stuff on my plate.'
- Take control of your working hours by creating your own flexible schedule. Let people know when you will be working and how to reach you. Report your progress regularly and be prepared to change your schedule in order to meet an emergency business need.
- Make a weekly date with your wife, *without* your children or other couples. If you don't have much money, go window shopping, take a walk or go to a coffee shop.
- Take your kids to work with you one day to help them to understand why you are not always available for them.
- Spend some time with each child individually. Rather than thinking of your weekend household chores as time away from your kids, get them to help you.
- Set aside time devoted exclusively to worrying, lasting anything from fifteen minutes to an hour. By focusing

your worries in a concentrated way you increase the
likelihood of finding a solution.

- Block out half an hour to an hour for yourself each day
  or every other day for some physical exercise, an evening
  walk or a hobby.
- Instead of using your journey to work to read office
  memos, read something for fun. If you drive, switch off
  news and play some music.
- Make sure you share the childcare fairly with your
  spouse.
- If your job requires you to travel, explain this to your
  children in terms they can understand. Fax drawings to
  your children and leave special notes to be put into their
  lunch box or under their pillow.

Daddy matters

From *Raising Cain*, Dan Kindlon and
Michael Thompson, 1999

Two important developments reflecting this new wave of father
research were an October 1996 conference on father involvement
sponsored by the American National Institutes of Health and the
publication in May 1998 of a special issue of the journal
Demography that was devoted to new research on fathers' influence on the lives of their children. These new research findings
are compelling and show clearly that having a father in the picture,
especially an involved one, is good for kids: they tend to be
smarter, have better psychological health, do better in school, and
get better jobs. When presenting their findings, some of these
researchers even depart from the normally arid language of science
to use words such as *remarkable* and *astonishing* to describe the
powerful influence they found fathers to have on their children's
development.

Dad

Berlie Doherty, *Another First Poetry Book*, 1987

Dad is the dancing-man
The laughing-bear, the prickle-chin,
The tickle-fingers, jungle-roars,
Bucking bronco, rocking-horse,
The helicopter roundabout
The beat-the-wind at swing-and-shout
Goal-post, scarey-ghost,
Climbing-jack, humpty-back.

But sometimes he's
A go-away-please!
A snorey-snarl, a sprawly slump
A yawny mouth, a sleepy lump,

And I'm a kite without a string
Waiting for Dad to dance again.

⌣

At least the big brown squiggle lives at home

Tom Kemp, *Daily Telegraph*, 26 June 1999

The first I knew that last Sunday was Father's Day was when my five-year-old shook me awake soon after dawn, shouted 'Happy Father's Day' and thrust a home-made card into my hand. School-made, I should say, because his teacher had set aside a lesson for all the children in his class to make Father's Day cards.

At the top of mine, on the front, was a thick stripe drawn in blue felt-tip. Beneath it, enclosed in square brackets, were two ant-like squiggles in brown, one bigger than the other, with a black dot between them. At the bottom was another thick stripe of felt-tip, this one green.

Inside the card, my son had written 'Happy Father's Day, with love', and I found myself wondering unpleasantly what the many children in his class with absentee fathers had written in theirs: 'Happy Male Carer's Day', perhaps. (I once had a letter from his

school that began, and I swear that this is true: 'Dear Male Carer
. . .' But that is by the way.)

It is always an awkward moment for me when the five-year-
old shows me one of his drawings. I have lost count of the times
when I have said, 'Gosh, what a lovely dinosaur', only to be told
with a hurt look: 'But it's a *spaceship*, Daddy.'

This time I was taking no chances. 'It's . . . it's *beautiful*,' I
said. 'Tell me what it is, exactly.'

'Can't you *see*?'

It was too early in the morning, and I didn't feel bright enough
to hazard a guess. 'I give up. You tell me.'

'It's you and me playing football, silly!'

Of course it was. The thick stripes, blue and green, were the
sky and the grass. The square brackets were the goals. The big
brown squiggle was me, the small one him, and the black dot
was the ball.

'I *see* now,' I said. 'It's brilliant. What an idiot I am.'

'Idiot, idiot,' he chanted and skipped out of the room.

I shouted after him: 'Oi! I'm allowed to call myself an idiot.
You're not.' He popped his head round the door, repeated 'Idiot,
idiot' and ran away. Happy Father's Day, indeed. The big brown
squiggle turned over and tried to get back to sleep. Five o'clock
. . . six o'clock . . . seven o'clock . . . Still no luck.

Of my three other sons, only the twelve-year-old, the nice one,
bothered to mark Father's Day. When I got up, he was already
out of the house and on his way to the newsagent to buy me
two bars of chocolate with his own pocket money. One of them
had a picture of Homer Simpson on its wrapper, slobbing on a
sofa with a can of beer on his stomach. The boy was obviously
worried that I might be offended by the joke, thinking it too
close to home. So he bought me a bar of Cadbury's Cappuccino
as well. He and I share a passion for cappuccino: the coffee, I
mean – I am not so sure about the chocolate. But I mustn't be
ungrateful. I admit that I was touched.

On the whole, however, I do not approve of Father's Day. I
do not know whether it is true that it was dreamt up by an
American greetings card company, as everybody says. But I do
know that we never marked Father's Day when I was a boy and
I suspect that my own father would have thrown up if we had.

I disapprove of it not only because the idea of Father's Day smacks of Disney sentimentality but because every year when it comes round, I find myself dwelling on my own shortcomings as a father. I hardly ever see my sons, except at weekends. They are on their way to school by the time I get up in the mornings, and they are usually fast asleep when I get home at night. I no longer do a stroke of housework, leaving everything to my wife.

I am exactly like those fathers in last week's survey, who said that they had given up the struggle to balance the demands of their jobs and their families. Nowadays, I concentrate entirely on the breadwinning, telling myself that I am doing it for my wife and the boys as much as for myself, yet at the same time feeling very bad about neglecting them.

But I am sick of feeling guilty. I may not be at home very often, but at least I live there. And it must be better, surely, for a child to have a benign male presence in the house from time to time than to have nobody to call an idiot at five o'clock in the morning on Father's Day.

~

True wealth

From Craig Raine, *Rich*, 1984

When I was eleven, I won a scholarship to a local public school where Robin, another rich cousin, a Mulholland, was already a pupil. His father, my uncle John, had made his money by selling birds' eggs. The scholarship paid my tuition fees and half my board. The remainder was paid for partly by the country education authority, partly by my mother's long stints at the sewing machine. The RAF Benevolent Fund made an initial contribution towards my clothes, and Mr Grice, their representative, would come round after work and help my mother fill in the forms. My father's way of showing his gratitude was to collect money for the Fund on Wings Day, which commemorates the Battle of Britain. He was busy trying to break all records in the charity business. No one was allowed to pass without a contribution: he knew everyone and covered the clubs, the pubs, the chip shops, the football ground. Each day he'd return with ten cans heavy with coins, five to a hand, the strings cutting his fingers. He broke all records, but it was my mother who filled in the forms.

I was bought a large trunk and Uncle Charlie came round one Saturday morning and sign-wrote my name on both ends, with my house number. On my last afternoon at home, surrounded by grey shirts and socks, I looked from the window and saw Bobby Bowen in his best suit with the extra-wide trousers walking quickly down the hill, whistling beautifully as he always did, with lots of grace notes. And I remembered how my father had once interfered when Bobby's wife Ena had lost her temper with one of her sons. The boy was cowering outside. She stood, fat, filling the doorway, holding a full-size plastic rifle, shouting, 'In. In. *In.*' Finally, the boy tried to squirm past her like a silverfish but she had him by the hair and was breaking the rifle over his head and shoulders when my father stopped her. He was, as he could be, abusive: he called her a 'fat sadist'. It was the first time I had come across the word. He came back and used another word I knew of course but had never heard my father, or any adult, say before. My mother dashed in from the kitchen, 'Norman, there's *no* excuse for *that*.' It was enough. We got on with our game of chess and, as usual, I exploded with anger when he cheated. 'Are you sure you want to move your queen there?' I'd say. 'When you take your finger off, you can't change it, you know. All right, you've taken your finger off. Are you sure? This is your last chance. OK?' But it wasn't OK and when I reached for my bishop, he'd wave his arms over the board like a referee who's just counted somebody out – and change his move.

I thought that by going away to school I would be leaving nothing behind. Bobby would still whistle in his brown double-breasted suit. My Rudd Cup football medal would nestle in its cotton wool till I got back in the holidays. In fact, I was leaving my father behind. I was completely proud of him and he was proud of me. He was the only father who ever came to our primary school football matches. He would race up and down the touchline, shouting advice and encouragement. At half-time, he'd come on to the pitch and give the whole team extra-strong mints, rearrange the tactics, change our positions, tell us we were playing downhill in the second half, tell us that a six-goal deficit was nothing. Mr Newby, the teacher nominally in charge, would suck a mint and listen like the rest of us. We won every game. He willed us to do it.

At my boarding school, I learned to be ashamed of him. It was a complicated process. I was very much his son and it was six or seven weeks before I learned that the self-confidence he'd given me, genetically and by example, to other people was mere boasting. Modesty wasn't something he'd taught me. I knew when I had played the best game on the rugby field. I remembered my father's story of how he'd played in a game 'against the pick, the *pick*, of Catterick Camp' and won it single-handed by tackling again and again a big winger from the Scots Guards. I had been brought up to be a hero. Gradually, I was made to feel unpopular and I applied these new standards to him. In the first few days, too, I was made to realise my relative poverty. My father had taught me to do a proper somersault. I would bounce on a bed till I was high enough, then I'd do the turn, backwards and forwards. I was showing this off in my first week – wishing I could walk on my hands too, like my father – when I broke the bed's cast-iron frame. The school bursar, to whom I had to report the damage, was stern but not unkind. 'You must realise, Raine 3,' he said, 'that you are different from the other boys. Your parents can't afford to pay for a new bed. The school won't charge you this time, but you must cut your coat according to your cloth.' I broke no more beds and when Humphreys, whose father was a market gardener, asked me what my father did, I said he was a football manager. I told Manders he was a brain surgeon.

I was at school for seven years. It wasn't until my second year that I told anything like the truth about my father. I had been taken out to lunch by Wakefield's grandparents one Sunday. 'What does your father do?' the old man asked, a trickle of fat in the cleft of his chin. 'He's war disabled,' I replied. I couldn't lie to an adult. 'So you're on a scholarship, then?' 'Yes,' I said. It wasn't so bad, after all.

Yet I must have conveyed some uneasiness to my parents. Perhaps my father couldn't be bothered, perhaps he was worried about his unpredictable epilepsy (I was), but he never came to see the school. My mother would visit on Speech Day and Sports Day, wearing a Jaeger-style home-made camel coat and a pillbox hat, or her green velvet coat that made her look, I thought, like the Queen. If she was uneasy, she disguised it well. I was sixteen before I took any of my school friends home. They adored my father. He told them dirty jokes, irrepressible as ever.

And I felt rich again.

Not even kissed by self-contempt.

～

Human bondage

Fathers and slavery in the ante-bellum South, recounted by Robert Griswold, *Fatherhood in America*, 1993

The bonds between slave fathers and children, of course, went well beyond teaching survival skills. In a brutal and exploitative world, they gave meaning to men's lives, a point made by fathers forced to cope with the sale of their children. Georgia slave Abream Scriven poignantly revealed his sentiments in a letter to his wife in 1858: 'Give my love to my father & mother and tell them good Bye for me. And if we Shall not meet in this world I hope to meet in heaven. My Dear wife for you and my Children my pen cannot Express the griffe I feel to be parted from you all.' Other men simply wept, while one expressed his sentiments more brutally: to prevent forced separation from his son, he chopped off his left hand with a hatchet.

～

Access denied

An article in *The Times*, 25 July 2000

When Paul Lander's marriage ended, his wife took their son, aged three, to live with her parents. Divorce proceedings and questions of custody and access followed.

Paul's high-pressure media job and lack of home help made it untenable for him to seek custody, and it was decided that he could see his son every two weeks. The legal fight was tough, and Paul believes it cost him his job. 'I was worn to jelly: something had to give,' he says.

Such stories have prompted a study at London's Birkbeck College into relations between fathers and their children after separation. Dr Helen Barrett, the research officer, points out that while much is known about the way women fare at such times, far less research has assessed the situations of fathers. As part of the project, funded by the Wellcome Trust, Dr Barrett hopes that 500 fathers will answer a questionnaire about contacts with their children, and that some will be interviewed.

'Many fathers are distressed by the difficulties of maintaining relationships with their children. I have been asked by some people how often suicide is connected with this issue,' she says.

When Tom, an unemployed father of eight-year-old twins, parted from their mother five years ago she took the children from the family home in Manchester to live in Dover. At first Tom was allowed to take them home at weekends, but after a year their mother stipulated that he could see them, in Dover, only for a week during school holidays. After a court hearing, Tom's access was reinstated, but there have been months when he didn't see them.

Inevitably, children suffer in such circumstances. Many agree that one of the key issues is not only fathers' rights to see their children, but the rights of children to have access to both parents. As Lander says: 'Agreements made between parents at the time of divorce to protect children's interests are often ignored by the custodial parent, harming the interests of the children. The court gives access to the parent, but what about the child's right of access to both parents? That should be top of the agenda.'

Some names have been changed.

FATHERS: LINKS
www.depressionalliance.org
Depression Alliance: 020–76330557

www.fnf.org.uk
Families Need Fathers: 020–76135060

Life is half made up of partings

Charles Dickens to his eldest son, on the latter's emigration to Australia in 1868

I need not tell you that I love you dearly, and am very, very sorry in my heart to part with you. But this life is half made up of partings, and these pains must be borne. It is my comfort and my sincere conviction that you are going to try the life for which you are best fitted. I think its freedom and wildness more suited to you than any experiment in a study or office would ever have been, and without that training, you could have followed no other occupation. . . .

Never take a mean advantage of anyone in any transaction, and never be hard upon people who are in your power. Try to do to others, as you would have them do for you, and do not be discouraged if they fail sometimes. It is much better for you that they should fail in obeying the greatest rule laid down by our Saviour, than that you should. . . .

Only one more thing on this head. The more we are in earnest as to feeling it, the less we are disposed to hold forth about it. Never abandon the wholesome practice of saying your own private prayers, night and morning. I have never abandoned it myself, and I know the comfort of it.

I hope you will always be able to say in life, that you had a kind father.

~

'Even if I cannot see you'

Isaac Austin Brooks, a Union soldier in the US Civil War, writes home

Camp Caldwell
13 October 1861

My Dear Children,

As there are so many of you in the nest at home, I cannot write to each one, and therefore send this to you all. I think you will be glad to hear from me, in a letter to you all, as well as to hear of me through Mothers letters, for I never forget you, even if I do not write to you. Mothers accounts of you are very gratifying to me, for I think you are all trying to be good children, to give Mother as little trouble as you can, & to improve yourselves. My life here, is not very pleasant, but I submit to it because I think it is for the best and it is the duty of us all, to do what we can for our country and to preserve its integrity even to the sacrifice of our lives, if that is necessary. It is a glorious country, and *must* be preserved to our children. It was given to *us entire*, and *we* must give it to you, entire and *you* must give it as you receive it, to those who come after you. Remember your *country* is next to your God, in love, and never see it injured, or disgraced, if you have a hand, or a mind, to put forth in its defence. I hope to return to you in due time, safe and well, and find *you* are well and happy, but should it be so ordered that we do not meet again on earth, remember to love, and serve your country in whatever way it may be your lot to do so. To do this, many things are needed, which you will all learn in due time, but one of the *foundations* will be, to be sober, honest, and industrious.

So be good children all of you, & remember I *think* of you all, *daily*, even if I can not see you.

Your Affectionate Father

◡

'Each night I sing out my love'

Letter from Corporal Samuel Furash, a US soldier, to his infant daughter at home in America

Somewhere in England
3 February 1944

My dearest Toby:
Probably by the time you receive this, you will have reached your first birthday; and by the time you will be able to read and understand it, we will be together as father and daughter, living through the days being missed now. Then again, there is always the possibility that never shall we know the relationship which is so deserving of us, but that possibility is quite remote. However, whatever the future holds in store for us, now is the

time for us to get acquainted. As difficult as it may be, your mother's words to me through letters are descriptive enough to offer a realisation of your habits, characteristics, personality, and other traits of you in different stages of your young life, the scene still remains incomplete, of course, because we are still strangers to each other. However, Toby darling, I'm speaking to you now, because the words I say are my sincere beliefs and always will be, and some day you, too, shall share these thoughts with your mother and me.

You were born into a world which was experiencing the second stage of the 'dark ages', a world filled with turmoil, suffering and grief, and a civilisation on the verge of destruction and total chaos. By this statement you might easily assume that the responsibility for all this lies upon the shoulders of all mankind; and you would be right! I do not mean by this, that man is evil; to the contrary, man is good, *but* he has been lax and smug and because of this has allowed his basic principle of life, freedom, to be snatched from his hands by the long, murderous talons of fascistic tyranny through the rule of a small group of individuals. At this moment, this group of men have not succeeded in their attempts in this nation and a few others, but even though the people of these nations are in an all-out war against fascists and the principles of fascism, these men are still in important positions in our own set-up of government. And that is where you come in Toby, dear. You see, though we are fighting a war now, which we will undoubtedly win, the victory alone will not bring about the complete and happy change in our way of life. No! The struggle will then only begin and you and your generation will be the spearhead and main body of our fighting forces. We have begun the drive; you will finish it! Our victory will destroy tyranny; yours will establish freedom, freedom in every sense of the word; and that job constitutes the renovation of our whole system of society. Your mother and I are the fighters of the present; *you* are the builders of the future.

You are lucky, Toby, because your life will be full of love. It can be no other way; you see, you were born out of love. Never has there been a more perfect relationship than your mother's and mine, for when we are together, we are united as one individual, laughing as one, crying as one, thinking as one. We are melody, harmony and rhythm, together with courage, forming the most stirring symphony of love. Your mother is the 'zenith' of kindness and understanding, and as you originated within her, and will learn from her now, you will be the same. You are under the watchful and loving eyes of four grandparents who cherish you as their own child; and you have a father, who as yet has offered you nothing materially, only a little help in the assurance of your free future.

You shall benefit by your parents' tutelage, and soon will be aiding us in the education of your younger brothers and sisters, for there will be more, and we shall be more than a family for we have a foundation which is stronger than the very earth that holds us, the belief in truth, righteousness, and the right of all men to live and work happily in a society of social and economic equality, and to receive all the fruits of his labours. You shall live to see this, for you shall believe as strongly as we, and shall fight to achieve such a glorious goal.

The things I am trying to say are difficult, but you will understand later for you will read the works of the great poets and authors, listen to the music of great composers, and their words and melodies shall fill your heart and mind with the understanding and spirit to carry on in the battle for freedom.

Though my body be miles away, my heart is with you and I remain forever, your father, whose heart is filled with love for you and your mother. You are the nearest stars in my heaven and each night I sing out my love and best wishes.

∼

Walking Away
(For Sean)

Cecil Day Lewis, *The Complete Poems*, 1992

It is eighteen years ago, almost to the day –
A sunny day with the leaves just turning,
The touch-lines new-ruled – since I watched you play
Your first game of football, then, like a satellite
Wrenched from its orbit, go drifting away

Behind a scatter of boys. I can see
You walking away from me towards the school

With the pathos of a half-fledged thing set free
Into a wilderness, the gait of one
Who finds no path where the path should be.

That hesitant figure, eddying away
Like a winged seed loosened from its parent stem,
Has something I never quite grasp to convey
About nature's give-and-take – the small, the scorching
Ordeals which fire one's irresolute clay.

I have had worse partings, but none that so
Gnaws at my mind still. Perhaps it is roughly
Saying what God alone could perfectly show –
How selfhood begins with a walking away,
And love is proved in the letting go.

⌒

Growing up and away

James Agee to Father Flye, 1950

Mia had to take Teresa to town yesterday, to start 'school' this morning. Another reason I feel the year, and all of existence so far as I'm concerned, is taking a deep turn under. She's been a lovely and happy child so far; and I've felt, however foolishly, always within my sight and reach. I know that from now on will be just as before, the usual mixture of good and terrible things and of utterly undiscernible things: but all I can feel is, God help her now. I begin to get just a faint sense of what heartbreak there must be in it even at the best, to see a child keep growing up.

⌒

When Willie Wet the Bed

Eugene Fields, 1850–95

When Willie was a little boy,
Not more than five or six,
Right constantly did he annoy

His mother with his tricks.
Yet not a picayune cared I
For what he did or said,
Unless, as happened frequently,
The rascal wet the bed.

Closely he cuddled up to me,
And put his hand in mine,
Till all at once I seemed to be
Afloat in seas of brine.
Sabean odours clogged the air
And filled my soul with dread,
Yet I could only grin and bear
When Willie wet the bed.

'Tis many times that rascal has
Soaked all the bedclothes through,
Whereat I'd feebly light the gas
And wonder what to do.
Yet there he lay so peaceful-like,
God bless his curly head!
I quite forgave the little tyke
For wetting of the bed.

Ah, me! Those happy days have flown,
My boy's a father, too,
And little Willies of his own
Do what he used to do.
And I, ah! all that's left for me
Are dreams of pleasures fled,
My life's not what it used to be
When Willie wet the bed!

The road not taken

From Carl Sandburg, *Always the Young Strangers*,
1952

I remember walking on Christmas morning with my hand in my father's. I had been reading in the books about stars and I had this early morning been taking a look now and then up at a sky of clear stars. I turned my face up toward my father's and said, pointing with the loose hand, 'You know, some of those stars are millions of miles away.' And my father, without looking down toward me, gave a sniff, as though I were a funny little fellow, and said, 'We won't bodder about dat now . . .' For several blocks neither of us said a word and I felt, while still holding his hand, that there were millions of empty miles between us.

⌒

'*I may have been mistaken*'

From Jean-Jacques Rousseau, *The Confessions*,
1782–9

Never, for a single moment in his life, could Jean-Jacques have been a man without feeling, without compassion, or an unnatural father. I may have been mistaken, never hardened. If I were to state my reasons, I should say too much. Since they were strong enough to mislead me, they might mislead many others, and I do not desire to expose young people, who may read my works, to the danger of allowing themselves to be misled by the same error. I will content myself with observing, that my error was such that, in handing over my children to the State to educate, for want of means to bring them up myself, in deciding to fit them for becoming workmen and peasants rather than adventurers and fortune-hunters, I thought that I was behaving like a citizen and a father, and considered myself a member of Plato's Republic. More than once since then, the regrets of my heart have told me that I was wrong; but, far from my reason having given me the same information, I have often blessed Heaven for having preserved them from their father's lot, and from the lot which threatened them as soon as I should have been obliged to abandon them. If I had left them with Madame d'Epinay or Madame de Luxembourg, who, from friendship, generosity, or some other motive, expressed themselves willing to take charge of them, would they have been happier, would they have been brought up at least as honest men? I do not know; but I do know that they would have been brought up to hate, perhaps to betray, their parents; it is a hundred times better that they have never known them.

My third child was accordingly taken to the Foundling Hospital, like the other two. The two next were disposed of in the same manner, for I had five altogether. This arrangement appeared to me so admirable, so rational, and so legitimate, that, if I did not openly boast of it, this was solely out of regard for the mother; but I told all who were acquainted with our relations. I told Grimm and Diderot. I afterwards informed Madame d'Epinay, and, later, Madame de Luxembourg, freely and voluntarily, without being in any way obliged to do so, and when I might easily have kept it a secret from everybody; for Gouin was an honourable woman, very discreet, and a person upon whom I could implicitly rely. The only one of my friends to whom I had any interest in unbosoming myself was M. Thierry, the physician who attended my poor 'aunt' in a dangerous confinement. In a word, I made no mystery of what I did, not only because I have never known how to keep a secret from my friends, but because I really saw no harm in it. All things considered, I chose for my children what was best, or, at least, what I believed to be best for them. I could have wished, and still wish, that I had been reared and brought up as they have been.

～

In Chalkwell Park

John Fowles, 1992

the staring-green October green
the common grass intent on thriving
out of step
when all else dies this is the season

we walk
this tired municipal park
and Sunday sky
we walk the grass
my slow father and I

and the sun is tepidly warm
the sky a non-committal blue
with a few clouds dying

the death of leaves
mourning chrysanthemums
Li Po
we inspect the Michaelmas daisies
a new dwarf stock
a milky blue

and death

I cannot say
swift passage
I cannot say

most natural thing
and cannot say
cannot say

he mumbles on
'I thought it would be fine,
the glass was high'

cannot say
do not die
my father my father do not die

⌒

Do not go gentle into that good night

Dylan Thomas, *The Poems*, 1974

Do not go gentle into that good night,
Old age should burn and rave at close of day;
Rage, rage against the dying of the light.

Though wise men at their end know dark is right,
Because their words had forked no lighting they
Do not go gentle into that good night.

Good men, the last wave by, crying how bright
Their frail deeds might have danced in a green bay,
Rage, rage against the dying of the light.

Wild men who caught and sang the sun in flight,
And learn, too late, they grieved it on its way,
Do not go gentle into that good night.

Grave men, near death, who see with blinding sight
Blind eyes could blaze like meteors and be gay,
Rage, rage against the dying of the light.

And you, my father, there on the sad height,
Curse, bless, me now with your fierce tears, I pray.
Do not go gentle into that good night.
Rage, rage against the dying of the light.

Dad

Elaine Feinstein, *Some Unease and Angels*, 1977

Your old hat hurts me, and those black
fat raisins you liked to press into
my palm from your soft heavy hand:
I see you staggering back up the path
with sacks of potatoes from some local farm,
fresh eggs, flowers. Every day I grieve

for your great heart broken and you gone.
You loved to watch the trees. This year
you did not see their Spring.
The sky was freezing over the fen
as on that somewhere secretly appointed day
you beached: cold, white-faced, shivering.

What happened, old bull, my loyal
hoarse-voiced warrior? The hammer
blow that stopped you in your track
and brought you to a hospital monitor
could not destroy your courage
to the end you were
uncowed and unconcerned with pleasing anyone.

I think of you now as once again safely
at my mother's side, the earth as

chosen as a bed, and feel most sorrow for
all that was gentle in
my childhood buried there
already forfeit, now forever lost.

～

To My Dead Father

Frank O'Hara, 1926–66

Don't call to me father
Wherever you are I'm
still your little son
running through the dark

I couldn't do what you
say even if I could hear
your roses no longer grow
my heart's black as their

bed their dainty thorns
have become my face's
troublesome stubble you
must not think of flowers

And do not frighten my
blue eyes with hazel flecks
or thicken my lips when
I face my mirror don't ask

that I be other than your
strange son understanding
minor miracles not death
father I am alive! father

forgive the roses and me

～

Lonely

From *Clinging to the Wreckage*, the autobiography
of John Mortimer, 1982

After my father died I had slept for two days without interruption. I wrote, at the end of a play: 'I'd been told of all the things you're meant to feel. Sudden freedom, growing up, the end of dependence, the step into the sunlight when no one is taller than you and you're in no one's shadow. I know what I felt. Lonely.'

⌒

His father's grave

Albert Camus, *The First Man*, 1994

The caretaker opened a large book bound in wrapping paper and with his dirty finger went down a list of names. His finger came to a stop. 'Cormery Henri,' he said, 'fatally wounded at the Battle of the Marne, died at Saint-Brieuc 11 October 1914.'

'That's it,' said the traveller.

The caretaker closed the book. 'Come,' he said. And he led the way to the first row of gravestones, some of them simple, others ugly and pretentious, all covered with that bead and marble bric-à-brac that would disgrace any place on earth. 'Was he related to you?' he asked absently.

'He was my father.'

'That's rough,' the other man said.

'No, it isn't. I was less than a year old when he died. So, you see.'

'Yes,' said the caretaker, 'but even so. Too many died.'

Jacques Cormery did not answer. Surely, too many had died, but, as to his father, he could not muster a filial devotion he did not feel. For all these years he had been living in France, he had promised himself to do what his mother, who stayed in Algeria, what she [*sic*] for such a long time had been asking him to do: visit the grave of his father that she herself had never seen. He thought this visit made no sense, first of all for himself, who had never known his father, who knew next to nothing of what he had been, and who loathed conventional gestures and behaviour; and then for his mother, who never spoke of the dead man and could picture nothing of what he was going to see. But since his old mentor had retired to Saint-Brieuc and so he would have an opportunity to see him again, Cormery had made up his mind to go and visit this dead stranger, and had even insisted on doing it before joining his old friend so that afterwards he would feel completely free.

'It's here,' said the caretaker. They had arrived at a square-shaped area, enclosed by small markers of grey stone connected with a heavy chain that had been painted black. The gravestones – and they were many – were all alike: plain inscribed rectangles set at equal intervals row on row. Each grave was decorated with a small bouquet of fresh flowers. 'For forty years the French Remembrance has been responsible for the upkeep. Look, here he is.' He indicated a stone in the first row. Jacques Cormery stopped at some distance from the grave. 'I'll leave you,' the caretaker said.

Cormery approached the stone and gazed vacantly at it. Yes, that was indeed his name. He looked up. Small white and grey clouds were passing slowly across the sky, which was paler now, and from it fell a light that was alternately bright and overcast. Around him, in the vast field of the dead, silence reigned. Nothing but a muffled murmur from the town came over the high walls. Occasionally a black silhouette would pass among the distant graves. Jacques Cormery, gazing up at the slow navigation of the clouds across the sky, was trying to discern, beyond the odour of damp flowers, the salty smell just then coming from the distant motionless sea when the clink of a bucket against the marble of a tombstone drew him from his reverie. At that moment he read on the tomb the date of his father's birth, which he now discovered he had not known. Then he read the two dates. '1885–1914', and automatically did the arithmetic: twenty-nine years. Suddenly he was struck by an idea that shook his very body. He was forty years old. The man buried under that slab, who had been his father, was younger than he.

And the wave of tenderness and pity that at once filled his heart was not the stirring of the soul that leads the son to the memory of the vanished father, but the overwhelming compassion that a grown man feels for an unjustly murdered child – something here was not in the natural order and, in truth, there was no order but only madness and chaos when the son was older than the father. The course of time itself was shattering around him while he remained motionless among those tombs he now no longer saw, and the years no longer kept to their places in the great river that flows to its end. They were no more than waves and surf and eddies where Jacques Cormery was now struggling in the grip of anguish and pity. He looked at the other inscriptions in that section and realised from the dates that this soil was strewn with children who had been the fathers of greying men who thought they were living in this present time. For he too believed he was living, he alone had created himself, he knew his own strength, his vigour, he could cope and he had himself well in hand. But, in the strange dizziness of that moment, the statue every man eventually erects and that hardens in the fire of the years, into which he then creeps and there awaits its final crumbling – that statue was rapidly cracking, it was already collapsing. All that was left was this anguished heart, eager to live, rebelling against the deadly order of the world that had been with him for forty years, and still struggling against the wall that separated him from the secret of all life, wanting to go farther, to go beyond, and to discover, discover before dying, discover at last in order to be, just once to be, for a single second, but for ever.

He looked back on his life, a life that had been foolish, courageous, cowardly, wilful, and always straining towards that goal which he knew nothing about, and actually that life had all gone by without his having tried to imagine who this man was who had given him that life and then immediately had gone off to die in a strange land on the other side of the seas. At twenty-nine, had he himself not been frail, been ailing, tense, stubborn, sensual, dreamy, cynical and brave? Yes, he had been all that and much else besides; he had been alive, in short had been a man, and yet he had never thought of the man who slept there as a living being, but as a stranger who passed by on the land where he himself was born, of whom his mother said that he looked like him and that he died on the field of battle. Yet the secret he had eagerly sought to learn through books and people now seemed to him to be intimately linked with this dead man, this younger father, with what he had been and what he had become, and it seemed that he himself had gone far afield in search of what was close to him in time and in blood. To tell the truth, he had received no help. In a family where they spoke little, where no one read or wrote, with an unhappy and listless mother, who would have informed him about this young and pitiable father? No one had known him but his mother and she had forgotten him. Of that he was sure. And he had died unknown on this earth where he had fleetingly passed, like a stranger. No doubt it was up to him to ask, to inform himself. But for someone like him, who has nothing and wants the world entire, all his energy is not enough to create himself and to conquer or to understand that world. After all, it was not too late; he could still search, he could learn who this man had been who now seemed closer to him than any other being on this earth. He could . . .

Now the afternoon was coming to its end. The rustle of a skirt, a black shadow, brought him back to the landscape of tombs and sky that surrounded him. He had to leave: there was nothing more for him to do here. But he could not turn away from this name, those dates. Under that slab were left only ashes and dust. But, for him, his father was again alive, a strange silent life, and it seemed to him that again he was going to forsake him, to leave his father to haunt yet another night the endless solitude he had been hurled into and then deserted. The empty sky resounded with a sudden loud explosion: an invisible aeroplane had crossed the sound barrier. Turning his back on the grave, Jacques Cormery abandoned his father.

～

Farewell words

Letter from Captain John Coull, of the
Royal Fusiliers, to his son

Coull was killed in September 1918, six weeks before
the end of the First World War.

France 2.4.17 1 pm

My dear boy Fred,

This is a letter you will never see unless your daddy falls in the field. It is his farewell words to you in case anything happens. My boy I love you dearly and would have greatly liked to get leave for a few days to kiss you and shake hands again, after a few months separation, but as this seems at the present moment unlikely, I drop you this few lines to say 'God bless you' and keep you in the true brave manly upright course which I would like to see you follow.

You will understand better as you get older that your daddy came out to France for your sakes and for our Empire's sake. If he died it was in a good cause and all I would ask of you dear boy, is that you will keep this note in memory of me, and throughout your life may all that is good attend you and influence you. May you be strong to withstand the temptations of life and when you come to the evening of your days may you be able to say with St Paul 'I have fought the good fight'.

Goodbye dear boy and if it is that we are not to meet again in this life, may it be certain that we shall meet in another life to come, which faith I trust you will hold on to and live up to.

I remain ever
Your loving Daddy
J. F. Coull

Broken heart

From Roald Dahl's autobiography, *Boy*, 1982

In 1920, when I was still only three, my mother's eldest child, my own sister Astri, died from appendicitis. She was seven years old when she died, which was also the age of my own eldest daughter, Olivia, when she died from measles forty-two years later.

Astri was far and away my father's favourite. He adored her beyond measure and her sudden death left him literally speechless for days afterwards. He was so overwhelmed with grief that when he himself went down with pneumonia a month or so afterwards, he did not much care whether he lived or died.

If they had had penicillin in those days, neither appendicitis nor pneumonia would have been so much of a threat, but with no penicillin or any other magical antibiotic cures, pneumonia in particular was a very dangerous illness indeed. The pneumonia patient, on about the fourth or fifth day, would invariably reach what was known as 'the crisis'. The temperature soared and the pulse became rapid. The patient had to fight to survive. My father refused to fight. He was thinking, I am quite sure, of his beloved daughter, and he was wanting to join her in heaven. So he died. He was fifty-seven years old.

⌒

Nothing compared to her

Plutarch, (*c.* 46–*c.* 120) writes to his wife about the death of their two-year-old daughter, Timoxena

. . . besides that natural fatherly affection which commonly men have toward little babes, there was one particular property that gave an edge thereto, and caused me to love her above the rest; and that was a special grace that she had, to make joy and pleasure, and the same without any mixture at all of curstnesse or frowardnesse, and nothing given to whining and complaint; for she was of a wonderful kind and gentle nature, loving she was again to those that loved her, and marvellous desirous to gratifie and pleasure others; in which regards, she both delighted me, and also yielded no small testimony of rare debonairity that nature had endued her withal, for she would make prety meanes to her nurse, and seem (as it were) to entreat her to give the brest or pap, not onely to other infants, like her selfe, her play feeres, but also to little babies and puppets, and such like gawds as little ones take joy in, and wherewith they use to play; as if upon a singular courtesie and humanity she could find in her heart to communicate and distribute from her own table, even the best things she had, among them that did her any pleasure. But I see no reason (sweet wife) why these lovely qualities and such like, wherein we took contentment and joy in her lifetime, should disquiet and trouble us now, after her death, when we either think or make relation of them: and I fear againe, lest by our dolour and grief we abandon and put clean away all the remembrance thereof, like as *Clymene* desired to do, when she said

I hate the bow so light of cornel tree:
All exercise abroad, farewell for me;

as avoiding alwayes and trembling at the remembrance and commemoration of her son, which did no other good but renew her grief and dolour; for naturally we seek to flee all that troubleth and offendeth us. We ought, therefore, so to demean ourselves that as whiles she lived, we had nothing in the world more sweet to embrace, more pleasant to see, or delectable to hear than our daughter; so the cogitation of her may still abide and live with us all our life time, having by many degrees our joy multiplyed more than our heavinesse augmented.

⚯

My Boy Jack

Rudyard Kipling's only son, Jack, was posted missing in action during the Battle of Loos on the Western Front in 1915; his body was never recovered.

'Have you news of my boy Jack?'
Not this tide.
'When d'you think that he'll come back?'
Not with this wind blowing, and this tide.

'Has any one else had word of him?'
Not this tide.
For what is sunk will hardly swim,
Not with this wind blowing, and this tide.

'Oh, dear, what comfort can I find?'
None this tide,
Nor any tide,
Except he did not shame his kind –
Not even with that wind blowing, and that tide.

Then hold your head up all the more,
This tide,
And every tide;
Because he was the son you bore,
And gave to that wind blowing and that tide!

⚯

Such a child I never saw

From the diary of John Evelyn, 1620–1706

27 January [1658]:
After six fits of a quartan ague with which it pleased God to visite him, died my deare son Richard, to our inexpressible griefe and affliction, 5 yeares and 3 days old onely, but at that tender age a prodigy for witt and understanding; for beauty of body a very angel; for endowment of mind of incredible and rare hopes. To give onely a little taste of some of them, and thereby glory to God, who out of the mouths of babes and infants does sometimes perfect his praises: at 2 yeares and halfe old he could perfectly reade any of the English, Latine, French, or Gottic letters, pronouncing the three first languages exactly. He had before the 5th yeare, or in that yeare, not onely skill to reade most written hands, but to decline all the nouns, conjugate the verbs regular, and most of the irregular; learn'd out Puerilis, got by heart almost the entire vocabularie of Latine and French primitives and words, could make congruous syntax, turne English into Latine, and *vice versa*, construe and prove what he read, and did the government and use of relatives, verbs, substantives, elipses, and many figures and tropes, and made a considerable progress in Comenius's Janua; began himselfe to write legibly, and had a stronge passion for Greeke. The number of verses he could recite was prodigious, and what he remember'd of the parts of playes; which he would also act; and when seeing a Plautus in one's hand, he ask'd what booke it was, and being told it was comedy, and too difficult for him, he wept for sorrow. Strange was his apt and ingenious application of fables and morals, for he had read Aesop; he had a wonderful disposition to mathematics, having by heart divers propositions of Euclid that were read to him in play, and he would make lines and demonstrate them. As to his piety, astonishing were his applications of Scripture upon occasion, and his sense of God; he had learn'd all his Catechisme early, and understood the historical part of the Bible and New Testament to a wonder, how Christ came to redeeme mankind, and how, comprehending these necessarys himselfe, his godfathers were discharg'd of their promise. These and the like illuminations far exceeded his age and experience, considering the prettinesse of his addresse

and behaviour, cannot but leave impressions in me at the memory of him. When one told him how many dayes a Quaker had fasted, he replied that was no wonder, for Christ had said man should not live by bread alone, but by the Word of God. He would of himselfe select the most pathetic psalms, and chapters out of Job, to reade to his mayde during his sicknesse, telling her when she pitied him that all God's children must suffer affliction. He declaim'd against the vanities of the world before he had seene any. Often he would desire those who came to see him to pray by him, and a yeare before he fell sick, to kneel and pray with him alone in some corner. How thankfully would he receive admonition, how soon be reconciled! how indifferent, yet continually cherefull! He would give grave advice to his brother John, beare with his impertinencies, and say he was but a child. If he had heard of or saw any new thing, he was unquiet till he was told how it was made; he brought to us all such difficulties as he found in books, to be expounded. He had learn'd by heart divers sentences in Latin and Greeke, which on occasion he would produce even to wonder. He was all life, all prettinesse, far from morose, sullen, or childish in any thing he said or did. The last time he had ben at church (which was at Greenwich), I ask'd him, according to costome, what he remembered of the sermon; two good things, father, said he, *bonum gratiae* and *bonum gloriae*, with a just account of what the preacher said. The day before he died he cal'd to me, and in a more serious manner than usual told me that for all I loved him so dearly I should give my house, land, and all my fine things, to his brother Jack, he should have none of them; the next morning, when he found himself ill, and that I persuaded him to keepe his hands in bed, he demanded whether he might pray to God with his hands unjoyn'd; and a little after, whilst in greate agonie, whether he should not offend God by using his holy name so often calling for ease. What shall I say of his frequent pathetical ejaculations utter'd of himselfe; Sweete Jesus save me, deliver me, pardon my sinns, let thine angels receive me! So early knowledge, so much piety and perfection! But thus God having dress'd up a Saint fit for himselfe, would not longer permit him with us, unworthy of the future fruites of this incomparable hopefull blossome. Such a child I never saw: for such a child I blesse God in whose bosome he is! May I and mine become as this little child, who now follows the child Jesus that Lamb of God in a white robe whithersoever he goes; Even so, Lord Jesus, *fiat voluntas tua!* Thou gavest him to us, Thou hast taken him from us, blessed be the name of the Lord! That I had any thing acceptable to Thee was from thy grace alone, since from me he had nothing but sin, but that Thou hast pardon'd! blessed be my God for ever, amen!

Would you like to see the baby?

From Vernon Scannell, *The Tiger and
the Rose*, 1971

At half-past nine I borrowed my father-in-law's car and drove to the hospital. I was a little early but the doctor saw me straight away. He was a dark, tired-looking man, mercifully unfussy and practical.

He said, 'I am afraid this is a very unpleasant shock for you. As you know, one of the babies seems to be perfectly normal. A normal delivery, quite an easy one. The second wasn't so easy. He's suffering from what is called a meningocele, that's a hernia of the meninges, the membranes over the brain and spinal cord. He's got a big swelling on the back of his head and this will have to be removed. I think the chances of his surviving this are pretty good but how much brain damage he's likely to suffer I couldn't possibly say. I'm not a specialist on this, you see. But I know enough about it to say that the damage might be very considerable indeed. Encephalitis is common with these cases and you can be certain that the child will never be able to lead a normal life. I'd go as far as to say that it's very doubtful that he'd be able to walk or talk, though – as I've said – you must wait for specialist opinion before you decide what you're going to do.'

I must have looked blank. 'Do?'

He said, 'I mean whether you would look after the child yourselves or leave him in the hospital he'd be sent to for the operation. That's St Mary's at Carshalton. They look after a lot of similar cases there.'

I said, 'I see.' But I did not see or feel much at all. A sense of unreality was settling over me, cushioning me against the sharper edges of what was happening.

'What about Jo?' I said. 'My wife. Does she know about this?'

'She's been told only that the second twin is weak and has a spinal injury. We thought it might be better if you told her the facts.'

'Yes, I suppose so.'

He said, 'Would you like to see the baby? I must warn you that he's not – that the growth is large and unsightly. You might prefer not to . . . for the present, anyway . . .'

'Yes, I'd like to see him.'

I was not so sure that I did want to see him, but I felt I could not tell Jo about his condition unless I knew what he looked like.

'Very well.'

I followed the doctor along some corridors and we stopped outside a door.

'You sure you wouldn't like to leave it till a bit later?' he said.

I felt a flutter at the heart, a blurring of vision and a weakness in the legs. Panic. Was the baby so hideous? Would I make a fool of myself, be sick on the spot or collapse in a dead faint?

'No. I want to see him now.' I was mildly surprised that my voice sounded quite calm and firm.

We went into the room. There were a dozen or so incubators in it, each one like a glass box with a doll inside.

The doctor said, 'Here we are, this is the one.'

I realised that my fists were tightly clenched and I was digging the fingernails into the palms of my hands. I looked and, for a second, I was utterly bewildered and, wildly, I wondered if I could be the victim of a lunatic hoax. Then I felt a surge of relief that was instantly followed by a drench of pure joy and wonder at the beauty of the child. I had never seen anything so beautiful. He lay on one side with his eyes closed, and the tiny features looked at once exquisitely carved yet tenderly human like the head of one of those babies you see in fifteenth-century Flemish paintings, an idealisation of the infant. I could see one tiny hand, perfectly formed, the minute fingers curved near his cheek. The swelling at the back of the head seemed irrelevant; it ballooned out, a dark congested purple, a little like the bulb on an old-fashioned motor horn, about the size of the head itself. It could have been something left there by mistake, touching the little skull but not really connected to it. I looked closer and saw that the meningocele was indeed a malignant appendage attached to the back of the little head but I could feel no horror, only wonder that a child so handicapped could be so beautiful.

The doctor said, 'All right, Mr Scannell?'

I said, 'He's marvellous.'

I felt his hand on my arm. I think he was afraid that I might behave in some unpredictable and embarrassing manner.

I said, 'All right, thank you,' and he took me out of the room and directed me to the ward where Jo lay, a cot beside her bed with the other twin in it.

She was awake and she looked pale but quite composed.

She said, 'Have you seen Benjamin?'

I nodded. 'That's his name, is it?'

'Yes. He's been baptised already. They said he was weak. They baptise them at once if they think . . . have you seen him? Yes, you just said you had. What's he like? Is he all right?'

'He's fine. He's beautiful. But there's something wrong with him. He's going to be okay, I think. I mean he's going to survive. But he'll be handicapped.' I knew that she would not wish me to tell her anything but the truth as I knew it so I repeated to her all that the doctor had told me.

I held her hand. 'Don't worry,' I said. 'Everything's going to be all right. He's going to be fine. Believe me. He's the nicest baby I've ever seen.'

I thought she was going to cry but she did not. She said, 'We'll keep him at home, won't we? Whatever he's like? Whatever happens?'

'Of course.'

'Good. I thought you'd say that.'

We sat for a while, not saying much. Then Jo said, 'You haven't looked at Toby.'

'Toby?'

'Tobias. Your other son.'

I looked into the cot at the bedside. It contained a baby, an ordinary baby.

Jo said, 'Isn't he lovely?'

'Yes, he's lovely.'

But all I could think of was the tiny creature in the glass box, his grave sleeping face, the little head resting against the swollen bulb of dark flesh.

Presently a nurse came along and told me that I must leave. I said goodbye to Jo and promised to return that evening. I went out of the hospital. Outside, the sun was still shining and the air was sweet after the hospital smell. I got into the car and drove back to Edenbridge.

We brought Benjamin home from Carshalton towards the end of May. The woman specialist I had spoken to at St Mary's gave us cautious encouragement but was careful not to raise false hopes.

'It is impossible to predict what progress he may make,' she had said. 'But you must realise that he will never be a normal human being. There is absolutely no question of that. At the same time, there's no doubt that a child like this responds far better to the love and care of parents and brothers and sisters in its own home than ever he could to the necessarily more impersonal attention he would get here.'

At nights it was my responsibility to feed Benjamin while Jo was attending to Toby's needs. Benjamin was very frail and, on the rare occasions when he cried, his voice was paper-thin, fluttering on silence like the wings of a dying moth. I still found his face beautiful though I had to admit that it showed none of the expression that Toby's was beginning to display. He would lie, almost weightlessly, in the crook of my arm, so small and so fragile that it seemed impossible that he could be a living human, and after he had taken the little nourishment that he could swallow, I would very softly pat and massage his back until he expelled a tiny gust of wind. I would nurse him for a while, looking into his face for some sign of animation, but it always remained quite expressionless, the eyes either closed or apparently unseeing, a small breathing statue. There was a little lump on the back of his head where the meningocele had been removed. Otherwise, apart from his smallness and impassivity, he looked like any baby except that, to me, his minuscule features were more delicately shaped than any I had seen or could imagine. . . .

Jo and I did not, I am sure, hide from the realities of the situation. We both knew that Benjamin, as he grew older, would become a restraint on our freedom. We both faced the fact that he might never even reach the stage of development that Mary attained, might never perhaps recognise or be able to communicate with us at all, and, as we sternly reminded each other, he would not remain a baby for long; he would grow big and, perhaps, monstrous. It did not matter. We would have to face the fresh problems as they arose. Here and now we were grateful for Benjamin; we, too, felt blessed.

We watched his progress with microscopic care, worrying when he would not take his milk, rejoicing when he seemed hungry, and at nights, however deep our sleep, we would be instantly awakened by his wispy cries. We noticed that there were times when he seemed to find difficulty in breathing and you could hear the faint rasping in the frail cage of his chest and the rate of his breathing seemed too fast. When we took him to our doctor we were told that there was some bronchial congestion but it would probably clear itself up.

One night in late August, or rather in the early hours of the morning, after I had fed Benjamin and seen him back into his cot, I was slipping back into sleep when I was jerked awake by a faint noise. I sat up and listened. Again I heard the sound; it was not his usual dry fluttering cry, but a noise I had never before heard him make, a brief and very soft chirrup and twitter like birds settling in their nests for the night but heard from a considerable distance. I slipped out of bed and went to his side. A night light burned on the chest-of-drawers and shadows made obeisances on the walls. I looked down and saw that Benjamin's eyes were not closed. I bent close and he seemed to be looking back at me.

I waited to see if he would make the sound again but all I could hear was the slight wheezing of his rapid breathing. The little head looked unbearably vulnerable. His eyes were still open. I wished that he would make his new sound again but he just lay there and seemed to return my scrutiny with incurious serenity. Then, just as I was about to go back to bed, the miracle occurred. Benjamin smiled. For the first time the small, almost mask-like face was illumined from within and it became, instead of an idealisation or caricature of infancy, wonderfully and unequivocally human, and the opening of the lips, the upwards curve of each corner of the mouth and the narrowing of eyes, disturbing the perfection of the features in repose, thrilled me with their sweet and mortal imperfection. The smile lasted for perhaps two or three seconds. Then his eyes closed, the little mask of gravity was resumed, and he slept. I have since been told that all I saw was a trick of the flickering candlelight playing over his face or a spasm of indigestion contorting his features, but I am not convinced. I am sure that he smiled.

The next afternoon I had to go to London. I stayed longer than I had intended and I had to hurry to catch the 7.10 from Victoria. It was a fine evening. I walked the mile or so from the station to the village and I reached home soon after eight o'clock. I went into the house and found no one downstairs. I looked in the garden but Jo was not there so I started to go upstairs just as she appeared from our bedroom. I waited for her to come down.

I saw immediately that something was wrong. She looked pale; her eyes had a fixed brightness and her mouth was hard and twisted as if she were biting on something that tasted very bitter.

My heart began to thump with a sudden alarm. I said, 'What's the matter?'

She shook her head with a single flick as if deflecting the question I had thrown at her.

I let her pass me and then I followed her into the kitchen at the back of the house. She sat down at the table. Then her mouth went loose, her face twisted as if she had felt a quick thrust of pain and tears began to stream down her cheeks.

She said, 'Benjamin's dead.'

I sat down. I could taste beer, sour and rebellious in the stomach and throat. I felt parched and sick and I began to tremble.

I said, 'Benjamin?' as if I could not believe what she had said, but it seemed that I had known before she had spoken.

Jo began to speak very quickly and all the time the tears were streaming down her face. 'It wasn't my fault. It was about two o'clock. He started to breathe fast and he couldn't – he didn't seem able to get enough air. Then his face went blue. He couldn't breathe. I picked him up and put him in the car and drove as fast as I could to the hospital. They took him away and I waited. I waited. It wasn't my fault. They said there was nothing I could have done. He just died.'

I sat opposite Jo and watched her cry. I knew I ought to do

something to comfort her but I did nothing. I saw that each of us was alone now. There was nothing, for the moment, that we could do to help one another. Later, perhaps, but not now. I got up and went into the garden. I thought, 'He's gone. There wasn't much of him and now there's nothing.' I did not feel angry – not then – but there was a wedge of pain, dry and abrasive, like a growth in my throat. I thought if I could cry it might help. It might flush the quinsy of grief. But I could not cry. I had not cried for longer than I could remember and, in any case, it would be absurd for a man of my age to be standing in his garden on a summer evening bawling his eyes out. Grown men did not cry. They knew it served no purpose. It was something that women and children did, something you outgrew; its impossibility defined the adult male. It might have helped though, had it been possible. It might, if only for the moment, ease the immediate pain. Then I noticed the hot prickle and itch on my face and I found that I had been crying all the time, but it did not help very much. The pain of loss was not to be washed away by a few drops of salty water. I would have to get accustomed to it; it would become familiar and therefore bearable, but it would stay with me for ever.

⌒

Yielded up his soul to God

A letter from William Wordsworth,
2 December 1812

Wednesday Evening

My dear Friend,

Symptoms of the measles appeared upon my Son Thomas last Thursday; he was most favourable held till tuesday, between ten and eleven at that hour was particularly lightsome and comfortable; without any assignable cause a sudden change took place, an inflammation had commenced on the lungs which it was impossible to check and the sweet Innocent yielded up his soul to God before six in the evening. He did not appear to suffer much in body, but I fear something in mind as he was of an age to have thought much upon death a subject to which his mind was daily led by the grave of his Sister. My Wife bears the loss of her Child with striking fortitude. My Sister was not at home but is returned to day, I met her at Threlkeld. Miss Hutchinson also supports her sorrow as ought to be done. For myself dear Southey I dare not say in what state of mind I am; I loved the Boy with the utmost love of which my soul is capable, and he is taken from me – yet in the agony of my spirit in surrendering such a treasure I feel a thousand times richer than if I had never possessed it. God comfort and save you and all our friends and us all from a repetition of such trials – O Southey feel for me! If you are not afraid of the complaint, I ought to have said if you have had it come over to us! Best love from everybody – you will impart this sad news to your Wife and Mrs Coleridge and Mrs Lovel and to Miss Barker and Mrs Wilson. Poor woman! she was most good to him – Heaven reward her.

> Heaven bless you
> Your sincere Friend
> W. Wordsworth

Will Mrs Coleridge please to walk up to the Calverts and mention these afflictive news with the particulars. I should have written but my sorrow over-powers me.

Remembrance of my deare Mary

From the diary of the Reverend Ralph Josselin

27 [May 1650]: This day a quarter past two in the afternoone my Mary fell asleepe in the Lord, her soule past into that rest where the body of Jesus, and the soules of the saints are, shee was: 8 yeares and 45 dayes old when shee dyed, my soule had aboundant cause to blesse god for her, who was our first fruites, and those god would have offered to him, and this I freely resigned up to him(,) it was a pretious child, a bundle of myrrhe, a bundle of sweetnes, shee was a child of ten thousand, full of wisedome, woman-like gravity, knowledge, sweet expre[*ssions of god, apt in her learning,*] tender hearted and loving, an [*obed*]ient child

[*to us.*] it was free from [*the rudenesse of*] litle children, it was to us as a boxe of sweet ointment, which now its broken smells more deliciously then it did before, Lord I rejoyce I had such a present for thee, it was patient in the sicknesse, thankefull to admiracion; it lived desired and dyed lamented, thy memory is and will bee sweete unto mee,

28: This day my deare Mary was buried in Earles Colne church by the 2 uppermost seats, shee was accompanyed thither with most of the towne; Mrs Margarett Harlakenden, and Mrs Mabel Elliston layd her in grave, those two and Mrs Jane Clench and my sister carryed her in their hands to the grave, I kist her lips last, and carefully laid up that body the soule being with Jesus it rests there till the resurrection.

16 [June]: God was in many outward mercies exceeding good to mee and mine, my deare wife somewhat faint and weakely but cheerfull, god helpes us under our great losses I am some-times ready to bee overwhelmed in remembrance of my deare Mary . . .

⌒

The Distress'd Father or, the Author's Tears over his Dear Darling Rachel

Henry Carey, *c.* 1687–1743

Oh! lead me where my Darling lies,
Cold as the Marble Stone;
I will recall her with my Cries,
And wake her with my Moan.

Come from thy Bed of Clay, my dear!
See! where thy Father stands;
His Soul he sheds out Tear by Tear,
And wrings his wretched Hands.

But ah! alas! thou canst not rise,
Alas! thou canst not hear,
Or, at thy tender Father's Cries,
Thou surely wouldst appear.

Since then my Love! my Soul's delight!
Thou canst not come to me,
Rather than want thy pleasing sight,
I'll dig my way to thee.

⌒

On My First Son

Ben Jonson, 1572–1637

Farewell, thou child of my right hand, and joy;
My sin was too much hope of thee, loved boy:
Seven years thou wert lent to me, and I thee pay,
Exacted by thy fate, on the just day.
O could I lose all father now! for why
Will man lament the state he should envy,
To have so soon 'scaped world's and flesh's rage,
And, if no other misery, yet age?
Rest in soft peace, and asked, say, 'Here doth lie
Ben Jonson his best piece of poetry.'
For whose sake henceforth all his vows be such
As what he loves may never like too much.

⌒

Three Years She Grew

William Wordsworth, 1770–1850

Three years she grew in sun and shower,
Then Nature said, 'A lovelier flower
On earth was never sown;
This Child I to myself will take;
She shall be mine, and I will make
A Lady of my own.

'Myself will to my darling be
Both law and impulse: and with me
The Girl, in rock and plain,
In earth and heaven, in glade and bower,
Shall feel an overseeing power
To kindle or restrain.

'She shall be sportive as the fawn
That wild with glee across the lawn
Or up the mountain springs;
And hers shall be the breathing balm,
And hers the silence and the calm
Of mute insensate things.

'The floating clouds their state shall lend
To her; for her the willow bend;
Nor shall she fail to see
Even in the motions of the Storm
Grace that shall mould the Maiden's form
By silent sympathy.

'The stars of midnight shall be dear
To her; and she shall lean her ear
In many a secret place
Where rivulets dance their wayward round,
And beauty born of murmuring sound
Shall pass into her face.

'And vital feelings of delight,
Shall rear her form to stately height,
Her virgin bosom swell;
Such thoughts to Lucy I will give
While she and I together live
Here in this happy dell.'

Thus Nature spake – the work was done –
How soon my Lucy's race was run!
She died, and left to me
This health, this calm, and quiet scene;
The memory of what has been,
And never more will be.

The Death of Jean

Mark Twain, 1911

Stormfield, Christmas Eve, *11 a.m., 1909. – Jean is dead!*

Has any one ever tried to put upon paper all the little happenings connected with a dear one – happenings of the twenty-four hours preceding the sudden and unexpected death of that dear one? Would a book contain them? would two books contain them? I think not. They pour into the mind in a flood. They are little things that have been always happening every day, and were always so unimportant and easily forgettable before – but now! Now, how different! how precious they are, how dear, how unforgettable, how pathetic, how sacred, how clothed with dignity!

Last night Jean, all flushed with splendid health, and I the same, from the wholesome effects of my Bermuda holiday, strolled hand in hand from the dinner table and sat down in the library and chatted, and planned, and discussed, cheerily and happily (and how unsuspectingly!) until nine – which is late for us – then went upstairs, Jean's friendly German dog following. At my door Jean said, 'I can't kiss you good night, father: I have a cold, and you could cath it.' I bent and kissed her hand. She was moved – saw it in her eyes – and she impulsively kissed my hand in return. Then with the usual gay 'Sleep well, dear!' from both, we parted.

At half past seven this morning I woke, and heard voices outside my door. I said to myself, 'Jean is starting on her usual horseback flight to the station for the mail.' Then Katy entered, stood quaking and gasping at my bedside a moment, then found her tongue:

'Miss Jean is dead!'

Possibly I know now what the soldier feels when a bullet crashes through his heart.

In her bath-room there she lay, the fair young creature, stretched upon the floor and covered with a sheet. And looking so placid, so natural, and as if asleep. We knew what had happened. She was an epileptic: she had been seized with a convulsion and heart failure in her bath. The doctor had to come several miles. His efforts, like our previous ones, failed to bring her back to life.

It is noon, now. How lovable she looks, how sweet and how tranquil! It is a noble face, and full of dignity; and that was a good heart that lies there so still . . .

There was never a kinder heart than Jean's. From her childhood up she always spent the most of her allowance on charities of one kind and another. After she became secretary and had her income doubled she spent her money upon these things with a free hand. Mine too, I am glad and grateful to say.

She was a loyal friend to all animals, and she loved them all, birds, beasts, and everything – even snakes – an inheritance from me. She knew all the birds: she was high up in that lore. She became a member of various humane socieites when she was still a little girl – both here and abroad – and she remained an active member to the last. She founded two or three societies for the protection of animals, here and in Europe.

She was an embarrassing secretary, for she fished my correspondence out of the waste-basket and answered the letters. She thought all letters deserved the courtesy of an answer. Her mother brought her up in that kindly error.

She could write a good letter, and was swift with her pen. She had but an indifferent ear for music, but her tongue took to languages with an easy facility. She never allowed her Italian, French and German to get rusty through neglect.

The telegrams of sympathy are flowing in, from far and wide, now, just as they did in Italy five years and a half ago, when this child's mother laid down her blameless life. They cannot heal the hurt, but they take away some of the pain. When Jean and I kissed hands and parted at my door last, how little did we imagine that in twenty-two hours the telegraph would be bringing words like these:

'From the bottom of our hearts we send our sympathy, dearest of friends.'

For many and many a day to come, wherever I go in this house, rememberancers of Jean will mutely speak to me of her. Who can count the number of them?

She was in exile two years with the hope of healing her malady – epilepsy. There are no words to express how grateful I am that she did not meet her fate in the hands of strangers, but in the loving shelter of her own home.

'Miss Jean is dead!'
     It is true. Jean is dead.
     A month ago I was writing bubbling and hilarious articles for magazines yet to appear, and now I am writing – this.

6

Patrimony

Echoing down the ages

Jean-Paul Richter, 1763–1825

The words a father speaks to his children in the privacy of the home are not heard at the time, but, as in whispering galleries, they will be clearly heard at the end and by posterity.

⌒

Heracles' last words to his son

From *Sophocles: Women of Trachis*, translated by
Ezra Pound, 1956

HERAKLES: Listen first, and show what you're made of,
my stock. My father told me long ago
that no living man should kill me,
but that someone from hell would, and
that brute of a Centaur has done it.
The dead beast kills the living me.
And that fits another odd forecast
breathed out at the Selloi's oak –
Those fellows rough it,
sleep on the ground, up in the hills there.
I heard it and wrote it down
under my Father's tree.
Time lives, and it's going on now.
I am released from trouble.

I thought it meant life in comfort.
It doesn't. It means that I die.
For amid the dead there is no work in service.
Come at it that way, my boy, what

SPLENDOUR,
IT ALL COHERES.

⌒

His father's voice

From Tony Parsons, *Man and Boy*, 1999

It was a brochure like any other – tastefully shot, beautifully presented – and the undertaker gently led me through it, starting with the cheapest, simplest pine numbers, going right up to the top of the range model, a large hardwood coffin lined with red satiny material and adorned with big brass handles.

My first instinct was to go for the most expensive one – let's push the boat out, nothing's too good for my old man. But my second instinct was that the top of the range coffin was just a touch too elaborate for my dad to sleep in for all eternity.

I hesitated, and told the undertaker that we would go for the second most expensive coffin. And when Uncle Jack and I were back on the street, I was pleased with my choice.

'Your old man would have had a fit at that posh coffin,' my Uncle Jack grinned.

'The most expensive one?' I smiled. 'Yeah, I thought that was a bit much.'

'Gold handles and a red velvet lining!' chuckled Uncle Jack. 'It looked more like a French knocking shop than a coffin!'

'Talk about turning in your grave,' I laughed. 'I know what he would have said if we'd gone for that one – "*Who do you think I am? Bloody Napoleon?*"'

I could hear his voice.

I would never hear his voice again.

I would always hear him.

To *thine own self be true*

Polonius to his son, Laertes, from Shakespeare's
Hamlet, Act I, Scene 3, written *c.* 1599

POLONIUS: Look thou character. Give thy thoughts no tongue,
              Nor any unproportion'd thought his act.
              Be thou familiar, but by no means vulgar.
              Those friends thou hast, and their adoption tried,

Grapple them to thy soul with hoops of steel.
But do not dull thy palm with entertainment
Of each new-hatch'd, unfledg'd courage. Beware
Of entrance to a quarrel. But, being in,
Bear't that th' opposed may beware of thee.
Give every man thine ear, but few thy voice.
Take each man's censure, but reserve thy judgment.
Costly thy habit as thy purse can buy,
But not express'd in fancy; rich, not gaudy;
For the apparel oft proclaims the man,
And they in France of the best rank and station
Are of a most select and generous chief in that.
Neither a borrower nor a lender be,
For loan oft loses both itself and friend,
And borrowing dulls the edge of husbandry.
This above all: to thine own self be true,
And it must follow, as the night the day,
Thou canst not then be false to any man.

⌒

Blessing

The exiled Walter de la Pole, Duke of Suffolk, writes
to his son, April 1450

Dear and only well-beloved Son,
I beseech our Lord in Heaven, the Maker of all the World, to
bless you, and to send you ever grace to love him, and to dread
him, to the which, as far as a Father may charge his child, I both
charge you, and pray you to set all your spirits and wits to do,
and to know his Holy Laws and Commandments, by the which
ye shall, with his great mercy, pass all the great tempests and
troubles of this wretched world.

And that, also weetingly, ye do nothing for love nor dread of
any earthly creature that should displease him. And there as any
Frailty maketh you to fall, beseech his mercy soon to call you to
him again with repentance, satisfaction, and contrition of your
heart, never more in will to offend him.

Secondly, next him above all earthly things, to be true Liege man in heart, in will, in thought, in deed, unto the King our alder-most high and dread Sovereign Lord, to whom both ye and I be much bound to; charging you, as Father can and may, rather to die than to be contrary, or to know any thing that were against the welfare or prosperity of his most Royal Person, but that as far as your body and life may stretch, ye live and die to defend it, and to let his Highness have knowledge thereof in all the haste ye can.

Thirdly, in the same wise, I charge you, my dear Son, alway as ye be bounden by the Commandment of God to do, to love, to worship, your Lady and Mother; and also that ye obey always her commandments, and to believe her counsels and advices in all your works, the which dread not but shall be best and truest to you.

And if any other body would steer you to the contrary, to flee the counsel in any wise, for ye shall find it nought and evil.

Furthermore, as far as Father may and can, I charge you in any wise to flee the company and counsel of proud men, of covetous men, and of flattering men, the more especially and mightily to withstand them, and not to draw nor to meddle with them, with all your might and power; and to draw to you and to your company good and virtuous men, and such as be of good conversation, and of truth, and by them shall ye never be deceived nor repent you of.

Moreover, never follow your own wit in no wise; but in all your works, of such folks as I write of above, ask your advice and counsel, and doing thus, with the mercy of God, ye shall do right well, and live in right much worship, and great heart's rest and ease.

And I will be to you as good Lord and Father as my heart can think.

And last of all, as heartily and as lovingly as ever Father blessed his child in earth I give you the Blessing of Our Lord and of me, which of his infinite mercy increase you in all virtue and good living; and that your Blood may by his grace from kindred to kindred multiply in this earth to his service, in such wise as after the departing from this wretched world here, ye and they may glorify him eternally amongst his Angels in heaven.

Written of mine hand,
The day of my departing from this Land,
Your true and loving Father,
Suffolk

The ABC of goodness

Samuel Taylor Coleridge to his son Derwent,
aged seven

Ashby de la Zouch, Coleorton,
Saturday night, 7 Feb. 1807.

My dear Derwent,

It will be many times the number of years, you have already lived, before you can know and feel thoroughly, how very much your dear Father wishes and longs to have you on his knees, and in his arms. Your Brother, Hartley, too whirls about, and wrings his hands at the thought of meeting you again: he counts the days and hours, and makes sums of arithmetic of the time, when he is again to play with you, and your sweet squirrel of a Sister. He dreams of you, and has more than once hugged me between waking and sleeping, fancying it to be you or Sara: and he talks of you before his eyes are fully open in the morning, and while he is closing them at night. And this is very right: for nothing can be more pleasing to God Almighty and to all good people, than that Brothers and Sisters should love each other, and try to make each other happy; but it is impossible to be happy without being good, and the beginning and the ABC of goodness is to be dutiful and affectionate to their Parents; to be obedient to them, when they are present, and to pray for them [and to write] frequent letters from a thankful and loving heart when both or either of them chance to be absent. For you are a big Thought, and take up a great deal of room in your Father's Heart: and his eyes are often full of tears thro' his Love of you, and his Forehead wrinkled from the labour of his Brain, planning to make you good, and wise and happy. And your *Mother* has fed and cloathed and taught you, day after day, all your life; and has passed many sleepless nights, watching and lulling you, when you were sick and helpless, and she gave *you* nourishment out of her own Breasts for so long a time, that the moon was at its least and its greatest sixteen times before you lived entirely on any other food, than what came out of her body, and she brought you into the world with shocking Pains, which she suffered for you, and before you were born for eight months together every drop of blood in your body, first beat in *her* Pulses and throbbed in *her* Heart. So it must needs be a horribly wicked thing ever to forget, or wilfully to vex a Father or a Mother, especially a Mother. God is above all: and only good and dutiful children can say their Lord's Prayer, and say to God, '*our Father*,' without being wicked even in their Prayers. But after God's name, the name of Mother is the sweetest and most holy. The next good thing and that without which you cannot either honour any person, or be esteemed by anyone, is *always to tell the truth*. For God gave you a tongue to tell the Truth, and to tell a Lie with it is as silly, as to try to walk on your Head instead of your Feet; besides it is such a base, hateful, and wicked thing, that when good men describe all wickedness put together in one wicked mind, they call it the Devil, which is Greek for *malicious Liar*: and the Bible names him a *Liar* from the beginning, and the Father of *Lies*. Never, never, tell a Lie – even tho' you should escape a whipping by it; for the pain of a whipping does not last above a few minutes, and the Thought of having told a Lie would make you miserable for days – unless, indeed, you are hardened in wickedness and then you must be miserable for ever –

But you are a dear Boy, and will scorn such a vile thing: and whenever you happen to do anything amiss, which *will* happen now and then, you will say to yourself 'Well whatever comes of it, I will *tell the Truth*, both for its own sake, and because my dear Father [spoke] and wrote so to me about it.'

I am greatly delighted that you are desirous to go on with your Greek; and shall finish this letter with a short Lesson of Greek. But more cannot be done till we meet, when we will begin anew, and, I trust, not to leave off, till you are a good scholar. And now go, and give a loving kiss to your little sister and tell her, that Papa sent it to her: and will give hundreds in a little time: for I am, my dear Child,

Your affectionate Father
S. T. Coleridge

P. S. I find that I cannot write in this space what I wished – therefore I will send you, dear child! a whole sheet of Greek Lessons in a few days.

One in ten

Report in *The Daily Telegraph*, November 1996

A new British Social Attitudes survey . . . shows that lack of contact with fathers is relatively high in adult life.

The survey, of more than 2,000 people, reveals that around one adult in 10 never sees his or her father. This compares with one in 33 who had no contact with his or her mother.

⌒

It makes you blind

Letter from John Evelyn to his son, November 1679, on the eve of the latter's marriage

. . . Take heed of those filthy lusts even with your own wife, nor delight to feed and satisfy your eyes or incite your fancy with nakedness, or unnatural figures & usages of yourselves, for they will breed impudence, loathing and contempt. . . . be none of those who brag how frequently they can be brutes in one night, for that intemperance will exhaust you, & possibly create importunate expectations when your inclinations are not so fierce. Such excesses do oft times dispose to . . . inconveniences through the straining of nature . . . which are sometimes incurable. . . .

It is likewise experimentally found that carnal caresses upon a full stomach, or in the daytime, or in the excessive heat and cold of weather are very pernicious, & too much frequency of embraces dulls the sight, decays the memory, induces the gout, palsies, enervates and renders effeminate the whole body & shortens life.

There should therefore repose succeed upon those wasting exercises, & therefore physicians permit it after the first concoction is made, namely the first sleep; but rarely in the morning, never totally fasting, as indisposing the body the whole day after.

These particulars I only touch, knowing that young married people will hardly be reasoned into that temperance, & perhaps they are to be indulged some liberties for a time, especially at first, But it is profitable to know these things once, and much better to use moderation. . . . I do not by these abridge you therefore any decent satisfaction; a man may eat . . . not only to satisfy hunger, but to cheer him, & if there were not some gratification of the inferior sense accompanying this & other natural action, the world would cease.

A declaration for dependence

Letter from Thomas Jefferson to his daughter
Martha, 28 November 1783

The acquirements which I hope you will make under the tutors I have provided for you will render you more worthy of my love, and if they cannot increase it they will prevent its diminution. Consider the good lady who has taken you under her roof, who has undertaken to see that you perform all your exercises, and to admonish you in all those wanderings from what is right or what is clever to which your inexperience would expose you, consider her I say as your mother, as the only person to whom, since the loss with which heaven has been pleased to afflict you, you can now look up; and that her displeasure or disapprobation on any occasion will be an immense misfortune which should you be so unhappy as to incur by any unguarded act, think no concession too much to regain her good will. With respect to the distribution of your time the following is what I should approve.

from 8. to 10 o'clock practise music.
from 10. to 1. dance one day and draw another
from 1. to 2. draw on the day you dance, and write a letter the next day.
from 3. to 4. read French.
from 4. to 5. exercise yourself in music.
from 5. till bedtime read English, write &c.

Strive to be good under every situation and to all living creatures, and to acquire those accomplishments which I have put in your power, and which will go far towards ensuring you the warmest love of your affectionate father.

P. S. Keep my letters and read them at times that you may

always have present in your mind those things which will endear you to me.

∽

Advice to a son about to depart America

Benjamin and Julia Rush to Jonathan Rush

Directions and advice to Jno. Rush from his father and mother composed the evening before he sailed for Calcutta, May 18th, 1796.

We shall divide these directions into four heads, as they relate to *morals, knowledge, health* and *business*.

I. MORALS

1. Be punctual in committing your soul and body to the protection of your Creator every morning and evening. Implore at the same time his mercy in the name of his Son, our Lord and Saviour Jesus Christ.
2. Read in your Bible frequently, more especially on Sundays.
3. Avoid swearing and even an irreverent use of your Creator's name. *Flee* youthful lusts.
4. Be courteous and gentle in your behaviour to your fellow passengers, and respectful and obedient to the captain of the vessel.
5. Attend public worship regularly every Sunday when you arrive at Calcutta.

II. KNOWLEDGE

1. Begin by studying Guthrie's *Geography*.
2. Read your other books *through* carefully, and converse daily upon the subjects of your reading.
3. Keep a diary of every day's studies, conversations, and transactions at sea and on shore. Let it be composed in a fair, legible hand. Insert in it an account of the population, manners, climate, diseases, &c., of the places you visit.
4. Preserve an account of every person's name and disease whom you attend.

III. HEALTH

1. Be temperate in eating, more especially of animal food. Never *taste* distilled spirits of any kind, and drink fermented liquors very sparingly.
2. Avoid the night air in sickly situations. Let your dress be rather warmer than the weather would seem to require. Carefully avoid fatigue from all causes both of body and mind.

IV. BUSINESS

1. Take no step in laying out your money without the advice and consent of the captain or supercargo.
2. Keep an exact account of all your expenditures. Preserve as vouchers of them all your bills.
3. Take care of all your instruments, books, clothes, &c.

Be sober and vigilant. Remember at all times that while you are seeing the world, the world will see you. Recollect further that you are always under the eye of the Supreme Being. One more consideration shall close this parting testimony of our affection. Whenever you are tempted to do an improper thing, fancy that you see your father and mother kneeling before you and imploring you with tears in their eyes to refrain yielding to the temptation, and assuring you at the same time that your yielding to it will be the means of hurrying them to a premature grave.

~~

Make yourself a delight to all eyes that behold you

Jack London to his daughter, 16 September 1915

Glen Ellen, California

Dear Joan,

First of all, I had Aunt Eliza send you the cheque for $7.00 so that you might buy the two pairs of boots for yourself and Bess.

Second of all, I promised to reply to your letter.

Third of all, and very important, please remember that your Daddy is a very busy man. When you write to society people, or to young people, who have plenty of time, write on your fine stationery and write on both sides of the paper. But, please, when you write to Daddy, take any kind of paper, the cheapest paper for that matter, and write on one side only. This makes it ever so much easier for Daddy to read. A two-sheet letter, such as yours that I am now looking at, written on both sides, is like a Chinese puzzle to a busy man. I take more time trying to find my way from one of the four portions into which your two-sided sheet is divided than I do in reading the letter itself.

Some day I should like to see your French heeled slippers. Joan, you are on the right track. Never hesitate at making yourself a dainty, delightful girl and woman. There is a girl's pride and a woman's pride in this, and it is indeed a fine pride. On the one hand, of course, never over-dress. On the other hand, never be a frump. No matter how wonderful are the thoughts that burn in your brain, always, physically, and in dress, make yourself a delight to all eyes that behold you.

I have met a number of philosophers. They were real philosophers. Their minds were wonderful minds. But they did not take baths, and they did not change their socks and it almost turned one's stomach to sit at table with them.

Our bodies are as glorious as our minds, and, just as one cannot maintain a high mind in a filthy body, by the same token one cannot keep a high mind and high pride when said body is not dressed beautifully, delightfully, charmingly. Nothing would your Daddy ask better of you in this world than that you have a high mind, a high pride, a fine body, and, just as all the rest, a beautifully dressed body.

~

The good news

Extracted from Thomas Fuller,
Scripture Observations, 1645

Rehoboam begat Abiam: a bad father begat a bad son. Abiam begat Asa: a bad father a good son. Asa begat Jehoshaphat: a good father a good son. Jehoshaphat begat Joram: a good father a bad son. I see, Lord, from hence, that my father's piety cannot be entailed; that is bad news for me. But I see also that actual impiety is not always hereditary; that is good news for my son.

⌒

Advice to a son

Ernest Hemingway, Berlin, 1931

Never trust a white man,
Never kill a Jew,
Never sign a contract,
Never rent a pew.
Don't enlist in armies;
Nor marry many wives;
Never write for magazines;
Never scratch your hives.
Always put paper on the seat,
Don't believe in wars,
Keep yourself both clean and neat,
Never marry whores.
Never pay a blackmailer,
Never go to law,
Never trust a publisher,
Or you'll sleep on straw.
All your friends will leave you
All your friends will die
So lead a clean and wholesome life
And join them in the sky.

⌒

Paternity and ambition

From Bertrand Russell, *Marriage and Morals*, 1929

As soon as the physiological fact of paternity is recognised, a quite new element enters into paternal feeling, an element which has led almost everywhere to the creation of patriarchal societies. As soon as a father recognises that the child is, as the Bible says, his 'seed', his sentiment towards the child is reinforced by two factors, the love of power and the desire to survive death. The achievements of a man's descendants are in a sense his achievements, and their life is a continuation of his life. Ambition no longer finds its termination at the grave, but can be indefinitely extended through the careers of descendants. Consider, for example, the satisfaction of Abraham when he is informed that his seed shall possess the land of Canaan. In a matrilineal society, family ambition would have to be confined to women, and as women do not do the fighting, such family ambition as they may have has less effect than that of men. One must suppose, therefore, that the discovery of fatherhood would make human society more competitive, more energetic, more dynamic and hustling than it had been in the matrilineal stage.

Shit

From Philip Roth, *Patrimony*, 1991

We were drinking our coffee when it occurred to me that he was still gone. I quietly left the table and, while the others were talking, slipped into the house, certain that he was dead.

He wasn't, though he might well have been wishing that he were.

I smelled the shit halfway up the stairs to the second floor. When I got to his bathroom, the door was ajar, and on the floor of the corridor outside the bathroom were his dungarees and his undershorts. Standing inside the bathroom door was my father, completely naked, just out of the shower and dripping wet. The smell was overwhelming.

At the sight of me he came close to bursting into tears. In a voice as forlorn as any I had ever heard, from him or anyone, he told me what it hadn't been difficult to surmise. 'I beshat myself,' he said.

The shit was everywhere, smeared underfoot on the bathmat, running over the toilet bowl edge and, at the foot of the bowl, in a pile on the floor. It was splattered across the glass of the shower stall from which he'd just emerged, and the clothes discarded in the hallway were clotted with it. It was on the corner of the towel he had started to dry himself with. In this smallish bathroom, which was ordinarily mine, he had done his best to extricate himself from his mess alone, but as he was nearly blind and just up out of a hospital bed, in undressing himself and getting into the shower he had managed to spread the shit over everything. I saw that it was even on the tips of the bristles of my toothbrush hanging in the holder over the sink.

'It's okay,' I said, 'it's okay, everything is going to be okay.'

I reached into the shower stall and turned the water back on and fiddled with the taps until it was the right temperature. Taking the towel out of his hand, I helped him back under the shower.

'Take the soap and start from scratch,' I said, and while he obediently began again to soap his body all over, I gathered his clothes and the towels and the bathmat together in a heap and went down the hall to the linen closet and got a pillowcase to dump them in. I also found a fresh bath towel for him. Then I got him out of the shower and took him straight into the hallway where the floor was still clean, and wrapped him up in the towel and began to dry him. 'You made a valiant effort,' I said, 'but I'm afraid it was a no-win situation.'

'I beshat myself,' he said, and this time he dissolved in tears.

I got him into his bedroom, where he sat on the edge of the bed and continued to towel himself while I went off and got a terry-cloth robe of mine. When he was dry I helped him into the robe and then pulled back the top sheet of the bed and told him to get in and take a nap.

'Don't tell the children,' he said, looking up at me from the bed with his one sighted eye.

'I won't tell anyone,' I said. 'I'll say you're taking a rest.'

'Don't tell Claire.'

'Nobody,' I said. 'Don't worry about it. It could have happened to anyone. Just forget about it and get a good rest.'

I lowered the shades to darken the room and closed the door behind me.

The bathroom looked as though some spiteful thug had left his calling card after having robbed the house. As my father was tended to and he was what counted, I would just as soon have nailed the door shut and forgotten that bathroom for ever. 'It's like writing a book,' I thought – 'I have no idea where to begin.' But I stepped gingerly across the floor and reached out and threw open the window, which was a start. Then I went down the back stairway to the kitchen, and keeping out of sight of Seth and Ruth and Claire, who were still in the summer room talking, I got a bucket, a brush, and a box of Spic and Span from the cabinet under the sink and two rolls of paper towels and came back upstairs to the bathroom.

Where his shit lay in front of the toilet bowl in what was more or less a contiguous mass, it was easiest to get rid of. Just scoop it up and flush it away. And the shower door and the windowsill and the sink and the soap dish and the light fixtures and the towel bars were no problem. Lots of paper towels and lots of soap. But where it had lodged in the narrow, uneven crevices of the floor, between the wide old chestnut planks, I had my work cut out for me. The scrub brush seemed only to make things worse, and eventually I took down my toothbrush and, dipping it in and out of the bucket of hot sudsy water, proceeded inch by inch, from wall to wall, one crevice at a time, until the floor was as clean as I could get it. After some fifteen minutes on my knees, I decided that flecks and particles down so deep that I still couldn't reach them we would simply all live with. I removed the curtain from the window, even though it looked to be clean, and shoved it in the pillowcase with all the other soiled things, and then I went into Claire's bathroom and got some eau de cologne, which I sprinkled freely over the swabbed and scoured room, flicking it off my fingertips like holy water. I set up a small summer fan in one corner and got it going, and I went back to Claire's bathroom and washed my arms and my hands and my face. There was a little shit in my hair, so I washed that out, too.

I tiptoed back into the bedroom where he was asleep, still breathing, still living, still with me – yet another setback outlasted by this man whom I had known unendingly as my father. I felt awful about his heroic, hapless struggle to cleanse himself before I had got up to the bathroom and about the shame of it, the disgrace he felt himself to be, and yet now that it was over and he was so deep in sleep, I thought I couldn't have asked anything more for myself before he died – this, too, was right and as it should be. You clean up your father's shit because it has to be cleaned up, but in the aftermath of cleaning it up, everything that's there to feel is felt as it never was before. It wasn't the first time that I'd understood this either: once you sidestep disgust

and ignore nausea and plunge past those phobias that are forti-
fied like taboos, there's an awful lot of life to cherish.

Though maybe once is enough, I added, addressing myself
mentally to the sleeping brain squeezed in by the cartilaginous
tumour; if I have to do this every day, I may not wind up feeling
quite so thrilled.

I carried the stinking pillowcase downstairs and put it into a
black garbage bag which I tied shut, and I carried the bag out
to the car and dumped it in the trunk to take to the laundry.
And *why* this was right and as it should be couldn't have been
plainer to me, now that the job was done. So *that* was the patrimony. And not because cleaning it up was symbolic of something
else but because it wasn't, because it was nothing less or more
than the lived reality that it was.

There was my patrimony: not the money, not the tefillin, not
the shaving mug, but the shit.

⌒

The four commandments

G. I. Gurdjieff, *Meetings with Remarkable Men*, 1963

My father had a very simple, clear, and quite definite view on
the aim of human life. He told me many times in my youth that
the fundamental striving of every man should be to create for
himself an inner freedom toward life and to prepare for himself
a happy old age. He considered that the indispensability and
imperative necessity of this aim in life was so obvious that it
ought to be understandable to everyone without any wiseacring.
But a man could attain this aim only if, from childhood up to
the age of eighteen, he had acquired data for the unwavering
fulfilment of the following four commandments:

First – To love one's parents.
Second – To remain chaste.
Third – To be outwardly courteous to all without distinction,
whether they be rich or poor, friends or enemies, power-possessors
or slaves, and to whatever religion they may belong, but inwardly

to remain free and never to put much trust in anyone or anything.

Fourth – To love work for work's sake and not for its gain.

My father, who loved me particularly as his first-born, had a great influence on me.

My personal relationship to him was not as toward a father, but as toward an elder brother; and he, by his constant conversations with me and his extraordinary stories, greatly assisted the arising in me of poetic images and high ideals.

‿

Aristocratic advice

Lord Chesterfield to his son, 15 July 1751

My dear Friend,

As this is the last, or the last letter but one, that I think I shall write before I have the pleasure of seeing you here, it may not be amiss to prepare you a little for our interview, and for the time we shall pass together. Before kings and princes meet, ministers on each side adjust the important points of precedence, armchairs, right hand and left, etc., so that they know previously what they are to expect, what they have to trust to: and it is right they should; for they commonly envy or hate, but most certainly distrust each other. We shall meet upon very different terms; we want no such preliminaries: you know my tenderness, I know your affection. My only object, therefore, is to make your short stay with me as useful as I can to you; and yours, I hope, is to co-operate with me. Whether, by making it wholesome, I shall make it pleasant to you, I am not sure. Emetics and cathartics I shall not administer, because I am sure you do not want them; but for alteratives you must expect a great many; and I can tell you, that I have a number of *nostrums*, which I shall communicate to nobody but yourself. To speak without a metaphor, I shall endeavour to assist your youth with all the experience that I have purchased at the price of seven and fifty years. In order to this, frequent reproofs, corrections, and admonitions will be necessary; but then, I promise you, that they shall be in a gentle, friendly, and secret manner; they shall not put you out of countenance in company, nor out of humour when we are alone. I do not expect that at nineteen, you should have that knowledge of the world, those manners, that dexterity, which few people have at nine and twenty. But I will endeavour to give them you; and I am sure you will endeavour to learn them, as far as your youth, my experience, and the time we shall pass together, will allow. You may have many inaccuracies (and to be sure you have, for who has not at your age?) which few people will tell you of, and some nobody can tell you of but myself. You may possibly have others, too, which eyes less interested, and less vigilant than mine, do not discover: all those you shall hear of from one whose tenderness for you will excite his curiosity and sharpen his penetration. The smallest inattention, or error in manners, the minutest inelegancy of diction, the least awkwardness in your dress and carriage, will not escape my observation, nor pass without amicable correction . . .

As fathers commonly go, it is seldom a misfortune to be fatherless; and considering the general run of sons, as seldom a misfortune to be childless. You and I form, I believe, an exception to that rule; for I am persuaded that we would neither of us change our relation, were it in our power. You will, I both hope and believe, be not only the comfort, but the pride of my age; and I am sure I will be the support, the friend, the guide of your youth. Trust me without reserve; I will advise you without private interest, or secret envy. Mr Harte will do so too; but still there may be some little things proper for you to know, and necessary for you to correct, which even his friendship would not let him tell you of so freely as I should; and some of which he may possibly not be so good a judge of as I am, not having lived so much in the great world.

One principal topic of our conversation will be, not only the purity but the elegancy of the English language; in both which you are very deficient. Another will be the constitution of this country, of which, I believe, you know less of than of most other countries in Europe. Manners, attentions and address, will also be the frequent subjects of our lectures; and whatever I know of that important and necessary art, the art of pleasing, I will unreservedly communicate to you. Dress too (which, as things are, I can logically prove, requires some attention) will not always escape our notice. Thus, my lectures will be more various, and in some respects more useful, than Professor Mascow's; and therefore, I can tell you, that I expect to be paid for them; but, as possibly you would not care to part with your ready money, and as I do not think that it would be quite handsome in me to accept it, I will compound for the payment, and take it in attention and practice.

Pray remember to part with all your friends, acquaintances, and mistresses, if you have any, at Paris, in such a manner as may make them not only willing but impatient to see you there again. Assure them of your desire of returning to them; and do it in a manner that they may think you in earnest, that is *avec onction et une espèce d'attendrissement* All people say pretty nearly the same things upon those occasions; it is the manner only that makes the difference; and that difference is great.

~

Don't bet on it

Charles Kingsley to one of his sons away at boarding school, *c*. 1860

My dearest Boy,

There is a matter which gave me great uneasiness when you mentioned it. You said you had put into some lottery for the Derby and had hedged to make it safe.

Now all this is bad, bad, nothing but bad. Of all the habits gambling is the one I hate most and have avoided most. Of all habits it grows most on eager minds. Success and loss alike make it grow. Of all habits, however much civilised man may give way to it, it is one of the most intrinsically *savage*. Historically it has been the peace excitement of the lowest brutes in human form for ages past. Morally it is unchivalrous and unchristian.

1. It gains money by the lowest and most unjust means, for it takes money out of your neighbour's pocket without giving him anything in return.
2. It tempts you to use what you fancy your superior knowledge of a horse's merits – or anything else – to your neighbour's harm.

If you know better than your neighbour, you are bound to give him your advice. Instead, you conceal your knowledge to win from his ignorance; hence come all sorts of concealments, dodges, deceits – I say the Devil is the only father of it. I'm sure, moreover, that B. would object seriously to anything like a lottery, betting, or gambling.

I hope you have not won. I should not be sorry for you to lose. If you have won I should not congratulate you. If you wish to please me, you will give back to its lawful owners the money you have won. If you are a loser in gross thereby, I will gladly reimburse your losses this time. As you had put in you could not in honour draw back till after the event. Now you can give back your money, saying you understand that Mr B. and your father disapprove of such things, and so gain a very great moral influence.

Recollect always that the stock argument is worthless. It is this: 'My friend would win from me if he could, *therefore* I have an equal right to win from him.' Nonsense. The same argument would prove that I have a right to maim or kill a man if only I give him leave to maim or kill me if he can and will.

I have spoken my mind once and for all on a matter on which I have held the same views for more than twenty years, and trust in God you will not forget my words in after life. I have seen many a good fellow ruined by finding himself one day short of money, and trying to get a little by playing or betting – and then the Lord have mercy on his simple soul for simple it will not remain long.

Mind, I am not in the least *angry* with you. Betting is the way of the world. So are all the seven deadly sins under certain rules and pretty names, but to the Devil they lead if indulged in, in spite of the wise world and its ways.

> Your loving,
> Pater

~

The Marxist theory of seduction

Letter from Groucho Marx to his son, Summer, 1940

Dear Arthur,

Glad to hear from you and to know that you are recovering. I am also pleased to learn that you have a rich dame who wants to put you up while you are recuperating. How does she have her money? – Is it in jewels or securities, or just plain gold? Some night, when you are grappling with her in the moonlight, you might find out. Do it discreetly, for God's sake. Don't come out bluntly and say, 'How much dough have you got?' That wouldn't be the Marxian way. Use finesse. Well, I will leave the whole thing to you.

Love,
Padre

~

Three little sentences that will get you through life

Advice from the supposedly dying Homer Simpson to son Bart in *The Simpsons*, episode 'One Fish, Two Fish, Blowfish, Blue Fish', 1991

Homer to Bart: '. . . Three little sentences that will get your through life . . . Number 1: (whispers) Cover for me. Number 2: Oh, good idea, Boss! Number 3: It was like that when I got here.'

~

In your dreams

From Sigmund Freud, *The Interpretation of Dreams*, 1913

The fact that dreams of a dead father were the first to furnish us with examples of absurdity in dreams is by no means accidental. The conditions for the creation of absurd dreams are here grouped together in a typical fashion. The authority proper to the father has at an early age evoked the criticism of the child, and the strict demands which he has made have caused the child, in self-defence, to pay particularly close attention to every weakness of his father's; but the piety with which the father's personality is surrounded in our thoughts, especially after his death, intensifies the censorship which prevents the expression of this criticism from becoming conscious.

~

Starlight memory

Samuel Taylor Coleridge, aged eight in 1780

My father was fond of me, & used to take me on his knee, and hold long conversations with me. I remember, that at eight years old I walked with him one winter evening from a farmer's house, a mile from Ottery – & he told me the names of the stars – and how Jupiter was a thousand times larger than our world – and that the other twinkling stars were Suns that had worlds rolling round them – & when I came home, he showed me how they rolled round . . . I heard him with a profound delight & admiration.

⌐⌐

Awakening

From James Dodson, *Final Rounds*, 1997

Eventually, when I calmed down and grew up, golf became much more than a game between my old man and me. It acted as my personal entry hatch to my father's morally advanced cosmos – a means of seeing who this funky, funny, oddball philosopher really *was*, and who I needed to become. I know no other game that would have permitted us the opportunity to compete so thoroughly, so joyfully, for so long. The golf course – any golf course, anywhere – became our playground and refuge, the place where we sorted things out or escaped them altogether, debated without rancor, found common ground, discovered joy, suspended grief, competed like crazy, and took each other's pocket change.

We played the day Neil Armstrong walked on the moon, and the day Martin Luther King was gunned down in Memphis. We played the day before I got married, and the day after my son Jack was born. We played through rain, wind, heat, birth, death. We played on holidays, birthdays, to celebrate nothing and everything, so many rounds in so many places, I couldn't possibly remember them all. We played some of the best courses in America, and some of the worst cow pastures and goat tracks, too. We discovered that in good company there is no such thing as a bad golf course.

We preferred to play late in the day, following our shadows in the last of the light, the fairway ahead of us robed in hues of red and gold and very often deserted. You could see the contours of the earth so well then, feel the coolness of approaching night, perhaps witness a sliver of moon rising over the creek poplars. Our routine almost never varied. My father would leave work early, I would ride my bike to the club, with my bag swaying on my back. After the round, he would put my bike in the trunk of his car. Sometimes we would grab dinner at the Boar and Castle on the way home, sit eating our Castle steaks in the rustling grapevine arbour while eavesdropping on the murmurous voices of teenage lovers in the musky foliage around us, or sit in the glowing foxfire of the Buick's radio, listening to the evening news report. There were race riots going on in Memphis and Miami one summer. A full-blown war was raging in Southeast Asia. Poor people marched on Washington, Bobby Kennedy was shot. A tidal wave of so much news – and yet so *far away* from us. A couple times, we stayed out on the golf course to look at stars. My father knew the constellations. He showed me Venus, the evening star, Aries the ram, how to find the North Star if I was ever lost in the woods. I never got lost in the woods, but I loved those times and never even knew it. It's as if I were sleepwalking and he was inviting me to awaken.

~

A model father

As remembered by George Bernard Shaw, 1856–1950

I cannot remember having ever heard a single sentence uttered by my mother in the nature of moral or religious instruction. My father made an effort or two. When he caught me imitating him by pretending to smoke a toy pipe he advised me very earnestly never to follow his example in any way; and his sincerity so impressed me that to this day I have never smoked, never shaved, and never used alcoholic stimulants. He taught me to regard him as an unsuccessful man with many undesirable habits, as a warning and not as a model. In fact, he did himself some injustice lest I should grow up like him; and I now see that this anxiety on his part was admirable and lovable; and that he was really just what he so carefully strove not to be: that is, a model father.

~

Smile

From Angela Carter, 'Sugar Daddy', 1983

Himself, he is a rich source of anecdote. He has partitioned off a little room in the attic of his house, constructed the walls out of cardboard boxes, and there he lies, on a camp-bed, listening to the World Service on a portable radio with his cap on. When he lived in London, he used to wear a trilby to bed but, a formal man, he exchanged it for a cap as soon as he moved. There are two perfectly good bedrooms in his house, with electric blankets and everything, as I well know, but these bedrooms always used to belong to his siblings, now deceased. He moves downstairs into one of these when the temperature in the attic drops too low for even his iron constitution, but he always shifts back up again, to his own place, when the ice melts. He has a ferocious enthusiasm for his own private space. My mother attributed this to a youth spent in the trenches, where no privacy was to be had. His war was the War to end Wars. He was too old for conscription in the one after that.

When he leaves this house for any length of time, he fixes up a whole lot of burglar traps, basins of water balanced on the tops of doors, tripwires, bags of flour suspended by strings, so that we worry in case he forgets where he's left what and ends up hoist with his own petard.

He has a special relationship with cats. He talks to them in a soft chirruping language they find irresistible. When we all lived in London and he worked on the night news desk of a press agency, he would come home on the last tube and walk, chirruping, down the street, accompanied by an ever-increasing procession of cats, to whom he would say good night at the front door. On those rare occasions, in my late teens, when I'd managed to persuade a man to walk me home, the arrival of my father and his cats always caused consternation, not least because my father was immensely tall and strong.

He is the stuff of which sitcoms are made.

His everyday discourse, which is conducted in the stately prose of a thirties *Times* leader, is enlivened with a number of stock phrases of a slightly eccentric, period quality. For example. On a wild night: 'Pity the troops on a night like this.' On a cold day:

> *Cold, bleak, gloomy and glum,*
> *Cold as the hairs on a polar bear's—*

The last word of the couplet is supposed to be drowned by the cries of outrage. My mother always turned up trumps on this one, interposing: 'Father!' on an ascending scale.

At random: 'Thank God for the Navy, who guard our shores.' On entering a room: 'Enter the fairy, singing and dancing.' Sometimes, in a particularly cheerful mood, he'll add to this formula: 'Enter the fairy, singing and dancing and waving her wooden leg.'

Infinitely endearing, infinitely irritating, irascible, comic, tough, sentimental, ribald old man, with his face of a borderline eagle and his bearing of a Scots Guard, who, in my imagination as when I was a child, drips chocolates from his pockets as, a cat dancing in front of him, he strides down the road bowed down with gifts, crying: 'Here comes the Marquess of Carrabas!' The very words, 'my father', always make me smile.

✑

Daddytrack

From Robert L. Griswold,
Fatherhood in America, 1993

A variety of other surveys introduced as evidence supported [James A.] Levine's findings. Forty-eight per cent of fathers in metropolitan Washington, DC, for example, claimed they reduced their working hours to spend more time with their children, and 23 per cent reported they had passed up a promotion for the same reason. In a 1990 poll by the *Los Angeles*

Times, 39 per cent of the fathers said they would quit their jobs if they could in order to spend more time with their children, and 28 per cent felt their parental obligations hurt their careers. *Time* magazine reported that 48 per cent of men between the ages of eighteen and twenty-four expressed an interest in staying home with their children. Another survey found that '74 per cent of men said they would rather have a "daddy track" job than a "fast track" job', and a *Washington Post*/ABC News poll found that 43 per cent of the fathers had actually cut back on their working hours to be with their children. *Fortune* magazine reported similar results, including the startling finding that more fathers than mothers thought companies should do more to help parents work out career and family responsibilities. Perhaps Peter Lynch, one of the most successful mutual fund managers in the country, can speak for millions of American men in describing why he left his position to spend more time with his family: 'Children are a great investment. They beat the hell out of stocks.'

Nothing good gets away

Letter from John Steinbeck to his son, aged fourteen

10 November 1958

Dear Thom,

We had your letter this morning. I will answer it from my point of view and of course Elaine will from hers.

First – if you are in love – that's a good thing – that's about the best thing that can happen to anyone. Don't let anyone make it small or light to you.

Second – There are several kinds of love. One is a selfish, mean, grasping, egotistical thing which uses love for self-importance. This is the ugly and crippling kind. The other is an outpouring of everything good in you – of kindness, and consideration and respect – not only the social respect of manners but the greater respect which is recognition of another person as unique and valuable. The first kind can make you sick and small and weak but the second can release in you strength, and courage and goodness and even wisdom you didn't know you had.

You say this is not puppy love. If you feel so deeply – of course it isn't puppy love.

But I don't think you were asking me what you feel. You know that better than anyone. What you wanted me to help you with is what to do about it – and that I can tell you.

Glory in it for one thing and be very glad and grateful for it.

The object of love is the best and most beautiful. Try to live up to it.

If you love someone – there is no possible harm in saying so – only you must remember that some people are very shy and sometimes the saying must take that shyness into consideration.

Girls have a way of knowing or feeling what you feel, but they usually like to hear it also.

It sometimes happens that what you feel is not returned for one reason or another – but that does not make your feeling less valuable and good.

Lastly, I know your feeling because I have it and I am glad you have it.

We will be glad to meet Susan. She will be very welcome. But Elaine will make all such arrangements because that is her province and she will be very glad to. She knows about love too and maybe she can give you more help than I can.

And don't worry about losing. If it is right, it happens – The main thing is not to hurry. Nothing good gets away.

Love

Fa

In heaven, as it is on earth

From the diary of Reverend Ralph Josselin

13 [July 1661]: My son Thomas came down from London to see us, so I saw my six children togither on earth, blessed bee god, and lett us all bee togither in heaven

A son departs

Extracted from *The Vicar of Wakefield*,
Oliver Goldsmith, 1776

As my eldest son was bred a scholar, I determined to send him to town, where his abilities might contribute to our support and his own. The separation of friends and families is, perhaps, one of the most distressful circumstances attendant on penury. The day soon arrived on which we were to disperse for the first time. My son, after taking leave of his mother and the rest, who mingled their tears with their kisses, came to ask a blessing from me. This I gave him from my heart, and which, added to five guineas, was all the patrimony I had now to bestow. 'You are going, my boy,' cried I, 'to London on foot, in the manner Hooker, your great ancestor, travelled there before you. Take from me the same horse that was given him by the good bishop Jewel, this staff, and take this book too, it will be your comfort on the way: these two lines in it are worth a million, *I have been young, and now am old; yet never saw I the righteous man forsaken, or his seed begging their bread*. Let this be your consolation as you travel on. Go, my boy, whatever be thy fortune, let me see thee once a-year; still keep a good heart, and farewell.' As he was possessed of integrity and honour, I was under no apprehensions from throwing him naked into the amphitheatre of life; for I knew he would act a good part whether vanquished or victorious.

∽

The crown and the glory

Proverbs, 17: 6

Children's children are the crown of old men;
And the glory of children are their fathers.

∽

Love Anyhow

F. Scott Fitzgerald's epistolic advice to his daughter

8 August 1933

Dear Pie,

I feel very strongly about you doing [your] duty. Would you give me a little more documentation about your reading in French? I am glad you are happy – but I never believe much in happiness. I never believe in misery either. Those are things you see on the stage or the screen or the printed page, they never really happen to you in life.

All I believe in in life is the rewards for virtue (according to your talents) and the *punishments* for not fulfilling your duties, which are doubly costly. If there is such a volume in the camp library, will you ask Mrs Tyson to let you look up a sonnet of Shakespeare's in which the line occurs *'lilies that fester smell far worse than weeds.'*

Have had no thoughts today, life seems composed of getting up a *Saturday Evening Post* story. I think of you, and always pleasantly; but if you call me 'Pappy' again I am going to take the White Cat out and beat his bottom *hard, six times for every time you are impertinent*. Do you react to that?

I will arrange the camp bill.

Halfwit, I will conclude.

Things to worry about:
    Worry about courage
    Worry about cleanliness
    Worry about efficiency
    Worry about horsemanship
    Worry about . . .
Things not to worry about:
    Don't worry about popular opinion
    Don't worry about dolls
    Don't worry about the past
    Don't worry about the future
    Don't worry about growing up
    Don't worry about anybody getting ahead of you
    Don't worry about triumph

Don't worry about failure unless it comes through your own fault
Don't worry about mosquitoes
Don't worry about flies
Don't worry about insects in general
Don't worry about parents
Don't worry about boys
Don't worry about disappointments
Don't worry about pleasures
Don't worry about satisfactions
Things to think about:
What am I really aiming at?
How good am I really in comparison to my contemporaries in regard to:
(a) Scholarship
(b) Do I really understand about people and am I able to get along with them?
(c) Am I trying to make my body a useful instrument or am I neglecting it?

With dearest love,
[Daddy]

P. S. My come-back to your calling me Pappy is christening you by the word Egg, which implies that you belong to a very rudimentary state of life and that I could break you up and crack you open at my will and I think it would be a word that would hang on if I ever told it to your contemporaries. 'Egg Fitzgerald'. How would you like that to go through life with – 'Eggie Fitzgerald' or 'Bad Egg Fitzgerald' or any form that might occur to fertile minds? Try it once more and I swear to God I will hang it on you and it will be up to you to shake it off. Why borrow trouble?

Love anyhow.

Acknowledgements

My greatest thanks are due to my wife, Penny, and children, Tristram and Freda, for simply being there.

The editor has made every effort to locate all persons having any rights in the selections appearing in this anthology and to secure permission from the holders of such rights. Queries regarding the use of material should be addressed to the editor c/o the publishers. If any errors have inadvertently been made, corrections will, of course, be made in future additions.

Beauvoir, Simone de
Extract from *The Second Sex* (*Le Deuxième Sex*), translation copyright © 1953 Jonathan Cape. Reprinted by permission of The Random House Group Ltd.

Berlin, Irving
'Mary Be Good' from *Daddy Come Home* by Irving Berlin, copyright © Irving Berlin 1913.

Blankenhorn, David
Extracts from *Fatherless America* by David Blankenhorn, copyright © Institute for American Values 1995. Reprinted by permission of Perseus Books Group.

Bly, Robert
Extract from *The Sibling Society* by Robert Bly, copyright © Robert Bly 1996. Reprinted by permission of Penguin UK (Hamish Hamilton).
    Extract from *Iron John* by Robert Bly, copyright © Robert Bly 1993. Reprinted by permission of Sheil Land Associates.

Booth, Philip
'First Lesson' from *Relations*, copyright © Philip Booth 1957. Reprinted by permission of Penguin Books USA Inc.

Bradshaw, Jonathan, Stimson, Carol, Skinner, Christine, and Williams, Julie
Extract from *Absent Fathers* by Jonathan Bradshaw, Carol Stimson, Christine Skinner, and Julie Williams, copyright © the authors 1999. Reprinted by permission of ITPS on behalf of Routledge.

Burgess, Adrienne
Extract from *Fatherhood Reclaimed* by Adrienne Burgess, copyright © Adrienne Burgess 1997. Reprinted by permission of The Random House Group Ltd.

Camus, Albert
Extract from *The First Man* by Albert Camus, translation copyright © David Hapgood 1994. Reprinted by permission of Penguin UK.

Carey, Peter
Extract from 'Letter to Our Son' by Peter Carey, from *The Granta Book of the Family*, copyright © Peter Carey 1995.

Carter, Angela
Selections from 'Sugar Daddy' by Angela Carter, copyright © Angela Carter 1983. First published in *Fathers*, 1983. Reprinted by permission of Rogers, Coleridge and White.

Carver, Raymond
'On an old photograph of my son' from *All of Us: The Collected Poems* by Raymond Carver. First published in Great Britain in 1996 by Harvill. Copyright © Tess Gallagher 1996. Reprinted by permission of The Harvill Press.

Cash, Johnny
'A Boy Named Sue'. Lyrics by Shel Silverstein, copyright © TRO Essex Music Ltd.

Cellini, Benvenuto
Extract from *The Autobiography of Benvenuto Cellini*, translation copyright © George Bull 1956. Reprinted by permission of Penguin UK.

Chapin, Harry and Sandra
'The Cat's in the Cradle' by Harry and Sandra Chapin, copyright © Story Songs 1974. Reprinted by permission of Warner Bros Publications Inc and International Music Publications (London).

Citino, David
'The Father and the Son' from *The House of Memory* by David Citino, copyright © the author 1990. Reprinted by permission of Ohio University Press and the author.

Coleridge, Samuel Taylor
Extract from *The Collected Letters of Samuel Taylor Coleridge*, 6 vols, edited by E. L. Griggs (Oxford, 1965–71), copyright © Oxford University Press 1965. Reprinted by permission of Oxford University Press.

Durcan, copyright © the author 1990. Reprinted by permission of The Blackstaff Press.

Dylan, Bob
'Forever Young', copyright © Ram's Horn Music 1973. First performed on the album *Planet Waves*, 1974.

Elman, Richard M.
Selection from *Fredi, Shirl & the Kids: The Autobiography in Fable of Richard M. Elman*, copyright © Richard M. Elman 1972.

Esquire magazine
'Things a Man Should Know About Fatherhood', copyright © *Esquire* (USA) 1999.

Faulkner, William
Extract from *Absalom, Absalom!* by William Faulkner, copyright © William Faulkner 1936. Reprinted by permission of The Random House Group Ltd.

Feinstein, Elaine
'Dad' by Elaine Feinstein, copyright © Elaine Feinstein 1977. Reprinted by permission of Rogers, Coleridge and White.

Fitzgerald, F. Scott
Selection from *The Letters of F. Scott Fitzgerald*, edited by Andrew Turnbull. Copyright © Frances Scott Lanahan 1962. Reprinted by permission of Harold Ober Associates.

Fowles, John
'In Chalkwell Park' by John Fowles, from *Fathers and Sons*, edited by J. Hoyland 1992, copyright © John Fowles 1992. Reprinted by permission of Sheil Land Associates.

Freud, Sigmund
Extract from *The Letters of Sigmund Freud*, Hogarth Press, edited by Ernest L. Freud. Copyright © The Estate of Sigmund Freud 1961. Reprinted by permission of Random House Archive and Library.
  Extract from *The Interpretation of Dreams* copyright ©

Sigmund Freud 1913. Reprinted by permission of ITPS on behalf of Routledge.

Geoffrey of Monmouth
'The Grief of Lear', quoted in *Anthology of English Prose*, 1914.

Gilmore, Mikal
Extract from *Shot in the Heart: One Family's History of Murder* by Mikal Gilmore, copyright © Mikal Gilmore 1994. Reprinted by permission of Penguin UK.

Graham, Harry
'Thoughtlessness' by Harry Graham, from *When Grandma Fell off the Boat*, copyright © V. Thesiger 1986. 'The Stern Parent' from *Ruthless Rhymes*, 1899.

Green, Maureen
Extract from *Goodbye Father* by Maureen Green, copyright © Maureen Green 1976. Reprinted by permission of ITPS Ltd on behalf of Routledge.

Griswold, Robert L.
Extracts from *Fatherhood in America* by Robert L. Griswold, copyright © Basic Books 1993. Reprinted by permission of the publisher.

Gurdjieff, G. I.
Extract from *Meetings with Remarkable Men* by G. I. Gurdjieff, copyright © Editions Janus 1963.

Hall, Donald
'My Son, My Executioner' from *One Day: Poems 1947–1990* by Donald Hall, Carcanet Press, copyright © Donald Hall 1988. Reprinted by permission of the publisher.

Harper, Sam
'Dad's Department' by Sam Harper, copyright © Sam Harper 1999. Reprinted by permission of the author.

Harrison, Fraser
Extracts from *A Father's Diary* by Fraser Harrison, copyright ©
Fraser Harrison 1985. Reprinted by permission of the author.

Hearn, Lafcadio
Extract from *The Life and Letters of Lafcadio Hearn*, copyright
© L. Hearn 1909. Reprinted by permission of Constable &
Robinson.

Hemingway, Ernest
'Advice to a Son' by Ernest Hemingway, copyright © the Ernest
Hemingway Foundation and Nicholas Georgiannis 1979.
Reprinted by permission of Harcourt Inc.

Hewlett, Barry
Extract from *Intimate Fathers* by Barry Hewlett, copyright ©
Barry Hewlett 1991. Reprinted by permission of the University
of Michigan Press.

Hogan, Phil
'The Children Are Revolting' by Phil Hogan, *The Observer*, 18
June 2000. Reprinted by permission of Guardian Newspapers
Ltd.

Horn, Dr Wade F.
Selections from *The Washington Times* by Dr Wade F. Horn,
copyright © Wade F. Horn 1999. Reprinted by permission of
Wade F. Horn, PhD, and *The Washington Times*.

Jennings, Charles
Extracts from *Father's Race* by Charles Jennings, copyright ©
Charles Jennings 1999. Reprinted by permission of Little, Brown
& Company (UK) and the author's agent, Sara Menguc.

Jones, Evan
'Generations' by Evan Jones, from *Two Centuries of Australian
Poetry*, edited by Mark O'Connor. Copyright © Evan Jones
1988.

Levine, James A., and Pittinsky, Todd L.
Extract from *Working Fathers: New Strategies for Balancing Work and Family* by James A. Levine and Todd L. Pittinsky, copyright © James A. Levine and Todd L. Pittinsky 1997.

Lewis, Cecil Day
'Walking Away' by Cecil Day Lewis, copyright © the estate of © Cecil Day Lewis 1992. Reprinted by permission of the Random House Archive and Library.

Lorenz, Konrad
Selection from *King Solomon's Ring* by Konrad Lorenz, translation copyright © Majorie Kerr Wilson and Methuen Ltd 1952.

McClain, Buzz
'Don't Call Me Mr Mom! Or, what not to say to a Stay-at-home Dad', by Buzz McClain, *slowlane.com* web page. Copyright © 2000 the author. Reprinted by permission of the author.

McCourt, Frank
Extract from *Angela's Ashes* by Frank McCourt, copyright © Frank McCourt 1996. Reprinted by permission of HarperCollins Publishers.

Marx, Groucho
Extract from *The Groucho Letters* by Groucho Marx, copyright © Groucho Marx 1967. Reprinted by permission of Penguin UK (Michael Joseph).

Mead, Margaret
Extract from *Male and Female* by Margaret Mead, copyright © Margaret Mead 1949. Reprinted by permission of The Orion Publishing Group (Victor Gollancz).

Meinke, Peter
'This is a poem to my son Peter' from *Liquid Paper* by Peter Meinke, University of Pittsburg Press, copyright © Peter Meinke 1991. Reprinted by permission of the publisher.

Miller, Henry
Extract from *My Life and Times* by Henry Miller, copyright © Henry Miller and Gemini Smith Inc 1971.

Mitchell, Adrian
'Beattie is Three' by Adrian Mitchell, copyright © Adrian Mitchell. First published in *Heart on the Left: Poems 1953–84* by Bloodaxe Books Limited. Reprinted by permission of PFD on behalf of Adrian Mitchell.

Mitchison, Naomi
Extract from *Small Talk: Memories of an Edwardian Childhood* by Naomi Mitchison, copyright © Naomi Mitchison 1973. Reprinted by permission of The Random House Group Ltd.

Morrison, Blake
Extracts from *And When Did You Last See Your Father?* by Blake Morrison, copyright © Blake Morrison 1985. Reprinted by permission of Penguin Books (Granta).

Mortimer, John
Extract from *Clinging to the Wreckage* by John Mortimer, copyright © John Mortimer 1982. Reproduced by permission of The Orion Publishing Group (Weidenfeld & Nicolson).

Murray, Les
'Fatherhood, from the German' from *Collected Poems* by Les Murray, copyright © the author 1991. Reprinted by permission of Carcanet Press Ltd.

Nabokov, Vladimir
Extract from *Speak, Memory: An Autobiography Revisited* by Vladimir Nabokov, copyright © Vladimir Nabokov 1964. Reprinted by permission of The Orion Publishing Group (Weidenfeld & Nicolson).

Narayan, R. K.
Extract from 'Forty-Five a Month', from *Malgudi Days* by R. K. Narayan, copyright © the author 1947, 1972. Reprinted by permission of the Wallace Literary Agency, Inc.

Nash, Ogden
Extract from *Candy is Dandy*, 1989. Copyright © 1989 The estate of Ogden Nash. Reprinted by permission of Curtis Brown USA.

Newson, John and Elizabeth
Extract from *Patterns of Infant Care in an Urban Community* by John and Elizabeth Newson, copyright © J. and E. Newson 1965. Reprinted by permission of ITPS on behalf of Routledge.

Nin, Anaïs
Extract from *The Journals of Anaïs Nin*, edited by Gunther Stuhlmann, copyright © Anaïs Nin 1966.

O'Hara, Frank
'To My Dead Father' by Frank O'Hara, copyright © Maureen Granville-Smith 1971. Reprinted by permission of Alfred A. Knopf, a division of Random House, Inc.

O'Neill, Hugh
Extract from *A Man Called Daddy* by Hugh O'Neill, copyright © Hugh O'Neill 1996. Reprinted by permission of the Rutledge Hill Press.

Parsons, Tony
Extracts from *Man and Boy* by Tony Parsons, copyright © Tony Parsons 1999. Reprinted by permission of HarperCollins Publishers.

Plath, Sylvia
'Daddy' from *Collected Poems* by Sylvia Plath, 1986, copyright © the estate of Ted Hughes 1960. Reprinted by permission of Faber & Faber.

Plutarch
Extract from *Vitae Parallae*, translated by Bernadotte Perrin 1914–26.

Po Chu-i
'Rising late and playing with A-ts'ui' from *170 Chinese Poems*,

right © Bertrand Russell 1929. Reprinted by permission of ITPS on behalf of Routledge.

Sandburg, Carl
Extract from *Always the Young Strangers* by Carl Sandburg, copyright © Carl Sandburg 1952. Reprinted by permission of Harcourt Inc.

Saroyan, Aram
Quoted in Jon Winokur, *Fathers*, Dutton Books 1993.

Saroyan, William
Extract from *Here Comes, There Goes, You Know Who* by William Saroyan, copyright © William Saroyan 1961. Reprinted by permission of Pocket Books, a division of Simon & Schuster.

Sartre, Jean-Paul
Extract from *The Words* by Jean-Paul Sartre, translation copyright © George Braziller Inc 1964.

Scannell, Vernon
'Growing Pain' and 'Nettles' from *Collected Poems 1950–1993* by Vernon Scannell, copyright © Vernon Scannell 1993. Reprinted by permission of Robson.
    'Poem for Jane' from *Selected Poems*, copyright © Vernon Scannell 1971. Reprinted by kind permission of Allison & Busby, London.
    Extract from *The Tiger and the Rose*, copyright © Vernon Scannell 1971. Reprinted by permission of the author.

Schulberg, Budd
Extract from 'A Short Digest of a Long Novel' by Budd Schulberg, first published in *Some Faces in the Crowd* by Budd Schulberg, copyright © the author 1953.

The Simpsons
Extract from script of *The Simpsons*, copyright © 20th Century-Fox Television 1991.

Trumbo, Dalton
Extract from *Additional Dialogue: Letters of Dalton Trumbo, 1942–1962*, copyright © Dalton Trumbo 1970.

Turner, Janine
Extract from *Behind Closed Doors* by Janine Turner, copyright © Janine Turner 1988.

Waugh, Auberon
Extracts from *Will This Do?* by Auberon Waugh, copyright © Auberon Waugh 1991. Reprinted by permission of Peters, Fraser & Dunlop.

Wells, H. G.
Extract from *Ann Veronica* by H. G. Wells, copyright © H. G. Wells 1909. Reprinted by permission of The Orion Publishing Group.

Williams, Hugo
Extract from 'What Shall We Do Now That We Have Done Everything?' by Hugo Williams, copyright © Hugo Williams 1992. First published in *Fatherhood*, edited by Sean French, Virago 1992. Reprinted by permission of the author.

Williams, William Carlos
Extracts from *The Selected Letters of William Carlos Williams*, edited by John Thirlwell, copyright © William Carlos Williams 1957.

Yeats, W. B.
'A Prayer for My Daughter' from *Collected Poems*, copyright © Macmillan Publishing Company 1924. Renewed 1952 B. G. Yeats. Reprinted by permission of A. P. Watt Ltd.

Julia QUINN

Because of Miss Bridgerton

PIATKUS

PIATKUS

First published in the US in 2016 by Avon Books,
An imprint of HarperCollins, New York
First published in Great Britain in 2016 by Piatkus
by arrangement with Avon Books
This paperback edition published in 2021 by Piatkus

1 3 5 7 9 10 8 6 4 2

A CIP catalogue record for this book
is available from the British Library.

ISBN 978-0-349-43013-3

Printed and bound in Great Britain by
Clays Ltd, Elcograf S.p.A.

Papers used by Piatkus are from well-managed forests
and other responsible sources.

Piatkus
An imprint of
Little, Brown Book Group
Carmelite House
50 Victoria Embankment
London EC4Y 0DZ

An Hachette UK Company
www.hachette.co.uk

www.littlebrown.co.uk

For Susan Cotter.
You amaze me every day.

And also for Paul.
A well-timed phone call is
the mark of an excellent husband.
May you touch the sky this time.

Top 10 Reasons to Read This Book

10. Because Julia Quinn has finally brought back historical romance's most beloved family.

9. Because where else are you going to get such a racy archery reference?

8. Because ROMANCE.

7. Because you totally want to see a one-armed man build a house of cards.

6. Because in the battle between hero, heroine, and cat, the cat wins.

5. Because WITTY REPARTEE.

4. Because you agree that croquet ought to be a blood sport.

3. Because George Rokesby is so hot he ought to star in his own BBC miniseries.

2. Because THAT KISS.

1. Because of Miss Bridgerton.

Chapter 1

---━━➤✴◀━---

The roof of an abandoned farmhouse
Midway between Aubrey Hall and Crake House
Kent, England
1779

It wasn't that Billie Bridgerton was lacking in common sense. On the contrary, she was quite sure that she was one of the most sensible people of her acquaintance. But like any thoughtful individual, she occasionally chose to ignore the little voice of reason that whispered through her mind. This could not, she was certain, be considered recklessness. When she ignored this cautionary voice, it was a conscious decision, made after a (somewhat) careful analysis of her situation. And to her credit, when Billie made a decision—one that most of humanity would deem beyond foolish—she usually landed quite sprightly on her feet.

Except when she didn't.

Like right now.

She glared down at her companion. "I ought to throttle you."

Her companion let out a rather unconcerned meow.

Billie let out a rather unladylike growl.

The cat assessed the noise, judged it to be beneath its notice, and began to lick its paws.

Billie considered the twin standards of dignity and decorum, decided they were both overrated, and returned volley with an immature scowl.

It didn't make her feel any better.

With a weary groan, she looked up at the sky, trying to gauge the time. The sun was wedged quite firmly behind a layer of clouds, which complicated her task, but it had to be at least four o'clock. She reckoned she'd been stuck here for an hour, and she'd left the village at two. If she factored in the time it took to walk . . .

Oh bloody hell, what did it matter what the time was? It wasn't going to get her off this damned roof.

"This is all your fault," she said to the cat.

Predictably, the cat ignored her.

"I don't know what you think you were doing up in that tree," she continued. "Any fool would have known you couldn't have got down."

Any fool would have left it up there, but no, Billie had heard the mewling, and she'd been halfway up the tree before it occurred to her that she didn't even *like* cats.

"And I *really* don't like you," she said.

She was talking to a cat. *This* was what she'd been reduced to. She shifted her position, wincing as her stocking caught on one of the weatherworn roof shingles. The snag jerked her foot sideways, and her already throbbing ankle howled in protest.

Or rather her mouth howled. She couldn't help it. It *hurt.*

She supposed it could have been worse. She'd been well up in the tree, easily a good eight feet above the roof of the farmhouse, when the cat had hissed at her, flung out a well-clawed paw, and sent them both tumbling.

The cat, needless to say, had made its descent with acrobatic grace, landing without injury, four paws on the roof.

Billie still wasn't sure how *she'd* landed, just that her elbow hurt, her hip stung, and her jacket was torn, likely from the branch that had broken her fall two-thirds of the way down.

But the worst was her ankle and foot, which were killing her. If she were home, she'd prop it up on pillows. She'd witnessed more than her fair share of twisted ankles—some on her own body, even more on others—and she knew what to do. Cold compress, elevation, a sibling forced to wait on her hand and foot . . .

Where were her minions when she needed them?

But then, off in the distance she saw a flash of movement, and unless the local beasts had recently made the move to bipedalism, it was quite clearly human.

"Hellooooooooo!" she called out, then thought the better of it and yelled, "Help!"

Unless Billie's eyesight was deceiving her—and it

wasn't, it really wasn't; even her best friend Mary Rokesby admitted that Billie Bridgerton's eyes wouldn't dare to be anything but perfect—the human in the distance was male. And there wasn't a male of her acquaintance who could ignore a feminine cry for help.

"Help!" she yelled again, feeling no small bit of relief when the man paused. She couldn't quite tell if he'd turned in her direction—perfect eyesight only went so far—so she let out another holler, this one quite as loud as she could make it, and nearly sobbed in relief when the gentleman—oh, *please* let him be a gentleman, if not by birth, then at least by nature— began to move in her direction.

Except she didn't sob. Because she never sobbed. She would never have been that sort of a female.

She did, however, take an unexpected breath—a surprisingly loud and high-pitched unexpected breath.

"Over here!" she called out, shrugging off her jacket so that she could wave it in the air. There was no point in trying to appear dignified. She was, after all, stuck on a roof with a twisted ankle and a mangy cat.

"Sir!" she all but hollered. "Help! Please!"

The gentleman's gait adjusted ever-so-slightly at the noise, and he looked up, and even though he was still too far away for Billie's perfect eyes to see his face, she *knew*.

No. No. *No*. Anyone but him.

But of course it was him. Because who else would stroll by at her lowest moment, at her most awkward and embarrassing, at the one bloody time *she* needed rescuing?

"Good afternoon, George," she said, once he'd drawn close enough to hear.

He put his hands on his hips and squinted up at her. "Billie Bridgerton," he said. She waited for him to add, "I might have known."

He didn't, and somehow that made her even more irritated. The world was not in balance when she couldn't predict every inflated, pompous word that rolled out of George Rokesby's mouth.

"Getting a bit of sun?" he inquired.

"Yes, I rather thought I could use a few more freckles," she snapped.

He did not immediately respond. Instead he removed his tricorn hat, revealing an unpowdered head of thick, tawny brown hair, and regarded her with a steady, assessing gaze. Finally, after carefully setting his chapeau down on what had once been a stone wall, he looked back up and said, "I cannot say that I'm not enjoying this. Just a little bit."

Any number of retorts danced on Billie's tongue, but she reminded herself that George Rokesby was the only human being in sight, and if she wished to touch her feet to the ground before May Day she was going to have to be nice to him.

Until he rescued her, at least.

"How'd you come to be up there, anyway?" he asked.

"Cat." Said in a voice that might charitably have been described as *seething*.

"Ah."

"It was in the tree," she explained, although heaven knew why. It wasn't as if he'd requested further explanation.

"I see."

Did he? She rather thought he didn't.

"It was crying," she ground out. "I couldn't very well ignore it."

"No, I'm sure you couldn't," he said, and even though his voice was perfectly cordial, she was convinced he was laughing at her.

"Some of us," she pried her teeth apart long enough to say, "are compassionate, considerate individuals."

He cocked his head. "Kind to small children and animals?"

"Quite."

His right brow arched in that monstrously aggravating Rokesby manner. "Some of us," he drawled, "are kind to *large* children and animals."

She bit her tongue. First figuratively, and then literally. *Be nice*, she reminded herself. *Even if it kills you* . . .

He smiled blandly. Well, except for that little smirk at the corner.

"Are you bloody well going to help me down?" she finally burst out.

"Such language," he scolded.

"Learned from *your* brothers."

"Oh, I know," he said. "Never could quite convince them you were actually a girl."

Billie sat on her hands. She actually *sat* on her

hands, she was so sure she would not be able to resist the urge to throw herself off the roof in an attempt to strangle him.

"Never could quite convince my*self* you were actually human," George added, rather offhandedly.

Billie's fingers hardened into claws. Which was *really* uncomfortable, all things considered. "*George,*" she said, and she heard a thousand different things in her tone—pleading, pain, resignation, remembrance. They had a history, they two, and no matter their differences, he was a Rokesby and she was a Bridgerton, and when push came to shove, they might as well be family.

Their homes—Crake House for the Rokesbys and Aubrey Hall for the Bridgertons—lay a mere three miles apart in this cozy green corner of Kent. The Bridgertons had been there longer—they had arrived in the early 1500s, when James Bridgerton had been made a viscount and granted land by Henry VIII—but the Rokesbys had outranked them since 1672.

A particularly enterprising Baron Rokesby (so the story went) had performed an essential service to Charles II and been named the first Earl of Manston in gratitude. The details surrounding this elevation of rank had become murky over time, but it was generally accepted that it had involved a stagecoach, a bolt of Turkish silk, and two royal mistresses.

Billie could well believe it. Charm was inherited, was it not? George Rokesby might be precisely the sort of stick-in-the-mud one would expect of the heir to an earldom, but his younger brother Andrew possessed the sort of devilish *joie de vivre* that would have endeared him to a notorious philanderer like Charles II. The other Rokesby brothers were not quite so roguish (although she supposed that Nicholas, at only fourteen, was still honing his skills), but they easily outstripped George in all contests involving charm and amiability.

George. They'd never liked each other. But Billie supposed she could not complain. George *was* the only available Rokesby at the moment. Edward was off in the colonies, wielding a sword or a pistol, or heaven only knew what, and Nicholas was at Eton, probably also wielding a sword or a pistol (although hopefully to considerably less effect). Andrew was here in Kent for the next few weeks, but he'd fractured his arm doing some such derring-do in the navy. He could hardly have been helpful.

No, it would have to be George, and she was going to have to be civil.

She smiled down at him. Well, she stretched her lips.

He sighed. Just a little. "I'll see if there's a ladder around back."

"Thank you," she said primly, but she didn't think he heard her. He'd always had a fast, long-legged stride, and he'd disappeared around the corner before she could be properly polite.

A minute or so later he came back into view, his arm slung over a ladder that looked like it had last seen use during the Glorious Revolution. "What actually happened?" he called up, setting it into place. "It's not like you to get stuck."

It was as close to a compliment as she'd ever heard from his lips. "The cat was not as grateful for my assistance as one might have expected," she said, every consonant a haughty ice pick directed at the monstrous little feline.

The ladder *thunked* into position, and Billie heard George climbing up.

"Is that going to hold?" she asked. The wood looked somewhat splintered and was emitting ominous creaking noises with every step.

The creaks paused for a moment. "It doesn't really matter if it holds or not, does it?"

Billie swallowed. Another person might not be able to translate his words, but she'd known this man since the dawn of her memory, and if there was one fundamental truth to George Rokesby, it was that he was a gentleman. And he would never leave a lady in distress, no matter how fragile a ladder's appearance.

She was in trouble, ergo he had no choice. He had to help, no matter how aggravating he found her.

And he did. Oh, she knew he did. He had never made any effort to disguise it. Although to be fair, neither had she.

His head popped into view, and his Rokesby-blue eyes narrowed. All the Rokesbys had blue eyes. Every last one of them.

"You're wearing breeches," George said with a heavy sigh. "Of course you're wearing breeches."

"I would hardly have attempted the tree in a dress."

"No," he said dryly, "you're much too sensible for that."

Billie decided to let this one pass. "It scratched me," she said, jerking her head toward the cat.

"Did it?"

"We fell."

George looked up. "That's quite a distance."

Billie followed his gaze. The nearest branch was five feet up, and she had not been on the nearest branch. "I hurt my ankle," she admitted.

"I reckoned as much."

She looked over at him in question.

"You would have just jumped to the ground, otherwise."

Her mouth twisted as she peered past him to the packed dirt that surrounded the ruins of the farmhouse. At one point the building must have belonged to a prosperous farmer because it was two full stories high. "No," she said, assessing the distance. "It's too far for that."

"Even for you?"

"I'm not an idiot, George."

He did not agree with her nearly as fast as he should have done. Which was to say, not at all.

"Very well," was what he *did* say. "Let's get you down."

She breathed in. Then out. Then said, "Thank you."

He looked over at her with a strange expression. Disbelief, maybe, that she'd uttered the words *thank* and *you* in the same sentence?

"It's going to be dark soon," she said, her nose

crinkling as she looked up at the sky. "It would have been awful to have been stuck—" She cleared her throat. "Thank you."

He acknowledged this with the briefest of nods. "Can you manage the ladder?"

"I think so." It would hurt dreadfully, but she could do it. "Yes."

"I could carry you."

"On the ladder?"

"On my back."

"I'm *not* getting on your back."

"It's not where I'd want you," he muttered.

She looked up sharply.

"Right, well," he continued, climbing another two rungs up. The edge of the roof was now even with his hips. "Can you stand?"

She stared at him dumbly.

"I would like to see how much weight you can put on that ankle," he explained.

"Oh," she mumbled. "Of course."

She probably shouldn't have attempted it. The slant of the roof was such that she'd need both her feet for balance, and her right was near to useless by this point. But she tried, because she hated showing weakness in front of this man, or maybe she tried just because it wasn't in her nature not to try—*anything*—or maybe she just didn't think the matter through in the first place, but she stood, and she stumbled, and she sat right back down.

But not before a choked cry of pain tore across her lips.

George was off the ladder and on the roof in a second. "You little fool," he muttered, but there was affection in his voice, or at least as much affection as he ever showed. "May I see it?"

Grudgingly, she poked her foot in his direction. She'd already removed her shoe.

He touched it clinically, cupping her heel in one hand as he tested her range of motion with the other. "Does it hurt here?" he asked, pressing lightly on the outside of her ankle.

Billie let out a hiss of pain before she could stop herself and nodded.

He moved to another spot. "Here?"

She nodded again. "But not quite as much."

"What about—"

A bolt of pain shot through her foot, so intense it was positively electric. Without even thinking, she yanked it back from his hands.

"I'll take that as a yes," he said with a frown. "But I don't think it's broken."

"Of course it's not broken," she practically snapped. Which was a ridiculous thing to say because there was no *of course* about it. But George Rokesby always brought out the worst in her, and it didn't help that her foot *hurt*, damn it all.

"A sprain," George said, ignoring her little outburst.

"I know." Petulantly. *Again.* She hated herself right now.

He smiled blandly. "Of course you do."

She wanted to kill him.

"I'll go first," George announced. "That way if you stumble I'll be able to stop you from falling."

Billie nodded. It was a good plan, the only plan, really, and she'd be stupid to argue just because he was the one who'd come up with it. Even if that *had* been her initial impulse.

"Ready?" he asked.

She nodded again. "You're not concerned that I'll knock you off the ladder?"

"No."

No explanations. Just no. As if it were absurd even to ponder the question.

She looked up sharply. He looked so solid. And strong. And *dependable*. He'd always been dependable, she realized. She was just usually too busy being irritated by him to notice.

He edged carefully back to the end of the roof, turning around so that he could set one foot on the top rung of the ladder.

"Don't forget the cat," Billie directed.

"The cat," he repeated, giving her a *surely you jest* look.

"I'm not going to abandon it after all this."

George gritted his teeth, said something quite unsavory under his breath, and reached out for the cat.

Which bit him.

"*Mother of—*"

Billie scooted back an inch. He looked ready to tear someone's head off, and she was closer than the cat.

"That cat," George growled, "can rot in hell."

"Agreed," she said, *very* quickly.

He blinked at her speedy acquiescence. She tried for a smile and settled for a shrug. She had two brothers by blood and three more who might as well have been brothers in the Rokesby household. Four if she included George, which she wasn't quite sure she did.

The point was, she understood men, and she knew when to keep her mouth shut.

Besides, she was *done* with that cursed animal. Never let it be said that Billie Bridgerton was in possession of a sentimental heart. She'd tried to save the mangy beast because it was the right thing to do, then she had tried to save it again, if only because it seemed like a waste of her previous efforts not to, but now . . .

She stared down at the animal. "You are on your own."

"I'll go first," George said, moving over to the ladder. "I want you right in front of me the whole way. That way if you stumble—"

"We'll both go down?"

"I'll catch you," he ground out.

She'd been joking, but it didn't seem the wisest course of action to point that out.

George turned to descend, but as he moved to set his foot on the highest rung, the cat, which had apparently not liked being ignored, let out a bloodcurdling screech and dashed through his legs. George pitched back, arms pinwheeling.

Billie didn't think. She didn't notice her foot, or

her balance, or anything. She just leapt forward and grabbed him, pulling him back to safety.

"The ladder!" she shrieked.

But it was too late. Together they watched the ladder pivot, spin, then fall with a strange balletic grace to the ground.

Chapter 2

It would be fair to say that George Rokesby, eldest son of the Earl of Manston and currently known to the civilized world as Viscount Kennard, was an even-tempered gentleman. He had a calm, steady hand, a relentlessly logical mind, and a way of narrowing his eyes *just-so* that ensured that his wishes were met with cool efficiency, his desires granted with breathless pleasure, and—and this was the most important part—all of this occurred according to *his* preferred schedule.

It would also be fair to say that if Miss Sybilla Bridgerton had any idea how close he was to going for her throat, she would look a lot more frightened of him than she was of the gathering darkness.

"That's *most* unfortunate," she said, peering down at the ladder.

George did not speak. He thought this best.

"I know what you're thinking," she said.

He unclenched his jaw for just long enough to say, "I am not certain that you do."

"You're trying to decide which of us you'd rather toss from the roof. Me or the cat."

She was a lot closer to the truth than one might have predicted.

"I was only trying to help," she said.

"I know." Said in a tone that was *not* meant to encourage future conversation.

But Billie just went right on talking. "If I hadn't grabbed you, you would have fallen."

"I *know.*"

She caught her lower lip between her teeth, and for one blessed moment he thought she was going to let the matter drop.

Then she said, "It was your foot, you know."

He moved his head about an inch. Just enough to indicate he'd heard. "I beg your pardon?"

"Your foot." She motioned with her head toward the extremity in question. "You kicked the ladder."

George gave up all pretense of ignoring her. "You are *not* blaming this on me," he all but hissed.

"No, of course not," she said quickly, finally showing a shred of self-preservation. "I merely meant— Just that you—"

He narrowed his eyes.

"Never mind," she mumbled. She let her chin rest on her bent knees and gazed out over the field. Not that there was anything to see. The only thing moving was the wind, declaring its presence through the light ruffling of the leaves on the trees.

"I think we have another hour before the sun goes down," she murmured. "Maybe two."

"We won't be here when it gets dark," he told her.

She looked at him, then down at the ladder. Then back at him with an expression that made him want to leave her in the proverbial dark.

But he didn't. Because apparently he couldn't. Twenty-seven years was a long time to have the tenets of gentlemanly behavior schooled into one's brain, and he could never be so cruel to a lady. Even *her.*

"Andrew should be along in thirty minutes or so," he said.

"What?" She looked relieved, then annoyed. "Why didn't you say something? I can't believe you let me think we would be stranded up here all night."

He looked at her. At Billie Bridgerton, the bane of his existence since her birth twenty-three years earlier. She was glaring at him as if he'd committed some unspeakable affront, her cheeks high with color, her lips pursed like a furious rose.

With great and icy enunciation he said, "One minute has passed between the time the ladder hit the ground and this moment, right now, as these words are leaving my lips. Pray, tell me, when, during your enlightening analysis of the motion by which my foot connected with the ladder was I meant to offer this information?"

The corners of her mouth moved, but it wasn't quite a smirk. It was nothing that indicated sarcasm. If she were anyone else, he would have thought her embarrassed, or maybe even sheepish. But this was

Billie Bridgerton, and she didn't *do* embarrassment. She just did as she pleased and damn the consequences. She had done her entire life, generally dragging half the Rokesby clan down with her.

And somehow everyone *always* forgave her. She had that way about her—it wasn't charm exactly—it was that crazy, reckless confidence that made people flock to her side. Her family, his family, the entire bloody village—they all adored her. Her smile was wide, and her laugh was infectious, and God in heaven but how was it *possible* he was the only person in England who seemed to realize what a danger she was to humanity?

That twisted ankle of hers? It wasn't the first. She'd broken her arm, too, in typically spectacular fashion. She'd been eight, and she had taken a tumble from a horse. A barely trained gelding she'd had no business riding, much less trying to jump a hedge on. The bone had healed perfectly—of course it did, Billie had always had the devil's own luck—and within months she was back to her old ways, and no one thought to scold her. Not when she rode astride. In breeches. On that same damned gelding over that same damned hedge. And when one of his younger brothers followed her lead and knocked his shoulder out of joint . . .

Everyone had laughed. His parents—and hers— had shaken their heads and laughed, and not a one of them thought it prudent to take Billie off the horse, shove her into a dress, or better yet, pack her off to one of those girls' schools that taught needlework and deportment.

Edward's arm had been hanging from its socket. Its socket!! And the sound it had made when their stablemaster had shoved it back in . . .

George shuddered. It had been the sort of sound one felt rather than heard.

"Are you cold?" Billie asked.

He shook his head. Although *she* probably was. His coat was considerably thicker than hers. "Are you?"

"No."

He looked at her closely. She was just the sort to try to tough it out and refuse to allow him to behave as a gentleman ought. "You would tell me if you were?"

She held up a hand as if to make a pledge. "I promise."

That was good enough for him. Billie didn't lie, and she didn't break promises.

"Was Andrew in the village with you?" she asked, squinting off at the horizon.

George gave a nod. "We had business with the blacksmith. He stopped in to speak to the vicar afterward. I didn't feel like waiting."

"Of course not," she murmured.

His head snapped around. "What is that supposed to mean?"

Her lips parted, then hovered for a moment in a delicate oval before she said, "I don't know, actually."

He scowled at her, then turned his attention back to the roof, not that there was a damned thing he could do at the moment. But it was not in his nature to sit and wait. At the very least he could examine the dilemma, reassess, and—

"There's nothing to be done," Billie said blithely. "Not without the ladder."

"I'm aware," he bit off.

"You were looking about," she said with a shrug, "as if—"

"I *know* what I was doing," he snapped.

Her lips pressed together in perfect concert with her brows, which rose into that annoying Bridgerton arch, as if to say—*Go ahead, think what you wish. I know better.*

They were silent a moment, and then, in a smaller voice than he was used to hearing from her, she asked, "Are you quite certain that Andrew will come this way?"

He gave a nod. He and his brother had walked to the village from Crake House—not their usual mode of transport, but Andrew, who had recently been made a lieutenant in the Royal Navy, had broken his arm doing some damn fool stunt off the coast of Portugal and had been sent home to recuperate. Walking was currently easier for him than riding, and it was an uncommonly lovely day for March.

"He's on foot," George said. "How would he come if not by here?" There were many footpaths in the area, but none that wouldn't add a mile to the journey home.

Billie tipped her head to the side, gazing out over the field. "Unless someone gave him a ride."

He turned slowly toward her, dumbfounded by the utter lack of . . . *anything* in her tone. There was no one-upmanship, no argument, not even a hint of worry. Just a bizarre, matter-of-fact—*Hmmm, here's a disastrous thing that might have happened.*

"Well, he could have done," she said with a shrug. "Everyone likes Andrew."

It was true, Andrew had the sort of devil-may-care, easy charm that endeared him to everyone, from the village vicar to the barmaids at the public house. If someone was heading his way, they'd offer a ride.

"He'll walk," George said firmly. "He needs the exercise."

Billie's face took on a decidedly dubious mien. "Andrew?"

George shrugged, not wanting to concede the point, even though Andrew had always been a superb athlete. "He'll want the fresh air, at the very least. He's been climbing the walls all week. Mother has been trying to put him on broth and bedrest."

"For a broken arm?" Billie's snort gave way to a giggle.

George glanced at her sideways. "Taking joy in the misery of others?"

"Always."

He smiled despite himself. It was difficult to take offense, not when he'd spent the last week enjoying—nay, encouraging—his younger brother's frustration.

Billie gingerly shifted her position, bending her legs so that she could rest her chin on her knees.

"Watch that foot," George said, almost absently.

She nodded, and together they lapsed into silence. George stared straight ahead, but he could feel every motion Billie made at his side. She brushed an errant strand of hair from her eyes, then stretched one arm out in front of her, her elbow creaking like an old wooden chair. Then, with the tenacity she displayed in all aspects of her life, she circled back around to their previous conversation and said, "All the same, he could have got a ride."

He almost smiled. "He could."

She was quiet for a few more seconds, then said, "It doesn't look like rain."

He looked up. It was overcast, but not thickly so. The clouds were too pale to be holding much water.

"And surely we will be missed."

He allowed himself a smirk. "I will, at least."

She elbowed him. Hard. Hard enough to make him laugh.

"You're a terrible person, George Rokesby." But she was grinning when she said it.

He chuckled again, surprised by how much he enjoyed the light fizz of amusement in his chest. He wasn't sure that he and Billie qualified as friends—they'd butted heads far too many times for that—but she was familiar. That wasn't always a good thing, but right now . . .

It was.

"Well," she announced, "I suppose there's no one with whom I'd rather be stranded on a roof."

He swung his head toward her. "Why, Miss Bridgerton, was that a compliment?"

"You can't tell?"

"From you?" he parried.

She smiled in an endearingly lopsided manner. "I

suppose I deserve that. But, you know, you're very dependable."

"Dependable," he repeated.

She nodded. "Very much so."

He felt himself scowl, although for all that was holy, he had no idea why.

"If I hadn't hurt my ankle," Billie continued blithely, "I'm sure I would have found a way down."

He regarded her with clear skepticism. Aside from the fact that this had nothing to with his dependability . . . "Didn't you just say that it's too far to jump?"

"Well, yes," she said, her hand making a dismissive little wave in front of her face, "but I would have thought of something."

"Of course," he said, mostly because he lacked the energy to say anything else.

"The point is," she continued, "that as long as I'm here with *you* . . ."

Her face went suddenly pale. Even her eyes, normally a fathomless shade of brown, seemed to blanch down to something decidedly more tepid.

George's heart stopped. He had never, *ever* seen Billie Bridgerton with such an expression on her face.

She was terrified.

"What is it?" he demanded.

She turned to him. "You don't think . . ."

He waited, but she seemed beyond words. "*What?*"

Her ashen face took on a greenish hue. "You don't think that someone would think that you . . . that we . . ." She swallowed. "That we disappeared . . . *together?*"

George's entire world lurched. "*God*, no," he said. Instantly.

"I know," she agreed. With equal alacrity. "I mean, you. And me. It's laughable."

"Absurd."

"Anyone who knows us . . ."

"Will know we'd never . . ."

"And yet . . ." This time Billie's words did not merely trail off, they sank into a desperate whisper.

He gave her an impatient look. "What?"

"If Andrew doesn't come along as expected . . . and you're missed . . . and I'm missed . . ." She looked up at him, her eyes huge and horrified in her face. "Eventually someone will realize that we've both been missed."

"Your point?" he snapped.

She turned to face him directly. "Just that why wouldn't someone assume . . . ?"

"Because they have a brain in their head," he shot back. "No one would ever think I would be with you on *purpose*."

She lurched back. "Oh, well, *thank* you."

"Are you saying you wish someone *did*?" he retorted.

"No!"

He rolled his eyes. *Women*. And yet, this was Billie. The least womanly woman of his acquaintance.

She let out a long, steadying breath. "Regardless of what you think of me, George . . ."

How did she make his name sound like an insult?

". . . I do have my reputation to consider. And

while my family knows me well enough, and"—
her voice took on a reluctant edge here—"I suppose
trusts *you* well enough to know that our concurrent
disappearances signify nothing untoward . . ."

Her words trailed off, and she chewed on her
lip, looking uncomfortable, and, if one was honest,
vaguely ill.

"The rest of the world might not be as kind," he
finished for her.

She looked at him for a moment, then said,
"Quite."

"If we're not found until tomorrow morning . . ."
George said, mostly to himself.

Billie finished the horrifying sentence. "You'd have
to marry me."

Chapter 3

ー➤✳◅ー

"What are you doing?" Billie nearly shrieked. George had sprung to his feet with speed that was *highly* reckless, and now he was peering over the edge of the building with a calculating, furrowed brow.

Honestly, it looked as if he was performing complicated mathematical equations.

"Getting off the damned roof," he grunted.

"You'll kill yourself."

"I might," he agreed grimly.

"Well, don't I feel special," Billie retorted.

He turned, staring down at her with heavy-lidded superiority. "Are you saying you *want* to marry me?"

She shuddered. "Never." But at the same time, a lady didn't want to think that a man would prefer to hurl himself from a roof just to avoid the possibility.

"In that, madam," George said, "we are agreed."

And it stung. Oh, how it stung. Ah, irony. She didn't *care* if George Rokesby didn't want to marry her. She didn't even like him most of the time. And she knew that when he did deign to choose a bride, the oh-so grateful lady wasn't going to be anything like *her*.

But still, it stung.

The future Lady Kennard would be delicate, feminine. She would have been trained to run a grand house, not a working estate. She would dress in the latest of fashions, her hair would be powdered and intricately styled, and even if she possessed a backbone of steel, she would hide it beneath an aura of genteel helplessness.

Men like George loved to think themselves manly and strong.

She watched him as he planted his hands on his hips. Very well, he *was* manly and strong. But he was like the rest of them; he'd want a woman who flirted over a fan. God forbid he married someone *capable*.

"This is a disaster," he spat.

Billie only somewhat resisted the urge to snarl. "You're just realizing this now?"

His response was an equally immature scowl.

"Why couldn't you be *nice*?" Billie blurted out.

"Nice?" he echoed.

Oh, God, why had she said that? Now she was going to have to explain. "Like the rest of your family," she clarified.

"Nice," he said again. He shook his head, as if he couldn't believe her gall. "Nice."

"*I'm* nice," she said. Then she regretted *that*, because she wasn't nice. At least not all the time, and she had a feeling she wasn't being particularly nice right now. But surely she could be excused, because this was George Rokesby, and she couldn't help herself.

And neither, it seemed, could he.

"Has it ever occurred to you," he said, in a voice that was positively bathed with a lack of niceness, "that I am nice to everyone but you?"

It hurt. It shouldn't have, because they'd never liked each other, and damn it, it shouldn't have hurt because she didn't *want* it to.

But she would never let it show.

"I *think* you were trying to insult me," she said, picking disdainfully through her words.

He stared at her, waiting for further comment.

She shrugged.

"But . . . ?" he prodded.

She shrugged again, pretending to look at her fingernails. Which of course meant that she *did* look at her fingernails, which were revoltingly filthy.

One more thing she didn't have in common with the future Lady Kennard.

She counted silently to five, waiting for him to demand an explanation in that cutting way he'd perfected before he'd been old enough to shave. But he didn't say a word, and finally she was the one to lose whatever asinine contest was simmering between them, and she lifted her head.

He wasn't even looking at her.

Damn him.

And damn her, because she just couldn't help herself. She knew that anyone with an ounce of restraint would have known when to hold her tongue, but no, she had to open her stupid, stupid mouth and say, "If you can't muster the—"

"Don't say it," he warned.

"—generosity of spirit to—"

"I'm warning you, Billie."

"Are you?" she shot back, "I rather think you're threatening me."

"I will do," he nearly spat, "if you don't *shut*—" He cut himself off with a muffled curse, snapping his head in the other direction.

Billie picked at a loose thread on her stocking, her mouth pressed into an angry, trembling pout. She shouldn't have said anything. She'd known that even as she spoke, because as pompous and annoying as George Rokesby was, it was entirely her fault that he was stuck up on the roof, and she'd had no call to be so provoking.

But there was something about him—some special talent that only he possessed—that stripped her of years of experience and maturity and made her act like a bloody six-year-old. If he were anyone else— *anyone* else—she'd be lauded as the most reasonable and helpful female in the history of Christendom. Tales would be spread—once they'd got off the roof—of her bravery and wit. Billie Bridgerton . . . so resourceful, so reasonable . . . It's what everyone said. It's what everyone had reason to say, because she *was* resourceful, and she *was* reasonable.

Just not with George Rokesby.

"I'm sorry," she mumbled.

His head turned slowly, as if even his muscles could not believe what they'd heard.

"I said I'm sorry," she repeated, louder this time. It felt like an antidote, but it was the right thing to do. But God help him if he made her say it again, because there was only so much of her pride she could swallow before she choked on it. And he ought to know that.

Because he was just the same.

His eyes met hers, and then they both looked down, and then after a few moments George said, "We are neither of us at our best just now."

Billie swallowed. She thought maybe she ought to say something more, but her judgment had not done her any favors thus far, so instead she nodded, vowing that she was going to keep her mouth shut until—

"Andrew?" George whispered.

Billie snapped to attention.

"Andrew!" George all but bellowed.

Billie's eyes did a frantic scan of the trees at the far end of the field, and sure enough . . . "Andrew!" she screamed, reflexively starting to rise before remembering her ankle.

"Ow!" she yelped, plunking back down on her bottom.

George did not spare her so much as a glance. He was too busy over by the edge of the roof, waving his arms through the air in wide, vigorous swoops.

There was no way Andrew could miss them, hollering like a pair of deranged banshees, but if he picked up his pace, Billie couldn't see it. But that was Andrew. She should probably be glad he hadn't fallen over with laughter at their predicament.

This was not something he was going to let either of them forget.

"Ahoy there!" Andrew called out, once he'd halved the distance between them.

Billie glanced over at George. She could only see him in profile, but he looked visibly relieved at his brother's appearance. Also, oddly grim. No not odd at all, she realized. Whatever ribbing she was going to get from Andrew, George would suffer it a hundredfold.

Andrew drew closer, a spring in his step despite the sling on his arm. "Of all the delightful surprises," he declared, his face nearly split by his grin. "If I thought and thought and thought . . ."

He stopped, holding up one elegant forefinger, the universal sign, Billie realized, to ask for a moment's pause. Then he tipped his head as if getting back into the swing of things, and said, "and *thought*—"

"Oh, for the love of Christ," George growled.

"All that thinking for *years* . . ." Andrew chortled. "I still couldn't have come up with—"

"Just get us off the bloody roof," George snapped.

Billie rather sympathized with his tone.

"I've always thought the two of you would make a splendid pair," Andrew said slyly.

"Andrew," Billie growled.

He rewarded her with a purse-lipped smile. "Truly,

you needn't have gone to such extremes for a moment of privacy. The rest of us would have been more than happy to oblige."

"Stop it," Billie ordered.

Andrew looked up, laughing even as he affected a frown. "Do you really want to take that tone, Billie-goat? I *am* the one on *terra firma*."

"Please, Andrew," she said, trying her very best to be civil and reasonable. "We would very much appreciate your help."

"Well, since you asked so nicely," Andrew murmured.

"I'm going to kill him," she said under her breath.

"*I'm* going to break his other arm," George muttered.

Billie choked down a laugh. There was no way that Andrew could have heard them, but she looked down at him, anyway, and that was when she realized he was frowning, his good hand on his hip.

"What is it now?" George demanded.

Andrew stared down at the ladder, his mouth twisting into a curious frown. "I'm not sure if it has occurred to either of you, but this isn't the sort of thing that's easy to do one-handed."

"Take it out of the sling," George said, but his last words were drowned out by Billie's shriek of "Don't take it out of the sling!"

"Do you really want to stay on the roof?" George hissed.

"And have him reinjure his arm?" she returned. They might have joked about breaking Andrew's good arm, but *really*. The man was a sailor in the navy. It was essential that his bone healed properly.

"You'd marry me for the sake of his arm?"

"I'm not going to marry you," she shot back. "Andrew knows where we are. He can go get help if we need it."

"By the time he gets back with an able-bodied man, we'll have been up here alone for several hours."

"And I suppose you've such a high opinion of your male prowess that you think people will believe you managed to compromise me on a roof."

"Believe me," George hissed, "any man with sense would know you are thoroughly uncompromisable."

Billie's brows came together for a second of confusion. Was he complimenting her moral rectitude? But then—

Oh!

"You are despicable," she seethed. Since that was her only choice of reply. Somehow she didn't think— *You have no idea how many men would like to compromise me* would earn her any points for dignity and wit.

Or honesty.

"Andrew," George called down, in that haughty *I-am-the-eldest-son* voice of his, "I will pay you one hundred pounds to take off that sling and fix the ladder into place."

One hundred pounds?

Billie turned on him with wild disbelief. "Are you *insane?*"

"I don't know," Andrew mused. "It might actually

be worth one hundred pounds to watch the two of you kill each other."

"Don't be an ass," George said, flicking a furious look at him.

"You wouldn't even inherit," Billie pointed out, not that Andrew had ever wished to succeed his father as Earl of Manston. He was far too enamored of his footloose life for that sort of responsibility.

"Ah, yes, Edward," Andrew said with an exaggerated sigh, referring to the second Rokesby son, who was two years his senior. "That does throw a fly in the ointment. It'd look deuced suspicious if both of you perish in curious circumstances."

There was a moment of awkward silence as they all realized that Andrew had, perhaps, made light of something far too heavy for offhand quips. Edward Rokesby had taken the proudest route of second sons and was a captain in His Majesty's 54th Regiment of Foot. He'd been sent to the American colonies over a year earlier and had served bravely in the Battle of Quaker Hill. He'd remained in Rhode Island for several months before being transferred to British Headquarters in New York Town. News of his health and welfare came far too infrequently for anyone's comfort.

"If Edward perishes," George said stiffly, "I do not believe that the circumstances would ever be described as 'curious'."

"Oh, come now," Andrew said, rolling his eyes at his older brother, "stop being so bloody serious all the time."

"Your brother risks his life for King and Country,"

George said, and truly, Billie thought, his voice was clipped and tense, even for him.

"As do I," Andrew said with a cool smile. He tipped his injured arm up toward the roof, his bent and bound limb hinging at the shoulder. "Or at least a bone or two."

Billie swallowed and looked hesitantly over at George, trying to gauge his reaction. As was common for third sons, Andrew had skipped university and gone straight into the Royal Navy as a midshipman. He had been raised to the rank of lieutenant a year earlier. Andrew didn't find himself in harm's way nearly so often as Edward, but still, he wore his uniform proudly.

George, on the other hand, had not been permitted to take a commission; as the heir to the earldom, he had been deemed far too valuable to throw himself in front of American musket balls. And Billie wondered . . . did that bother him? That his brothers served their country and he did not? Had he even wanted to fight?

Then she wondered . . . why had she never wondered about this? True, she did not devote much thought to George Rokesby unless he was standing in front of her, but the lives of the Rokesbys and Bridgertons were thoroughly intertwined. It seemed odd that she did not know this.

Her eyes moved slowly from brother to brother. They had not spoken for several moments. Andrew was still staring up with a measure of challenge in his icy blue eyes, and George was looking right back down with . . . well, it wasn't anger exactly. At least not any longer. But nor was it regret. Or pride. Or anything she could identify.

There was far more to this conversation than rose to the surface.

"Well, *I* have risked life and limb for an unappreciative feline," she declared, eager to direct the conversation back to less controversial topics. Namely, her rescue.

"Is that what happened?" Andrew murmured, bending over the ladder. "I thought you didn't like cats."

George turned to her with an expression that went somewhere beyond exasperation. "You don't even like cats?"

"Everyone likes cats," Billie said quickly.

George's eyes narrowed, and she knew there was no way he believed that her bland smile was anything but a placation, but thankfully Andrew chose that moment to let out a muffled curse, causing both of them to return their attention to his struggles with the ladder.

"Are you all right?" Billie called out.

"Splinter," Andrew bit off. He sucked on the side of his little finger. "Bloody hell."

"It's not going to kill you," George snapped.

Andrew took a moment to fix his brother with a livid glare.

George rolled his eyes. "Oh, for the love of God."

"Don't provoke him," Billie hissed.

George made an odd, growly sound, but he remained silent, crossing his arms as he stared down at his younger brother.

Billie scooted a tiny bit closer to the end for a better view of Andrew as he wedged one of his feet against the bottom of the rail and then bent over to grasp a rung. He grunted audibly as he pulled the ladder upright. The physics of the maneuver were all wrong, but there was only so much a one-armed man could do.

But at least he was a strong one-armed man, and with great exertion and not a little inappropriate language, he managed to set the ladder into place against the side of the building.

"Thank you," George breathed, although from his tone Billie wasn't sure if he was thanking his brother or the Almighty.

With Andrew to brace the ladder—and no cats underfoot—the descent was considerably simpler than their first attempt. But it hurt. By God, the pain in her ankle stole the very breath from her body. And there was nothing she could do about it. She couldn't very well hop down the rungs, so with each step she had to put some weight on her injured ankle. By the time she reached the third-to-last rung, it was all she could do to keep her tears silent.

Strong hands settled at her waist. "I've got you," George said quietly, and she let herself collapse.

Chapter 4

---◆❖◆---

$\mathcal{G}$eorge had had a feeling that Billie was in more pain than she'd let on, but he didn't realize how much until they finally made their way down the ladder. He briefly considered taking her down on his back, but it seemed safer to have her follow him instead. He moved down three rungs before she set her good foot onto the ladder, then he watched as she gingerly followed with its injured companion. For a moment she stood still, probably trying to decide how best to proceed to the next rung.

"I'd lead with the good one," he said quietly, "and grip the rails hard to absorb some of your weight."

She gave a tense nod of acknowledgment and followed his instructions, her breath escaping with an agonized hiss when her good foot was solid and secure, and she was able to lift the injured one from the upper rung.

She'd been holding her breath. He didn't blame her.

He waited as she composed herself, well aware that he needed to remain only a few rungs ahead; if she fell—and she might; he could see that her ankle was very weak—he had to be close enough to stop her from tumbling all the way to the ground.

"Maybe if I try it the other way . . ." she said, breathing hard through her pain.

"I wouldn't," he replied, keeping his voice purposefully even and humble. Billie had never taken well to being told what to do. He supposed he understood this better than anyone. "You don't want your lower foot to be the weak one," he said. "Your leg could buckle—"

"Of course," she said tightly. Not angrily, just tightly. He knew that tone. It was the tone of one who had conceded a point and *really* didn't want any further elucidation on the matter.

It was one he himself used quite often.

Well, as often as he deigned to concede points.

"You can do this," he said. "I know it hurts."

"It really does," she admitted.

He smiled a little. He wasn't sure why, but he was glad she couldn't see his face. "I won't let you fall."

"Everything all right up there?" Andrew called out.

"Tell him to shut up," Billie ground out.

George laughed despite himself. "Miss Bridgerton requests that you shut the hell up," he called down.

Andrew let out a bark of laughter. "It's all good, then."

"I wouldn't say *that*," Billie grumbled, gasping her way through another step.

"You're almost halfway there," George said encouragingly.

"You're lying, but I do appreciate the show of support."

He smiled, and this time he did know why. Billie might be a right pain in the ass most of the time, but she'd always had a good sense of humor. "You're halfway to halfway, then," he said.

"Such an optimist," she muttered.

She made it down another rung without incident, and George realized that their conversation was proving an able distraction. "You can do this, Billie," he said.

"You said that already."

"It bears repeating."

"I think—" She hissed, then sucked in her breath as she moved down another rung.

He waited while she collected herself, her body quivering as she balanced for a moment on her good foot.

"I think," she said again, her voice more carefully modulated, as if she were determined to get the sentence out in an orderly manner, "that this might be the most amiable you have ever behaved in my presence."

"I could say the same," he commented.

She made it down to the halfway mark. "Touché."

"There is nothing quite so invigorating as an able opponent," he said, thinking of all the times they had crossed verbal swords. Billie had never been an easy person to best in conversation, which was why it was always so delicious when he did.

"I'm not sure that holds true on the battle—oh!"

George waited as she gritted her teeth and continued.

"—on the battlefield," she said, after a rather angry-sounding inhalation. "My God, this hurts," she muttered.

"I know," he said encouragingly.

"No you don't."

He smiled yet again. "No, I don't."

She gave a terse nod and took another step. Then, because she was Billie Bridgerton and thus fundamentally unable to allow an unfinished point to lay dormant, she said, "On the battlefield, I think I might find an able opponent inspiring."

"Inspiring?" he murmured, eager to keep her talking.

"But not invigorating."

"One would lead to the other," he said, not that he had any firsthand experience. His only battles had taken place in fencing salons and boxing rings, where the most serious risk was to one's pride. He eased down another step, giving Billie room to maneuver, then peered over his shoulder at Andrew, who appeared to be whistling while he waited.

"Can I help?" Andrew asked, catching his glance.

George shook his head, then looked back up to Billie. "You're almost to the bottom," he told her.

"Please tell me you're not lying this time."

"I'm not lying."

And he wasn't. He hopped down, skipping the last two rungs, and waited for her to draw close enough for him to grab her. A moment later she was within reach, and he swept her into his arms.

"I've got you," he murmured, and he felt her collapse a little, for once in her life allowing someone else to take charge of her.

"Well done," Andrew said cheerfully, poking his head in close. "Are you all right there, Billie-goat?"

Billie nodded, but she didn't look all right. Her jaw was still clenched, and from the way her throat worked, it was clear she was trying her damnedest not to cry.

"You little fool," George murmured, and then he knew she wasn't all right, because she let that pass without a word of protest. In fact, she apologized, which was so wholly unlike her as to be almost alarming.

"Time to go home," George said.

"Let's take a look at that foot," Andrew said, his voice still an obnoxiously bright note in the tableau. He peeled off her stocking, let out a low whistle, and said with some admiration, "Ech, Billie, what did you do to yourself? That looks brutal."

"Shut up," George said.

Andrew just shrugged. "It doesn't look broken—"

"It's not," Billie cut in.

"Still, you'll be off it for a week, at least."

"Perhaps not quite so long," George said, even though he rather thought Andrew was correct in his assessment. Still, there was no point in debating her condition. They weren't saying anything Billie didn't already know. "Shall we go?" he said.

Billie closed her eyes and nodded. "We should put the ladder away," she mumbled.

George tightened his arms around her and headed east toward Aubrey Hall, where Billie lived with her parents and three younger siblings. "We'll get it tomorrow."

She nodded. "Thank you."

"For what?"

"Everything."

"That covers quite a lot," he said in a dry voice. "Are you sure you wish to be in such debt?"

She looked up at him, her eyes tired but wise. "You're far too much of a gentleman to hold me to it."

George chuckled at that. She was right, he supposed, although he'd never treated Billie Bridgerton like any other female of his acquaintance. Hell, no one did.

"Will you still be able to come to dinner tonight?" Andrew asked, loping alongside George.

Billie turned to him distractedly. "What?"

"Surely you haven't forgotten," he said, laying one dramatic hand over his heart. "The Family Rokesby is welcoming the prodigal son—"

"You're not the prodigal son," George said. Good God.

"A prodigal son," Andrew corrected with good cheer. "I have been gone for months, even years."

"Not years," George said.

"Not years," Andrew agreed, "but it felt like it, didn't it?" He leaned down toward Billie, close enough to give her a little nudge. "You missed me, didn't you, Goatrix? Come now, admit it."

"Give her some room," George said irritably.

"Oh, she doesn't mind."

"Give *me* some room."

"An entirely different matter," Andrew said with a laugh.

George started to scowl, but then his head snapped up. "*What* did you just call her?"

"He frequently likens me to a goat," Billie said in the flat tone of one who has given up taking offense.

George looked at her, then looked at Andrew, then just shook his head. He'd never understood their sense of humor. Or maybe it was just that he'd never been a part of it. Growing up, he had always felt so separate from the rest of the Rokesbys and Bridgertons. Mostly by virtue of his age—five years older than Edward, who was the next one down the line—but also by his position. He was the eldest, the heir. He, as his father was quick to remind him, had responsibilities. He couldn't bloody well frolic about the countryside all day, climbing trees and breaking bones.

Edward, Mary, and Andrew Rokesby had been born in quick succession, separated from each other by barely a year. They, along with Billie, who was almost precisely Mary's age, had formed a tight little pack that did everything together. The Rokesby and Bridgerton homes were a mere three miles apart, and more often than not the children had met somewhere in the middle, at the brook that separated the estates, or in the treehouse Lord Bridgerton had had built at Billie's insistence in the ancient oak by the trout pond. Most of the time George wasn't sure what specific mischief they'd got up to, but his siblings had tended to come home filthy and hungry and in blooming good spirits.

He hadn't been jealous. Really, they were more annoying than anything else. The last thing he'd wanted to do when he came home from school was muck about with a pack of wild urchins whose average age didn't even scrape into the double digits.

But he had been occasionally wistful. What would it have been like if he'd had such a close cadre of companions? He'd not had a true friend his own age until he left for Eton at the age of twelve. There simply hadn't been anyone to befriend.

But it mattered little now. They were all grown, Edward in the army and Andrew in the navy and Mary married off to George's good friend Felix Maynard. Billie, too, had passed the age of majority, but she was still Billie, still romping around her father's property, still riding her too-spirited mount like her bones were forged of steel and flashing her wide smile around the village that adored her.

And as for George . . . He supposed he was still himself, too. Still the heir, still preparing for responsibility even as his father relinquished none of it, still doing absolutely nothing while his brothers took up their arms and fought for the Empire.

He looked down at his own arms, currently cradling Billie as he carried her home. It was quite possibly the most useful thing those arms had done in years.

"We should take you to Crake," Andrew said to Billie. "It's closer, and then you'll be able to stay for dinner."

"She's hurt," George reminded him.

"Pfft. When has that ever stopped her?"

"Well, she's not dressed properly," George said. He sounded like a prig and he knew it, but he was feeling unaccountably irritated, and he couldn't very well take it out on Billie while she was injured.

"I'm sure she can find something to wear in Mary's wardrobe," Andrew said dismissively. "She didn't take everything with her when she got married, did she?"

"No," Billie said, her voice muffled against George's chest. It was funny, that, how one could *feel* sound through one's body. "She left quite a bit behind."

"That settles it, then," Andrew said. "You'll come for supper, you'll spend the night, and all will be right with the world."

George gave him a slow look over his shoulder.

"I'll stay for supper," Billie agreed, moving her head so that her voice slid out into the air instead of George's body, "but then I'll go home with my family. I'd much rather sleep in my own bed, if you don't mind."

George stumbled.

"You all right?" Andrew queried.

"It's nothing," George muttered. And then, for no

reason he could discern, he was compelled to add, "Just one of those things when one of your legs goes weak for a moment and bends a bit."

Andrew gave him a curious look. "Just one of those things, eh?"

"Shut up."

Which only made Andrew laugh.

"I have those," Billie said, looking up at him with a little smile. "When you're tired and you don't even realize it. And your leg surprises you."

"Exactly."

She smiled again, a smile of kinship, and it occurred to him—although not, he realized with some surprise, for the first time—that she was actually rather pretty.

Her eyes were lovely—a deep shade of brown that was always warm and welcoming, no matter how much ire might lie in their depths. And her skin was remarkably fair for one who spent as much time out of doors as she did, although she did sport a light sprinkling of freckles across her nose and cheeks. George couldn't remember if they'd been there when she was young. He hadn't really been paying attention to Billie Bridgerton's freckles.

He hadn't really been paying attention to her at all, or at least he'd been trying not to. She was—and always had been—rather difficult to avoid.

"What are you looking at?" she asked.

"Your freckles." He saw no reason to lie.

"Why?"

He shrugged. "They're there."

Her lips pursed, and he thought that would be the end of the conversation. But then she said, somewhat abruptly, "I don't have very many of them."

His brows rose.

"Sixty-two," she said.

He almost stopped walking. "You counted?"

"I had nothing else to do. The weather was beastly, and I couldn't go outside."

George knew better than to inquire about embroidery, or watercolors, or any of a dozen other indoor pursuits commonly taken up by ladies of his acquaintance.

"Probably a few more now," Billie admitted. "It's been a prodigiously sunny spring."

"What are we talking about?" Andrew asked. He'd got a bit ahead of them and they'd only just caught up.

"My freckles," Billie said.

He blinked. "My God, you *are* boring."

"Or bored," Billie countered.

"Or both."

"Must be the company."

"I've always thought George was dull," Andrew said.

George rolled his eyes.

"I was talking about *you*," Billie said.

Andrew only grinned. "How's the foot?"

"It hurts," she said plainly.

"Better? Worse?"

Billie thought about that for a moment, then answered, "The same. No, better, I suppose, since I'm not putting weight on it." She looked back up at George. "Thank you," she said. "Again."

"You're welcome," he replied, but his voice was brusque. He didn't really have a place in their conversation. He never had.

The path forked, and George turned off to the right, toward Crake. It *was* closer, and with Andrew's arm in a sling, he was going to have to carry Billie the entire way.

"Am I too heavy?" she asked, sounding a touch sleepy.

"It wouldn't really matter if you were."

"*Gad*, George, no wonder you're starved for female companionship," Andrew groaned. "That was a clear invitation to say, 'Of course not. You are a delicate petal of womanhood.'"

"No, it wasn't," Billie said.

"It was," Andrew said firmly. "You just didn't realize it."

"I'm not starved for female companionship," George said. Because *really*.

"Oh, yes, of course not," Andrew said with great sarcasm. "You've got Billie in your arms."

"I think you might have just insulted me," she said.

"Not at all, m'dear. Just a statement of fact."

She scowled, her chestnut brows drawing down hard toward her eyes. "When do you go back to sea?"

Andrew gave her an arch look. "You'll miss me."

"I don't believe I will."

But they all knew she was lying.

"You'll have George, at any rate," Andrew said,

reaching up and swatting a low-hanging branch. "You two make quite a pair."

"Shut up," Billie said. Which was a lot tamer than what came out of George's mouth.

Andrew chuckled, and the three of them continued on toward Crake House, walking in amiable silence as the wind whistled lightly through the newly budded tree leaves.

"You're not too heavy," George suddenly said.

Billie yawned, shifting slightly in his arms as she looked up at his face. "What did you just say?"

"You're not too heavy." He shrugged. For some reason, it had seemed important to say it.

"Oh. Well." She blinked a few times, her brown eyes equal parts puzzled and pleased. "Thank you."

Up ahead, Andrew laughed, although for the life of him, George didn't know why.

"Yes," Billie said.

"I beg your pardon?"

"Yes," she said again, answering the question he didn't think he'd asked, "he's laughing at us."

"I had a feeling."

"He's an idiot," she said, sighing into George's chest. But it was an affectionate sigh; never had the words *he's an idiot* been imbued with more love and fondness.

"It's nice to have him home, though," George said quietly. And it was. He'd spent years being annoyed by his younger brothers, Andrew most especially, but now that they were grown and pursuing a life beyond the ordinariness of Kent and London, he missed them.

Almost as much as he envied them.

"It is nice, isn't it?" Billie gave a wistful smile, then she added, "Not that I'd ever tell him so."

"Oh no. Definitely not."

Billie chuckled at their shared joke, then let out a yawn. "Sorry," she mumbled. She couldn't very well cover her mouth with her arms around his neck. "Do you mind if I close my eyes?"

Something odd and unfamiliar lurched in George's chest. Something almost protective. "Of course not," he said.

She smiled—a sleepy, happy thing—and said, "I never have trouble falling asleep."

"Never?"

She shook her head, and her hair, which had long since given up any attempt to remain confined with pins, crept up and tickled his chin. "I can sleep anywhere," she said with a yawn.

She dozed the rest of the way home, and George did not mind it at all.

Chapter 5

━━━━◆➤✳❮◆━━━━

$\mathcal{B}$illie had been born just seventeen days after Mary Rokesby, and according to their parents, they had been the best of friends from the moment they'd been placed in the same cradle when Lady Bridgerton called upon Lady Manston for their regular Thursday morning visit.

Billie wasn't sure why her mother had brought along a two-month-old baby when there had been a perfectly able nanny back at Aubrey Hall, but she suspected it had something to do with her rolling over from front to back at the improbably early age of six weeks.

The Ladies Bridgerton and Manston were devoted and loyal friends, and Billie was quite sure that each would lay down her life for the other (or for the other's children), but it had to be said, there had always been a strong element of competition in their relationship.

Billie also suspected that her stunning prowess in the art of rolling over had less to do with innate genius and more to do with the tip of her mother's forefinger against her shoulder, but as her mother pointed out, there were no witnesses.

But what *was* witnessed—by both their mothers and a housemaid—was that when Billie had been placed in Mary's spacious cradle, she had reached out and grabbed the other baby's tiny hand. And when their mothers tried to pull them apart, they both started howling like banshees.

Billie's mother told her that she had been tempted to just leave her there at Crake House overnight; it was the only way to keep both babies calm.

That first morning was surely a portent of things to come. Billie and Mary were, as their nannies like to say, two peas in a pod. Two very different peas that happened to be quite fond of each other.

Where Billie was fearless, Mary was careful. Not timid, just careful. She always looked before she leapt. Billie looked, too; she just tended to do it in a somewhat more perfunctory manner.

And then she leapt high and far, often outdoing both Edward and Andrew, who had been more or less forced to befriend her after they realized that Billie would A) follow them to the ends of the earth except that B) she'd probably get there before they did.

With Mary—after a careful consideration of the ambient danger—right at her heels.

And so they became a foursome. Three wild children and one voice of reason.

They did listen to Mary occasionally. Truly, they did. It was probably the only reason all four had reached adulthood without permanent injury.

But like all good things, it came to an end, and a few years after both Edward and Andrew left home, Mary had fallen in love, got married, and moved away. She and Billie exchanged letters regularly, but it wasn't the same. Still, Billie would always call Mary her best friend, and thus, when she found herself at Crake House with a sprained ankle and nothing to wear but men's breeches and a rather dusty shirt and coat, she had no compunction raiding her friend's wardrobe for a garment suitable for a family dinner. Most of the dresses were a few years out of fashion, but that didn't bother Billie. In all truth, she likely wouldn't have even noticed if the maid who was helping her to dress for dinner hadn't apologized for it.

And they were certainly more stylish than anything she possessed in her own closet.

Billie rather thought that the bigger problem was the length, or rather, the excess of it. Mary was taller than she was, by at least three inches. It had always irked Billie (and amused Mary) to no end; it had always *seemed* like she should be the taller of the two. But as Billie couldn't even walk, this was less of an issue than it might have been.

Mary's gowns were also a bit too large in the chest. But beggars could never be choosers, and so Billie tucked two extra fichus into the bodice and decided instead to be grateful that Mary's wardrobe had contained a relatively simple round gown in a shade of forest green that Billie liked to think flattered her complexion.

The maid was tucking a few final pins into Billie's hair when a knock sounded on the door to Mary's old room, where Billie had taken up residence.

"George," she said with surprise when she saw his strong form filling the doorway. He was elegantly dressed in a midnight blue coat that she suspected would complement his eyes if he wore it in the full light of day. Gold buttons twinkled in the candlelight, adding to his already regal mien.

"My lady," he murmured, executing a small bow. "I've come to help you down to the drawing room."

"Oh." Billie wasn't sure why she was surprised. Andrew couldn't very well do it, and her father, who was surely already downstairs, wasn't as strong as he used to be.

"If you prefer," George said, "we could summon a footman."

"No, no, of course not," Billie replied. A footman seemed most awkward. At least she *knew* George. And he had already carried her once.

He came into the room, clasping his hands behind his back when he reached her side. "How is your ankle?"

"Still quite painful," she admitted, "but I bound it with some wide ribbon, and that seems to be helping."

His lips curved, and his eyes took on an azure sparkle of amusement. "Ribbon?"

To her maid's horror, Billie hiked up her over-long skirt and stuck out her foot, revealing an ankle bound in a length of festive pink ribbon.

"Very stylish," George commented.

"I could not justify tearing up a bedsheet when this would do just as well."

"Ever practical."

"I like to think so," Billie said, her jaunty voice giving way to a slight frown when it occurred to her that this might not have been a compliment. "Well," she said, brushing an invisible speck of dust off her arm, "they're your sheets, at any rate. You should thank me."

"I'm sure I do."

Her eyes narrowed.

"Yes," he said, "I'm mocking you. But only a little."

Billie felt her chin rise an inch or so. "So long as it's only a little."

"I wouldn't dare otherwise," he replied. He leaned in, just a bit. "At least not in your presence."

Billie stole a glance at the maid. She appeared thoroughly scandalized by the exchange.

"In all seriousness, though, Billie," George said, proving that a sympathetic heart did beat somewhere in his chest, "are you certain you're well enough to dine?"

She fastened an earring. Again, Mary's. "I have to eat. I might as well do it in good company."

He smiled at that. "It has been too long since we have had everyone—well, at least as many as we have tonight—together."

Billie nodded, feeling wistful. When she was a child, the Rokesbys and Bridgertons had dined together several times each month. With nine children between the two families, suppers—or luncheons, or whatever odd holiday they'd elected to celebrate—could not be anything but loud and boisterous affairs.

But one by one, the boys left for Eton, first George, then Edward, and then Andrew. Billie's two younger brothers, Edmund and Hugo, were boarding there now, along with the youngest Rokesby, Nicholas. Mary had found love and moved to Sussex, and now the only ones left in regular residence were Billie and her younger sister Georgiana, who at fourteen was perfectly pleasant but no bosom bow for a grown woman of three and twenty.

And George of course, but—eligible unmarried gentleman that he was—he split his time between Kent and London.

"Penny for them," George said, crossing the room to where Billie sat at the vanity.

She shook her head. "Not worth even that, I'm afraid. It's all quite maudlin, really."

"Maudlin? You? I must learn more."

She gave him a look, then said, "We are so diminished in number now. There used to be so many of us."

"There still are," he pointed out.

"I know, but we're so rarely together. It makes me sad." She could hardly believe she was speaking so frankly with George, but it had been such an odd, trying day. Perhaps it was making her less guarded.

"We shall all be together again," he said gamely. "I'm quite sure of it."

Billie lifted a brow. "Have you been assigned to cheer me up?"

"Your mother offered me three quid."

"*What?*"

"I jest."

She scowled, but with no real feeling behind it.

"Here, come now. I'll carry you down." He bent down to take her into his arms, but when he moved to the right, she moved to the left, and their heads bumped.

"Ooof, sorry," he muttered.

"No, it was my fault."

"Here, I'll . . ." He made to put his arms behind her back and under her legs, but there was something inescapably awkward about it, which was the oddest thing, since he had carried her for over a mile just a few hours earlier.

He lifted her into the air, and the maid, who had been standing at quiet attention throughout the conversation, jolted out of the way as Billie's legs swung around in an arc.

"A little less pressure on my neck, if you would," George said.

"Oh, so sorry." Billie adjusted her position. "It was just the same as this afternoon."

He moved out into the hall. "No, it wasn't."

Maybe not, Billie conceded to herself. She'd felt so at ease when he had carried her through the woods. Far more at ease than she'd had any right to in the arms of a man who was not her relation. Now it was just plain uncomfortable. She was excruciatingly aware of his nearness, of the bold heat of his body, seeping through his clothing. His coat collar was properly high, but when her finger grazed the very top of it, a little lock of his light brown hair curled down over her skin.

"Is aught amiss?" he asked as they reached the top of the staircase.

"No," she said quickly, then cleared her throat. "Why would you think so?"

"You haven't stopped fidgeting since I picked you up."

"Oh." She couldn't really think of anything to say to that. "It's just that my foot hurts." No, apparently she *could* think of something. Pity it was completely irrelevant.

He paused, gazing down at her with concern. "Are you sure you want to come to dinner?"

"I'm *sure*." She let out an exasperated snuff of air. "For heaven's sake, I'm already *here*. It would be ridiculous to quarantine myself in Mary's room."

"It's hardly a quarantine."

"It would feel like quarantine," she muttered.

He regarded her with a curious expression. "You don't like being by yourself, do you?"

"Not when the rest of the world is making merry without me," she retorted.

He was quiet for a moment, his head cocking just far enough to the side to indicate that he found her words curious. "What about the rest of the time?"

"I beg your pardon?"

"When the world isn't gathering without you," he said with a vaguely condescending tone. "Do you mind being on your own?"

She felt her brows come together as she gazed up at him. What on earth could be prompting such probing?

"It's not a difficult query," he said, something slightly provocative bringing his voice down to a murmur.

"No, of course I don't mind being alone." She pressed her lips together, feeling rather peeved. And peevish. But he was asking her questions she never even asked herself. But then, before she realized she was planning to speak, she heard herself say, "I don't like—"

"What?"

She gave her head a shake. "Never mind."

"No, tell me."

She let out a sigh. He wasn't going to let up. "I don't like being cooped up. I can spend all day in my own company if I'm out of doors. Or even down in the drawing room, where the windows are tall and let in so much light."

He nodded slowly, as if he agreed with her.

"Are you much the same way, then?" she asked.

"Not at all," he said.

Well, then, so much for her being able to interpret his gestures.

"I quite enjoy my own company," he continued.

"I'm sure you do."

His mouth managed half a smile. "I thought we weren't insulting each other tonight."

"We weren't?"

"I *am* carrying you down a flight of stairs. You'd do well to speak kindly to me."

"Point taken," she acceded.

George rounded the landing, and she thought they were done with the conversation when he said, "The other day it rained . . . all day long, unremittingly."

Billie tipped her head to the side. She knew which day he was talking about. It had been miserable. She had been planning to take her mare Argo out to inspect the fences at the southern end of her father's lands. And maybe stop at the wild strawberry patch. It was much too early in the season for fruit, but the blossoms would be starting to emerge, and she was curious as to their abundance.

"I stayed indoors, of course," George continued. "There was no reason to go out."

She wasn't quite sure where he was going with this, but obliged him by inquiring, "How did you occupy yourself?"

"I read a book." He sounded quite pleased with himself. "I sat in my study and read an entire book from start to finish, and it was quite the most pleasant day in recent memory."

"You need to get out more," she deadpanned.

He ignored that entirely. "All I'm saying is, I spent the day cooped up, as you call it, and it was delightful."

"Well. That just proves my point."

"We were making points?"

"We're always making points, George."

"And always keeping score?" he murmured.

Always. But she didn't say it out loud. It seemed childish. And petty. And worse, like she was trying too hard to be something she wasn't. Or rather, something she *was* but that society would never allow her to be. He was Lord Kennard, and she was Miss Sybilla Bridgerton, and while she'd gleefully stack her inner fortitude up against his any day of the week, she was no fool. She understood how the world worked. Here in her little corner of Kent, she was queen of her domain, but in any contest held outside the homey little circle drawn 'round Crake and Aubrey Hall . . .

George Rokesby would win. Always. Or if not, he'd give the appearance of having done so.

And there was nothing she could do about it.

"You look uncommonly serious all of a sudden," he said, stepping onto the polished parquet of the ground floor hall.

"Thinking about *you*," she said truthfully.

"A dare if ever I heard one." He reached the open door to the drawing room, and his lips moved closer to her ear. "And one I shall not take."

Her tongue touched the top of her mouth, readying a reply, but before she could make a sound, George had stepped through the entry to Crake House's formal drawing room.

"Good evening, everyone," he said grandly.

Any hope Billie might have had at making a subtle entrance were squashed immediately when she realized they were the last to arrive. Her mother was seated next to Lady Manston on the long sofa with

Georgiana in a nearby chair looking vaguely bored. The men had congregated over by the window. Lords Bridgerton and Manston were chatting with Andrew, who was happily accepting a glass of brandy from his father.

"Billie!" her mother exclaimed, practically hopping to her feet. "In your message you wrote that it was just a sprain."

"It *is* just a sprain," Billie replied. "I'll be as good as new by the end of the week."

George snorted. She ignored him.

"It's nothing, Mama," Billie assured her. "I've certainly done worse."

Andrew snorted. She ignored him, too.

"With a cane, she might have made it down on her own," George said as he set her down on the settee, "but it would have taken her thrice as long, and neither of us has the patience for that."

Billie's father, who had been standing by the window with a glass of brandy, let out a hearty guffaw.

Billie gave him a bit of an evil eye, which only made him laugh with more vigor.

"Is that one of Mary's gowns?" Lady Bridgerton asked.

Billie nodded. "I was in breeches."

Her mother sighed but made no comment. It was an endless argument between them, and their truce was maintained only by Billie's promise to always dress properly for dinner. And among guests. And at church.

There was actually a rather long list of events for which she was required to attire herself to her mother's specifications. But in the matter of Billie wearing breeches while conducting business around the estate, Lady Bridgerton had acquiesced.

To Billie, it had felt like a victory. As she had explained to her mother—repeatedly—all she really needed was permission to dress sensibly when out and about. The tenants surely called her something more colorful than eccentric, but she knew she was well-liked. And respected.

The affection had come naturally; according to Billie's mother, she'd emerged from the womb smiling, and even as a child, she'd been the tenants' favorite.

The respect, however, had been earned, and for that reason it was all the more fiercely treasured.

Billie knew that her younger brother would one day inherit Aubrey Hall and all its lands, but Edmund was still a child, eight years her junior. Most of the time he was away at school. Their father wasn't getting any younger, and someone had to learn how to properly manage such a large estate. Besides, Billie was a natural at it; everyone said so.

She'd been an only child for so many years; there had been two babies between her and Edmund's births, but neither had lived past infancy. During those years of prayers and hopes and wishing for an heir, Billie had become something of a mascot to the tenants, a living, smiling symbol of Aubrey Hall's future.

Unlike most highborn daughters, Billie had always accompanied her parents on their duties around the estate. When her mother brought baskets of food to the needy, she was right there with apples for the children. When her father was out surveying the land, she could more often than not be found at his feet, digging up worms as she explained why she thought rye would be a much better choice than barley in such a sun-starved field.

At first she'd been a source of amusement—the energetic little five-year-old who insisted upon measuring grain when the rents were collected. But eventually she became a fixture, and now it was expected that she would see to the needs of the estate. If a cottage roof was leaking, she was the one who made sure it was mended. If a harvest was lean, she went out and tried to figure out why.

She was, for all intents and purposes, her father's eldest son.

Other young ladies might read romantic poetry and Shakespearean tragedies. Billie read treatises on agricultural management. And she loved them. Honestly. They were ripping good reads.

It was difficult to imagine a life that might suit her better, but it had to be said: it was all much easier to conduct without a corset.

Much as it pained her mother.

"I was out seeing to the irrigation," Billie explained. "It would have been impractical in a frock."

"I didn't say anything," Lady Bridgerton said, even though they all knew she'd been thinking it.

"Not to mention difficult to climb that tree," Andrew put in.

That did get her mother's attention. "She was climbing a tree?"

"Saving a cat," Andrew confirmed.

"One might assume," George said, his voice purring with authority, "that had she been wearing a frock, she would not have attempted the tree."

"What happened to the cat?" Georgiana asked.

Billie looked to her sister. She'd almost forgotten she was there. And she had definitely forgotten the cat. "I don't know."

Georgiana leaned forward, her blue eyes impatient. "Well, did you save it?"

"If so," Billie said, "it was entirely against its wishes."

"It was a most ungrateful feline," George said.

Billie's father chuckled at the description and gave him a manly slap on the back. "George, m'boy, we must get you a drink. You'll need it after your trials."

Billie's mouth fell open. "*His* trials?"

George smirked, but no one else saw it, the bloody man.

"Mary's gown looks lovely on you," Lady Bridgerton said, steering the conversation back to more ladylike pursuits.

"Thank you," Billie replied. "I rather like this shade of green." Her fingers flitted to the lace along the round neckline. It was really most becoming.

Her mother stared at her in shock.

"I like pretty dresses," Billie insisted. "I just don't like wearing them when it's impractical to do so."

"The *cat*," Georgiana persisted.

Billie flicked her an impatient look. "I told you, I don't know. Honestly, it was a horrid little creature."

"Agreed," George said, raising his glass in salute.

"I can't believe you're toasting to the possible demise of a cat," Georgiana said.

"*I'm* not," Billie replied, glancing around to see if someone might bring her a drink. "But I'd like to."

"It's all right, darling," Lady Bridgerton murmured, giving her younger daughter a reassuring smile. "Don't fret so."

Billie looked back at Georgiana. If their mother used such a tone on her, she would likely go mad. But Georgiana had been sickly as a child, and Lady Bridgerton had never quite learned to treat her with anything less than solicitous concern.

"I'm sure the cat survived its ordeal," Billie told Georgiana. "He was quite a scrappy fellow. Had the look of a survivor in his eye."

Andrew loped over and leaned down near Georgiana's shoulder. "Always lands on its feet, that one."

"Oh, stop!" Georgiana batted him away, but it was clear she wasn't angry about the joke. No one was ever angry at Andrew. Not for long, at least.

"Is there any news of Edward?" Billie asked Lady Manston.

Lady Manston's eyes clouded as she shook her head. "None since the last letter. The one we received last month."

"I'm sure he's well," Billie said. "He is such a talented soldier."

"I'm not sure how much talent plays into it when someone is aiming a gun at your chest," George said darkly.

Billie turned to glare. "Don't listen to him," she said to Lady Manston. "He's never been a soldier."

Lady Manston smiled at her, an expression that was sad and sweet and loving, all at once. "I think he would like to have been," she said, peering up at her eldest. "Wouldn't you, George?"

Chapter 6

George forced his face into an impassive mask. His mother meant well; she always did. But she was a woman. She could never understand what it meant to fight for one's king and country. She could never understand what it meant *not* to do so.

"It doesn't matter what I wanted," he said gruffly. He took a large gulp of his brandy. Then he took another. "I was needed here."

"For which I am grateful," his mother declared. She turned back to the other ladies with a determined smile, but her eyes were overbright. "I don't need *all* of my sons going off to war. God willing, this nonsense will be over before Nicholas is of an age to take a commission."

At first no one spoke. Lady Manston's voice had been just a little too loud, her words just a little too shrill. It was one of those awkward moments that no one quite knew how to break. George finally took a small sip of his drink and said in a low voice, "There will always be nonsense among men."

That seemed to let some of the tension out of the air, and sure enough, Billie looked up at him with a defiant tilt to her chin. "Women would do a far better job if we were allowed to govern."

He returned her volley with a bland smile. She was trying to goad him. He refused to indulge her.

Billie's father, however, was hooked quite neatly on her bait. "I'm certain you would," he said, with enough placation in his voice for everyone to know he did not mean it.

"We would," Billie insisted. "Certainly there would be less war."

"I would have to agree with her there," Andrew said, lifting his glass in her direction.

"It's a moot point," Lord Manston said. "If God had wanted women to govern and fight, he would have made them strong enough to wield swords and muskets."

"I can shoot," Billie said.

Lord Manston looked at her and blinked. "Yes," he said, almost as if he were contemplating an odd scientific curiosity, "you probably can."

"Billie brought down a stag last winter," Lord Bridgerton said, shrugging as if this were a normal occurrence.

"Did you?" Andrew said admiringly. "Well done."

Billie smiled. "It was delicious."

"I can't believe you allow her to hunt," Lord Manston said to Lord Bridgerton.

"Do you really think I could stop her?"

"No one can stop Billie," George muttered. He turned abruptly and crossed the room to get another drink.

There was a long silence. An uncomfortable silence. George decided that this time he didn't care.

"How *is* Nicholas?" Lady Bridgerton asked. George smiled into his glass. She'd always known how to deflect a conversation from delicate topics. Sure enough, her perfect social smile was evident in her voice as she added, "Better behaved than Edmund and Hugo, I'm sure."

"I'm sure he *isn't*," Lady Manston returned with a laugh.

"Nicholas wouldn't—" Georgiana started to say.

But Billie's voice came out on top. "It's difficult to imagine anyone getting sent down more often than Andrew."

Andrew held up a hand. "I hold the record."

Georgiana's eyes grew wide. "Among Rokesbys?"

"Among everyone."

"That cannot be true," Billie scoffed.

"I assure you, it is. There's a reason I left early, you know. I reckon if I showed up for a visit, they would not let me back through the gate."

Billie gratefully accepted the glass of wine the footman finally brought over and then lifted it toward Andrew in a skeptical salute. "*That* only shows that the headmaster should be applauded for his great good sense."

"Andrew, stop your exaggerations," Lady Man-

ston said. She rolled her eyes as she turned back to
Lady Bridgerton. "He did get sent down from Eton
more than once, but I assure you, he has not been
banished."

"Not for want of trying," Billie quipped.

George let out a long breath and turned back to the
window, peering out into the inky night. Perhaps he
was an insufferable prig—an insufferable prig who,
as it happened, had never been sent down from Eton
or Cambridge—but he really didn't feel like listening
to Andrew and Billie's endless banter.

It never changed. Billie would be deliciously clever,
and then Andrew would play the rogue, and then
Billie would say something utterly deflating, and
then Andrew would laugh and twinkle, and then *everyone* would laugh and twinkle, and it was always,
always the same damned thing.

He was just so bored of it all.

George glanced briefly at Georgiana, sitting mo-
rosely in what was, in his opinion, the least comfortable chair in the house. How was it possible that no
one noticed she'd been left out of the conversation?
Billie and Andrew were lighting up the room with
their wit and vivacity, and poor Georgiana couldn't
get a word in. Not that she appeared to be trying, but
at fourteen, how could she hope to compete?

Abruptly, he crossed the room to the younger girl's
side and leaned down. "I saw the cat," he said, his
words disappearing into her gingery hair. "It dashed
off into the woods."

It hadn't, of course. He had no idea what had become of the cat. Something involving brimstone and the wrath of the devil, if there was any justice in the world.

Georgiana started, then turned to him with a wide smile that was disconcertingly like her sister's. "Did you? Oh, *thank you* for letting me know."

George glanced over at Billie as he straightened. She was regarding him with a keen eye, silently admonishing him for lying. He returned the expression with equal insolence, his quirked brow almost daring her to call him out on it.

But she didn't. Instead she dismissed him with a one-shouldered shrug so tiny no one could possibly have noticed it but him. Then she turned back to Andrew with her usual sparkle and charm. George returned his attention to Georgiana, who was clearly a cleverer girl than he'd ever realized, because she was watching the scene with slow-rising curiosity, her eyes moving back and forth between all of them, as if they were players on a field.

He shrugged. Good for her. He was glad she had a brain in her head. She was going to need it with her family.

He took another sip of his brandy, losing himself in his thoughts until the conversation around him descended into a low hum. He felt restless tonight, unusually so. Here he was, surrounded by people he'd known and loved his entire life, and all he wanted . . .

He stared toward the window, searching for an answer. All he wanted was to . . .

He didn't know.

There was the problem. Right there. He didn't know what he wanted, just that it wasn't here.

His life, he realized, had reached a new depth of banality.

"George? George?"

He blinked. His mother was calling his name.

"Lady Frederica Fortescue-Endicott has become betrothed to the Earl of Northwick," she said to him. "Had you heard?"

Ah. So this was to be tonight's conversation. He finished his drink. "I had not."

"The Duke of Westborough's eldest daughter," his mother said to Lady Bridgerton. "Such a charming young lady."

"Oh, of course, lovely girl. Dark hair, yes?"

"And such beautiful blue eyes. Sings like a bird."

George stifled a sigh.

His father slapped him on the back. "The duke set her up with a good dowry," he said, coming straight to the point. "Twenty thousand *and* a piece of property."

"As I've missed my chance," George said with a diplomatically impassive smile, "there can be no benefit to the catalogue of her many attributes."

"Of course not," his mother said. "It's far too late for that. But if you had listened to me last spring—"

The supper gong sounded—*thank God*—and his mother must have decided that there was no use in further pressing her matchmaking points because the next words out of her mouth had to do with the evening's menu, and the apparent lack of good fish this week at market.

George made his way back to Billie's side. "Shall I?" he murmured, holding out his arms.

"Oh," she exclaimed lightly, although for the life of him, he couldn't imagine why she'd be surprised. Nothing had changed in the past quarter of an hour; who else was going to carry her into the dining room?

"How very gallant of you, George," his mother said, taking her husband's hand and allowing him to lead her across the room.

He gave her a dry smile. "I confess it's a heady feeling to have Billie Bridgerton at my mercy."

Lord Bridgerton laughed. "Enjoy it while you can, son. She doesn't like to lose, that one."

"Does anyone?" Billie retorted.

"Of course not," her father replied. "It's more of a question of how gracefully one concedes."

"I'm perfectly gr—"

George scooped her into his arms. "Are you sure you want to finish that sentence?" he murmured. Because they all knew. Billie Bridgerton was rarely graceful in defeat.

Billie clamped her mouth together.

"Two points for honesty," he said.

"What would it take to earn three?" she shot back.

He laughed.

"And anyway," Billie said to her father, fundamentally unable to let a point drop, "I didn't *lose* anything."

"You lost the cat," Georgiana said.

"And your dignity," Andrew added.

"Now *that* earns three points," George said.

"I sprained my ankle!"

"We know, dear," Lady Bridgerton said, giving her daughter a little pat on the arm. "You'll feel better soon. You said so."

Four points, George started to say, but Billie fixed him with a murderous glare.

"Don't you dare," she ground out.

"But you make it so *easy*."

"Are we mocking Billie?" Andrew asked, catching up as they entered the hall. "Because if we are, I'll have you know I'm hurt that you would begin without me."

"*Andrew*," Billie all but growled.

Andrew laid his good hand on his heart in feigned affront. "Hurt. Hurt, I say."

"Do we think we could not mock me?" Billie asked in an exasperated voice. "Just for one evening?"

"I suppose," Andrew said, "but George isn't nearly so much fun."

George started to say something, but then he caught a glance at Billie's face. She was tired. And in pain. What Andrew had taken as customary banter was actually a plea for relief.

He brought his lips close to her ear, lowering his voice to a quiet murmur. "Are you certain you're up to supper?"

"Of course!" she replied, visibly chagrined that he'd asked. "I'm fine."

"But are you well?"

Her lips tightened. Then trembled.

George slowed his pace, allowing Andrew to amble ahead of them. "There is no shame in needing a rest, Billie."

She looked up at him, something almost rueful in her eyes. "I'm hungry," she said.

He nodded. "I can ask that a small ottoman be placed under the table so that you might elevate your leg."

Billie blinked up at him in surprise, and for a moment he could have sworn he could hear the sound of her breath passing across her lips. "That would be most welcome," she said. "Thank you."

"Consider it done." He paused. "You do look rather fetching in that gown, by the way."

"*What*?"

He had no idea why he'd said that. And judging from her shocked expression, neither did she.

He shrugged, wishing he had a free hand to adjust his cravat. It felt unaccountably tight. And of course he would say something complimentary about her gown; wasn't that what gentlemen did? Plus, she'd looked as if she could use a little boost. And it did suit her quite well. "It's a nice color," he improvised. He could be occasionally charming. "It, ehrm . . . brings out your eyes."

"My eyes are brown."

"It still brings them out."

She looked vaguely alarmed. "Good heavens,

George. Have you ever paid a lady a compliment before?"

"Have you ever *received* one?"

Too late he realized how awful that sounded, and he stammered something that was meant to approximate an apology, but Billie was already shaking with laughter. "Oh, I'm sorry," she gasped, wiping her eyes on her shoulder since her hands were around his neck. "Oh, that was funny. Your face . . ."

Amazingly, George felt himself smile. "I was trying to ask if you'd ever *accepted* one," he was compelled to say. Then he muttered, "Obviously, you've received them."

"Oh, obviously."

He shook his head. "Truly, I'm sorry."

"You're such a gentleman," she teased.

"This surprises you?"

"Not at all. I think you would die before insulting a lady, however inadvertently."

"I'm fairly certain I've insulted you at some point in our history."

She waved that off. "I'm not sure I count."

"I will confess," he said, "you do seem more of a lady than usual this evening."

Her expression grew shrewd. "There is an insult in there somewhere, I'm sure."

"*Or* a compliment."

"No," she said, pretending to give it serious thought, "I don't think there is."

He laughed, full and throaty, and it was only when

his mirth had subsided to a light chuckle that he realized how unfamiliar it had felt. It had been a long time since he had given himself over to laughter, allowing it to tickle through his body.

It was a far cry from the social titters one encountered in London.

"I *have* received a compliment before," Billie said, her voice softening when she added, "but I will own that I am not well-skilled in accepting them. At least not for the color of my gown."

George slowed his pace yet again as he turned a corner and the door to the dining room came into view. "You never did go to London for a Season, did you?"

"You know I didn't."

He wondered why. Mary had done so, and she and Billie usually did everything together. But it didn't seem polite to ask, at least not now, just as supper was about to commence.

"I didn't want to," Billie said.

George did not point out that he had not asked for an explanation.

"I'd have been dreadful at it."

"You'd have been a breath of fresh air," he lied. She *would* have been dreadful at it, and then he'd have been conscripted to be her social savior, making sure her dance card was at least halfway filled, and then defending her honor every time some brainless young lord assumed she was lax of morals because she was a bit too loud and free.

It would have been exhausting.

"Excuse me," he murmured, pausing to ask a footman to find her an ottoman. "Shall I hold you until he returns?"

"Hold me?" she echoed, as if she had suddenly lost her command of English.

"Is something wrong?" his mother asked, watching them with undisguised curiosity through the open doorway. She, Lady Bridgerton, and Georgiana had already taken their seats. The gentlemen were waiting for Billie to be set down.

"Sit," George told them, "please. I've asked a footman to bring something for under the table. So that Billie may elevate her foot."

"That's very kind of you, George," Lady Bridgerton said. "I should have thought of that."

"I've turned an ankle before," he said, carrying Billie into the room.

"And I have not," Lady Bridgerton returned, "although one would think I'd be an expert on them by now." She looked over at Georgiana. "I think you might be the only one of my children who hasn't broken a bone or twisted a joint yet."

"It's my special skill," Georgiana said in a flat voice.

"I must say," Lady Manston said, looking over at George and Billie with a deceptively placid smile, "the two of you make quite a pair."

George speared his mother with a stare. *No.* She might want to see him married, but she was not going to try *this*.

"Don't tease so," Billie said, with exactly the right amount of affectionate admonishment in her voice to put a halt to that line of thinking. "Who else would carry me if not George?"

"Alas, my fractured limb," Andrew murmured.

"How did you break it?" Georgiana asked.

He leaned forward, his eyes sparkling like the sea. "Wrestled with a shark."

Billie snorted.

"No," Georgiana said, unimpressed, "what really happened?"

Andrew shrugged. "I slipped."

There was a little beat of silence. No one had expected anything so mundane as that.

"The shark makes for a better story," Georgiana finally said.

"It does, doesn't it? The truth is rarely as glamorous as we'd like."

"I thought at the very least you'd fallen from the mast," Billie said.

"The deck was slippery," Andrew said in a matter-of-fact manner. And while everyone was pondering the utter banality of this, he added, "It gets that way. Water, you know."

The footman returned with a small tufted ottoman. It was not as tall as George would have liked, but he still thought it would be better for Billie than letting her foot dangle.

"I was surprised Admiral McClellan allowed you to recuperate at home," Lady Manston said as the footman crawled under the table to set the ottoman into place. "Not that I'm complaining. It's delightful to have you at Crake where you belong."

Andrew gave his mother a lopsided smile. "Not much use for a one-armed sailor."

"Even with all those peg-legged pirates?" Billie quipped as George set her down in her seat. "I thought it was practically a requirement to be missing a limb at sea."

Andrew tipped his head thoughtfully to the side. "Our cook is missing an ear."

"Andrew!" his mother exclaimed.

"How gruesome," Billie said, eyes aglow with macabre delight. "Were you there when it happened?"

"Billie!" her mother exclaimed.

Billie whipped her head around to face her mother, protesting, "You can't expect me to hear about an earless sailor and *not* ask."

"Nevertheless, it is not appropriate conversation at a family supper."

Gatherings between the Rokesby and Bridgerton clans were always classified as family, no matter that there wasn't a drop of shared blood between them. At least not within the last hundred years.

"I can't imagine where it would be more appropriate," Andrew said, "unless we all head out to the public inn."

"Alas," Billie said, "I'm not allowed this time of night."

Andrew flashed her a cheeky grin. "Reason seven hundred and thirty-eight why I'm glad I was not born a female."

Billie rolled her eyes.

"Are you allowed during the day?" Georgiana asked her.

"Of course," Billie said, but George noticed that her mother didn't look happy about it.

Neither did Georgiana. Her lips were pursed into a frustrated frown, and she had one hand on the table, her index finger tapping impatiently against the cloth.

"Mrs. Bucket makes the most delicious pork pie," Billie said. "Every Thursday."

"I'd forgotten," Andrew said, shuddering with delicious culinary memory.

"How on earth could you? It's heaven in a crust."

"Agreed. We shall have to sup together. Shall we say at noo—"

"Women are bloody," Georgiana blurted out.

Lady Bridgerton dropped her fork.

Billie turned to her sister with an expression of cautious surprise. "I'm sorry?"

"Women can be bloody, too," Georgiana said, her tone approaching truculence.

Billie seemed not to know what to make of that. Normally George would be enjoying her discomfiture, but the conversation had taken such a sharp turn into the bizarre that he could not bring himself to feel anything but sympathy.

And relief that he wasn't the one questioning the young girl.

"What you said earlier," Georgiana said. "About women, and how we would wage war less frequently than men. I don't think that's true."

"Oh," Billie said, looking mightily relieved. Truth was, George was relieved, too. Because the only other explanation for women being bloody was a conversation he did *not* want to have at the dining table.

Or anywhere for that matter.

"What about Queen Mary?" Georgiana continued. "No one could call her a pacifist."

"They didn't call her Bloody Mary for nothing," Andrew said.

"Exactly!" Georgiana agreed with an enthusiastic nod. "And Queen Elizabeth sank an entire armada."

"She had her *men* sink the armada," Lord Bridgerton corrected.

"*She* gave the orders," Georgiana shot back.

"Georgiana has a point," George said, happy to give credit where it was due.

Georgiana gave him a grateful look.

"Indeed," Billie said with a smile.

At that, Georgiana seemed ridiculously pleased.

"I did not mean to say that women couldn't be violent," Billie said, now that Georgiana was done with her argument. "Of course we can, given proper motivation."

"I shudder to think," Andrew murmured.

"If someone I loved was in danger," Billie said with quiet intensity, "I'm quite certain I could be moved to violence."

For years George would wonder about that moment. Something changed. Something shook and twisted. The air crackled electric, and everyone— every last Rokesby and Bridgerton at the table—sat almost suspended in time, as if waiting for something none of them understood.

Even Billie.

George studied her face. It was not difficult to imagine her as a warrior, fierce and protective of the people she loved. Was he counted among that number? He rather thought he was. Anyone with his surname would fall beneath her protection.

No one spoke. No one even breathed until his mother let out a laugh that was really nothing more than a breath, and then declared, "Such a depressing topic."

"I disagree," George said softly. He didn't think she'd heard him. But Billie did. Her lips parted, and her dark eyes met his with curiosity and surprise. And maybe even a hint of gratitude.

"I do not understand why we are talking of such things," his mother continued, thoroughly determined to steer the conversation back to sweetness and light.

Because it's important, George thought. Because it means something. Because nothing had meant anything for years, not for those who had been left behind. He was sick of being useless, of pretending that he was more valuable than his brothers by virtue of his birth.

He looked down at his soup. He'd lost his appetite. And of course that was when Lady Bridgerton exclaimed, "We should have a party!"

Chapter 7

ーーーー⇒⚜⇐ーーーー

$\mathcal{A}$ party?

Billie carefully set down her napkin, a vague sense of alarm washing over her. "Mother?"

"A house party," her mother clarified, as if *that* had been what she'd been asking about.

"This time of year?" her father asked, his soup-spoon pausing only briefly on its way to his mouth.

"Why not this time of year?"

"We usually have one in the autumn."

Billie rolled her eyes. What typically male reasoning. Not that she disagreed. The last thing she wanted right now at Aubrey Hall was a house party. All those strangers tramping around her home. Not to mention the time it would take to play the part of the dutiful daughter of the hostess. She'd be stuck in her frocks all day, unable to tend to the very real responsibilities of running the estate.

She tried to catch her father's eye. Surely he realized what a bad idea this was, no matter the season. But he was oblivious to anything but his wife. And his soup.

"Andrew won't be home in the autumn," Lady Bridgerton pointed out. "And we should celebrate now."

"I do love a party," Andrew said. It was true, but Billie had a feeling he'd said it more to smooth the tension at the table. Because it was quite tense. And it was oddly clear to her that no one knew why.

"It's settled, then," her mother said. "We shall have a house party. Just a small one."

"Define small," Billie said warily.

"Oh, I don't know. A dozen guests, perhaps?" Lady Bridgerton turned to Lady Manston. "What do you think, Helen?"

Lady Manston surprised no one when she replied, "I think it sounds delightful. But we shall have to act quickly, before Andrew is sent back to sea. The admiral was quite explicit that his leave was for the duration of his convalescence and not a moment longer."

"Of course," Lady Bridgerton murmured. "Shall we say in one week's time?"

"One week?" Billie exclaimed. "You can't possibly ready the house in one week."

"Oh, pish. Of course I can." Her mother gave her a look of amused disdain. "I was born for this sort of thing."

"That you were, my dear," her father said affectionately.

He would be no help at all, Billie realized. If she

was going to put a stop to this madness, she was going to have to do it herself. "Think of the guests, Mama?" she persisted. "Surely you must give them more notice. People lead busy lives. They will have plans."

Her mother waved this away as if it were of no consequence. "I'm not planning to send invitations across the country. We've plenty of time to reach friends in the nearby counties. Or London."

"Who will you invite?" Lady Manston asked.

"You, of course. Do say you'll come and stay with us. It will be so much more fun to have everyone under one roof."

"That hardly seems necessary," George said.

"Indeed," Billie agreed. For the love of God, they lived only three miles apart.

George gave her a look.

"Oh, please," she said impatiently. "You can't possibly take offense."

"*I* can," Andrew said with a grin. "In fact I think I will, just for the fun of it."

"Mary and Felix," Lady Bridgerton said. "We cannot possibly have a celebration without them."

"It would be nice to see Mary," Billie admitted.

"What about the Westboroughs?" Lady Manston asked.

George groaned. "Surely that ship has sailed, Mother. Didn't you just tell me that Lady Frederica has become engaged?"

"Indeed." His mother paused, delicately lifting her soupspoon to her lips. "But she has a younger sister."

Billie let out a choked laugh, then quickly schooled her face into a frown when George threw her a furious scowl.

Lady Manston's smile grew positively terrifying. "And a cousin."

"Of course she does," George said under his breath.

Billie would have expressed some sort of sympathy, but of course *that* was the moment her own mother chose to say, "We shall have to find some nice young men, too."

Billie's eyes widened in horror. She should have known that her turn was coming. "Mother, *don't*," she cautioned.

Cautioned? Ordered was more like it.

Not that this had any effect on her mother's enthusiasm. "We'll be uneven if we don't," she said briskly. "Besides, you're not getting any younger."

Billie closed her eyes and counted to five. It was either that or go for her mother's throat.

"Doesn't Felix have a brother?" Lady Manston asked.

Billie bit her tongue. Lady Manston knew perfectly well that Felix had a brother. Felix Maynard was married to her only daughter. Lady Manston had likely known the names and ages of his every first cousin before the ink was dry on the betrothal papers.

"George?" his mother prompted. "Doesn't he?"

Billie stared at Lady Manston in fascinated amazement. Her single-minded determination would do an army general proud. Was it some kind of inborn trait? Did females spring from the womb with the urge to match men and women into neat little pairs? And if so, how was it possible that *she'd* been skipped?

Because Billie had no interest in matchmaking, for herself or anyone else. If that made her some kind of strange, unfeminine freak, so be it. She would much rather be out on her horse. Or fishing at the lake. Or climbing a tree.

Or anything, really.

Not for the first time Billie wondered what her Heavenly Father had been thinking when she'd been born a girl. She was clearly the least girlish girl in the history of England. Thank heavens her parents had not forced her to make her debut in London when Mary had done so. It would have been miserable. *She* would have been a disaster.

And no one would have wanted her.

"George?" Lady Manston said again, impatience sharpening the edge of her voice.

George started, and Billie realized he'd been looking at her. She couldn't begin to imagine what he had seen on her face . . . what he'd *thought* he'd seen there.

"He does," George confirmed, turning toward his mother. "Henry. He's two years younger than Felix, but he's—"

"Excellent!" Lady Manston exclaimed, clapping her hands together.

"But he's what?" Billie asked. Or rather, pounced. Because this was her potential mortification they were talking about.

"Nearly engaged," George told her. "Or so I've heard."

"It doesn't count until it's official," his mother said airily.

Billie stared at her in disbelief. This, from the woman who had been planning Mary's wedding from the first time Felix had kissed her hand.

"Do we like Henry Maynard?" Lady Bridgerton asked.

"We do," Lady Manston confirmed.

"I thought she wasn't even sure he had a brother," Billie said.

Beside her, George chuckled, and she felt his head draw close to hers. "Ten pounds says she knew every last detail of his current courtship before she even mentioned his name," he murmured.

Billie's lips flickered with a hint of a smile. "I would not take that bet."

"Smart girl."

"Always."

George chuckled, then stopped. Billie followed his gaze across the table. Andrew was watching them with an odd expression, his head tilted at the slightest of angles and his brow pleated into a thoughtful frown.

"What?" she said, while the mothers continued their plans.

Andrew shook his head. "Nothing."

Billie scowled. She could read Andrew like the back of her hand. He was up to something. "I don't like his expression," she murmured.

"I never like his expression," George said.

She glanced at him. How odd this was, this silly

little kinship with George. It was usually Andrew with whom she was sharing muttered quips. Or Edward. But not George.

Never George.

And while she supposed this was a good thing—there was no reason she and George *had* to be at constant loggerheads—it still made her feel strange. Off-balance.

Life was better when it puttered along without surprises. It really was.

Billie turned to her mother, determined to escape this growing sense of unease. "Do we really *have* to have a party? Surely Andrew can feel celebrated and adored without a twelve-course meal and archery on the lawn."

"Don't forget the fireworks and a parade," Andrew said. "And I might want to be carried in on a litter."

"You want to *encourage* this?" Billie asked, gesturing to him with an exasperated hand.

George snorted into his soup.

"Will I be permitted to attend?" Georgiana asked.

"Nothing in the evening," her mother said, "but certainly some of the afternoon entertainments."

Georgiana sat back with a cat-in-the-cream smile. "Then I think it's an excellent idea."

"*Georgie*," Billie said.

"*Billie*," Georgiana mocked.

Billie's lips parted in surprise. Was the entire world tipping on its axis? Since when did her younger sister talk back to her like *that*?

"It's settled, Billie," her mother said in a tone that

brooked no dissent. "We are having a party, and you will attend. In a dress."

"Mother!" Billie cried out.

"I don't think it's an unreasonable demand," her mother said, glancing about the table for confirmation.

"I *know* how to behave at a house party." Good Lord, what did her mother think she would do? Come to dinner with riding boots under her gown? Race the hounds through the drawing room?

She knew the rules. She did. And she didn't even mind them under the right circumstances. That her own mother thought her so inept . . . And that she would say so in front of all the people Billie cared most about . . .

It hurt more than she could ever have imagined.

But then the strangest thing happened. George's hand found hers and squeezed. Under the table, where no one could see. Billie jerked her head to look at him—she couldn't help it—but he'd already let go and was saying something to his father about the price of French brandy.

Billie stared at her soup.

What a day.

LATER THAT EVENING, after the men had gone off to have their port and the ladies were congregated in the drawing room, Billie stole away to the library, wanting nothing more than a spot of peace and quiet.

Although she wasn't really sure if it counted as

stealing away when she was required to beg a footman to carry her there.

Still, she'd always liked the library at Crake House. It was smaller than the one they had at Aubrey Hall, and it felt less imposing. Almost cozy. Lord Manston had a habit of falling asleep on the soft leather sofa, and as soon as Billie settled into the cushions she understood why. With a fire in the grate and a knitted blanket thrown over her legs, it was the perfect place to rest her eyes until her parents were ready to return home.

She wasn't sleepy, though. Just weary. It had been a long day, and her entire body ached from her fall, and her mother had been spectacularly insensitive, and Andrew hadn't even noticed that she wasn't feeling well, and George *had*, and then Georgiana had gone and turned into someone she didn't recognize, and—

And, and, and. It was all *ands* this evening, and the sum of it all was exhausting.

"Billie?"

She let out a softly startled shriek as she lurched into a more upright position. George was standing in the open doorway, his expression made unreadable by the dim, flickering candlelight.

"Sorry." She squeezed her eyes shut, taking a moment to catch her breath. "You surprised me."

"My apologies. It was not my intention." He leaned against the doorjamb. "Why are you here?"

"I needed a bit of quiet." She still could not see his face clearly, but she could well imagine his bemused countenance, so she added, "Even I need quiet every now and again."

He smiled faintly. "You don't feel cooped up?"

"Not at all." She tipped her head, acknowledging the riposte.

He took a moment to consider this, then said, "Would you like me to leave you to your solitude?"

"No, it's all right," Billie said, surprising herself with her statement. George's presence was oddly calming, in a way Andrew's or her mother's or really any of the others' never were.

"You're in pain," he said, finally stepping into the room.

How had he known? Nobody else had. But then again, George had always been uncomfortably observant. "Yes," she said. There was little point pretending otherwise.

"A great deal?"

"No. But more than a little."

"You should have rested this evening."

"Perhaps. But I enjoyed myself, and I think it was worth it. It was lovely to see your mother so happy."

George's head cocked to the side. "You thought she was happy?"

"Didn't you?"

"To see Andrew, perhaps, but in some ways his presence only serves to remind her that Edward is not here."

"I suppose. I mean, of course she'd rather have two sons home, but the reminder of Edward's absence is surely outweighed by the joy of Andrew's presence."

George's lips pressed into a wry, one-sided curve. "She did have two sons home."

Billie stared at him for a moment before— "Oh! I'm so sorry. Of course she did. I was just thinking of the sons who aren't normally at home. I . . . Good God, I'm really sorry." Her face was burning. Thank heavens the candlelight hid her blush.

He shrugged. "Think nothing of it."

She couldn't, though. No matter how even his mien, she couldn't help but think she'd hurt his feelings. Which was mad; George Rokesby did not care enough for her good opinion to be bothered by anything she said.

But still, there had been something in his expression . . .

"Does it bother you?" she asked.

He came further into the room, stopping by the shelf where the good brandy was kept. "Does what bother me?"

"Being left behind." She bit her lip. There had to be a better way of saying it. "Remaining home," she amended, "when everyone else is gone."

"You're here," he pointed out.

"Yes, but I'm hardly a comfort. To you, I mean."

He chuckled. Well, not really, but he did exhale a bit through his nose, and it sounded amused.

"Even Mary's gone to Sussex," Billie said, shifting her position so that she could watch him over the back of the sofa.

George poured himself a brandy, setting the glass down as he returned the stopper to the decanter. "I can't begrudge my sister a happy marriage. To one of my closest friends, no less."

"Of course not. Nor could I. But I still miss her. And you're still the only Rokesby in regular residence."

He brought his glass to his lips, but he didn't quite take a sip. "You do have a way of cutting right to the heart of the matter, don't you?"

Billie held her tongue.

"Does it bother *you*?" he asked.

She didn't pretend to misunderstand the question. "My siblings aren't all gone. Georgiana is still home."

"And you have so much in common with her," he said in a dry voice.

"More than I used to think," Billie told him. It was true. Georgiana had been a sickly child, worried over by her parents, stuck inside while the rest of the children ran wild across the countryside.

Billie had never disliked her younger sister; but at the same time, she hadn't found her very interesting. Most of the time, she'd forgotten she was even there. There were nine years between them. Really, what could they possibly have had in common?

But then everyone else went away, and now Georgiana was finally growing close enough to adulthood to become interesting.

It was George's turn to speak, but he did not seem to have noticed this fact, and the silence stretched for long enough to be vaguely unsettling.

"George?" Billie murmured. He was looking at her in the oddest manner. As if she were a puzzle—no, not that. As if he were thinking, quite deeply, and she just happened to be in the way of his eyes.

"George?" she repeated. "Are you all—"

He looked up suddenly. "You should be nicer to her." And then, as if he hadn't just said the most appalling thing, he motioned to the brandy. "Would you like a glass?"

"Yes," Billie said, even though she was well aware that most ladies would have refused, "and what on earth do you mean, I should be nicer to her? When have I ever been unkind?"

"Never," he agreed, splashing a bit of liquid into a glass, "but you ignore her."

"I do not."

"You forget about her," he amended. "It amounts to the same thing."

"Oh, and you pay so much attention to Nicholas."

"Nicholas is at Eton. I can hardly shower him with attention from here."

He handed her a brandy. She noticed her glass was considerably less full than his had been.

"I don't ignore her," Billie muttered. She didn't like being scolded, especially by George Rokesby. Especially when he was right.

"It's all right," he said, surprising her with his sudden kindness. "I'm sure it's different when Andrew isn't home."

"What does Andrew have to do with anything?"

He turned to her with an expression that hovered somewhere between surprised and amused. "Really?"

"I don't know what you're talking about." Maddening man.

George took a long sip, and then—without even turning toward her—he managed to give her a condescending look. "He should just marry you and be done with it."

"What?" Her surprise was unfeigned. Not that she might marry Andrew. She'd always thought she'd one day marry him. Or Edward. She didn't really care which; it was all the same to her. But that George was actually speaking of it in such a manner . . .

She didn't like it.

"I'm sure you're aware," she said, quickly regaining her composure, "that Andrew and I have no understanding."

He waved that off with a roll of his eyes. "You could do worse."

"So could he," she retorted.

George chuckled. "True enough."

"I'm not going to marry Andrew," she said. Not yet, anyway. But if he asked . . .

She would probably say yes. It was what everyone expected.

George took a sip of his brandy, watching her enigmatically over the rim of his glass.

"The last thing I'd want to do," Billie said, unable to leave the silence be, "is get engaged to someone who is going to turn around and leave."

"Oh, I don't know," George said with a thoughtful frown. "Many military wives follow their husbands. And you're more adventurous than most."

"I like it here."

"In my father's library?" he quipped.

"In Kent," she said pertly. "At Aubrey Hall. I'm needed."

He made a patronizing sound.

"I am!"

"I'm sure you are."

Her spine stiffened. If her ankle weren't throbbing, she'd have probably jumped to her feet. "You have no idea all I do."

"Please don't tell me."

"What?"

He made a dismissive motion with his hand. "You have that look about you."

"What loo—"

"The one that says you're about to launch into a very long speech."

Her lips parted with shock. Of all the condescending, supercilious . . . Then she saw his face. He was enjoying himself!

Of course he was. He lived to get under her skin. Like a needle. A dull, rusty needle.

"Oh, for heaven's sake, Billie," he said, leaning against a bookcase as he chuckled. "Can't you take a ribbing? I know you help your father from time to time."

From time to time? She ran the bloody place. Aubrey Hall would fall apart without her direction. Her father had all but ceded the ledgers to her, and the steward had long since given up protesting about having to answer to a woman. Billie had, for all intents and purposes, been raised as her father's eldest son. Except that she couldn't inherit anything. And eventually Edmund would grow up, take his rightful place. Her younger brother wasn't stupid; he'd learn what to do quickly enough, and when he did . . . when Edmund showed all of Aubrey how capable he was, everyone would breathe a sigh of relief and say something about natural order being restored.

Billie would be superfluous.

Replaced.

The ledgers would be quietly removed from her purview. No one would ask her to inspect the cottages or settle disputes. Edmund would become lord of the manor, and she'd be his long-toothed older sister, the one people quietly pitied and mocked.

God, maybe she *should* marry Andrew.

"Are you sure you're not unwell?" George asked.

"I'm fine," she said curtly.

He shrugged. "You looked rather ill all of a sudden."

She'd felt rather ill all of a sudden. Her future had finally danced before her, and there was nothing bright and beautiful about it.

She tossed back the rest of her brandy.

"Careful there," George cautioned, but she was already coughing, unaccustomed to setting her throat on fire. "It's better to sip it slowly," he added.

"I *know*," she ground out, well aware that she sounded like an idiot.

"Of course you do," he murmured, and just like that, she felt better. George Rokesby was being a pompous ass. Everything was back to normal. Or almost normal.

Normal enough.

Chapter 8

Lady Bridgerton began planning her assault on the social Season the very next morning. Billie hobbled into the small dining room to break her fast, fully prepared to be drafted into service, but to her relief and amazement her mother said that she did not require Billie's assistance with the planning. All she asked was that Billie write a note of invitation to Mary and Felix. Billie nodded her grateful agreement. This she could do.

"Georgiana has offered to help me," Lady Bridgerton said as she signaled to a footman to prepare a breakfast plate. Billie was agile on her crutches, but even she could not fix her own meal from the sideboard while balanced on a pair of sticks.

Billie glanced at her younger sister, who appeared quite pleased at this prospect. "It will be great fun," Georgiana said.

Billie swallowed a retort. She couldn't think of

much that would be *less* fun, but she did not need to insult her sister by saying so. If Georgiana wanted to spend the afternoon penning invitations and planning menus, she was welcome to it.

Lady Bridgerton prepared a cup of tea for Billie. "How do you plan to spend your day?"

"I'm not sure," Billie said, nodding her thanks to the footman as he set her plate in front of her. She gazed wistfully out the window. The sun was just beginning to break through the clouds, and within an hour the morning dew would have evaporated. A perfect day to be out of doors. On horseback. Being useful.

And she had so much to do. One of the tenants was rethatching the roof of his cottage, and even though his neighbors knew they were expected to offer their aid, Billie still suspected that John and Harry Williamson would try to weasel out of it. Someone needed to make sure that the brothers did their share, just like someone needed to make sure that the western fields were being planted properly and the rose garden had been pruned to her mother's exact specifications.

Someone needed to do all that, and Billie had no idea who that would be if not her.

But no, she was stuck inside with a stupid swollen foot, and it wasn't even her fault. All right, maybe it was a little bit her fault, but certainly more the cat's fault, and the bloody thing hurt like the devil—her foot, that was, not the cat, although she was small-minded enough to hope that the beastly little creature also had reason to limp.

She paused to consider that. When it came right down to it . . .

"Billie?" her mother murmured, eyeing her above the rim of her bone china teacup.

"I think I'm not a very nice person," Billie mused.

Lady Bridgerton choked so hard tea came out her nose. It was quite a sight, really, and not one Billie had ever expected to see in her lifetime.

"I could have told you *that*," Georgiana said.

Billie flashed a scowl at her sister that was, all things considered, rather immature.

"Sybilla Bridgerton," came her mother's brook-no-dissent voice. "You are a perfectly nice person."

Billie opened her mouth to speak, not that she had anything intelligent to say.

"If you're not," her mother continued, her voice leaping into the moment with a *don't-you-dare-think-of-contradicting-me* punch of volume, "it reflects badly upon *me*, and I refuse to believe I am so derelict a mother as that."

"Of course not," Billie said quickly. Very quickly.

"Therefore I will repeat my question," her mother said. She took a delicate sip of her tea and gazed upon her elder daughter with remarkable impassivity. "What do you plan to do today?"

"Well," Billie stalled. She glanced over at her sister, but Georgiana was no help. She just lifted her shoulders in a helpless little shrug that could have meant anything from *I-have-no-idea-what's-got-into-her* to *I-am-enjoying-your-discomfort-immensely*.

Billie scowled. Wouldn't it be lovely if people just said what they thought?

Billie turned back to her mother, who was still regarding her with a deceptively placid expression. "Well," she stalled again. "I might read a book?"

"A book," her mother repeated. She dabbed at the corner of her mouth with her napkin. "How delightful."

Billie eyed her cautiously. Any number of sarcastic retorts sprang to mind, but despite her mother's serene demeanor, there was a gleam in her eye that told Billie she'd be wise to keep her mouth shut.

Lady Bridgerton reached for the teapot. She always drank more tea at breakfast than the rest of the family combined. "I could recommend something, if you like," she said to Billie. She also generally read more books than the rest of the family combined.

"No, that's all right," Billie replied, cutting her sausage into rounds. "Father bought the latest volume of *Prescott's Encyclopaedia of Agriculture* when he was in London last month. I should have already started it, but the weather has been so fine I haven't had the chance."

"You could read outside," Georgiana suggested. "We could put down a blanket. Or drag out a chaise."

Billie nodded absently as she stabbed a sausage disc. "It would be better than remaining in, I suppose."

"You could help me plan the entertainments for the house party," Georgiana said.

Billie gave her a condescending look. "I don't think so."

"Why not, darling?" Lady Bridgerton put in. "It might be fun."

"You just told me I didn't have to take part in the planning."

"Only because I didn't think you wanted to."

"I don't want to."

"Of course not," her mother said smoothly, "but you *do* want to spend time with your sister."

Oh, hell. Her mother was *good*. Billie pasted a smile on her face. "Can't Georgie and I do something else?"

"If you can convince her to read your agricultural treatise over your shoulder," her mother said, her hand flitting delicately through the air.

Delicately like a bullet, Billie thought. "I'll help with *some* of the planning," she conceded.

"Oh, that will be marvelous!" Georgiana exclaimed. "And so very helpful. You'll have much more experience with this sort of thing than I."

"Not really," Billie said frankly.

"But you've *been* to house parties."

"Well, yes, but . . ." Billie didn't bother finishing her sentence. Georgiana looked so happy. It would be like kicking a puppy to tell Georgiana that she had hated being dragged to house parties with their mother. Or if hate was too strong a word, she certainly hadn't enjoyed herself. She really didn't like traveling. She'd learned that much about herself.

And she did not enjoy the company of strangers. She wasn't shy; not at all. She just preferred being among people she knew.

People who knew *her*.

Life was so much easier that way.

"Look at it this way," Lady Bridgerton said to Billie. "You don't want a house party. You don't like house parties. But I am your mother, and I have decided to host one. Therefore, you have no choice but to attend. Why not take the opportunity to mold this gathering into something you might actually enjoy?"

"But I'm not going to enjoy it."

"You certainly won't if you approach it with that attitude."

Billie took a moment to compose herself. And to hold down the urge to argue her point and defend herself and tell her mother that she would not be spoken to as if she was a child . . .

"I would be delighted to assist Georgiana," Billie said tightly, "as long as I get some time to read my book."

"I wouldn't dream of pulling you away from *Prescott's*," her mother murmured.

Billie glared at her. "You shouldn't mock it. It's exactly that sort of book that has enabled me to increase productivity at Aubrey Hall by a full ten percent. Not to mention the improvements to the tenant farms. They are all eating better now that—"

She cut herself off. Swallowed. She'd just done exactly what she'd told herself not to do.

Argue her point.

Defend herself.

Act like a child.

She shoveled as much of her breakfast into her

mouth as she could manage in thirty seconds, then stood and grabbed her crutches, which were leaning against the table. "I will be in the library if anyone needs me." To Georgiana she added, "Let me know when the ground is dry enough to spread a blanket."

Georgiana nodded.

"Mother," Billie said to Lady Bridgerton with a nod to replace the normal bob of a curtsy she gave when she took her leave. Yet another thing one couldn't manage on crutches.

"Billie," her mother said, her voice conciliatory. And perhaps a little frustrated. "I wish you wouldn't . . ."

Billie waited for her to finish her sentence, but her mother just shook her head.

"Never mind," she said.

Billie nodded again, pressing a crutch into the ground for balance as she pivoted on her good foot. She *thunked* the crutches on the ground, then swung her body between them, her shoulders held tight and straight as she repeated the motion all the way to the door.

It was bloody hard to make a dignified exit on crutches.

GEORGE STILL WASN'T sure how Andrew had talked him into accompanying him to Aubrey Hall for a late morning visit, but here he was, standing in the grand entry as he handed his hat to Thamesly, butler to the Bridgertons since before he was born.

"You're doing a good deed, old man," Andrew said, slapping George's shoulder with surely more force than was necessary.

"Don't call me old man." God, he hated that.

But this only made Andrew laugh. Of course. "Whomever you might be, you're still doing a good deed. Billie will be out of her mind with boredom."

"She could use a little boredom in her life," George muttered.

"True enough," Andrew conceded, "but my concern was for her family. God only knows what madness she'll inflict upon them if no one shows up to entertain her."

"You talk as if she's a child."

"A child?" Andrew turned to look at him, his face taking on an enigmatic serenity that George knew well enough to find suspicious in the extreme. "Not at all."

"Miss Bridgerton is in the library," Thamesly informed them. "If you will wait in the drawing room, I will alert her to your presence."

"No need," Andrew said cheerily. "We will join her in the library. The last thing we want is to force Miss Bridgerton to hobble about more than is necessary."

"Very kind of you, sir," Thamesly murmured.

"Is she in a great deal of pain?" George inquired.

"I would not know," the butler said diplomatically, "but it may be worth noting that the weather is very fine, and Miss Bridgerton is in the library."

"So she's miserable, then."

"Very much so, my lord."

George supposed *this* was why he'd allowed Andrew to drag him away from his weekly meeting with their father's steward. He'd known Billie's ankle could not have been much improved. It had been grotesquely swollen the night before, no matter how festively she'd wrapped it with that ridiculous pink ribbon. Injuries like that did not resolve themselves overnight.

And while he and Billie had never been friends, precisely, he felt a strange responsibility for her well-being, at least as pertained to her current situation. What was that old Chinese proverb? If you saved a life, you were responsible for it forever? He certainly had not saved Billie's life, but he had been stuck up on a roof with her, and . . .

And bloody hell, he had no idea what any of this meant, just that he thought he ought to make sure she was feeling at least somewhat better. Even though she was the _most_ exasperating female, and she bloody well set his teeth on edge half the time.

It was still the right thing to do. That was all.

"Oh, Billie . . ." Andrew called as they made their way to the back of the house. "We've come to rescue you . . ."

George shook his head. How his brother survived in the navy he would never know. Andrew had not a serious bone in his body.

"Billie . . ." he called again, his voice warbling into a ridiculous singsong. "Where aaaaaarrrrrre you?"

"In the library," George reminded him.

"Well, of course she is," Andrew said with a blinding grin, "but isn't this more fun?"

Naturally, he did not wait for an answer.

"Billie!" he called again. "Oh, *Billiebilliebilliebill*—"

"For heaven's sake!" Billie's head popped out of the doorway to the library. Her chestnut hair had been pulled back into the loose coiffure of a lady with no plans to socialize. "You're loud enough to wake the dead. What are you doing here?"

"Is that any way to greet an old friend?"

"I saw you last night."

"So you did." Andrew leaned down and dropped a brotherly kiss on her cheek. "But you had to go without for so very long. You need to stock up."

"On your company?" Billie asked dubiously.

Andrew patted her arm. "We are so fortunate that you have this opportunity."

George leaned to the right so that he could see her from behind his brother. "Shall I strangle him or will you?"

She rewarded him with a devious smile. "Oh, it must be a joint endeavor, don't you think?"

"So that you may share the blame?" Andrew quipped.

"So that we may share the joy," Billie corrected.

"You wound me."

"Happily, I assure you." She hopped to the left and looked at George. "What brings you here this fine morning, Lord Kennard?"

He gave her a bit of a look at her use of his title. The Bridgertons and Rokesbys never stood on occasion when it was just the two families. Even now, no one so much as blinked at Billie being alone with two unmarried gentlemen in the library. It wasn't the sort of thing that would be permitted during the upcoming house party, though. They were all well aware that their relaxed manners would not stand in extended company.

"Dragged along by my brother, I'm afraid," George admitted. "There was some fear for your family's safety."

Her eyes narrowed. "Really."

"Now, now, Billie," Andrew said. "We all know you don't do well trapped indoors."

"I came for *his* safety," George said with a jerk of his head toward Andrew. "Although it is my belief that any injury you might do to him would be entirely justified."

Billie threw back her head and laughed. "Come, join me in the library. I need to sit back down."

While George was recovering from the unexpectedly marvelous sight of Billie in full joy, she hopped back to the nearest reading table, holding her light blue skirts above her ankles for easier motion.

"You should use your crutches," he told her.

"Not worth it for such a short trip," she replied, settling back down into her chair. "Besides, they tipped over and it was far too much trouble to retrieve them."

George followed her gaze to where the crutches lay askew on the ground, one slightly atop the other. He leaned down and picked them up, setting them gently against the side of the library table. "If you need help," he said in a quiet voice, "you should ask for it."

She looked at him and blinked. "I didn't need help."

George started to tell her not to be so defensive, but then he realized she *hadn't* been defensive. She was merely stating a fact. A fact as *she* saw it.

He shook his head. Billie could be so bloody literal.

"What was that?" she asked.

He shrugged. He had no idea what she was about.

"What were you going to say?" she demanded.

"Nothing."

Her mouth tightened at the corners. "That's not true. You were definitely going to say something."

Literal *and* tenacious. It was a frightening combination. "Did you sleep well?" he asked politely.

"Of course," she said, with just enough of an arch to her brows to tell him that she was well aware that he'd changed the subject. "I told you yesterday. I never have trouble sleeping."

"You said you never have trouble falling asleep," he corrected, somewhat surprised that he recalled the distinction.

She shrugged. "It's much the same thing."

"The pain did not wake you up?"

She glanced down at her foot as if she'd quite forgotten it was there. "Apparently not."

"If I might interrupt," Andrew said, bowing to Billie with a ridiculous sweep of his arm, "we are here to offer our assistance and succor in any way you deem necessary."

She gave Andrew the sort of look George normally reserved for small, recalcitrant children. "Are you sure you want to make such a sweeping promise?"

George leaned down until his lips were at the same latitude as her ear. "Pray remember that he uses 'we' as a grandiose gesture, not as a plural pronoun."

She grinned. "In other words, you want no part of it?"

"None whatsoever."

"You insult the lady," Andrew said without a hint of protest in his voice. He sprawled in one of the Bridgertons' fine wingback chairs, his long legs stretched out so that the heels of his boots rested against the carpet.

Billie gave him an exasperated glance before turning back to George. "Why *are* you here?"

George took a seat at the table across from her. "What he said, but without the hyperbole. We thought you might need company."

"Oh." She drew back a touch, clearly surprised by his frankness. "Thank you. That's very kind of you."

"*Thank you, that's very kind of you?*" Andrew echoed. "Who *are* you?"

She whipped her head to face him. "Was I supposed to curtsy?"

"It would have been nice," he demurred.

"Impossible on crutches."

"Well, if *that's* the case . . ."

Billie turned back to George. "He's an idiot."

He held up his hands. "You will find no argument here."

"The plight of the younger son," Andrew said with a sigh.

Billie rolled her eyes, tipping her head toward Andrew as she said to George, "Don't encourage him."

"To be ganged up upon," Andrew went on, "never respected . . ."

George craned his neck, trying to read the title of Billie's book. "What are you reading?"

"And," Andrew continued, "apparently ignored as well."

Billie rotated her book so that the gold leaf lettering faced George. "*Prescott's Encyclopaedia of Agriculture.*"

"Volume Four," he said approvingly. He had volumes one through three in his own personal library.

"Yes, it was only recently published," Billie confirmed.

"It must have been very recently, or I would have purchased it when I was last in London."

"My father brought it back from his most recent trip. You can read it when I'm done if you wish."

"Oh, no, I'm sure I'll need a copy of my own."

"As a reference," she said with an approving nod.

"This might be the dullest conversation I have ever beheld," Andrew said from behind them.

They ignored him.

"Do you often read such tomes?" George asked, nodding at the Prescott book. He'd always thought ladies preferred slim volumes of poetry or plays by Shakespeare and Marlowe. It was what his sister and mother seemed to enjoy reading.

"Of course," she replied, scowling as if he'd insulted her with the very question.

"Billie helps her father with the land management," Andrew said, apparently bored of making fun of them. He pushed himself to his feet and wandered over to the wall of shelves, selecting a book seemingly at random. He leafed through a few pages, frowned, and put it back.

"Yes, you mentioned you'd been assisting him," George said. He looked at Billie. "Very singular of you."

Her eyes narrowed.

"That was not meant as an insult," he got in before she could open her rash little mouth, "just an observation."

She did not look convinced.

"You will concede," he said smoothly, "that most young ladies do not assist their fathers in such a manner. Hence, your singularity."

"I swear, George," Andrew said, glancing up from the book he was paging through, "you even give your compliments like a conceited ass."

"I'm going to kill him," George muttered.

"You'll have to form a line," Billie remarked. But then she lowered her voice. "It's a little bit true, though."

He drew back. "I beg your pardon?"

"You did sound a little . . ." She waved her hand in the air as a substitute for actually finishing her sentence.

"Like an ass?" George supplied.

"No!" She said this with enough speed and conviction for him to believe her. "Just a little bit . . ."

He waited.

"Are you talking about me?" Andrew asked, settling back in his chair with a book in his hand.

"No," they said in unison.

"I don't mind if it's complimentary," he murmured.

George ignored him, keeping his eyes on Billie. She was frowning. Two small lines formed between her brows, curving against each other like an hourglass, and her lips tightened into a curious pucker, almost as if she were anticipating a kiss.

He'd never watched her think, he realized.

Then he realized what a staggeringly odd observation *that* was.

"You did sound a *little* conceited," Billie finally said. Her voice was quiet, meant for their ears only. "But I think that's understandable?"

Understandable? He leaned forward. "Why are you saying that like it's a question?"

"I don't know."

He sat back and crossed his arms, quirking one brow to indicate that he was waiting for her to continue.

"Fine," she said, less than graciously. "You're the eldest, the heir. You're the brilliant, the handsome, oh, and we must not forget, the *eligible* Earl of Kennard."

George felt a slow smile spread across his face. "You think I'm handsome?"

"This is exactly what I'm talking about!"

"Brilliant, too," George murmured. "I had no idea."

"You're acting like Andrew," Billie muttered.

For some reason, this made him chuckle.

Billie's eyes narrowed into a glare.

George's smile stretched into a full-fledged grin. By God, it was fun to needle her.

She leaned forward, and in that moment he realized just how well people could speak through clenched teeth. "I was trying to be considerate," she ground out.

"I'm sorry," George said immediately.

Her lips pressed together. "You asked me a question. I was trying to give you an honest, thoughtful answer. I thought you deserved as much."

Well, *now* he felt like an ass.

"I'm sorry," he said again, and this time it was more than an ingrained bit of polite manners.

Billie let out a breath, and she caught the inside of her lower lip between her teeth. She was thinking again, George realized. How remarkable it was to see another person think. Was everyone this expressive as they pondered their ideas?

"It's how you were brought up," she finally said. "You're no more to blame than . . ." She exhaled again, but George was patient. She would find the right words.

And after a few moments, she did. "You've been raised—" But this time she stopped herself quite suddenly.

"To be conceited?" he said softly.

"To be confident," she corrected, but he had a feeling that his statement was a lot closer to what she had been about to say. "It's not your fault," she added.

"Now who's being patronizing?"

She gave him a wry smile. "Me, I'm sure. But it's true. You can't help it any more than I can help being a . . ." She waved her hands again, which was apparently her all-purpose gesture for things that were too awkward to say aloud.

"What I am," she finally finished.

"What you are." He said it softly. He said it because he had to say it, even if he didn't know why.

She looked up at him, but only with her eyes. Her face remained tipped slightly down, and he had the oddest notion that if he did not meet her gaze, if he did not hold it with his own, she would return hers to her tightly clutched hands, and the moment would be lost forever.

"What are you?" he whispered.

She shook her head. "I have no idea."

"Is anyone hungry?" Andrew suddenly asked.

George blinked, trying to snap himself out of whatever spell had been cast over him.

"Because I am," Andrew continued. "Famished. Utterly. I ate only one breakfast this morning."

"*One* breakfast?" Billie started to say, but Andrew was already on his feet, bounding over to her side.

He set his hands on the table, leaning down to murmur, "I was hoping I'd be invited to tea."

"Of course you're invited to tea," Billie said, but she sounded just as off-balance as George felt. She frowned. "It's a little early, though."

"It's never too early for tea," Andrew declared. "Not if your cook has been making shortbread." He turned to George. "I don't know what she puts in it, but it's divine."

"Butter," Billie said absently. "Quite a lot of it."

Andrew cocked his head to the side. "Well, that makes sense. Everything tastes better with quite a lot of butter."

"We should ask Georgiana to join us," Billie said, reaching for her crutches. "I'm meant to be helping her plan the entertainments for the house party." She rolled her eyes. "My mother's orders."

Andrew let out a bark of laughter. "Does your mother even *know* you?"

Billie threw an irritated look at him over her shoulder.

"Seriously, Billie-goat, what will you have us do? Head out to the south lawn to plant barley?"

"Stop," George said.

Andrew swung around. "What was that?"

"Leave her alone."

Andrew stared at him for so long George could not help but wonder if he'd been speaking in tongues.

"It's Billie," Andrew finally said.

"I know. And you should leave her alone."

"I can fight my own battles, George," Billie said.

He glanced over at her. "Of course you can."

Her lips parted, but she seemed not to know how to respond to that.

Andrew looked back and forth between the two of them before offering Billie a small bow. "My apologies."

Billie nodded awkwardly.

Chapter 9

Four days later

It was remarkable—no, *inspirational*—Billie decided, how quickly she'd weaned herself from her crutches. Clearly, it was all in the mind.

Strength. Fortitude.

Determination.

Also, the ability to ignore pain was helpful.

It didn't hurt *that* much, she reasoned. Just a twinge. Or maybe something closer to a nail being hammered into her ankle at intervals corresponding to the speed at which she took her steps.

But not a very big nail. Just a little one. A pin, really.

She was made of stern stuff. Everybody said so.

At any rate, the pain in her ankle wasn't nearly as bad as the chafing under her arms from the crutches. And she wasn't planning to go for a five-mile hike. She just wanted to be able to get about the house on her own two feet.

"Perhaps I might help in the planning," Andrew suggested.

"You'll certainly be better at it than I am," Billie said.

"Well, *that* goes without saying."

She poked him in the leg with one of her crutches.

And just like that, George realized, all was back to normal.

Except it wasn't. Not for him.

Nevertheless, her pace was considerably slower than her usual stride as she headed toward the drawing room a few hours after breakfast. Andrew was waiting for her, Thamesly had informed her. This was not terribly surprising; Andrew had called upon her every day since her injury.

It was really quite sweet of him.

They'd been building card houses, a characteristically perverse choice for Andrew, whose dominant arm was still immobilized in a sling. He'd said that as long as he was coming over to keep her company, he might as well do something useful.

Billie didn't bother pointing out that building a house of cards might very well be the definition of *not* useful.

As for his having only one working arm, he needed help getting the first few cards balanced, but after that, he could set up the rest just as well as she could.

Or better, really. She'd forgotten how freakishly good he was at building card houses—*and* how freakishly obsessed he became during the process. The day before had been the worst. As soon as they'd completed the first level he'd banned her from construction. Then he banned her from the entire area, claiming that she breathed too hard.

Which of course left her with no choice but to sneeze.

She might also have kicked the table.

There had been a fleeting moment of regret when it had all come down in a spectacular earthquake of destruction, but the look on Andrew's face had been worth it, even if he had gone home immediately following the collapse.

But that was yesterday, and knowing Andrew, he'd want to start again, bigger and better the fifth time around. So Billie had collected another two decks on her way to the drawing room. It should be enough for him to add another story or two to his next architectural masterpiece.

"Good morning," she said as she entered the drawing room. He was standing over by a plate of biscuits someone had left out on the table that ran behind the sofa. A maid, probably. One of the sillier ones. They were always giggling over him.

"You've jettisoned the crutches," he said with an approving nod. "Congratulations."

"Thank you." She glanced about the room. Still no George. He had not visited since that first morning in the library. Not that she had expected him to. She and George were not friends.

They weren't *enemies*, of course. Just not friends. They never had been. Although maybe they were a little bit . . . now.

"What's wrong?" Andrew asked.

Billie blinked. "Nothing's wrong."

"You're scowling."

"I'm not scowling."

His expression turned condescending. "You can see your own face?"

"And you're here to cheer me up," she drawled.

"Gad no, I'm here for the shortbread." He reached

out and took some of the playing cards from her. "And maybe to build a house."

"At last, some honesty."

Andrew laughed and flopped down on the sofa. "I have hardly been hiding my motives."

Billie acknowledged this with a flick of her eyes. He had eaten a prodigious amount of shortbread in the past few days.

"You'd be kinder to me," he continued, "if you knew how horrid the food is on a ship."

"Scale of one to ten?"

"Twelve."

"I'm so sorry," she said with a grimace. She knew how Andrew liked his sweets.

"I knew what I was getting into." He paused, frowning with thought. "No, actually I don't think I did."

"You wouldn't have entered the navy if you'd realized there would be no biscuits?"

Andrew sighed dramatically. "Sometimes a man must make his own biscuits."

Several playing cards slid from her grasp. "*What*?"

"I believe he's substituting biscuits for destiny," came a voice from the door.

"George!" Billie exclaimed. With surprise? With delight? What *was* that in her voice? And why couldn't she, of all people, figure it out?

"Billie," he murmured, offering a polite bow.

She stared. "What are you doing here?"

His mouth moved into a dry expression that in all honesty could not be called a smile. "Ever the model of gentility."

"Well"—she bent down to gather the cards she'd dropped, trying not to trip on the lace trim of her skirt—"you haven't visited for four days."

Now he did smile. "You've missed me, then."

"No!" She glared at him, reaching out to snatch up the knave of hearts. The annoying little rascal had slid halfway under the sofa. "Don't be ridiculous. Thamesly said nothing about your being here. He mentioned only Andrew."

"I was seeing to the horses," George said.

She immediately looked to Andrew, surprise coloring her features. "Did you ride?"

"Well, I tried," he admitted.

"We went very slowly," George confirmed. Then his eyes narrowed. "Where are your crutches?"

"Gone," she replied, smiling proudly.

"I can *see* that." His brow pulled down into a scowling vee. "Who told you you were allowed to stop using them?"

"No one," she bristled. Who the devil did he think he was? Her father? No, definitely not her father. That was just . . .

Ugh.

"I rose from bed," she said with exaggerated patience, "took a step, and decided for myself."

George snorted.

She drew back. "What is that supposed to mean?"

"Allow me to translate," Andrew said from the sofa, where he was still stretched out in a boyish sprawl.

"I *know* what it meant," Billie snapped.

"Oh, Billie," Andrew sighed.

She swung around to glare at him.

"You need to get out of the house," he said.

Please, as if she didn't know *that*. She turned back to George. "Pray, excuse my impoliteness. I wasn't expecting you."

His brows arched, but he accepted her apology with a nod and took a seat when she did.

"We need to feed him," Billie said, tilting her head toward Andrew.

"Water him, too?" George murmured, as if Andrew were a horse.

"I'm right here!" Andrew protested.

George motioned to the day-old copy of the *London Times*, which lay freshly ironed on the table next to him. "Do you mind if I read?"

"Not at all," Billie said. Far be it from her to expect him to entertain her. Even if that had been his implied purpose in stopping by. She leaned forward, giving Andrew a little tap on his shoulder. "Would you like me to get you started?"

"Please," he said, "and then don't touch it."

Billie looked at George. The newspaper was still folded in his lap, and he was watching the two of them with amused curiosity.

"In the center of the table," Andrew said.

Billie gave him a bit of a look. "Autocratic as always."

"I am an artist."

"Architect," George said.

Andrew looked up, as if he'd forgotten his brother was there. "Yes," he murmured. "Quite."

Billie slid from her chair and knelt in front of the low table, adjusting her weight so as not to put pressure on her bad foot. She selected two cards from the messy pile near the table's edge and balanced them into the shape of a *T*. Carefully, she released her fingers and waited to see if it was secure.

"Nicely done," George murmured.

Billie smiled, absurdly pleased by his compliment. "Thank you."

Andrew rolled his eyes.

"I swear, Andrew," Billie said, using a third card to transform the *T* into an *H*, "you turn into the *most* annoying person when you're doing this."

"But I get the job done."

Billie heard George chuckle, followed by the crinkling sound of the newspaper opening and then folding into a readable shape. She shook her head, decided that Andrew was extraordinarily fortunate she was his friend, and set a few more cards into place. "Will that be enough to get you started?" she asked Andrew.

"Yes, thank you. Mind the table when you get up."

"Is this what you're like at sea?" Billie asked, limping across the room to get her book before settling back down. "It's a wonder anyone puts up with you."

Andrew narrowed his eyes—at the card structure, not at her—and placed a card into position. "I get the job done," he repeated.

Billie turned back to George. He was watching Andrew with a peculiar expression on his face. His brow was furrowed, but he wasn't precisely frowning. His eyes were far too bright and curious for that. Every time he blinked, his lashes swept down like a fan, graceful and—

"Billie?"

Oh, God, he'd caught her looking at him.

Wait, *why* was she looking at him?

"Sorry," she mumbled. "Lost in thought."

"I hope it was something interesting."

She choked on her breath before answering, "Not really." Then she felt kind of terrible, insulting him without his even knowing it.

And without her really meaning to.

"He's like a different person," she said, motioning to Andrew. "I find it very disconcerting."

"You've never seen him like this before?"

"No, I have." She looked from the chair to the sofa and decided on the sofa. Andrew was now on the floor, and he wasn't likely to want his spot back anytime soon. She sat down, leaning against the arm and stretching her legs out in front of her. Without really thinking about what she was doing she reached for the blanket that lay folded over the back and spread it over her legs. "I still find it disconcerting."

"He is unexpectedly precise," George said.

Billie considered that. "Unexpected because . . . ?"

George shrugged and motioned to his brother. "Who would think it of him?"

Billie thought for a moment, then decided she agreed with him. "There's an odd sort of sense to that."

"I can still hear you, you know," Andrew said.

He'd got about a dozen more cards into place and had pulled back a few inches to examine the house from several angles.

"I don't believe we were aiming for stealth," George said mildly.

Billie smiled to herself and slid her finger into the correct spot in her book. It was one of those volumes that came with an attached ribbon to use as a bookmark.

"Just so you are aware," Andrew said, moving to the other side of the table, "I will kill you if you knock this down."

"Brother," George said with impressive gravity, "I am barely breathing."

Billie stifled a giggle. She rarely saw this side of George, teasing and dry. Usually he was so irritated by the rest of them that he was left entirely without humor.

"Is that *Prescott's*?" George asked.

Billie turned to look at him over her shoulder. "Yes."

"You're making good progress."

"Despite myself, I assure you. It's very dry."

Andrew didn't look up, but he did say, "You're reading an encyclopedia of agriculture and you're complaining that it's dry?"

"The last volume was brilliant," Billie protested. "I could hardly put it down."

Even from the back of his head, it was obvious that Andrew was rolling his eyes.

Billie returned her attention to George, who, it

had to be said, had not once maligned her for her reading choices. "It must be the subject matter. He seems terribly stuck on mulch this time."

"Mulch is important," George said, his eyes twinkling in what was an impressively somber face.

She met his gaze with equal seriousness. And perhaps just the littlest twitch of her lips. "Mulch is mulch."

"God," Andrew grunted, "the two of you are enough to make me want to tear my hair out."

Billie tapped him on the shoulder. "But you love us."

"Don't touch me," he warned.

She looked back over at George. "He's very touchy."

"Bad pun, Billie," Andrew growled.

She let out a light laugh and returned to the book in her hands. "Back to the mulch."

She tried to read. She really did. But *Prescott's* seemed so dull this time around, and every time George moved, his newspaper crinkled and then she *had* to look up.

But then *he* would look up. And then she'd have to pretend she'd been watching Andrew. And then she really *was* watching Andrew, because it was bizarrely riveting to watch a one-armed man build a house of cards.

Back to *Prescott's*, she admonished herself. As dull as mulch was, she had to get through it. And she did, somehow. An hour drifted by in companionable silence, she on the sofa with her book, George in his chair with the newspaper, and Andrew on the floor with his cards. She got through the straw mulch, and she got through the peat mulch, but when she got to sour mulch, she just couldn't do it any longer.

She sighed, and not elegantly. "I am so bored."

"Just the sort of thing one says to company," Andrew quipped.

She gave him the side eye. "You don't count as company."

"Does George?"

George looked up from his newspaper.

She shrugged. "I suppose not."

"I count," he said.

Billie blinked. She had not realized he'd even been listening.

"I count," he said again, and if Billie hadn't been looking at him she would have missed it. She would have missed the blaze of fire in his eyes, hot and intense, burning for less than a second before he banked it and returned his attention to his newspaper.

"You treat Andrew like a brother," he said, turning a page with slow, deliberate movements.

"And I treat you . . ."

He looked at her. "Not like a brother."

Billie's lips parted. She couldn't look away. And then she *had* to look away, because she felt very strange, and it was suddenly imperative that she get back to the sour mulch.

But then George made a noise, or maybe he just breathed, and she couldn't stop herself, she was looking at him again.

He had nice hair, she decided. She was glad he didn't powder it, at least not for everyday. It was thick, with just a hint of a wave, and it looked like it would curl if he grew it long. She gave a little snort. Wouldn't her maid love hair like that? Billie usually just tied her hair back in a queue, but sometimes she had to fancify herself. They had tried everything with her hair—hot tongs, wet ribbons—but it just wouldn't take a curl.

She liked the color of George's hair, too. It was like caramel, rich and sweet, tipped with strands of gold. She would wager he sometimes forgot to wear his hat in the sun. She was the same way.

It was interesting how all the Rokesbys had the exact same color eyes, but their hair ran the gamut of browns. No one was blond, and no one ginger, but even though they were all brunet, no one had quite the same coloring.

"Billie?" George asked, his voice somewhere between confused and amused.

Oh, bloody hell, he'd caught her looking at him again. She winced out a smile. "I was just thinking how you and Andrew resemble each other," she said. It was sort of the truth.

Andrew glanced up at that. "Do you really think so?"

No, she thought, but she said, "Well, you both have blue eyes."

"As does half of England," Andrew said dryly. He shrugged and got back to work, his tongue catching between his teeth as he pondered his next move.

"My mother has always said that we have the same ears," George commented.

"*Ears?*" Billie's jaw fell about an inch. "I've never heard of anyone comparing ears."

"As far as I know, no one does, aside from my mother."

"Dangling lobes," Andrew put in. He didn't look at her, but he did use his good hand to tweak his lobe. "Hers are attached."

Billie touched her own earlobe. There was no way *not* to, now. "I didn't even realize there was more than one kind."

"Yours are also attached," Andrew said without looking up.

"You know this?"

"I notice ears," he said unapologetically. "I can't help it now."

"Nor can I," George admitted. "I blame Mother."

Billie blinked a few times, still pinching her lobe between her fingers. "I just don't . . ." She frowned and swung her legs off the sofa.

"Watch out!" Andrew snapped.

She shot him a look of great irritation, not that he was paying attention to her, and bent forward.

Andrew turned slowly. "Are you examining my ears?"

"I'm just trying to see what the difference is. I told you, I didn't even realize there was more than one type."

He flicked his hand toward his brother. "Go look at George's if you must. You're too close to the table here."

"I vow, Andrew," she said, carefully edging herself

sideways until she was out of the space between the sofa and the table, "this is like a disease with you."

"Some men turn to drink," he said archly.

George stood, having seen that Billie had come to her feet. "Or cards," he said with a sly half-smile.

Billie snorted a laugh.

"How many levels do you think he's laid down?" George asked.

Billie leaned to the right; Andrew was blocking her view. One, two, three, four . . .

"Six," she told him.

"That's remarkable."

Billie quirked a smile. "Is this what it takes to impress you?"

"Quite possibly."

"Stop talking," Andrew snapped.

"We move the air with our breath," Billie explained, giving the statement gravity it absolutely didn't deserve.

"I see."

"Yesterday I sneezed."

George turned to her with full admiration. "Well done."

"I need more cards," Andrew said. He backed up from the table very slowly, scooting along the carpet like a crab until he was far enough away to rise without risking knocking into anything.

"I don't have any," Billie said. "I mean, I'm sure we do, but I wouldn't know where to find them. I brought you the last two decks from the game room earlier."

"This won't do," Andrew muttered.

"You could ask Thamesly," she suggested. "If anyone would know, it would be he."

Andrew nodded slowly, as if he were working it all out in his head. Then he turned and said, "You'll have to move."

She stared at him. "I beg your pardon."

"You can't stand there. You're too close."

"Andrew," she said plainly, "you've gone mad."

"You're going to knock it down."

"Just go," Billie said.

"If you—"

"Go!" she and George yelled together.

Andrew threw an evil eye at them both and left the room.

Billie looked at George. He looked at her.

They burst into laughter.

"I don't know about you," Billie said, "but I'm moving to the other side of the room."

"Ah, but then you are admitting defeat."

She tossed him a glance over her shoulder as she walked away. "I prefer to think of it as self-preservation."

George chuckled and followed her to the bank of windows. "The irony," he said, "is that he's terrible at cards."

"He is?" She wrinkled her nose. It was odd, really, but she didn't think she and Andrew had ever played cards.

"All games of chance, actually," George went on. "If you ever need some money, he's your man."

"Alas, I don't gamble."

"With cards," he countered.

She had a feeling he'd meant to sound droll, but to her ears it was patronizing in the extreme. She scowled. "What do you mean by that?"

He looked at her as if he were mildly surprised by her question. "Just that you gamble quite happily with your life all the time."

She felt her chin draw back. "That's absurd."

"Billie, you fell out of a tree."

"Onto a *roof*."

He almost laughed. "This counters my argument *how*?"

"You would have done the exact same thing I did," she insisted. "In fact, you did."

"Oh, really."

"I went up the tree to save a cat." She jabbed him in the shoulder with her index finger. "You went up to save me."

"First of all," he shot back, "I did not go up the tree. And secondly, you're comparing yourself to a cat?"

"Yes. No!" For the first time she was grateful she'd injured her foot. She might have stamped it, otherwise.

"What would you have done if I hadn't come along?" he demanded, "Truly, Billie. What would you have done?"

"I'd have been fine."

"I'm sure you would have. You've the devil's own luck. But your family would have been frantic, and likely the entire village would have been called out to search for you."

He was right, damn it, and that just made it worse. "Do you think I'm not aware of that?" she demanded, her voice dropping to a low hiss.

He regarded her for just long enough to make her uncomfortable. "No," he said, "I don't."

She sucked in her breath. "Everything I do, I do for the people here. My whole life . . . everything. I'm reading a bloody encyclopedia of agriculture," she said, her arm jerking back toward the book in question. "Volume *Four*. Who else do you know who—" Her words came to a choking halt, and several moments passed before she was able to continue. "Do you really believe me to be so uncaring?"

"No." His voice was devastatingly low and even. "I believe you to be unthinking."

She lurched back. "I can't believe I thought we were starting to be friends."

He didn't say anything.

"You're a terrible person, George Rokesby. You are impatient and intolerant and—"

He grabbed her arm. "Stop this."

Billie yanked back, but his fingers were too firmly wrapped around her flesh. "Why did you even come here this morning? You only look at me to find fault."

"Don't be absurd," he scoffed.

"It's true," she shot back. "You don't see yourself when you're near me. All you do is frown and scold and—and—everything about you. Your manner, your expressions. You are so disapproving."

"You're being ridiculous."

She shook her head. She felt almost revelatory. "You disapprove of everything about me."

He stepped toward her, his hand tightening on her arm. "That is so far from the truth as to be laughable."

Billie's mouth fell open.

Then she realized that George looked as shocked by his words as she did.

And that he was standing very close.

Her chin tipped up, bringing her eyes to his.

She stopped breathing.

"Billie," he whispered, and his hand rose, as if to touch her cheek.

Chapter 10

———— ➤※◅ ————

$\mathcal{H}$e almost kissed her.

Dear God, he almost kissed Billie Bridgerton.

He had to get out of here.

"It's late," George blurted.

"What?"

"It's late. I need to go."

"It's not late," she said, blinking rapidly. She looked confused. "What are you talking about?"

I don't know, he almost said.

He'd almost kissed her. His eyes had dropped to her mouth and he heard the tiny rush of her breath across her lips, and he'd felt himself leaning, wanting . . .

Burning.

He prayed she hadn't realized. Surely she'd never been kissed before. She wouldn't have known what was happening.

But he'd wanted her. By God, he'd wanted her. It had hit him like a swell, sneaking up and then washing over him so fast and hard he'd barely been able to think straight.

He still wanted her.

"George?" she said. "Is something wrong?"

His lips parted. He needed to breathe.

She was watching him with an almost wary curiosity. "You were scolding me," she reminded him.

He was fairly certain his brain had not resumed its normal workings. He blinked, trying to absorb her words. "Did you want me to continue?"

She shook her head slowly. "Not particularly."

He raked a hand through his hair and tried to smile. It was the best he could do.

Billie's brow knitted with concern. "Are you sure you're well? You look very pale."

Pale? He felt like he was on *fire*. "Forgive me," he said. "I think I'm somewhat—" What? Somewhat *what*? Tired? Hungry? He cleared his throat and decided on: "Light-headed."

She did not look as if she believed him. "Light-headed?"

"It came on suddenly," he said. That much was true.

She motioned toward the bellpull. "Shall I get you something to eat? Do you want to sit down?"

"No, no," he said stupidly. "I'm fine."

"You're fine," she repeated, her lack of belief in this statement practically radiating from her.

He gave a nod.

"No longer light-headed."

"Not at all."

She was staring at him as if he'd gone mad. Which

was quite possible. He couldn't think of any other explanation.

"I should go," he said. He turned, striding to the door. He could not get out of there fast enough.

"George, wait!"

So close. But he stopped. He had to. He could no more leave the room when a gentlewoman was calling his name than spit in the face of the king. It had been bred into his bones.

When he turned around he saw that she'd moved several steps closer. "Don't you think you should wait for Andrew?" she asked.

He exhaled. Andrew. Of course.

"He'll need help, won't he? With his mount?"

Bloody hell. George exhaled. "I will wait."

Billie caught her lower lip between her teeth. The right side. She only ever worried the right side, he realized.

"I can't imagine what is taking him so long," she said, glancing at the door.

George shrugged.

"Maybe he couldn't find Thamesly."

He shrugged again.

"Or perhaps my mother waylaid him. She can be a nuisance that way."

He started to shrug for a third time, realized how inane he looked and instead opted for a *who-can-guess* sort of smile.

"Well," Billie said, apparently out of suggestions. "Hmmm."

George clasped his hands behind his back. Looked

at the window. At the wall. But not at Billie. Any-where but Billie.

He still wanted to kiss her.

She coughed. He managed to look at her feet.

This was awkward.

Insane.

"Mary and Felix arrive in two days," she said.

He gave a shove to the part of his brain that knew how to make conversation. "Doesn't everyone arrive in two days?"

"Well, of course," Billie replied, sounding some-what relieved to have an actual question to answer, "but they're the only ones I care about."

George smiled despite himself. How like her to throw a party and hate every minute of it. Although in truth she hadn't had much choice; they all knew that the house party had been Lady Bridgerton's idea.

"Has the guest list been finalized?" he asked. He knew the answer, of course; the guest list had been drawn up for days, and the invitations had gone out with swift messengers with orders to wait for replies.

But this was a silence that needed filling. She was no longer on the sofa with her book and he in the chair with the newspaper. They had no props, noth-ing but themselves, and every time he looked at her, his eyes fell to her lips, and nothing—*nothing* could have been more wrong.

Billie wandered aimlessly toward a writing desk and tapped her hand on the table. "The Duchess of Westborough is coming," she said. "Mother is very pleased that she has accepted our invitation. I'm told it's a coup."

"A duchess is always a coup," he said wryly, "and usually also a great bother."

She turned and looked back at him. "Do you know her?"

"We've been introduced."

Her expression turned rueful. "I imagine you've been introduced to everyone."

He thought about that. "Probably," he said. "Everyone who comes to London, at least." Like most men of his station, George spent several months each year in the capital. He generally enjoyed it. He saw friends, he kept himself up-to-date on affairs of the state. Lately he'd been eyeing prospective brides; it had been a far more tedious endeavor than he had anticipated.

Billie caught her lip between her teeth. "Is she very grand?"

"The duchess?"

She nodded.

"No grander than any other duchess."

"George! You know that's not what I'm asking."

"Yes," he said, taking pity on her, "she's quite grand. But you will—" He stopped, looked at her. Really looked at her, and finally caught the way her eyes lacked their usual sparkle. "Are you nervous?"

She picked a piece of lint off her sleeve. "Don't be silly."

"Because—"

"Of course I'm nervous."

That drew him up short. She was nervous? *Billie*?

"What?" she demanded, seeing the incredulity on his face.

He shook his head. For Billie to admit to nerves after all the things she'd done . . . all the things she'd done with a mad grin on her face . . . It was inconceivable.

"You jumped out of a tree," he finally said.

"I fell out of a tree," she returned pertly, "and what has that to do with the Duchess of Westborough?"

"Nothing," he admitted, "except that it's difficult to imagine you nervous about . . ." He felt his head shaking, slow, tiny movements, and a reluctant admiration rose within him. She was fearless. She had always been fearless. "About anything," he finished.

Her lips pressed together. "Have you ever danced with me?"

He gaped at her. "What?"

"Have you ever danced with me?" she repeated, her voice edging toward impatience.

"Yes?" The word was drawn out, a question.

"No," she said, "you haven't."

"That can't be possible," he said. Of course he'd danced with her. He'd known her all of her life.

She crossed her arms.

"You can't dance?" he asked.

She shot him a look of pure irritation. "Of course I can dance."

He was going to kill her.

"I'm not very good," she continued, "but I'm good enough, I suppose. That's not the point."

George was fairly certain they had reached the point where there *was* no point.

"The point is," Billie went on, "you have never danced with me because I don't *go* to dances."

"Perhaps you should."

She scowled mightily. "I don't glide when I walk, and I don't know how to flirt, and the last time I tried to use a fan I poked someone in the eye." She crossed her arms. "I certainly don't know how to make a gentleman feel clever and strong and better than me."

He chuckled. "I'm fairly certain the Duchess of Westborough is a lady."

"George!"

He drew back, surprised. She was truly upset. "Forgive me," he said, and he watched her carefully, warily even. She looked hesitant, picking nervously at the folds of her skirt. Her brow was knit not into a frown but into a rueful wrinkle. He had never seen her like this.

He did not know this girl.

"I don't do well in polite company," Billie said in a low voice. "I don't—I'm not good at it."

George knew better than to make another joke, but he did not know what sort of words she needed. How did one comfort a whirlwind? Reassure the girl who did everything well and then did it all backwards for fun? "You do perfectly well when you dine at Crake," he said, even though he knew this wasn't what she was talking about.

"That doesn't count," she said impatiently.

"When you're in the village . . ."

"Really? You're going to compare the villagers to a *duchess*? Besides, I've known the villagers all my life. They know *me*."

He cleared his throat. "Billie, you are the most confident, competent woman I know."

"I drive you mad," she said plainly.

"True," he agreed, although that madness had been taking on a disturbingly different hue lately. "But," he continued, trying to get his words in the proper order, "you are a Bridgerton. The daughter of a viscount. There is no reason why you cannot hold your head high in any room in the land."

She let out a dismissive snort. "You don't understand."

"Then make me." To his great surprise, he realized that he meant it.

She didn't answer right away. She wasn't even looking at him. She was still leaning on the table, and her eyes seemed locked on her hands. She glanced up, briefly, and it occurred to him that she was trying to determine if he was sincere.

He was outraged, and then he wasn't. He wasn't used to having his sincerity questioned, but then again, this was Billie. They had a long history of needling one another, of searching for the perfect weak spot, tiny and undefended.

But it was changing. It *had* changed, just over this past week. He didn't know why; neither of *them* had changed.

His respect for her was no longer so grudging. Oh, he still thought she was beyond headstrong and reckless in the extreme, but underneath all that, her heart was true.

He supposed he'd always known that. He'd just been too busy being aggravated by her to notice.

"Billie?" He spoke softly, his voice a gentle prod.

She looked up, one corner of her mouth twisting forlornly. "It's not a case of holding my head high."

He made sure to keep any hint of impatience out of his voice when he asked, "Then what is the problem?"

She looked at him for a long moment, lips pressed together, before saying, "Did you know that I was presented at court?"

"I thought you didn't have a Season."

"I didn't"—Billie cleared her throat—"after that."

He winced. "What happened?"

She did not quite look at him when she said, "I may have set someone's dress on fire."

He nearly lost his footing. "*You set someone's dress on fire?*"

She waited with exaggerated patience, as if she'd been through this conversation before and knew exactly how long it was going to take to get through it.

He stared at her, dumbfounded. "You set someone's dress on fire."

"It wasn't on purpose," she snipped.

"Well," he said, impressed despite himself, "I suppose if anyone was going to—"

"Don't say it," she warned.

"How did I not hear of this?" he wondered.

"It was a very small fire," she said, somewhat primly.

"But still . . ."

"Really?" she demanded. "I set someone's dress on fire, and your biggest question is how you missed the gossip?"

"I apologize," he said immediately, but then he could not help but ask (somewhat gingerly), "Are you inviting me to inquire *how* you set this dress on fire?"

"No," she said irritably, "and it's not why I brought it up."

His first inclination was to tease her further, but then she sighed, and the sound was so tired and disconsolate that his mirth slid away. "Billie," he said, his voice as gentle as it was sympathetic, "you can't—"

But she did not let him finish. "I don't fit the mold, George."

No, she didn't. And hadn't he been thinking the same thing just a few days earlier? If Billie had gone to London for a Season with his sister it would have been an unmitigated disaster. All the things that made her wonderful and strong would have been her downfall in the rarefied world of the *ton*.

They would have used her for target practice.

They weren't *all* cruel, the lords and ladies of high society. But the ones who were . . . Their words were their weapons, and they wielded them like bayonets.

"Why are you telling me this?" he suddenly asked.

Her lips parted, and a flash of pain shot through her eyes.

"I mean, why me?" he said quickly, lest she think he didn't care enough to listen. "Why not Andrew?"

She didn't say anything. Not right away. And then— "I don't know. I don't . . . Andrew and I don't talk about such things."

"Mary will be here soon," he said helpfully.

"For the love of God, George," she nearly spat, "if you don't want to talk to me, you can just say so."

"No," he said, grabbing her wrist before she could whirl away. "That's not what I meant. I'm happy to talk with you," he assured her. "I'm happy to listen. I just thought you'd rather have someone who . . ."

She stared at him, waiting. But he could not bring himself to say the words that had been on the tip of his tongue.

Someone who cares.

Because it was hurtful. And it was petty. And most of all, it wasn't true.

He did care.

He cared . . . quite a lot.

"I will . . ." The word trailed off, lost in his turbulent thoughts, and all he could do was watch her. Watch her watching him as he tried to remember how to speak his mother tongue, as he tried to figure out which words were right, which words were reassuring. Because she looked sad. And she looked anxious. And he hated that.

"If you wish," he said, slowly enough to allow him to pick over his thoughts as he spoke, "I will watch out for you."

She eyed him cautiously. "What do you mean?"

"Make sure you . . ." He made an air motion with his hands, not that either one of them knew what it meant. "That you're . . . well."

"That I'm well?" she echoed.

"I don't know," he said, frustrated with his inability to put together a complete thought, much less translate it into actual sentences. "Just that if you need a friend, I will be there."

Her lips parted, and he saw movement in her throat, all her words trapped there, all her emotions in check.

"Thank you," she said. "That's . . ."

"Don't say it's kind of me," he ordered.

"Why not?"

"Because it's not kindness. It's . . . I don't know what it is," he said helplessly. "But it's not kindness."

Her lips quivered into a smile. A mischievous smile. "Very well," she said. "You're not kind."

"Never."

"May I call you selfish?"

"That would be going too far."

"Conceited?"

He took a step in her direction. "You're pushing your luck, Billie."

"Arrogant." She ran around the table, laughing as she put it between them. "Come now, George. You cannot deny arrogant."

Something devilish rose up within him. Something devilish and hot. "What do I get to call you?"

"Brilliant?"

He moved closer. "How about maddening?"

"Ah, but that's in the eye of the beholder."

"Reckless," he said.

She feinted left when he feinted right. "It's not recklessness if you know what you're doing."

"You fell onto a *roof*," he reminded her.

She grinned wickedly. "I thought you said I jumped."

He growled her name and lunged, chasing her as she shrieked, "I was trying to save the cat! I was being noble!"

"I'll show you noble . . ."

She yelped and jumped back.

Straight into the house of cards.

It did not fall gracefully.

Neither did Billie, to tell the truth. When the dust had settled, she was sitting squarely on the table, the wreckage of Andrew's masterpiece scattered around like a Chinese firecracker had been lit beneath it.

She looked up and said in a very small voice, "I don't suppose the two of us can put it back together."

Mutely, he shook his head.

She swallowed. "I think I might have reinjured my ankle."

"Badly?"

"No."

"In that case," he told her, "I'd advise you to lead with *that* when Andrew returns."

And of course that was when he walked through the door.

"I hurt my ankle," Billie all but yelled. "It really hurts."

George had to turn away. It was the only way to keep from laughing.

Andrew just stared. "Again," he finally said. "You did it again."

"It was a very nice house," she said weakly.

"I suppose it's a talent," Andrew said.

"Oh, indeed," Billie said brightly. "You're brilliant at it."

"No, I meant you."

"Oh." She swallowed—her pride, most likely—and stretched out a smile. "Well, yes. There's no point in doing something if you're not going to do it well, wouldn't you agree?"

Andrew said nothing. George had the urge to clap his hands in front of his face. Just to make sure he wasn't sleepwalking.

"I'm truly sorry," Billie said. "I'll make it up to you." She pushed herself off the table and limped her way upright. "Although I don't really know how."

"It was my fault," George said suddenly.

She turned to him. "You don't need to take the blame."

He held up his hands in supplication. "I was chasing you."

That snapped Andrew out of his daze. "You were chasing her?"

Damn. He had not thought that one through. "Not in so many words," George said.

Andrew turned to Billie. "He was chasing you?"

She didn't blush, but her expression turned most sheepish. "I might have been somewhat provoking . . ."

"Provoking?" George said with a snort. "You?"

"It's really the cat's fault," she returned. "I would never have fallen if my ankle wasn't so weak." She frowned thoughtfully. "I may blame everything on that mangy beast from now on."

"What is happening here?" Andrew asked, his face turning slowly from Billie to George and back again. "Why aren't you killing each other?"

"The small matter of the gallows," George murmured.

"Not to mention your mother would be very displeased," Billie added.

Andrew just stared at them, his mouth slack. "I'm going home," he finally said.

Billie giggled.

And George . . . his breath caught. Because he'd heard Billie giggle before. A thousand times he'd heard her giggle. But this time was different. It sounded exactly the same, but when the light laugh reached his ears . . .

It was the loveliest sound he'd ever heard.

And quite possibly the most terrifying. Because he had a feeling he knew what it meant. And if there was one person in this world he was *not* going to fall in love with, it was Billie Bridgerton.

————— ❧※❧ —————

$\mathcal{B}$illie wasn't exactly certain what she'd done to her ankle when she crashed into Andrew's house of cards, but it felt only a little bit worse than before, so on the last day before the house party she decided that she was well enough to ride, as long as she did so sidesaddle.

She really didn't have any choice. Honestly, if she didn't get out to the west fields to monitor the progress of the barley crops, she had no idea who would. But dismounting was difficult, which meant she'd had to take a groom with her. Which neither of them enjoyed. The last thing the groom wanted was to inspect barley, and the last thing Billie wanted was to be watched by a groom while she inspected barley.

Her mare was in bad spirits as well, just to round out the cranky triumvirate. It had been a long time since Billie had sat in a sidesaddle, and Argo didn't like it one bit.

Neither did Billie. She had not forgotten how much she hated riding sidesaddle, but she *had* forgotten how much it hurt the next day when one was out of practice. With every step her right hip and thigh groaned with pain. Factor in her ankle, which was still twinging like mad, and it was a wonder she wasn't lurching around the house like a drunken sailor.

Or maybe she was. The servants gave her very odd looks when she made her way down the next morning to break her fast.

She supposed it was for the best that she was too sore to get back in the saddle. Her mother had made it explicitly clear that Billie was to remain at Aubrey Hall throughout the day. There were four Bridgertons currently in residence, she said, and there would be four Bridgertons standing in the drive to greet each and every guest.

And so Billie stood between her mother and Georgiana at one o'clock, when the Duchess of Westborough arrived in her grand coach and four, accompanied by her daughters (one engaged, one not) and niece.

Billie stood between her mother and Georgiana at half two, when Henry Maynard drove up in his racy little curricle with his good friend Sir Reginald McVie.

And she stood between her mother and Georgiana at twenty minutes past three, when Felix and Mary arrived with their neighbors Edward and Niall Berbrooke, who were both of good family and, it just so happened, of marriageable age.

"Finally," Lord Bridgerton grumbled, stretching a

crick from his neck as they waited in their neat little row for Felix and Mary's carriage to come to a halt, "someone I know."

"You know the Berbrookes?" Georgiana asked, leaning forward to speak to him past her sister and mother.

"I know Felix and Mary," he replied. He looked at his wife. "When do the Rokesbys arrive?"

"An hour before supper," she said without turning her head. The carriage had come to a stop, and, consummate hostess that she was, her eyes were on the door, awaiting her guests.

"Remind me why they're sleeping over?" he asked.

"Because it will be infinitely more festive."

Lord Bridgerton frowned, but he very wisely chose not to question her further.

Billie, however, showed no such restraint. "If it were me," she said, tugging on the sleeve of her printed cotton dress, "I would want to sleep in my own bed."

"It's not you," her mother replied tartly, "and stop fidgeting."

"I can't help it. It's itchy."

"I think it looks lovely on you," Georgiana said.

"Thank you," Billie said, momentarily nonplussed. "I'm not so sure about the front." She looked down. The bodice draped in a crisscross fashion, rather like a shawl. She'd never worn anything quite like it, although her mother assured her it had been in style for several years.

Was she revealing too much décolletage? She

reached for the pin that secured the linen near her waist. It looked like she could adjust it with a little—

"Stop it," her mother hissed.

Billie sighed.

The carriage finally came to a complete stop, and Felix alighted first, holding out his hand to assist his wife. Mary Maynard (née Rokesby) wore a chintz traveling jacket and shawl that even Billie could tell was the height of fashion. It looked absolutely perfect on her, Billie realized. Mary looked happy and jaunty from her light brown curls right down to the tips of her elegantly shod feet.

"Mary!" Lady Bridgerton gushed, striding forward with outstretched arms. "You are blooming!"

Georgiana elbowed Billie. "Does that mean what I think it means?"

Billie gave her a lopsided grimace and a shrug— code universal for *I-haven't-a-clue.* Was Mary pregnant? And if so, why on earth did her mother know this before she did?

Georgiana leaned slightly in, whispering out the corner of her mouth. "She doesn't *look*—"

"Well, if she *is*," Billie cut in, whispering out the corner of *her* mouth, "she can't be very far along."

"Billie!" Mary exclaimed, hurrying over to greet her good friend with a hug.

Billie leaned forward, speaking in a low voice. "Is there something you need to tell me?"

Mary didn't even pretend to misunderstand. "I don't know how your mother knows," she said.

"Did you inform *your* mother?"

"Yes."

"Well, there's your answer."

Mary laughed, her Rokesby-blue eyes crinkling just the way George's did when he—

Billie blinked. Just one moment . . . What the devil was *that* about? Since when did George have the right to plague her thoughts? Perhaps they were getting on somewhat better than they had done in the past, but still, he was not a welcome distraction.

Mary, she reminded herself. She was talking to Mary. Or rather, Mary was talking to her.

"It is *so* good to see you," Mary was saying. She clasped both of Billie's hands in her own.

Billie felt something warm and tingly behind her eyes. She'd known she was missing Mary, but she hadn't realized how very *much* until now. "I agree," she said, working hard to keep the choke of emotion out of her voice. It wouldn't do to turn into a watering pot in the front drive.

It wouldn't do to turn into a watering pot, period. Goodness, her mother would probably send for the *physician* before the first tear reached her chin. Billie Bridgerton was *not* a crier.

She did not cry. What could be the use of it?

She swallowed, and somehow this reclaimed her equilibrium enough to smile at Mary and say, "Letters just aren't the same."

Mary rolled her eyes. "Especially with *you* as a correspondent."

"What?" Billie's mouth fell open. "That's not true. I am a brilliant letter-writer."

"When you write," Mary retorted.

"I send you a letter every two—"

"Every three."

"—every three weeks," Billie finished, keeping her voice filled with enough outrage to masque the fact that she had changed her story. "Without fail."

"You really should come to visit," Mary said.

"You know I can't," Billie replied. Mary had been inviting her for a visit for over a year, but it was so difficult for Billie to get away. There was always something that needed to be done around the estate. And truly, didn't it make more sense for Mary to come to Kent, where she already knew everyone?

"You *can*," Mary insisted, "you just won't."

"Perhaps in the winter," Billie said, "when there isn't as much to do in the fields."

Mary's brows rose doubtfully.

"I would have visited last winter," Billie insisted, "but there was no point. You had already decided to come home for Christmas."

Mary's dubious expression did not alter in the least, and she gave Billie's hand one final squeeze before turning to Georgiana. "My goodness," she said, "I think you've grown three inches since I last saw you."

"Unlikely," Georgiana replied with a smile. "You were just here in December."

Mary glanced from sister to sister. "I think you're going to be taller than Billie."

"Stop saying that," Billie ordered.

"But it's true." Mary grinned, fully enjoying Billie's scowl. "We are *all* going to be taller than you." She turned back toward her husband, who was introducing the Berbrooke brothers to Lord and Lady Bridgerton. "Darling," she called out, "don't you think Georgiana has grown tremendously since we last saw her?"

Billie bit back a smile as she watched a flash of utter incomprehension cross Felix's face before he carefully schooled his features into indulgent affection.

"I have no idea," he said, "but if you say it, it must be true."

"I hate when he does that," Mary said to Billie.

Billie didn't bother to hide her smile that time.

"Billie," Felix said as he stepped forward to greet them. "And Georgiana. It is so good to see you both again."

Billie bobbed a curtsy.

"Allow me to introduce Mr. Niall Berbrooke and Mr. Edward Berbrooke," Felix continued, motioning to the two sandy-haired gentlemen at his side. "They live just a few miles away from us in Sussex. Niall, Ned, this is Miss Sybilla Bridgerton and Miss Georgiana Bridgerton, childhood friends of Mary's."

"Miss Bridgerton," one of the Berbrookes said, bowing over her hand. "Miss Georgiana."

The second Berbrooke repeated his brother's felicitations, then straightened and gave a somewhat eager smile. He reminded her of a puppy, Billie decided, with nothing but endless good cheer.

"Have my parents arrived?" Mary asked.

"Not yet," Lady Bridgerton told her. "We expect them just before dinner. Your mother preferred to dress at home."

"And my brothers?"

"Coming with your parents."

"I suppose that makes sense," Mary said with a bit of grumble, "but you would think Andrew could have ridden ahead to say hello. I haven't seen him for ages."

"He's not riding much right now," Billie said off-handedly. "His arm, you know."

"That must be driving him mad."

"I think it would do, were he not so proficient at milking the injury for all it's worth."

Mary laughed and linked her arm through Billie's. "Let us go inside and catch up. Oh, you're limping!"

"A silly accident," Billie said with a wave of her hand. "It's nearly healed."

"Well, you must have loads to tell me."

"Actually, I don't," Billie said as they ascended the portico stairs. "Nothing has changed around here. Not really."

Mary gave her a curious look. "Nothing?"

"Other than Andrew being home, it's all just as it ever was." Billie shrugged, wondering if she ought to be disappointed in all the sameness. She supposed she had been spending a little more time with George, but that hardly counted as an event.

"Your mother's not trying to marry you off to the new vicar?" Mary teased.

"We don't have a new vicar, and I believe she's trying to marry me off to Felix's brother." She tipped her head. "Or one of the Berbrookes."

"Henry is practically engaged," Mary said authoritatively, "and you do *not* want to marry one of the Berbrookes. Trust me."

Billie gave her a sideways glance. "Do tell."

"Stop that," Mary admonished. "It's nothing salacious. Or even interesting. They're lovely, both of them, but they're dull as sticks."

"Here, let's go up to my room," Billie said, steering them toward the main staircase. "And you know," she added, mostly to be contrary, "some sticks are actually quite pointy."

"Not the Berbrookes."

"Why did you offer to bring them, then?"

"Your mother begged! She sent me a three-page letter."

"*My* mother?" Billie echoed.

"Yes. With an addendum from mine."

Billie winced. The collective might of the Ladies Rokesby and Bridgerton was not easily ignored.

"She needed more gentlemen," Mary continued. "I don't think she was anticipating that the Duchess of Westborough would bring both of her daughters *and* her niece. And anyway, Niall and Ned are both very good-natured. They will make lovely husbands for someone." She gave Billie a pointed look. "But not for you."

Billie decided there was no point taking affront. "You don't see me marrying someone good-natured?"

"I don't see you marrying someone who can barely read his name."

"Oh, come now."

"Fine. I exaggerate. But this is important." Mary stopped in the middle of the upstairs hall, forcing Billie to a halt beside her. "You know I know you better than anyone."

Billie waited while Mary fixed her with a serious stare. Mary liked to dispense advice. Billie didn't ordinarily like to receive it, but it had been so long since she'd had the company of her closest friend. Just this once she could be patient. Placid, even.

"Billie, listen to me," Mary said with an odd urgency. "You cannot treat your future so flippantly. Eventually you are going to have to choose a husband, and you will go mad if you do not marry a man of at least equal intelligence to yourself."

"That presupposes that I marry anyone." Or, Billie did not add, that she might actually have a *choice* of husbands.

Mary drew back. "Don't say such a thing! Of course you will get married. You need only to find the right gentleman."

Billie rolled her eyes. Mary had long since succumbed to that sickness that seemed to afflict all recently married individuals: the fever to see everyone else blissful and wed. "I'll probably just marry Andrew," Billie said with a shrug. "Or Edward."

Mary stared at her.

"What?" Billie finally asked.

"If you can say it like *that*," Mary said with hot

disbelief, "like you don't care *which* Rokesby you meet at the altar, you have no business marrying either one of them."

"Well, I *don't* care. I love them both."

"As *brothers*. Goodness, if you're going to take that view of it, you might as well marry George."

Billie stopped short. "Don't be daft."

She, marry George? It was ludicrous.

"Honestly, Mary," she said with a stern little hiss to her voice. "That's not even something to joke about."

"You said that one Rokesby brother would be as good as another."

"No, *you* said that. I said *either* Edward or Andrew would do." Really, she did not understand why Mary was so upset. Marriage to either brother would have the same effect. Billie would become a Rokesby, and she and Mary would be sisters in truth. Billie thought it sounded rather lovely.

Mary clapped her hand to her forehead and groaned. "You are so unromantic."

"I don't necessarily see that as a flaw."

"No," Mary grumbled, "you wouldn't."

She'd meant it as criticism, but Billie just laughed. "Some of us need to view the world with practicality and sense."

"But not at the price of your happiness."

For the longest moment, Billie said nothing. She felt her head tipping slightly to the side, her eyes narrowing with thought as she watched Mary's face. Mary wanted what was best for her; she understood that. But Mary didn't know. How could she know?

"Who are you," Billie asked softly, "to decide what constitutes another person's happiness?" She made sure to keep her words gentle, her tone without edge. She did not want Mary to feel attacked by the question; she did not *mean* the question as such. But she did want Mary to think about this, to stop for one moment and try to understand that despite their deep friendship, they were fundamentally different people.

Mary looked up with stricken eyes. "I didn't mean—"

"I know you didn't," Billie assured her. Mary had always longed for love and marriage. She'd pined for Felix since the moment she'd first met him—at the age of twelve! When Billie was twelve all she'd been concerned about was the litter of puppies in the barn and whether she could climb the old oak tree faster than Andrew.

Truth be told, she was still concerned about this. It would be a massive blow if he could make it to the top branch before she could. Not that they'd be conducting a test anytime soon, what with his arm and her ankle. But still, these things were *important*.

Not that Mary would ever see them as such.

"I'm sorry," Mary said, but her smile was a little too tight. "I've no call to be so grave when I've only just arrived."

Billie almost asked her if that meant she had plans for later in the visit. But she didn't.

Such restraint. When had she developed such maturity?

"Why are you smiling?" Mary asked.

"What? I'm not smiling."

"Oh, you are."

And because Mary was her best friend, even when she was trying to tell her how to live her life, Billie laughed and linked their arms back together. "If you must know," she said, "I was congratulating myself on not making a smart comment at you."

"Such restraint," Mary said, echoing Billie's thoughts precisely.

"I know. It's so unlike me." Billie tipped her head toward the end of the hall. "Can we continue on to my bedroom? My foot hurts."

"Of course. How did you injure it?"

Billie smiled wryly as she resumed walking. "You're never going to believe who ended up being my hero . . ."

Chapter 12

❦t dinner that night, it became quickly apparent to George that one side of the table was the "fun" side.

He was not seated on that side.

To his left was Lady Frederica Fortescue-Endicott, who spoke incessantly of her new fiancé, the Earl of Northwick. To his right was Lady Frederica's younger sister, Lady Alexandra.

Who also spoke incessantly about the Earl of Northwick.

George was not quite sure what to make of this. For Lady Alexandra's sake, he hoped Northwick had a brother.

Billie was seated directly across from George, not that he could see her over the elaborate fruited epergne that graced the center of table. But he could hear her laughter, rich and deep, inevitably followed by Andrew's guffaw and then some asinine *bon mot* delivered by the absurdly handsome Sir Reginald McVie.

Sir *Reggie*, as he had instructed everyone to call him. George disliked him intensely.

Never mind that they had been introduced only one hour earlier; sometimes an hour was all it took. In this case, a minute had been enough. Sir Reggie had sauntered up to George and Billie, who were enjoying a private laugh about something entirely inconsequential (but nonetheless private), and then he'd flashed a smile that was positively blinding.

The man's teeth were so straight they might have been laid into place with a yardstick. Really, who had teeth like that? It was unnatural.

Then the lout had taken Billie's hand and kissed it like some French count, proclaiming her a beauty beyond the sea, sand, stars, and skies (in French, no less, despite the loss of alliteration).

It was beyond ridiculous; George had been sure that Billie would burst out laughing. But no, she blushed.

She blushed!

And then she had batted her eyelashes. It was quite possibly the least Billie Bridgerton-like thing he'd ever seen.

All for a set of freakishly straight teeth. And she didn't even speak French!

Of *course* they had been seated next to each other at dinner. Lady Bridgerton had eyes like an eagle when it came to the marriage prospects of her eldest daughter; George did not doubt she had noticed Sir Reggie flirting with Billie within seconds of the first pearly white grin. If Billie hadn't been seated next to him earlier that day, she would be by the dinner gong.

With Andrew on Billie's other side, there was no stopping her. Laughter rang like church bells as *that* side of the table ate, drank, and made merry.

George's side continued to extoll the many virtues of the Earl of Northwick.

The many, many virtues.

By the time the soup was removed, George was ready to put the man forth for a sainthood. To hear the Ladies Frederica and Alexandra tell it, nothing less would do him justice. The two ladies were regaling him with some nonsense involving Northwick and a parasol he had held for the both of them on a particularly rainy day, and George was just about to comment that it all sounded very crowded, when yet another peal of laughter rang out from the other side of the table.

George glowered, not that Billie could see him. She wouldn't have seen him even if they didn't have that damned fruit bowl between them. She was far too busy being the life of the party. The girl was a veritable shining star. Honestly, he wouldn't have been surprised if she was *literally* sparkling.

And he'd offered to watch out for her.

Please. She was doing quite well on her own.

"What do you suppose they are talking about?" Lady Alexandra queried after a particularly loud burst of merriment.

"Teeth," George muttered.

"What did you say?"

He turned with a bland smile. "I have no idea."

"They seem to be enjoying themselves a great deal," Lady Frederica said with a thoughtful frown.

George shrugged.

"Northie is such a wonderful conversationalist," she said.

"Is he?" George murmured, stabbing a piece of roasted beef.

"Oh, yes. Surely you know him?"

George nodded absently. Lord Northwick was a few years his senior, but they had crossed paths at both Eton and Cambridge. George couldn't remember much about him other than his shock of violently blond hair.

"Then you know," Lady Frederica said with an adoring smile, "he's perfectly droll."

"Perfectly," George echoed.

Lady Alexandra leaned forward. "Are you talking about Lord Northwick?"

"Er, yes," George replied.

"He is so delightful at a house party," Lady Alexandra concurred. "I wonder why you did not invite him."

"Strictly speaking," George reminded her, "I did not draw up the guest list."

"Oh, yes, of course. I'd quite forgotten that you are not a member of the family. You seem so at home at Aubrey Hall."

"The Bridgertons and Rokesbys have long been amiable neighbors," he told her.

"Miss Sybilla is practically his sister," Lady Frederica said, leaning forward to keep herself in the conversation.

Billie? His sister? George frowned. That wasn't right. "I wouldn't say . . ." he began.

But Lady Alexandra was already talking again. "Lady Mary said as much earlier this evening. She told *the* most amusing tales. I do so adore your sister."

George had a mouthful of food, so he nodded and hoped she'd take that as a thank you.

Lady Alexandra leaned forward. "Lady Mary said the lot of you ran wild together as children. It sounded dreadfully exciting."

"I was a bit older," he said. "I rarely—"

"—and then it *ran off*!" Andrew chortled from across the table, loudly enough to put a (thankful) halt to George's conversation with the two Fortescue-Endicott ladies.

Lady Frederica peered at them through the fruit display. "What do you think they are talking about?" she inquired.

"Lord Northwick," George said firmly.

Her entire face lit up. "Really?"

"But Mr. Rokesby said 'it'," Lady Alexandra pointed out. "Surely he would not refer to Northie as an it."

"I'm sure you misheard," George lied. "My brother very much admires Lord Northwick."

"He does?" She leaned forward, far enough to attract her sister's attention. "Frederica, did you hear that? Lord Kennard said that his brother admires Lord Northwick."

Lady Frederica blushed prettily.

George wanted to plant his face in his potatoes.

". . . ungrateful feline!" Billie's voice wafted over the asparagus terrine. More laughter ensued, followed by: "I was furious!"

George sighed. He never thought he would yearn for Billie Bridgerton, but her smile was bright, her laughter infectious, and he was quite sure that if he had to endure another moment seated between the Ladies Frederica and Alexandra his brain was going to start washing out his ears.

Billie must have caught him moping, because she moved just a bit to the side. "We're talking about the cat," she said.

"Yes, I'd gathered."

She smiled—a rather encouraging and pleasant smile that had the effect of making him feel rather discouraged.

And unpleasant.

"Do you know what she meant?" Lady Alexandra asked. "I believe she said something about a cat."

"Northie adores cats," Lady Frederica said.

"I can't stand them myself," George said with a renewed sense of affability. The statement wasn't precisely true, but one couldn't discount the pleasure to be found in being contrary.

Lady Frederica blinked with surprise. "Everybody likes cats."

"Not me!"

Both Fortescue-Endicott sisters stared at him in shock. George supposed he couldn't blame them; his tone had been downright gleeful. But as he was finally starting to enjoy himself, he decided he didn't care. "I prefer dogs," he said.

"Well, of course everyone likes dogs," Lady Frederica said. But she sounded hesitant.

"And badgers," George said cheerfully, popping a bit of bread into his mouth.

"Badgers," she repeated.

"And moles." He grinned. She was now regarding him with visible unease. George congratulated himself on a job well done. A few more minutes of this, and she would surely think him insane.

He couldn't recall the last time he'd had so much fun at a formal dinner.

He looked over at Billie, suddenly eager to tell her about his conversation. It was exactly the sort of thing she'd find amusing. They would have such a good laugh over it.

But she was busy with Sir Reginald, who was now gazing at her as if she were a rare creature.

Which she was, George thought violently. She just wasn't *his* rare creature.

George had a sudden urge to leap across the table and rearrange Sir Reggie's perfect teeth into something far more abstract.

For the love of God, who was born with teeth like that? The man's parents had clearly sold their souls to the devil.

"Oh, Lord Kennard," Lady Alexandra said, "do you plan to observe the ladies' archery tournament tomorrow?"

"I wasn't aware there was one," he replied.

"Oh yes. Frederica and I both plan to take part. We've practiced extensively."

"With Lord Northwick?" he could not help but ask.

"Of course not," she said. "Why on earth would you think that?"

He shrugged helplessly. Dear God, how much longer would this meal last?

She laid her hand on his arm. "I do hope you will come to watch."

He glanced down at her hand. It looked so *very* wrong on his sleeve. But he had a feeling she misinterpreted his gesture, because if anything her fingers tightened. He couldn't help but wonder what had happened to Lord Northwick. God help him if he'd replaced the earl in her affections.

George wanted to shake her off, but there was that damned gentlemanly nature of his, so instead he gave a tight smile and said, "I will of a certain come to watch."

Lady Frederica leaned forward and beamed. "Lord Northwick very much enjoys observing archery, too."

"Of course he does," George said under his breath.

"Did you say something?" Lady Alexandra asked.

"Merely that Miss Bridgerton is a very accomplished archer," he said. It was the truth, even if that hadn't been what he'd said. He looked over at Billie, intending to motion to her with his head, but she was already staring at him with a ferocious expression.

He leaned to the right to see her better.

Her mouth tightened.

He cocked his head.

She rolled her eyes and turned back to Sir Reginald.

George blinked. What the hell had that been about?

And honestly, why did he care?

BILLIE WAS HAVING a marvelous time. Truly, she wasn't quite certain just what she'd been so nervous about. Andrew was always an amusing dinner companion, and Sir Reggie was so kind and handsome; he'd put her right at ease even if he had started speaking in French when they had been introduced.

She hadn't understood a word of it, but she'd figured it must be complimentary, so she'd nodded and smiled, and even blinked a few times the way she'd seen other ladies do when they were trying to act particularly feminine.

No one could say she wasn't trying her best.

The one fly in the proverbial ointment was George. Or rather George's predicament. She felt desperately sorry for him.

Lady Alexandra had seemed like a perfectly pleasant sort of lady when they had been introduced in the drive, but the moment she arrived in the drawing room for pre-dinner drinks, the little shrew had latched on to George like a barnacle.

Billie was appalled. She knew the man was rich and handsome and going to be an earl, but did the grasping little wench need to be quite so obvious about it?

Poor George. Was this what he'd had to contend

with every time he went to London? Perhaps she ought to have had more compassion for him. At the very least she should have taken a peek into the dining room before the guests filed in to check on the seating arrangement. She could have saved him from a full evening of Lady Alexandra Four-handed-Endicott.

Blergh. She could come up with something better than that.

Formidable . . . For-heaven's-sake . . . For-the-last-time . . .

Fine. She couldn't come up with something better. But really, the woman might as well have had four hands with the way she kept clutching on to George in the drawing room.

At dinner she was even worse. It was difficult to see George across the table with her mother's monstrous fruit epergne blocking the way, but she had a clear view of Lady Alexandra, and it had to be said— the lady was displaying a highly impractical expanse of bosom.

Billie wouldn't have been surprised if she had an entire tea service hiding down there.

And then. And then! She'd put her hand on George's forearm like she *owned* it. Even Billie wouldn't have dared such a familiar gesture in such a formal setting. She leaned in her chair, trying to get a look at George's face. He could not be happy about this.

"Are you all right?"

She turned. Andrew was regarding her with an expression that hovered somewhere between suspicion and concern.

"I'm fine," she said in a clipped voice. "Why?"

"You're about to fall in my lap."

She lurched upright. "Don't be absurd."

"Has Sir Reginald broken wind?" Andrew murmured.

"Andrew!"

He gave her an unrepentant smirk. "It was either that or you've developed a new fondness for me."

She glared at him.

"I do love you, Billie," he drawled, "but not that way."

She rolled her eyes because . . . Well, because. Andrew was a wretch. He had always been a wretch. And she didn't love him that way, either.

But he didn't have to be quite so mean-spirited about it.

"What do you think of Lady Alexandra?" she whispered.

"Which one is she?"

"The one who is crawling over your brother," she said impatiently.

"Oh, that one." Andrew sounded like he was trying not to laugh.

"He looks very unhappy."

Andrew tipped his head as he regarded his brother. Unlike Billie, he did not have a gargantuan fruit display to contend with. "I don't know," he mused. "He doesn't look like he minds."

"Are you blind?" Billie hissed.

"Not that I'm aware."

"He— Oh, never mind. You're of no use."

Billie leaned again, this time toward Sir Reggie. He was talking with the woman on his left, so hopefully he wouldn't notice.

Lady Alexandra's hand was *still* on George's arm.

Billie's jaw clenched. He could not be happy about this. George was a very private person. She looked up, trying to catch a glimpse of his face, but he was saying something to Lady Alexandra, something perfectly pleasant and polite.

He didn't look the least bit perturbed.

She fumed.

And then he looked up. He must have caught her looking at him because he leaned to his right just far enough to catch her eye.

His brows rose.

She flicked her gaze toward the ceiling and turned back to Sir Reggie, even though he was still speaking to the duchess's niece.

She waited for a moment, but he seemed in no rush to return his attention to her, so she picked up her fork and knife and cut her meat into ever-tinier pieces.

Maybe George *liked* Lady Alexandra. Maybe he'd court her, and maybe they'd get married and have a flock of little Rokesby babies, all blue-eyed and plump-cheeked.

If that was what George wanted, that was what he should do.

But why did it seem so very wrong? And why did it hurt so much just to think about it?

Chapter 13

By one o'clock the following afternoon, George was remembering why he disliked house parties. Or rather, he was remembering *that* he disliked house parties.

Or maybe he just disliked *this* house party. Between the Northwick-besotted Fortescue-Endicott girls, Lord Reggie of the snow white teeth, and Ned Berbrooke, who had accidentally spilled port all over George's boots the previous night, he was ready to *crawl* back to Crake House.

It was only three miles away. He could do it.

He'd skipped the midday meal—the only way to avoid Lady Alexandra, who seemed to have decided he was the next best thing to Northwick—and now he was in a very bad mood. He was hungry and he was tired, twin demons guaranteed to reduce a grown man's disposition to that of a querulous three-year-old.

The previous night's sleep had been . . .

Unsatisfying.

Yes, that seemed the most appropriate word. Desperately inadequate, but appropriate.

The Bridgertons had put all of the Rokesbys in the family wing, and George had sat in the cushioned chair by his fireplace, listening to the regular, ordinary sounds of a family ending the day—the maids attending the ladies, doors opening and closing . . .

It should have been of no consequence. They were all the same noises one heard at Crake. But somehow, here at Aubrey Hall it felt too intimate, almost as if he were eavesdropping.

With every soft and sleepy sound, his imagination took flight. He knew he couldn't hear Billie moving about; her bedroom was across the hall and three doors down. But it *felt* like he heard her. In the silence of the night he sensed her feet lightly padding across her carpet. He felt the whisper of her breath as she blew out a candle. And when she settled into her bed, he was sure he could hear the rustling of her sheets.

She'd said she fell asleep immediately—but what then? Was she a restless sleeper? Did she wriggle about, kicking the covers, pushing the sheets to the bottom of the bed with her feet?

Or did she lie still, sweetly on her side with her hands tucked under her cheek?

He'd wager she was a squirmer; this was Billie, after all. She'd spent her entire childhood in constant motion. Why would she sleep any other way? And if she shared a bed with someone . . .

His brandy nightcap turned into three, but when he'd finally laid his head against his pillow, it had taken him hours to fall asleep. And then when he did, he'd dreamed of her.

And the dream . . . Oh, the dream.

He shuddered, the memory washing over him anew. If he'd ever thought of Billie as a sister . . .

He certainly didn't now.

It had started in the library, in the moonlit dark, and he didn't know what she'd been wearing—just that it wasn't like anything he'd ever seen her in before. It had to have been a nightgown . . . white and diaphanous. With every breeze it molded to her body, revealing perfectly lush curves designed to fit his hands.

Never mind that they were in the library, and there was no logical reason for a breeze. It was his dream, and it was breezy, and then it didn't matter anyway because when he took her hand and pulled her hard against him they were suddenly in his bedroom. Not the one here at Aubrey Hall but back at Crake, with his mahogany four-poster bed, the mattress large and square, with room for all sorts of reckless abandon.

She didn't say a word, which he had to admit was very unlike her, but then again, it *was* a dream. When she smiled, though, it was pure Billie—wide and free—and when he laid her on the bed, her eyes met his, and it was as if she had been born for that moment.

As if *he* had been born for that moment.

His hands opened the folds of her gown, and she arched beneath him, her perfect breasts thrusting toward him like an offering.

It was mad. It was madness. He shouldn't know what her breasts looked like. He shouldn't even be able to imagine it.

But he did, and in his dream, he worshipped them. He cupped them, squeezed them, pushed them together until that intoxicatingly feminine valley formed between them. Then he bent down and took her nipple between his teeth, teasing and tempting until she moaned with delight.

But it didn't end there. He slid his hands to the junction of her legs and her hips and he pushed her thighs open, his thumbs coming torturously close to her center.

And then he stroked . . . closer . . . closer . . . until he could sense the wet heat of her, and he knew that their joining was inevitable. She would be his, and it would be glorious. His clothes melted away, and he positioned himself at her opening . . .

And woke up.

Bloody goddamn bleeding *bollocks*.

He woke up.

Life was spectacularly unfair.

The following morning was the ladies' archery competition, and if George had felt a bit of irony while watching, surely he could be forgiven. There was Billie with a stiff, pointy thing, and there was he, *still* with a stiff, pointy thing, and it had to be said: only one of them was having any fun.

It had taken a full hour, of very icy thoughts before he was able to move from his carefully cross-legged position in the chairs that had been set up at the edge of the field. Every other gentleman had got up at some point to inspect the targets, but not George. He'd smiled, and he'd laughed, and he made up some sort of nonsense about enjoying the sun. Which was ridiculous, because the one spot of blue in the sky was about the size of his thumbnail.

Desperate for a moment of his own company, he made for the library immediately after the tournament. No one in the party struck him as much of a reader; surely he could find some peace and quiet.

Which he did, for all of ten minutes before Billie and Andrew came squabbling through the door.

"George!" Billie exclaimed, limping in his direction. She looked glowingly well-rested.

She never had difficulty falling asleep, George thought irritably. *She* probably dreamed of roses and rainbows.

"Just the person I'd hoped to find," she said with a smile.

"Words to strike terror in his heart," Andrew drawled.

So true, George thought, although not for the reasons Andrew supposed.

"Stop." Billie scowled at him before turning back to George. "We need you to settle a point."

"If it's who can climb a tree faster, it's Billie," George said without missing a beat. "If it's who can shoot with more accuracy, it's Andrew."

"It's neither," Billie said with a light frown. "It's got to do with Pall Mall."

"Then God help us all," George muttered, getting up and heading for the door. He'd played Pall Mall with his brother and Billie; it was a vicious, bloodthirsty sport involving wooden balls, heavy mallets, and the constant risk of grievous head injury. Definitely not something for Lady Bridgerton's gentle house party.

"Andrew accused me of cheating," Billie said.

"When?" George asked, honestly perplexed. As far as he knew, the entire morning had been taken up by the ladies' archery tournament. (Billie had won, not that anyone named Rokesby or Bridgerton was surprised.)

"Last April," Billie said.

"And you're arguing about it now?"

"It's the principle of the matter," Andrew said.

George looked at Billie. "Did you cheat?"

"Of course not! I don't need to cheat to beat Andrew. Edward maybe," she allowed with a flick of her eyes, "but not Andrew."

"Uncalled for, Billie," Andrew scolded.

"But true," she returned.

"I'm leaving," George said. Neither was listening, but it seemed only polite to announce his departure. Besides, he wasn't sure it was a good idea for him to be in the same room as Billie just then. His pulse had already begun a slow, inexorable acceleration and he knew he didn't want to be near her when it reached its crescendo.

This way lies ruin, his mind was screaming. Miraculously, his legs didn't put up any resistance, and he made it all the way to the door before Billie said, "Oh, don't go. It's just about to get interesting."

He managed a small but exhausted smile as he turned around. "With you it's always about to get interesting."

"Do you think so?" she asked delightedly.

Andrew gave her a look of pure disbelief. "That wasn't a compliment, Billie."

Billie looked at George.

"I have no idea what it was," he admitted.

Billie just chuckled, then jerked her head toward Andrew. "I'm calling him out."

George knew better—oh, he definitely knew better—but he couldn't stop himself from turning the rest of the way around to gape at her.

"You're calling me out?" Andrew repeated.

"Mallets at dawn," she said with flair. Then she shrugged. "Or this afternoon. I'd rather avoid getting up early, wouldn't you?"

Andrew raised one brow. "You'd challenge a one-armed man to a game of Pall Mall?"

"I'd challenge *you*."

He leaned in, blue eyes glittering. "I'll still beat you, you know."

"George!" Billie yelled.

Damn it. He'd almost escaped. "Yes?" he murmured, poking his head back through the doorway.

"We need you."

"No you don't. You need a nanny. You can barely walk."

"I can walk perfectly well." She limped a few steps. "See? I can't even feel it."

George looked at Andrew, not that he expected him to exhibit anything remotely approaching sense.

"I have a broken arm," Andrew said, which George supposed was meant to serve as an explanation. Or an excuse.

"You're idiots. The both of you."

"Idiots who need more players," Billie said. "It doesn't work with only two."

Technically that was true. The Pall Mall set was meant to be played with six, although anything over three would do in a pinch. But George had played this scene before; the rest of them were bit players to Andrew and Billie's tragic, vicious leads. For the two of them, the game was less about winning than it was making sure the other didn't. George was expected merely to move his ball along in their fray.

"You still don't have enough players," George said.

"Georgiana!" Billie yelled.

"Georgiana?" Andrew echoed. "You know your mother doesn't let her play."

"For the love of heaven, she hasn't been ill for years. It's time we stopped coddling her."

Georgiana came skidding around the corner. "Stop bellowing, Billie. You're going to give Mama a palpitation, and then *I'll* have to be the one to deal with her."

"We're playing Pall Mall," Billie told her.

"Oh. That's nice. I'll—" Georgiana's words tumbled to a halt, and her blue eyes went wide. "Wait, I get to play, too?"

"Of course," Billie said, almost dismissively. "You're a Bridgerton."

"Oh, brilliant!" Georgiana practically leapt into the air. "Can I be orange? No, green. I wish to be green."

"Anything you want," Andrew said.

Georgiana turned to George. "Are you playing, as well?"

"I suppose I must."

"Don't sound so resigned," Billie said. "You'll have a splendid time of it. You know you will."

"We still need more players," Andrew said.

"Perhaps Sir Reggie?" Georgiana asked.

"No!" came George's instant reply.

Three heads swiveled in his direction.

In retrospect, he might have been a bit forceful in his objection.

"He doesn't strike me as the sort of gentleman to enjoy such a rough and tumble game," George said with a haphazard shrug. He glanced down at his fingernails since he couldn't possibly look anyone in the eye when he said, "His teeth, you know."

"His teeth?" Billie echoed.

George didn't need to see her face to know that she was staring at him as if she were afraid he'd lost his mind.

"I suppose he does have a very elegant smile,"

Billie said, apparently prepared to concede the point. "And I suppose we did knock out one of Edward's teeth that one summer." She looked over at Andrew. "Do you remember? I think he was six."

"Precisely," George said, although in truth he did not recollect the incident. It must have been a milk tooth; Edward was no Sir Reginald McVie, but as far as George knew, his brother's smile was fully populated.

"We can't ask Mary," Billie went on. "She spent the entire morning hunched over a chamber pot."

"I really didn't need to know that," Andrew said.

Billie ignored him. "And besides, Felix would never permit it."

"Then ask Felix," George suggested.

"That would be unfair to Mary."

Andrew rolled his eyes. "Who cares?"

Billie crossed her arms. "If she can't play, he shouldn't, either."

"Lady Frederica went to the village with her mother and cousin," Georgiana said. "But I saw Lady Alexandra in the drawing room. She didn't seem to be doing anything important."

George was not keen to spend the afternoon listening to more tales of Lord Northwick, but after his vehement refusal of Sir Reginald, he did not think he could reasonably lodge another objection. "Lady Alexandra would make a fine addition to the game," he said diplomatically. "Provided, of course, that she wishes to play."

"Oh, she'll play," Billie said ominously.

Georgiana looked perplexed.

Billie looked at her sister but jerked her head in George's direction. "Tell her that Lord Kennard will be among the players. She'll be here with bells on her toes."

"Oh, for God's sake, Billie," George muttered.

Billie let out a self-righteous huff. "She was talking to you all night!"

"She was sitting next to me," George retorted. "She could hardly have done otherwise."

"Not true. Felix's brother was on her left. He's a perfectly acceptable conversationalist. She could have spoken with him about any number of things."

Andrew stepped between them. "Are the two of you going to snipe like jealous lovers or are we going to play?"

Billie glared.

George glared.

Andrew looked quite pleased with himself.

"You're an idiot," Billie said to him before turning back to Georgiana. "I suppose it will have to be Lady Alexandra. Get her and whomever else you can find. A gentleman if at all possible so we've equal numbers."

Georgiana nodded. "But not Sir Reginald?"

"George is too worried about his teeth."

Andrew made a choking sound.

Which came to a halt when George elbowed him in the ribs.

"Shall I meet you here?" Georgiana asked.

Billie thought for a moment, then said, "No, it will

be quicker if we meet you on the west lawn." She turned back to George and Andrew. "I'll see to getting the set pulled out."

She and Georgiana exited the room, leaving George alone with his younger brother.

"His teeth, eh?" Andrew murmured.

George glowered at him.

Andrew leaned in, just far enough to be annoying. "I'd wager he has very good oral hygiene."

"Shut up."

Andrew laughed, then leaned in with what was clearly meant to be an expression of concern. "You've got a little something . . ." He motioned to his teeth.

George rolled his eyes and shoved past him.

Andrew hopped to attention, caught up, and then overtook him, tossing a grin over his shoulder as he loped down the hall. "Ladies do love a dazzling smile."

He was going to kill his brother, George decided as he followed him outside. And he was going to use a mallet.

Chapter 14

Ten minutes later George, Andrew, and Billie were standing on the lawn, watching as a footman plodded toward them, dragging the Pall Mall set behind them.

"I love Pall Mall," Billie announced, rubbing her hands together in the brisk afternoon air. "This is a brilliant idea."

"It was your idea," George pointed out.

"Of course it was," she said merrily. "Oh, look, here comes Georgiana."

George shaded his eyes as he peered across the lawn. Sure enough, she was leading Lady Alexandra in their direction. And, if he wasn't mistaken, one of the Berbrooke brothers.

"Thank you, William," Billie said as the footman brought the set into place.

He nodded. "Milady."

"Wait a moment," Andrew said. "Didn't we break one of the mallets last year?"

"Father commissioned a new set," Billie informed him.

"Same colors?"

She shook her head. "We're not having red this time around."

George turned to look at her. "Why not?"

"Well," she stalled, looking slightly sheepish, "we've had very bad luck with red. The balls keep ending up in the lake."

"And you think a different color might rectify the problem?"

"No," she said, "but I'm hoping yellow will be easier to spot beneath the surface."

A few moments later, Georgiana and her little band of players arrived on the scene. George took an instinctive step toward Billie, but he was too slow. Lady Alexandra had already taken hold of his sleeve.

"Lord Kennard," she said. "What a delight it will be to play Pall Mall. Thank you for inviting me."

"It was Miss Georgiana, actually," he said.

She smiled knowingly. "At your behest, I'm sure."

Billie looked as if she might gag.

"And Lieutenant Rokesby," Lady Alexandra continued, her hand a tight little claw on George's arm even as she turned to Andrew. "We hardly had a chance to speak last night."

Andrew bowed with all due chivalry.

"Are you acquainted with Lord Northwick?" she asked.

George desperately tried to catch his brother's eye.

This was not an avenue of conversation any of them wished to pursue.

Luckily for all, the footman had just pulled the cover off the Pall Mall set, and Billie was taking efficient charge.

"Here we are," she said, pulling one of the mallets from its position. "Andrew already promised Georgiana the green, so let's see, Mr. Berbrooke will take blue, Lady Alexandra can have pink, I'll be yellow, Lieutenant Rokesby will be purple, and Lord Kennard will be black."

"Can't I be purple?" Lady Alexandra asked.

Billie looked at her as if she'd asked to have the Magna Carta revised.

"I like purple," Lady Alexandra said coolly.

Billie's back stiffened. "Take it up with Lieutenant Rokesby. It makes no difference to me."

Andrew gave Billie a curious look, then offered his mallet to Lady Alexandra with a gallant bow. "As the lady wishes . . ."

Lady Alexandra nodded graciously.

"Very well," Billie said with a sniff, "Georgiana is green, Mr. Berbrooke is blue, Lieutenant Rokesby is pink, I'm yellow, Lord Kennard is black, and Lady Alexandra is"—she gave her the side eye—"purple."

George was coming to realize that Billie *really* did not like Lady Alexandra.

"I've never played this before," Mr. Berbrooke said. He swung his mallet a few times, narrowly missing George's leg. "It looks like jolly good fun."

"Right," Billie said briskly. "The rules are quite

simple. The first person to hit his ball through all the wickets in the correct order wins."

Lady Alexandra looked at the collection of wickets currently hooked onto the set. "How will we know the correct order?"

"Just ask me," Billie said. "Or Lieutenant Rokesby. We've done this a million times."

"Which one of you usually wins?" Mr. Berbrooke asked.

"Me," they both said.

"Neither," George said firmly. "They rarely manage to finish a game. You'd all do well to watch your feet. This may turn vicious."

"I can't wait," Georgiana said, practically thrumming with excitement. She turned to Lady Alexandra. "You've also got to hit the pole at the end. Billie didn't mention that."

"She likes to leave out some of the rules," Andrew said. "So she can penalize you later if you're winning."

"That is not true!" Billie protested. "At least half the times I've beaten you I've done so without cheating."

"Should you ever play Pall Mall again," George advised Lady Alexandra, "I would ask for a full recitation of the rules and regulations. Nothing you learn here will be the least bit applicable."

"I *have* played before, you know," Lady Alexandra said. "Lord Northwick has a set."

Georgiana turned to her with a puzzled expression. "I thought Lord Northwick was engaged to your sister."

"He is," Lady Alexandra replied.

"Oh. I thought . . ." Georgiana paused, her mouth open for a second or two before she finally settled on, "You speak of him so often."

"He has no sisters of his own," Lady Alexandra said crisply. "Naturally, we have become quite devoted."

"I have a sister," Mr. Berbrooke piped up.

This was met with a beat of silence, and then Georgiana said, "That's wonderful."

"Nellie," he confirmed. "Short for Eleanor. She's very tall."

No one seemed quite to know what to say to that.

"Well then," Andrew said, breaking the now decidedly awkward moment. "It's time to set the wickets out."

"Can't the footman do it?" Lady Alexandra inquired.

Billie and Andrew both turned on her as if she'd gone mad.

George took pity, stepping forward to murmur, "They can be somewhat particular about the placement."

Lady Alexandra's chin rose an inch. "Lord Northwick always says the wickets should be laid out in the shape of a cross."

"Lord Northwick's not here," Billie snapped.

Lady Alexandra gasped.

"Well, he's not," Billie protested, looking to the rest of the group for affirmation.

George narrowed his eyes, the visual translation of an elbow in the ribs, and Billie must have realized that she had crossed a line—an absurd line, but a line nonetheless. She was the hostess, and she needed to behave as such.

It was fascinating to watch, though. Billie was a born competitor, and she had never been known for an abundance of patience. And she certainly was not inclined to acknowledge Lady Alexandra's suggestion. Still, she straightened her shoulders and fixed an almost pleasant smile on her face as she turned back to her guest.

"I think you will like it this way," she said primly. "And if you don't, you can tell Lord Northwick all about it, and then you will know for certain that his layout is superior."

George snorted.

Billie ignored him.

"The wickets," Andrew reminded everyone.

"George and I will do it," Billie said, grabbing them from Andrew's proffered hand.

George looked at her with some indulgence. "Oh we will, will we?"

"Lord Kennard," she said through clenched teeth, "will you be so kind as to help me set out the wickets?"

He glanced down at her injured ankle. "What, you mean because you cannot walk?"

She gave him an over-sweet smile. "Because I delight in your company."

He almost laughed.

"Andrew can't do it," she went on, "and no one else knows where they go."

"If we played in the shape of a cross," Lady Alexandra said to Mr. Berbrooke, "any one of us could set the wickets out."

Mr. Berbrooke nodded.

"We would start at the nave," Lady Alexandra instructed, "then move on to the transept and then the altar."

Mr. Berbrooke looked down at his mallet and frowned. "Doesn't seem like a very churchy game."

"It could be," Lady Alexandra replied.

"But we don't want it to be," Billie said sharply.

George grabbed her arm. "The wickets," he said, pulling her away before the two ladies came to blows.

"I really don't like that woman," she grumbled once they were out of earshot.

"Really?" George murmured. "I would never have known."

"Just help me with the wickets," she said, turning toward a large oak at the edge of the clearing. "Follow me."

He watched her for a few steps. She was still limping, but it was different somehow. More awkward. "Did you hurt yourself again?"

"Hmmm? Oh, that." She let out an irritated snort. "It was the sidesaddle."

"I beg your pardon?"

She shrugged. "I can't put my bad foot in a stirrup. So I had to ride sidesaddle."

"And you needed to ride because . . ."

She looked at him as if he were an idiot. Which he was fairly certain he was not.

"Billie," he said, grabbing her by the wrist so they

were both yanked to a halt, "what was so important that you had to ride with an injured ankle?"

"The barley," she said plainly.

He must have misheard. "What?"

"Someone had to make sure it was being planted properly," she said, deftly pulling her hand free.

He was going to kill her. Or rather he *would*, except that she would probably end up doing it herself first. He took a breath, then asked, as patiently as he could, "Isn't that the job of your steward?"

Her brows pulled together. "I don't know what you think I do all day when I'm not flitting away at house parties, but I am an extremely busy person." Something changed in her expression; something George could not quite name, and then she said, "I am a useful person."

"I can't imagine anyone would think otherwise," George said, although he had a feeling he'd thought otherwise, and not too long ago.

"What the devil are you two doing over there?" Andrew bellowed.

"I am going to massacre him," Billie seethed.

"The wickets," George said. "Just tell me where you want them."

Billie separated one from the bunch and held it out. "Over there. Under the tree. But over the root. Make sure you put it over the root. Otherwise it will be too easy."

George very nearly saluted her.

When he returned from his task, she was already a ways down the field, jamming another wicket into place. She'd left the rest in a pile, so he leaned down and scooped them up.

She looked up as she secured the wicket. "What have you against Sir Reginald?"

George grit his teeth. He should have known he wouldn't get off so easily. "Nothing," he lied. "I simply did not think he would enjoy the game."

She stood. "You can't know that."

"He spent the entire archery competition lounging on a lawn chair and complaining of the heat."

"*You* didn't get up."

"I was enjoying the sun." It hadn't been sunny, but he wasn't about to tell her the real reason he'd been stuck in his chair.

"Very well," Billie acceded, "Sir Reggie is probably not the best candidate for Pall Mall. But I still maintain that we could have done better than Lady Alexandra."

"I agree."

"She—" She blinked. "You do?"

"Of course. I had to spend all last night talking with her, as you so eloquently pointed out."

Billie looked about ready to throw her arms up in frustration. "Then why didn't you say something when Georgiana suggested her?"

"She's not evil, merely annoying."

Billie muttered something under her breath.

George could not stem the amused smile that spread across his face. "You really don't like her, do you?"

"I really don't."

He chuckled.

"Stop that."

"Laughing, you mean?"

She jammed a wicket into the ground. "You're just as bad as I am. One would think Sir Reggie had committed treason with the way you were carrying on."

Carrying on? George planted his hands on his hips. "That's entirely different."

She glanced up from her work. "How is that?"

"He is a buffoon."

Billie snorted out a laugh. It was not particularly feminine, but on her it was charming. She leaned toward him, her expression pure dare. "I think you're jealous."

George felt his stomach flip. Surely she didn't realize . . . *No.* These thoughts he'd been having about her . . . temporary madness. Brought on by proximity. That had to be it. He'd spent more time with her in the past week than he had in years. "Don't be ridiculous," he said scornfully.

"I don't know," Billie teased. "All the ladies are flocking to his side. You said yourself he has a handsome smile."

"I *said*," George bit out before realizing he didn't remember precisely what he'd said. Luckily for him, Billie had already interrupted him.

"The only lady who hasn't fallen under his spell is the illustrious Lady Alexandra." She tossed him a look over her shoulder. "Probably because she's so busy trying to gain *your* favor."

"Are *you* jealous?" he countered.

"Please," she scoffed, moving on to the next spot.

He followed, one step behind. "You didn't say no . . ."

"*No*," she said with great emphasis. "Of course I'm not jealous. I think she's touched in the head quite honestly."

"Because she's trying to gain my favor?" he could not help but ask.

She held her hand out for another wicket. "Of course not. That's probably the most sensible thing she's ever done."

He paused. "Why does that sound like an insult?"

"It's not," Billie assured him. "I would never be so ambiguous."

"No, that's true," he murmured. "You insult with pure transparency."

She rolled her eyes before returning to the topic of Lady Alexandra. "I was talking about her obsession with Lord Northwick. He's engaged to her sister, for heaven's sake."

"Ah, that."

"Ah, that," she mimicked, shoving another wicket into the ground. "*What* is wrong with her?"

George was saved from answering by Andrew, who was bellowing their names again, along with a rather vehement exhortation to hurry along.

Billie snorted. "I can't believe he thinks he can beat me with a broken arm."

"You do realize that if you win—"

"When I win."

"*Should* you win, you will look the worst sort of champion, taking advantage of the weakness of others."

She looked at him with wide, innocent eyes. "I can barely walk myself."

"You, Miss Bridgerton, have a convenient grasp on reality."

She grinned. "Convenient for me, yes."

He shook his head, smiling despite himself.

"Now then," she said, lowering her voice even though no one was within earshot, "you're on my team, are you not?"

George narrowed his eyes. "Since when are there teams?"

"Since today." She leaned closer. "We must *crush* Andrew."

"You're beginning to frighten me, Billie."

"Don't be silly, you're just as competitive as I am."

"Do you know, I don't think I am."

"Of course you are. You just show it differently."

He thought she might elucidate, but of course she did not.

"You don't want Andrew to win, do you?" she asked.

"I'm not certain how much I care."

She drew back.

He laughed. He couldn't help it. She looked so affronted. "No, of course I don't want him to win," he said. "He's my brother. But at the same time, I'm not sure I feel the need to resort to espionage to ensure the outcome."

She stared at him with heavy, disappointed eyes.

"Oh, fine," he gave in. "Who's on Andrew's team, then?"

She brightened up immediately. "No one. That's the beauty of it. He won't know that we've formed an alliance."

"There is no way this ends well," he said, sending the words out to the world at large.

He was fairly certain the world was not listening.

Billie set the last wicket into place. "This one's evil," she told him. "Overshoot and you're in the rosebushes."

"I shall take that under advisement."

"Do." She smiled, and his breath caught. No one smiled like Billie. No one ever had. He'd known this for years and yet . . . it was only now . . .

He indulged in a mental curse. This had to be the most inconvenient attraction in the history of man. *Billie Bridgerton*, for God's sake. She was everything he'd never wanted in a woman. She was headstrong, stupidly reckless, and if she'd ever had a mysterious, feminine moment in her life, he'd never seen it.

And yet . . .

He swallowed.

He wanted her. He wanted her like he'd never wanted anything in his life. He wanted her smile, and he wanted it exclusively. He wanted her in his arms, beneath his body . . . because somehow he knew that in his bed, she would be everything mysterious and feminine.

He also knew that every single one of these delightful activities required that he marry her, which was so patently ludicrous that—

"Oh, for God's sake," Billie muttered.

George snapped back to attention.

"Andrew's coming over," she said. "Hold your horses!" she bellowed. "I swear," she said to George, "he is so impatient."

"Said the—"

"*Don't* call me a kettle." She started marching back to the beginning of the course. As best as she could; she really did look ridiculous with her two-part limp.

He waited for a moment, grinning at her back. "Are you sure you don't want the black mallet?"

"I hate you!" she called.

He couldn't help but smile. It was quite the merriest declaration of hate he'd ever heard.

"I hate you, too," he murmured.

But he didn't mean it, either.

Chapter 15

***

Billie was humming quite happily by the time she reached the beginning of the Pall Mall course. She was in a remarkably cheerful mood, all things considered. Andrew was still being abominably impatient, and Lady Alexandra was still the most awful person in the history of the world, but none of that seemed to matter.

She peeked over her shoulder at George. He'd been following her the whole way, trading insults with a wolfish smile.

"What are you so happy about?" Andrew demanded.

She smiled enigmatically. Let him stew for a bit. Besides, she wasn't sure *why* she was so happy. She just was.

"Who plays first?" Lady Alexandra asked.

Billie opened her mouth to reply, but Andrew beat her to it.

"We usually play youngest to oldest," he said, "but it does seem somewhat rude to inquire . . ."

"I am certainly first, then," Georgiana announced, plopping the green ball down near the starting stick. "No question about it."

"I should think I am second," Lady Alexandra said, sending a pitying glance over at Billie.

Billie ignored her. "Mr. Berbrooke, might we inquire as to your age?"

"What? Oh, I'm twenty-five." He smiled broadly. He did that a lot. "Quarter of a century, you know."

"Very well, then," Billie said, "the order of play shall be Georgiana, Lady Alexandra . . . *we assume*, Andrew, me, Mr. Berbrooke, and George."

"Don't you mean Lord Kennard?" Lady Alexandra asked.

"No, I'm quite sure I mean George," Billie snipped. Good God but that woman grated on her.

"I rather like playing with the black ball," George said, smoothly changing the subject. But Billie had been watching him; she couldn't be positive, but she *thought* she'd seen him hiding a smile.

Good.

"It's a very manly color," Lady Alexandra confirmed.

Billie nearly gagged.

"It's the color of death," Andrew said, rolling his eyes.

"The Mallet of Death," George said thoughtfully. He swung it back and forth a few times, like a macabre pendulum. "It has quite a ring to it."

Andrew snorted.

"You laugh," George dared, "but you know you want it."

Billie rang out with laughter that only grew in volume when Andrew leveled a peevish glare in her direction. "Oh, come now, Andrew, you know it's the truth," she said.

Georgiana looked up from her position at the starting pole. "Who would want the Mallet of Peonies and Petunias when one could have the Mallet of Death?" she put in, tipping her head toward Andrew's pink equipment.

Billie smiled approvingly. When had her sister got so witty?

"My peonies and petunias shall triumph," Andrew said with a wiggle of his brows. "Just you watch."

"Your peonies and petunias are missing a vital petal," Billie countered, motioning toward his injured arm.

"I don't think I know what we're talking about," Mr. Berbrooke admitted.

"It's just silly fun," Georgiana told him as she readied for her first swing. "Billie and Andrew love to tease one another. They always have." She gave her ball a whack, and it shot through the two starting wickets. It didn't go much farther but she didn't seem to mind.

Lady Alexandra stepped up, setting her ball into place. "Lieutenant Rokesby plays after me, yes?" she confirmed. She glanced up at Billie with a deceptively placid expression. "I did not realize that you were older than he is, Miss Bridgerton."

"I am older than a great many people," Billie said coolly.

Lady Alexandra sniffed and slammed her mallet against her ball, sending it hurtling across the lawn.

"Well done!" Mr. Berbrooke cheered. "I say, you *have* played this before."

Lady Alexandra smiled modestly. "As I mentioned, Lord Northwick has a set."

"And he plays in the shape of a holy cross," Billie said under her breath.

George elbowed her.

"My turn," Andrew announced.

"Petunias ahoy!" Billie said jauntily.

Beside her she heard George chuckle. It was ridiculously satisfying, making him laugh.

Andrew ignored her completely. He dropped the pink ball, then nudged it into place with his foot.

"I still don't understand how you're going to play with a broken arm," Georgiana said.

"Watch and learn, my dear girl," he murmured. And then, after several practice swings—one of which included a full three-hundred-and-sixty-degree rotation—he whacked his ball rather impressively through the starting wickets and across the lawn.

"Almost as far as Lady Alexandra," Georgiana said admiringly.

"I do have a broken arm," he demurred.

Billie walked to the starting spot and set down her ball. "How did that happen again?" she asked innocently.

"Shark attack," he said without missing a beat.

"No!" Lady Alexandra gasped.

"A shark?" Mr. Berbrooke said. "Isn't that one of those toothy fish things?"

"Extremely toothy," Andrew confirmed.

"I shouldn't like to come across one myself," Mr. Berbrooke said.

"Has Lord Northwick ever been bitten by a shark?" Billie asked sweetly.

George made a choking sound.

Lady Alexandra's eyes narrowed. "I can't say that he has."

"Pity." Billie smacked her mallet against her ball with thundering force. It went flying across the lawn, well past the others.

"Well done!" Mr. Berbrooke again exclaimed. "Jolly good at this, you are, Miss Bridgerton."

It was impossible to remain unmoved in the face of his relentless good cheer. Billie offered him a friendly smile as she said, "I've played quite a bit over the years."

"She often cheats," Andrew said in passing.

"Only with you."

"I suppose I'd better have a go," Mr. Berbrooke said, crouching down to set the blue ball next to the starting pole.

George took a cautionary step back.

Mr. Berbrooke frowned down at the ball, testing out his mallet a few times before finally swinging. The ball went flying, but unfortunately so did one of the wickets.

"Oh! Terribly sorry," he said.

"It's no trouble," Georgiana said. "We can put it back into place."

The course was reset, and George took his turn. His black ball ended up somewhere between Lady Alexandra and Billie.

"Mallet of Death indeed," Andrew mocked.

"It's a strategic sort of assassination," George replied with an enigmatic smile. "I'm taking the longitudinal view."

"My turn!" Georgiana called out. She didn't have far to walk to reach her ball. This time she hit it much harder, and it went sailing across the field toward the next wicket, stopping about five yards short of its destination.

"Well done!" Mr. Berbrooke exclaimed.

Georgiana beamed. "Thank you. I do believe I might be getting the hang of this."

"By the end of the game you shall be trouncing us all," he pronounced.

Lady Alexandra was already in place near the purple ball. She took nearly a minute to adjust her aim, then gave it a careful tap. The ball rolled forward, stopping directly in front of the wicket.

Billie made a noise deep in her throat. Lady Alexandra was actually quite skilled.

"Did you just growl?" George asked.

She nearly jumped. She hadn't realized he was so close. He was standing almost right behind her, and she could not see him unless she turned her head away from the play.

But she could feel him. He might not be touching

her, but he was so close . . . Her skin tingled, and she could feel her heart beating, low and insistent in her chest.

"I have to ask," he said, his voice intoxicatingly close to her ear, "how exactly are we meant to work as a team?"

"I'm not sure," Billie admitted, watching Andrew take his turn. "I expect that it will become obvious as we go along."

"Your turn, Billie!" Andrew yelled.

"Excuse me," Billie said to George, suddenly eager to put some space between them. She felt almost light-headed when he was standing so close.

"What are you going to do, Billie?" Georgiana asked as she approached the ball.

Billie frowned. She wasn't far from the wicket, but Lady Alexandra's purple ball was squarely in her way.

"A difficult shot," Andrew said.

"Shut up."

"You could use blunt force." He looked up at the crowd. "Her usual *modus operandi*." His voice dropped to a confidential undertone. "In Pall Mall and in life."

Billie briefly considered giving up the game right then and there and slamming the ball toward his feet.

"Wouldn't that put Lady Alexandra through the wicket?" Georgiana asked.

Andrew shrugged as if to say—*c'est la vie*.

Billie focused on her ball.

"Or she could be patient," Andrew continued,

"and queue up for the wicket after Lady Alexandra. But we all know that's not like her."

Billie made a noise. This time it was definitely a growl.

"A third option—"

"Andrew!" she ground out.

He grinned.

Billie lined up her mallet. There was no way to get through the wicket without knocking Lady Alexandra through, but if she edged it on the side . . .

She let fly.

Billie's yellow ball careened toward the wicket and smacked the purple one left of center. They all watched as Lady Alexandra's ball rolled to the right, settling into position at such an angle that she couldn't possibly hope to make it through the wicket on the next turn.

Billie's ball now sat almost precisely where Lady Alexandra's had been.

"You did that on purpose!" Lady Alexandra accused.

"Of course I did." Billie looked at her disparagingly. Honestly, what had she expected? "That's how one plays."

"That's not how *I* play."

"Well, we're not on a cross," Billie snapped, losing patience. Gad, the woman was awful.

Someone made a choking sound.

"What is that supposed to mean?" Lady Alexandra demanded.

"I think," Mr. Berbrooke said thoughtfully, "that

she means that she would play more piously if the game were a religious endeavor. Which I don't think it is."

Billie gave him an approving glance. Maybe he was cleverer than he seemed.

"Lord Kennard," Lady Alexandra said, turning to George. "Surely you do not approve of such underhanded tactics."

George gave a shrug. "It's how they play, I'm afraid."

"But not how *you* play," Lady Alexandra persisted.

Billie gave him a stare, waiting for his answer.

He did not disappoint. "It's how I play when I play with them."

Lady Alexandra drew back with a huff.

"Don't worry," Georgiana said, jumping into the breach. "You'll get the hang of it."

"It's not in my nature," Lady Alexandra sniffed.

"It's in everyone's nature," Andrew barked. "Whose turn is it?"

Mr. Berbrooke gave a jump. "Oh, mine I think." He walked back to his ball. "Am I allowed to aim for Miss Bridgerton?"

"Absolutely," Andrew replied, "but you might want to—"

Mr. Berbrooke whacked his ball without waiting for the rest of Andrew's instructions, which surely would have been *not* to hit her ball dead-on, which was exactly what he did.

The yellow ball went through the wicket and beyond, making it an additional three feet before coming to a stop. The blue ball also rolled through the wicket, but, having transferred its force to the yellow ball, it came to a stop only directly on the other side.

"Well done, Mr. Berbrooke!" Billie cheered.

He turned to her with a wide smile. "Thank you!"

"Oh for heaven's sake," Lady Alexandra snapped. "She doesn't mean it. She's only happy you knocked *her* through the wicket."

"I take everything back," Billie murmured to George. "Forget Andrew. It's *her* we must crush."

Mr. Berbrooke appealed to the rest of the crowd. "Miss Bridgerton would have gone through on the next turn, anyway, wouldn't she?"

"I would," Billie confirmed. "You really didn't set me too far ahead, I promise."

"And you got yourself through the wicket," Georgiana added. "That puts you in second place."

"It does, doesn't it?" Mr. Berbrooke said, looking inordinately pleased with this development.

"*And*," Billie added with great flair, "look how you're blocking everyone else. Well done, you."

Lady Alexandra let out a loud huff. "Whose turn is it?"

"Mine, I believe," George said smoothly.

Billie smiled to herself. She loved the way he said so much with nothing but a polite murmur. Lady Alexandra would hear a gentleman making a casual comment, but Billie knew him better. She knew him better than that pompous duke's daughter ever would.

She heard his smile. He was amused by the entire exchange, even if he was too well-bred to show it.

She heard his salute. Billie had won this round; he was congratulating her.

And she heard his gentle scolding, a warning of sorts. He was cautioning her not to carry this too far.

Which she probably would. He knew her every bit as well as she knew him.

"Take your turn, George," Andrew said.

Billie watched as George stepped forward and set up his play. He squinted as he aimed. It was kind of adorable.

What a thought. George Rokesby, adorable? It was just the most ridiculous thing.

She let out a little chuckle, just as George hit his ball. It was a good shot, landing him directly in front of the wicket.

"Oh, my goodness," Georgiana said, blinking at the field. "Now we'll never get through."

She was right. The black and blue balls were mere inches apart, flanking both sides of the wicket. Anyone who attempted the wicket would just add to the jam.

George stepped back toward Billie, clearing the way for the next few players. He leaned toward her, his mouth drawing close to her ear. "Were you laughing at me?" he murmured.

"Just a little bit," she replied, watching Georgiana trying to figure out her shot.

"Why?"

Her lips parted before she realized she couldn't

possibly give him an honest reply. She turned to look at him, and again he was closer than she'd expected, closer than he ought to have dared.

She was suddenly *aware*.

Of his breath, warm across her skin.

Of his eyes, so blue and so magnetically fastened upon her own.

Of his lips, fine, full, and carrying a hint of a smile.

Of *him*. Simply of him.

She whispered his name.

He cocked his head to the side in question, and she realized she had no idea why she'd beckoned, just that there was something so right about standing here with him, and when he looked at her like that, like he thought she was remarkable, she *felt* remarkable.

She felt beautiful.

She knew it couldn't be true, because he'd never thought of her that way. And she didn't want him to.

Or did she?

She gasped.

"Something wrong?" he murmured.

She shook her head. *Everything* was wrong.

"Billie?"

She wanted to kiss him. She wanted to kiss *George*. She'd reached the age of three-and-twenty without wanting to even so much as flirt with a gentleman and now she wanted George *Rokesby*?

Oh, this was wrong. This was very, very wrong. This was panic-inducing, world-flipping, heart-stopping wrong.

"Billie, is something wrong?"

She snapped to attention, then remembered to breathe. "Nothing," she said, rather too brightly. "Nothing at all."

But what would he do? How would he react if she marched up to him, grabbed him by the back of his head, and dragged his mouth down to hers?

He'd tell her she was raving mad, that's what he'd do. To say nothing of the four other Pall Mall players not twenty yards away.

But what if no one else were here? What if the rest of the world fell away, and there was no one to witness her insanity? Would she do it?

And would he kiss her back?

"Billie? *Billie*?"

She turned, dazed, toward the sound of his voice.

"Billie, what is wrong with you?"

She blinked, bringing his face into focus. He looked concerned. She almost laughed. He ought to be concerned.

"Billie . . ."

"I'm fine," she said quickly. "Really. It's . . . ah . . . are you warm?" She fanned herself with her hand. "I'm very warm."

He didn't answer. He didn't need to. It wasn't the least bit warm.

"I think it's my turn!" she blurted.

She had no idea if it was her turn.

"No," George said, "Andrew's still going. I daresay Lady Alexandra is in for trouble."

"Is she," she murmured, her thoughts still on her imaginary kiss.

"Damn it, Billie, now I know something is wrong." He scowled. "I thought you wanted to crush her."

"I do," she said, slowly regaining possession of her brain. Dear heavens, she could not let herself get so discomfited. George wasn't stupid. If she descended into idiocy every time he looked at her he was going to realize that something was amiss. And if he realized that she might possibly be just a little bit *infatuated* . . .

No. He could never know.

"Your turn, Billie!" Andrew bellowed.

"Right," she said. "Right, right, right." She looked over at George without actually looking at him. "Excuse me." She hurried over to her ball, gave the field a cursory examination, and whacked it toward the next wicket.

"I do believe you've overshot," Lady Alexandra said, sidling up next to her.

Billie forced a smile, trying to look enigmatic.

"Watch out!" someone yelled.

She jumped back just before the blue ball slammed into her toes. Lady Alexandra was equally nimble, and they both watched as Mr. Berbrooke's ball settled a few feet away from the wicket.

"I suppose it would serve us both right if that idiot won the game," Lady Alexandra said.

Billie stared at her in surprise. It was one thing to trade insults with her; she could certainly give as good as she got. But to disparage Mr. Berbrooke, who was quite possibly the most genial man she'd ever met . . .

Honestly, the woman was a monster.

Billie glanced back up the course. The purple ball was still firmly fixed behind the first wicket. "It's almost your turn," she said sweetly.

Lady Alexandra narrowed her eyes and made a surprisingly unpleasant sound before stalking off.

"What did you say to her?" George asked a moment later. He'd just taken his turn and was presently well-situated to take the second wicket.

"She is a terrible person," Billie muttered.

"Not what I asked," George said, glancing back at the lady in question, "but probably answer enough."

"She— Oh, never mind." Billie gave her head a shake. "She's not worth my breath."

"Certainly not," George agreed.

Billie's heart did a flip at the compliment, and she turned. "George, have you—" She frowned, cocking her head to the side. "Is that Felix coming toward us?"

George shaded his eyes as he peered in the direction she was pointing. "I believe so, yes."

"He's moving very quickly. I hope nothing is amiss."

They watched as Felix approached Andrew, who was closer than they were to the house. They spoke for a few moments and then Andrew took off at a full sprint.

"Something's wrong," George said. Mallet still in hand, he started walking toward Felix, picking up speed with every step.

Billie hurried after him as best she could, half-limping half-hopping, the rest of their Pall Mall equipment forgotten on the lawn. Frustrated with her lack of speed, she hiked up her skirts and just ran, pain be damned. She caught up with George moments after he reached Felix.

"There was a messenger," Felix was saying.

George's eyes searched his face. "Edward?"

Billie's hand flew to her mouth. *Not Edward. Oh, please, not Edward.*

Felix nodded grimly. "He's gone missing."

Chapter 16

George was already halfway to Aubrey Hall before he realized that Billie was scurrying alongside him, forced to run just to keep up with his long, swift stride.

Running. She was running.

On her ankle.

He stopped short. "What are you—"

But then it occurred to him, without even pausing for thought. This was Billie. Of course she was going to run on her injured ankle. She was headstrong. She was reckless.

She *cared*.

He did not say another word. He simply scooped her into his arms and continued on toward the house, his pace only fractionally slower than before.

"You didn't have to carry me," she said.

He heard the pain in her voice. "Yes," he said. "I did."

"Thank you," she whispered, her words melting into his shirt.

But he couldn't respond. He was beyond words now, at least beyond meaningless platitudes. He didn't need to say anything for Billie to know that he'd heard her. She would understand. She would know that his head was somewhere else, somewhere far beyond *please* and *you're welcome*.

"They're in the private drawing room," Felix said when they reached the house. George could only assume that *they* meant the rest of his family. And maybe the Bridgertons, as well.

They were family, too, he realized. They'd always been family.

When he reached the drawing room, the sight that awaited him was one to make any grown man blanch. His mother was on the sofa, sobbing in Lady Bridgerton's arms. Andrew looked to be in shock. And his father . . .

His father was crying.

Lord Manston stood removed from the rest of the group, not quite facing them but not turned entirely away. His arms were sticks at his sides, and his eyes were squeezed tightly shut, as if that might possibly halt the slow trickle of tears down his cheeks. As if maybe, if he could not see the world around him, then none of this would have happened.

George had never seen his father cry. He had not imagined it even possible. He tried not to stare, but the sight was so stunning, so soul-altering, that he could not quite look away.

His father was The Earl of Manston, solid and stern. Since George was a child he had led the Rokesby family with a firm but fair hand. He was a pillar; he was strength. He was unquestionably in charge. He treated his children with scrupulous fairness, which occasionally meant that no one was satisfied with his judgments, but he was always obeyed.

In his father George saw what it meant to lead a family. And in his father's tears, he saw his own future.

Soon, it would be time for George to lead.

"Dear heavens," Lady Bridgerton exclaimed, finally noticing them in the doorway. "What happened to Billie?"

George just stared for a moment. He'd forgotten he was holding her. "Here," he said, setting Billie down near her mother. He looked around the room. He didn't know to whom he should apply for information. Where was the messenger? Was he even still here?

"George," he heard Felix say. He looked up and saw his friend holding out a sheet of paper. Wordlessly, he took it.

> *To the Earl of Manston,*
>
> *I regret to inform you that Captain the Hon. Edward Rokesby went missing on 22 March 1779 in Connecticut Colony. We are making every effort to recover him safely.*
>
> *God bless and Godspeed,*
> *Brigadier General Geo. Garth*

"Missing," George said, looking helplessly around the room. "What does that even mean?"

No one had an answer.

George stared down at the paper in his hands, his eyes taking in every last loop of the script. The message was spectacular in its lack of information. Why was Edward in Connecticut Colony? The last they'd heard he was in New York Town, boarded at a loyalist tavern while keeping an eye on General Washington's troops across the Hudson River.

"If he's missing . . ." he said, thinking out loud. "They have to know."

"Know what?" Billie asked. She was looking up at him from her position on the sofa, probably the only person close enough to hear his words.

He shook his head, still trying to make sense of it. From the (admittedly sparse) wording of the missive, it seemed that the army was certain that Edward was still alive. Which meant that the general had at least some idea where he was.

If that were the case, why didn't he just say so?

George raked his fingers through his hair, the ball of his hand rubbing hard against his forehead. "How can a decorated soldier go missing?" he asked, turning back to the rest of the room. "Was he kidnapped? Is that what they are trying to tell us?"

"I'm not sure they know," Felix said quietly.

"Oh, they bloody well know," George nearly spat. "They just don't want—"

But Andrew cut him off. "It's not like here," he said, his voice hollow and dull.

George shot him an irritated glance. "I know, but what—"

"It's not like here," Andrew said again, this time with rising anger. "The villages are far apart. The farms don't even border each other. There are giant swaths of land that nobody owns."

Everyone stared at him.

"And there are savages," Andrew said.

George stepped closer, trying to block his mother's view of Andrew's tortured face. "This is not the time," he said in a harsh whisper. His brother might be in shock, but so were they all. It was time for Andrew to grow up and bloody well take hold of his emotions before he shattered what little composure remained in the room.

But Andrew's tongue remained loose and indiscreet. "It would be easy to go missing there."

"You haven't been there," George snapped.

"I've heard."

"You've *heard*."

"Stop," someone said. "Stop it now."

The two men were now nearly nose to nose.

"There are men on my ship who fought in the colonies," Andrew bit off.

"Oh, and *that's* going to help us recover Edward," George practically spat.

"I know more about it than you do."

George nearly flinched. He hated this. He hated this so much. The impotence. The worthlessness. He'd been outside playing bloody Pall Mall and his brother was missing in some godforsaken colonial wilderness.

"I am still your older brother," he hissed, "and I will be head of this family—"

"Well, you're not now."

He might as well have been. George cast a fleeting glance at his father, who had not said a word.

"Oh, that was subtle," Andrew jeered.

"Shut up. Just shut—"

"Stop!" Hands came between them and forcibly pushed them apart, and when George finally looked down he realized they belonged to Billie.

"This isn't helping," she said, practically shoving Andrew into a chair.

George blinked, trying to regain his equilibrium. He didn't know why he was yelling at Andrew. He looked at Billie, still standing between them like a tiny warrior. "You shouldn't be on that foot," he said.

Her mouth fell open. "*That's* what you want to say?"

"You've probably reinjured it."

She stared at him. George knew he sounded a fool, but her ankle was the one bloody thing he actually could do something about.

"You should sit down," she said softly.

He shook his head. He didn't want to sit down. He wanted to act, to *do* something, anything that might bring his brother safely home. But he was tied here, he'd always been tied here, to this land, to these people.

"I can go," Andrew choked out.

They all turned to look at him. He was still in the chair that Billie had forced him into. He looked terrible. Thunderstruck. Andrew looked, George had a feeling, rather like he himself felt.

But with one massive difference. Andrew at least believed that he could help.

"Go where?" someone finally asked.

"To the colonies." Andrew looked up, the bleak desperation in his face slowly giving way to hard determination. "I will ask to be assigned to a different ship. There's probably one leaving in the next month."

"No," Lady Manston cried. She sounded like a wounded animal. She sounded like nothing George had ever heard.

Andrew rose to his feet. "Mother—"

"No," she said again, this time with fortitude as she pulled herself from Lady Bridgerton's comforting arms. "I will not permit it. I won't lose another son."

Andrew stood stiffly, looking more like a soldier than George had ever seen him. "It's no more dangerous than serving where I do now."

George closed his eyes. *Wrong thing to say, Andrew.*

"You can't," Lady Manston said, struggling to her feet. "You can't."

Her voice began to break again, and George silently cursed Andrew for his lack of tact. He stepped forward. "Mother . . ."

"He can't," she choked out, her tortured eyes coming to rest on George's face. "You must tell him . . . he can't."

George pulled his mother into his arms, meeting Andrew's eyes over her head before murmuring, "We can discuss it later."

"You're just saying that."

"I think you should lie down."

"We should go home," Lord Manston said.

They all turned. It was the first he had spoken since the terrible message had been delivered.

"We need to be at home," he said.

It was Billie who sprang into action. "Of course," she said, going quickly to his side. "You will be more comfortable there." She looked over at George. "The last thing you need is this house party."

George nearly groaned. He'd forgot all about the other guests. The thought of having to actually converse with any of them was excruciating. There would be questions, and condolences, never mind that none of them knew the first thing about Edward.

God, it was all so insignificant. This. The party. Everything but the people in this room.

He looked at Billie. She was still watching him, concern evident in every line of her face. "Has anyone told Mary?" she asked.

"I will do so now," Felix said. "We will join you at Crake, if that suits. I'm sure she will wish to be with her family. We have no need to go back to Sussex immediately."

"What will we do?" Lady Manston said in a lost voice.

George looked to his father. It was his right to decide.

But the earl looked lost. He'd said they should go home; apparently that was all he could manage.

George turned back to the rest of the room and

took a breath. "We will take a moment," he said firmly. "We will pause to collect ourselves and decide how best to proceed."

Andrew opened his mouth to speak, but George had had enough. With a hard stare, he added, "Time is of the essence, but we are too far removed from the military theater for one day to make a difference."

"He's right," Billie said.

Several pairs of eyes turned to her in surprise, George's included.

"None of us is in a state to make a proper decision just now." She turned to George. "Go home. Be with your family. I will call tomorrow to see how I may help."

"But what can you do?" Lady Bridgerton asked.

Billie looked at her with quiet, steely grace. "Anything that is required."

George swallowed, surprised by the rush of emotion behind his eyes. His brother was missing; his father was shattered, and *now* he thought he might cry?

He ought to tell her that they did not need help, that her offer was appreciated but unnecessary.

That was the polite thing to do. It was what he would have said, to anyone else.

But to Billie he said, "Thank you."

BILLIE DROVE HERSELF to Crake House the following day, taking a simple one-horse buggy. She wasn't sure how her mother had managed it, but the house party had been cut short by several days, and everyone had either left or was planning to do so by the following morning.

It had taken her a ridiculous amount of time to decide what to wear. Breeches were most certainly out. Despite what her mother thought, Billie did know how and when to dress appropriately, and she would never don her work clothes for a social call.

But this was no ordinary social call. Bright colors would not do. But she could not wear black. Or lavender or gray or anything that even hinted of mourning. Edward was *not* dead, she told herself fiercely.

In the end she settled on a comfortable day dress she'd got the year before. Her mother had picked out the pattern—a springlike floral with greens and pinks and oranges set against cream muslin—but Billie had loved it from the first. It made her think of a garden on a cloudy day, which somehow seemed exactly right for calling upon the Rokesbys.

Crake was quiet when she arrived. It felt wrong. It was an enormous house; like Aubrey Hall, one could theoretically go days without seeing another member of the family. But even so, it always seemed vibrant, alive. Some Rokesby or another was always about, ever happy, ever busy.

Crake House was huge, but it was a home.

Right now, however, it felt subdued. Even the servants, who normally worked with diligence and discretion, were quieter than usual. No one smiled, no one spoke.

It was almost heartbreaking.

Billie was directed to the sitting room, but before

she exited the hall George appeared, obviously having been alerted to her arrival.

"Billie," he said, bowing his head in greeting. "It is good to see you."

Her first impulse was to ask if there had been any news, but of course there would not be. There would be no swift rider, down from London with a report. Edward was far too far away. It would likely be months before they learned his fate.

"How is your mother?" she asked.

He smiled sadly. "As well as can be expected."

Billie nodded, following him into the sitting room. "And your father?"

George paused, but he did not turn to face her. "He sits in his study and stares out the window."

Billie swallowed, her heart breaking at George's bleak posture. She did not need to see his face to know his pain. He loved Edward, just as she did. Just as they all did.

"He is useless," George said.

Billie's lips parted in surprise at such harsh words, but then she realized that George had not meant them as scorn.

"He is incapacitated," he clarified. "The grief . . ."

"I don't think any of us knows how we will react to a crisis until we are forced into one."

He turned, one corner of his mouth tipping up. "When did you grow so wise?"

"It isn't wisdom to repeat platitudes."

"It is wisdom to know which ones bear repeating."

To her great surprise, Billie felt a bubble of humor rising within. "You are determined to compliment me."

"It's the only bloody bright spot in the day," George muttered.

It was the sort of comment that would normally make her heart leap, but like the rest of them, she was too blunted by pain and worry. Edward was missing, and George was hurting—

She took a breath. This wasn't about George. George was *fine*. He was here, right in front of her, healthy and hale.

No, this wasn't about George.

It couldn't be about George.

Except . . . lately it seemed as if everything was about George. She thought about him constantly, and heaven above, was it just the day before that they'd been playing Pall Mall and she'd practically *kissed* him?

She'd wanted to. Dear God, she'd wanted to, and if he'd shown any interest—and if there hadn't been four other people milling about with Pall Mall mallets— she'd have done it. She'd never kissed anyone before, but when had that ever stopped her? She'd jumped her first fence when she was six. She'd never so much as jumped a shrub before that, but she'd taken one look at that five-foot fence and known that she had to take it. So she'd just hopped on her mare, and she'd done it. Because she'd wanted to.

And also because Edward had dared her. But she wouldn't have tried it if she hadn't thought she could do it.

And known she would love it.

She'd known even then that she wasn't like other girls. She didn't want to play the pianoforte or pick at her sewing. She wanted to be outside, to fly through the air on the back of her horse, sunlight dancing across her skin as her heart skipped and raced with the wind.

She wanted to soar.

She still did.

If she kissed George . . . if he kissed her . . . Would it feel the same way?

She trailed her fingers along the back of the sofa, trying to fill the moment with idle movement. But then she made the mistake of looking up . . .

He was staring at her, his eyes fierce and curious and something else, too, something she could not precisely name.

But whatever it was . . . she felt it. Her heart leapt, and her breath quickened, and she realized it was just like when she raced on her mare. Breathless and giddy and determined and wild . . . It was all there within her, bursting to get free.

All because he'd looked at her.

Dear God, if he actually *kissed* her she might fall apart.

She tapped nervous fingers on the edge of the sofa, then gestured stupidly to a chair. "I should sit."

"If you wish."

But her feet wouldn't move. "I seem not to know what to do with myself," she admitted.

"Join the club," he muttered.

"Oh, George . . ."

"Do you want a drink?" he asked suddenly.

"Now?" It was barely past eleven.

His shrug bordered on insolence. Billie could only wonder at how much he'd already had.

But he didn't head for the brandy decanter. Instead he stood by the window, staring out over the garden. It had started to rain; a light misty drizzle that made the air thick and gray.

She waited for several moments, but he did not turn around. His hands were clasped behind his back—the classic stance of a gentleman. But it wasn't quite right. There was a certain harshness to his pose, a tension in his shoulders that she wasn't used to seeing there.

He was brittle. Bleak.

"What will you do?" she finally forced herself to ask. She did not think she could bear the silence for another moment.

His posture changed, a slight movement in his neck maybe, and then he turned his head to the side. But not far enough to actually look at her. Instead she was treated to his profile as he said, "Go to London, I suppose."

"To London?" she echoed.

He snorted. "There's not much else I can do."

"You don't want to go to the Colonies to look for him?"

"Of course I want to go to the Colonies," he snapped, whirling around to face her. "But that's not what I *do*."

Billie's lips parted, but the only sound was her pulse, racing wildly through her veins. His outburst was unexpected. Unprecedented.

She had seen George lose his temper before. She could hardly have grown up alongside his younger brothers and *not* have done so. But she had never seen *this*.

There was no missing the contempt in his voice, nor the fact that it was directed entirely within.

"George," she said, trying to keep her voice calm and reasonable, "if you want to—"

He stepped forward, his eyes hard and furious. "Don't tell me I can do what I want because if you believe that, you're just as naïve as the rest of them."

"I wasn't going to—" But it was just as well that he cut her off with a mocking snort, because that was exactly what she had been about to say, and it was only now that she realized how ludicrous it would have been. He couldn't take off and go to the Colonies; they all knew that.

He would never be as free as his brothers. The order of their birth had ensured that. George would inherit the title, the house, the land. Most of the money. But with privilege came responsibility. He was tied to this place. It was in his blood, the same way Aubrey Hall was in hers.

She wanted to ask him if he minded. If given the chance, would he trade places with Andrew or Edward?

"What will you do in London?" she said instead. Because she could never have asked him what she really wanted to know. Not while Edward's fate was uncertain.

He shrugged, although not so much with his shoulders as his head and eyes. "Speak to people. Make inquiries." He laughed bitterly. "I'm very good at speaking to people and making inquiries."

"You know how to get things done," she agreed.

"I know how to get other people to do things," he said derisively.

She pressed her lips together before she could utter something inane like, "That's an important skill." But it *was* an important skill, even if she'd never demonstrated it herself. She never left anything to her father's steward; he was surely the most overpaid clerk in the land. She acted first and thought later; she always had. And she could not bear to let someone else perform a task when she could do it better herself.

And she could almost always do it better herself.

"I need a drink," George suddenly muttered. Billie didn't dare point out again that it was still rather early for spirits.

He walked over to the side table and poured himself a brandy from the decanter. He took a sip. A long one. "Do you want one?"

Billie shook her head.

"Surprising," George muttered.

There was something hard in his voice. Something almost nasty. She felt her spine grow rigid. "I beg your pardon?"

But George only laughed, his brows arching into a mocking salute. "Oh, come now, Billie. You live to shock. I can hardly believe you wouldn't take a brandy when offered."

She grit her teeth, reminding herself that George was not himself at the moment. "It's not even noon."

He shrugged and kicked back the rest of his brandy.

"You shouldn't be drinking."

"*You* shouldn't be telling me what to do."

She held herself still, stiff even, allowing the long pause to express her disapproval. Finally, because she needed to be as brittle as he, she gave him a cool stare, and said, "Lady Alexandra sends her regards."

He gave her a look of disbelief.

"She leaves today."

"How kind of you to convey her salutations."

She felt a cutting retort rising through her throat, but at the last minute she blurted, "No! This is ridiculous. I'm not going to stand here and speak in rhymes. I came to help."

"You can't help," he bit off.

"Certainly not when you're like this," she retorted.

He slammed his glass down and stalked toward her. "What did you just say?" he demanded. His eyes were wild and furious, and she almost took a step back.

"How much have you had to drink?"

"I'm not drunk," he said in a dangerous voice. "This . . . *that*," he corrected, waving an arm back toward the glass he'd left on the sideboard, "was my first and only drink of the day."

Billie had a feeling she was supposed to apologize, but she couldn't make herself do it.

"I'd like to be drunk," he said, moving closer with the silent grace of a large cat.

"You don't mean that."

"Don't I?" He laughed stridently. "Drunk, I might not remember that my brother is lost in some god-forsaken wilderness where the locals are not predisposed to favor anyone in a red coat."

"George," she tried to say, but he would not be deterred.

"Drunk," he said again, the word punching harshly through the air, "I might not have noticed that my mother has spent the entire morning weeping in her bed. But best of all"—his hands came down heavily on a side table, and he looked at her with fury-laden despair—"if I were drunk, I might somehow forget that I am at the mercy of the rest of the goddamn world. If Edward is found—"

"When he's found," Billie cut in fiercely.

"Either way, it won't be because of me."

"What do you *want* to do?" she asked quietly. Because she had a feeling he didn't know. He said he wanted to go to the Colonies, but she wasn't sure she believed him. She didn't think he'd even allowed himself to think about what he wanted to do. He was so stuck on his restrictions that he could not think clearly about what was truly in his heart.

"What do I *want* to do?" he echoed. He looked . . . not surprised, exactly, but maybe a little dumbfounded. "I want . . . I want . . ." He blinked, then brought his eyes to hers. "I want you."

The breath left her body.

"I want you," he repeated, and it was as if the entire room shifted. The dazed look left his eyes, replaced by something fierce.

Predatory.

Billie could not speak. She could only watch as he came ever closer, the air between them heating to a simmering pitch.

"You don't want to do this," she said.

"Oh, I do. I really do."

But he didn't. She knew that he didn't, and she could feel her heart breaking because she *did*. She wanted him to kiss her like she was the only woman he could ever dream of kissing, like he'd die if he didn't touch his lips to hers.

She wanted him to kiss her and *mean* it.

"You don't know what you're doing," she said, edging back a step.

"Is that what you think?" he murmured.

"You've been drinking."

"Just enough to make this perfect."

She blinked. She didn't have a clue what that meant.

"Come now, Billie," he mocked. "Why so hesitant? That's not like you."

"This isn't like *you*," she countered.

"You have no idea." He came even closer, his eyes glittering with something she was terrified to define. He reached out and touched her arm, just one finger to her flesh, but it was enough to make her tremble. "When have you ever backed down from a dare?"

Her stomach was flipping and her heart was pounding, but still her shoulders fell into a stiff, straight line. "Never," she declared, staring him straight in the eye.

He smiled, and his gaze grew hot. "That's my girl," he murmured.

"I'm not—"

"You will be," he growled, and before she could utter another word, his mouth captured hers in a searing kiss.

Chapter 17

He was kissing her.

It was the very definition of madness.

He was kissing *Billie Bridgerton*, the last woman in the world he should ever dream of wanting, but by God, when she'd glared up at him, and her chin had trembled and jutted out, all he could see were her lips and all he could smell was her scent.

And all he could feel was the heat of her skin beneath his fingers, and he wanted more. More of *that*.

More of her.

His other hand came around her with stunning speed, and he wasn't thinking, he *couldn't* be thinking. He just pulled her up against him, hard, and then he was kissing her.

He wanted to devour her.

He wanted to own her.

He wanted to fold her into his arms and hold her tight and kiss her until she finally saw sense, until she stopped doing crazy things and stopped taking crazy risks, and started behaving the way a woman ought while still being *her* and—

He couldn't think. His thoughts were jumbled, torn to bits by the sheer heat of the moment.

More . . . his mind was begging. *More* was the only thing that made any sense to him. More of this. More of Billie.

He captured her face in his hands, holding her still. But she wasn't still. Her lips were moving beneath his, kissing him back with the sort of fervor that was exactly Billie. She rode hard and she played hard and by God she kissed the same way, like he was her triumph and she was going to glory in it.

It was all so mad, so completely wrong and yet so deliciously perfect. It was every sensation in the world, wrapped into one woman, and he could not get enough. In that moment, in that room, he could never get enough.

His palm moved to her shoulder, then to her back, pulling her closer until his hips pressed hard against her belly. She was small, and she was strong, but she curved in all the best places.

George was no monk. He had kissed women before, women who knew how to kiss him back. But he had never wanted anyone as much as he wanted Billie. He had never wanted anything as much as this kiss.

This kiss . . . and all that could come after.

"Billie," he groaned. "Billie."

She made a sound. It might have been his name. And somehow that was what it took.

Good God. Reason came slamming back into him. His brain woke and his sanity returned, and he stumbled back, the electricity that had sparked so hot between them now jolting him away.

What the hell had just happened?

He breathed. No, he *tried* to breathe. It was an entirely different thing.

She had asked him what he wanted.

And he'd answered. He wanted *her.* He hadn't even had to think about it.

Clearly, he *hadn't* thought about it, because if he had, he wouldn't have done it.

He raked a hand through his hair. Then another. Then he just gave up and squeezed both, pulling on his scalp until he let out a growl of pain.

"You kissed me," she said, and he had just enough presence of mind not to say that she'd kissed him back. Because he'd started it. He had started it, and they both knew that she never would have done so.

He shook his head, tiny unthinking movements that did nothing to clear his mind. "I'm sorry," he said stiffly. "That wasn't—I mean—"

He swore. This was apparently the extent of his coherency.

"You kissed me," she said again, and this time she sounded suspicious. "Why did—"

"I don't know," he bit off. He swore again, raking his hand through his hair as he turned away from her. Bloody hell. Bloody, bloody—

He swallowed. "That was a mistake," he said.

"What?"

It was just one word. Not nearly enough for him to decipher her tone. Which was probably for the best. He turned around, forcing himself to look at her while at the same time not allowing himself to *see*.

He didn't want to see her reaction. He didn't want to know what she thought of him. "That was a mistake," he said, because it was what he had to say. "Do you understand me?"

Her eyes narrowed. Her face grew hard. "Perfectly."

"For God's sake, Billie, don't take bloody offense—"

"Don't take offense? Don't take offense? You—" She stopped herself, shot a furtive glance at the open door, and lower her voice to a furious hiss. "I did not start this."

"I am well aware."

"What were you thinking?"

"Obviously, I wasn't," he practically spat.

Her eyes widened, flashing with pain, and then she turned, hugging her arms to her body.

And George finally knew the true meaning of remorse. He let out an unsteady breath, raking his hand through his hair. "I apologize," he said, for the second time in as many minutes. "I will marry you, of course."

"*What?*" She whirled around. "No."

George stiffened. It was like someone had taken an iron rod and shoved it right up his spine. "I beg your pardon?"

"Don't be daft, George. You don't want to marry me."

It was true, but he was not stupid enough to say so out loud.

"And you know I don't want to marry you."

"As you are making increasingly clear."

"You only kissed me because you're upset."

This was *not* true, but he kept his mouth shut on this point as well.

"So I accept your apology." Her chin rose. "And we will never speak of this again."

"Agreed."

They stood there for a moment, frozen in their painfully awkward tableau. He ought to be jumping for joy. Any other young lady would be screaming for the trees. Or for her father. And the vicar. And a special license woven into the shape of a noose.

But not Billie. No, Billie just looked at him with an almost preternatural haughtiness and said, "I hope *you* will accept *my* apology."

"Your—" *What?* His jaw dropped. What the devil did she have to apologize for? Or was she merely trying to get the upper hand? She'd always known how to unsettle him.

"It's not as if I can pretend that I didn't return the . . . ah . . ." She swallowed, and he took some pleasure in the fact that she blushed before she finished the statement. "The . . . ah . . ."

He took quite a bit of pleasure in the fact that she couldn't finish the statement at all.

"You liked it," he said with a slow smile. It was colossally unwise to goad her at such a moment, but he could not help himself.

She shifted her weight. "Everyone has to have a first kiss."

"Then I am honored," he said with a courtly bow.

Her lips parted in surprise, maybe even consternation. Good. He'd turned the tables.

"I was not expecting it to be you, of course," she said.

He stifled his irritation and instead murmured, "Perhaps you were hoping for someone else?"

She gave a jerky little shrug. "No one in particular."

He chose not to analyze the burst of pleasure that rushed through him at that statement.

"I suppose I always thought it would be one of your brothers," she continued. "Andrew, maybe—"

"*Not* Andrew," he bit off.

"No, probably not," she agreed, her head tilting to the side as she considered it. "But it used to seem plausible."

He stared at her with mounting irritation. While she was not wholly *un*affected by the situation, she was certainly not *as* affected as he thought she should have been.

"It wouldn't have been the same," he heard himself say.

She blinked. "I beg your pardon."

"If you had kissed someone else." He stepped toward her, unable to ignore the way his blood buzzed with anticipation. "It would not have been the same."

"Well . . ." She looked flustered, delightfully so. "I would expect not," she finally said. "I mean . . . different people . . ."

"Very different," he agreed.

Her mouth opened, and several seconds passed

before words emerged. "I'm not sure to whom you're comparing yourself."

"Anyone." He moved even closer. "Everyone."

"George?" Her eyes were huge, but she wasn't saying no.

"Do you want me to kiss you again?" he asked.

"Of course not." But she said it too quickly.

"Are you sure of that?"

She swallowed. "It would be a very bad idea."

"Very much so," he said softly.

"So we . . . shouldn't?"

He touched her cheek, and this time he whispered it. "Do you want me to kiss you again?"

She moved . . . a little. He couldn't tell whether she was shaking her head *yes* or *no*. He had a feeling she didn't know, either.

"Billie?" he murmured, coming close enough so that his breath whispered across her skin.

Her breath hitched, and she said, "I said I wouldn't marry you."

"You did."

"Well, I said you didn't *have* to marry me."

He nodded.

"That would still be true."

"If I kissed you again?"

She nodded.

"So this means nothing?"

"No . . ."

Something warm and lovely unfurled in his chest. This could never mean nothing. And she knew it.

"It just means . . ." She swallowed, her lips trembling as they pressed together. ". . . that there are no consequences."

He brushed his lips against her cheek. "No consequences," he softly repeated.

"None."

"I could kiss you again . . ." His hand stole around to the small of her back, but he exerted only the barest of pressure. She could step away at any moment. She could remove herself from his embrace, cross the room, and leave. He needed her to know this. *He* needed to know that she knew this. There would be no recriminations, no telling herself that she had been swept away by his passion.

If she was swept away by passion, it would be her own.

His lips touched her ear. "I could kiss you again," he repeated.

She gave a little nod. A tiny nod. But he felt it. "Again," she whispered.

His teeth found her earlobe, gently nipping. "And again."

"I think—"

"What do you think?" He smiled against her skin. He couldn't quite believe how utterly delightful this was. He'd known kisses of passion, of raw, primal hunger and overwhelming lust. This was all that, but there was something more.

Something joyful.

"I think . . ." She swallowed. "I think you *should* kiss me again." She looked up, her eyes remarkably clear. "And I think you should shut the door."

George had never moved so fast in his life. He had half a mind to shove a chair under the door handle just to keep the damned thing closed.

"This still doesn't mean nothing," she said as his arms wrapped around her.

"Absolutely not."

"But no consequences."

"None."

"You don't have to marry me."

"I don't have to, no."

But he could. The thought flicked across his mind with warm surprise. He *could* marry her. There was no reason why not.

His sanity, perhaps. But he had a feeling he'd lost that the first moment his lips had touched hers.

She stood on her tiptoes, tilting her face to his. "If you're my first kiss," she said, her lips curving with subtle mischief, "then you might as well be my second."

"Maybe your third," he said, capturing her mouth with his.

"It's important to know," she said, getting just those four words out between kisses.

"To know?" His mouth moved to her neck, causing her to arch provocatively in his arms.

She nodded, gasping as one of his hands moved along her rib cage. "How to kiss," she clarified. "It's a skill."

He felt himself smile. "And you like to be skilled."

"I do."

He kissed her neck, then her collarbone, giving

thanks to the current bodice styles, round and deep, baring creamy skin from her shoulders to the top swell of her breasts. "I predict great things for you."

Her only response was a gasp of surprise. About what, he wasn't quite sure—perhaps his tongue, flicking out along the sensitive skin peeking out from the lacy edge of her dress. Or maybe it was his teeth, nipping gently along the side of her neck.

He didn't dare tumble her onto the chaise; he did not trust himself that far. But he did nudge her until she was leaning against the sofa, lifting her the scant few inches required to set her atop the back.

And God love her, but Billie knew instinctively what to do. Her legs parted, and when he rucked up her skirts, she wrapped herself around him. Maybe it was just for balance, but as he pressed himself against her, he didn't care. Her skirt was still in the way, as were his breeches, but he *felt* her. He was hard, exquisitely so, and he pressed against her, his body knowing where it wanted to go. She was a country girl; she had to know what this meant, but she was lost in the same passion, and she pulled him closer, her legs tightening around his hips.

Dear God, at this rate he was going to spend himself like a green boy.

He took a breath. "It's too much," he gasped, forcing himself to pull away.

"No," was all she said, but her hands moved to his head, allowing him to kiss her even as he put a little distance between their bodies.

And so he kissed her. He kissed her endlessly. He

kissed her carefully, skirting the edge of his own desire, all too aware how close he was to the brink of reason.

And he kissed her tenderly, because this was Billie, and somehow he knew that no one ever thought to be tender with her.

"George," she said.

He lifted his lips from hers, just a bit, just a breath. "Hmmm."

"We have to . . . we have to stop."

"Mmmm," he agreed. But he didn't stop. He could have done; he had a grip on his passion now. But he didn't want to.

"George," she said again. "I hear people."

He drew back. Listened.

Swore.

"Open the door," Billie hissed.

He did. With alacrity. Nothing sparked suspicion like a closed door. He looked at her. "You might . . ." He cleared his throat and made a motion near his head. "You might want to . . ."

He was no expert on ladies' coiffures, but he was fairly certain her hair did not look as it should.

Billie blanched and frantically smoothed her hair, her nimble fingers tugging on pins and then jamming them back into place. "Better?"

He grimaced. There was a spot behind her right ear where a chestnut lock looked as if it was sprouting from her head.

They heard a voice from the hall. "*George?*"

His mother. Good God.

"George!"

"In the drawing room, Mother," he called back, heading to the doorway. He could stall her in the hall for a few seconds at least. He turned back to Billie, sharing one last urgent glance. She took her hands from her hair and held them out, as if to say, "*Well?*"

It would have to do.

"Mother," he said, stepping into the hall. "You're up."

She offered her cheek, which he dutifully kissed. "I can't stay in my room forever."

"No, although surely you are allowed time to—"

"Grieve?" she interrupted. "I refuse to grieve. Not until we receive more definite news."

"I was going to say 'rest,'" he told her.

"I've done that."

Well done, Lady Manston, he thought. Funny how his mother still managed to surprise him with her resilience.

"I was thinking," his mother began, walking past him into the drawing room. "Oh, hello, Billie, I did not realize you were here."

"Lady Manston." Billie bobbed a curtsy. "I was hoping I might be of some assistance."

"That is very kind of you. I'm not sure what can be done, but your company is always appreciated." Lady Manston's head tilted to the side. "Is it very windy out?"

"What?" Billie's hand flew self-consciously to her hair. "Oh. Yes, a bit. I forgot my bonnet."

They all looked at the bonnet she'd left on a table.

"What I meant to say was that I forgot to put it

on," Billie said with a nervous chuckle that George dearly hoped his mother did not detect. "Or rather, truthfully, I didn't forget. The air was so very fine."

"I won't tell your mother," Lady Manston said with an indulgent smile.

Billie nodded her thanks, and then an awkward silence fell over the room. Or maybe it wasn't awkward at all. Maybe George only thought it was awkward, because he knew what Billie was thinking, and he knew what *he* was thinking, and it seemed impossible somehow that his mother could be thinking of anything else.

But apparently she was, because she looked at him with a smile he knew was forced, and asked, "Have you given further thought to going to London?"

"Some," he replied. "I know a few people at the War Office."

"George was thinking of traveling to London to make inquiries," his mother said to Billie.

"Yes, he'd told me. It's an excellent idea."

Lady Manston gave a tiny nod and turned back to George. "Your father knows people as well, but . . ."

"I can go," George said swiftly, saving his mother the pain of having to describe her husband's current state of incapacitation.

"You probably know the same people," Billie said.

George glanced over. "Just so."

"I believe I will go with you," his mother said.

"Mother, no, you should stay home," George immediately said. "Father will need you, and it will be easier for me to do what needs to be done on my own."

"Don't be silly. Your father doesn't need anything but news of his son, and I can't do anything to further that cause from here."

"And you will in London?"

"Probably not," she admitted, "but at least there is a chance."

"I'm not going to be able to accomplish anything if I'm worried about you."

His mother raised one perfectly arched brow. "Then don't worry."

He grit his teeth. There was no arguing with her when she was like this, and the truth was, he wasn't even sure *why* he didn't want his mother to come with him. Just this strange, niggling feeling that some things were best done alone.

"It will all work out," Billie said, trying to smooth over the tension between mother and son. George shot her a look of gratitude, but he didn't think she saw it. She was more like her own mother than anyone gave her credit for, he realized. She was a peacemaker, in her own inimitable way.

He watched as she took one of his mother's hands in hers. "I know that Edward will come home to us," she said with a light squeeze.

A warm, almost homey sense of pride swirled through him. And he could have sworn he could feel her, giving his hand a squeeze as well.

"You're such a dear, Billie," his mother said. "You and Edward were always so close."

"My best friend," Billie said. "Well, besides Mary, of course."

George crossed his arms. "Don't forget Andrew."

She glanced over at him with a frown.

Lady Manston leaned forward and kissed Billie on the cheek. "What I wouldn't give to see you and Edward together one more time."

"And you shall," Billie said firmly. "He will be home—if not soon, then at least eventually." She gave an excellent approximation of a reassuring smile. "We will be together again. I know it."

"We will *all* be together again," George said peevishly.

Billie gave him another frown, this one considerably more remonstrative.

"I keep seeing his face," his mother said. "Every time I close my eyes."

"I do, too," Billie admitted.

George saw red. He'd just bloody kissed her—and he was fairly certain her eyes had been closed.

"George?" his mother inquired.

"What?" he bit off.

"You made a noise."

"I cleared my throat," he lied. Had Billie been thinking of Edward when she kissed him? No, she wouldn't do that. Or would she? How would he know? And could he blame her? If she had been thinking of Edward, it wasn't anything she'd done on purpose.

Which somehow made it even worse.

He watched as Billie spoke quietly with his mother. Was she in love with Edward? No, she couldn't be.

Because if she *was*, Edward would never have been so foolish as to not return the affection. And if that were the case, they'd be married by now.

Besides, Billie had said she had not been kissed. And Billie didn't lie.

Edward was a gentleman—maybe even more of one than George, after the events of today—but if he was in love with Billie, there was no way he'd have left for America without kissing her.

"George?"

He looked up. His mother was regarding him with some concern. "You don't look well," she said.

"I don't feel well," he said curtly.

His mother drew back ever-so-slightly, the only indication of her surprise. "I don't imagine any of us does," she said.

"I wish I could go to London," Billie said.

George snapped to attention. "Are you joking?" Good God, that would be a disaster. If he was worried about his *mother* being a distraction . . .

She drew back, visibly offended. "Why would I be joking?"

"You hate London."

"I've only been the once," she said stiffly.

"What?" Lady Manston exclaimed. "How is that possible? I know you didn't have a Season, but it's barely even a full day's ride."

Billie cleared her throat. "There was some hesitation on the part of my mother after what happened at my presentation at court."

Lady Manston cringed a little, then made a full recovery with a brightly declared: "Well, that settles it, then. We cannot live in the past."

George regarded his mother with a slow dose of dread. "Settles what, exactly?"

"Billie must go to London."

Chapter 18

And so it was that less than one week later Billie found herself stripped down to her unmentionables with two seamstresses jabbering on in French while they jabbed *her* with pins and needles.

"I could have used one of my gowns from home," she told Lady Manston for what was probably the fifth time.

Lady Manston did not even look up from the book of fashion plates she was perusing. "No, you couldn't."

Billie sighed as she stared out at the richly brocaded fabrics that draped the walls of the fancy dress shop that had become her second home here in London. It was very exclusive, she'd been told; the discreet sign hanging above the door said merely *Mme. Delacroix, tailoress*, but Lady Manston referred to the petite French dynamo as Crossy, and Billie had been told to do the same.

Normally, Lady Manston said, Crossy and her girls would come to *them*, but they hadn't much time to get Billie properly fitted and kitted, and in this instance it seemed more efficient to visit the shop.

Billie had tried to protest. She wasn't coming to London for a Season. It wasn't even the right time of year. Well, it would be soon, but it wasn't yet. And they absolutely had not traveled to London to attend parties and balls. Truth be told, Billie wasn't entirely certain why she was there. She had been utterly shocked when Lady Manston made her announcement, and it must have shown on her face.

"You just said you wished to go," Lady Manston had said, "and I will confess I am not being entirely unselfish. *I* wish to go, and I require a companion."

George had protested, which, under the circumstances, Billie had found sensible *and* insulting, but his mother was unstoppable.

"I can't bring Mary," she said firmly. "She's far too ill, and I doubt Felix would permit it in any case." At that she had looked over to Billie. "He's very protective."

"Quite so," Billie had mumbled . . . rather stupidly, in her opinion. But she couldn't think of anything else to say. Honestly, she never felt less sure of herself than in the face of an indomitable society matron, even one she'd known since birth. Most of the time Lady Manston was her beloved neighbor, but every now and then the Leader of Society shone through, issuing orders and directing people, and generally just being an expert on everything. Billie had no idea how to assert herself. It was the same way with her own mother.

But then George had jettisoned *sensible* and gone completely over to *insulting*.

"Forgive me, Billie," he'd said (while looking at his mother), "but she would be a distraction."

"A welcome one," Lady Manston said.

"Not to *me*."

"George Rokesby!" His mother was instantly incensed. "You apologize this minute."

"She knows what I meant," he said.

At that, Billie could not keep her mouth shut. "I do?"

George turned back to Billie with an expression of vague irritation. And clear condescension. "You don't really want to go to London."

"Edward was my friend, too," she said.

"There is no 'was' about it," George snapped.

She wanted to smack him. He was deliberately misunderstanding her. "Oh, for heaven's sake, George, you know what I meant."

"I do?" he mocked.

"What on earth is going on here?" Lady Manston had exploded. "I know the two of you have never been close, but there is no call for this sort of behavior. Good God, one would think the both of you were three years old."

And that was that. Both Billie and George were shamed into silence, and Lady Manston went off to pen a note to Lady Bridgerton, explaining that Billie had graciously agreed to accompany her to town.

Naturally, Lady Bridgerton had thought this a splendid idea.

Billie had thought she'd spend her days taking in the sights, perhaps attending the theater, but the day after their arrival, Lady Manston had received an invitation to a ball being given by a dear, dear friend, and much to Billie's surprise, she had decided to accept.

"Are you certain you're up to it?" Billie had asked. (At that point she had not thought that she was going to be roped in to attending as well, so it had to be said, her motives were purely altruistic.)

"My son is not dead," Lady Manston said, surprising Billie with her bluntness. "I am not going to act as if he is."

"Well, no, of course not, but—"

"Besides," Lady Manston said, giving no indication that she had heard Billie speak, "Ghislaine is a dear, dear friend, and it would be impolite to decline."

Billie had frowned, looking down at the sizable stack of invitations that had mysteriously appeared in the delicately scalloped porcelain dish resting atop Lady Manston's writing table. "How does she even know you're here in London?"

Lady Manston shrugged as she perused the rest of her invitations. "I expect she heard it from George."

Billie smiled tightly. George had reached London two days before the ladies. He'd ridden the whole way on horseback, lucky dog. Since her arrival, however, she'd seen him precisely three times. Once at supper, once at breakfast, and once in the drawing room when he came in for a brandy while she was reading a book.

He'd been perfectly polite, if a little distant. She supposed this could be forgiven; as far as she could tell he was busy trying to obtain news of Edward, and she certainly did not want to distract him from his objective. Still she had not thought that "no consequences" would mean "Oh, I'm sorry, is that you on the sofa?"

She didn't think that he had been unaffected by their kiss. She didn't have much—oh, very well, *any*—experience with men, but she knew George, and she knew that he had wanted her every bit as much as she wanted him.

And she had. Oh, how she had.

She still did.

Every time she closed her eyes she saw his face, and the crazy thing was, it wasn't the kiss she relived endlessly in her mind. It was the moment right before it, when her heart beat like a hummingbird and her breath ached to mingle with his. The kiss had been magical, but the moment before, the split second when she knew . . .

She'd been transformed.

He had awakened something inside of her she had not even known existed, something wild and selfish. And she wanted more.

Problem was, she had no idea how to get it. If ever there were a time to develop feminine wiles, this was probably it. But she was entirely out of her element here in London. She knew how to act back in Kent. Maybe she wasn't her mother's ideal version of womanhood, but when she was at home, at Aubrey or Crake, she knew who she was. If she said something strange or did something out of the ordinary it didn't matter, because she was Billie Bridgerton, and everyone knew what that meant.

She knew what it meant.

But here, in this formal town home, with its unfamiliar servants and pursed-lipped matrons coming to call, she was adrift. She second-guessed every word.

And now Lady Manston wanted to attend a ball?

"Ghislaine's daughter is eighteen, I believe," Lady Manston mused, flipping over the invitation and glancing at the back. "Maybe nineteen. Certainly of an age to marry."

Billie held her tongue.

"A lovely girl. So pretty and genteel." Lady Manston looked up with a wide, devious smile. "Shall I insist that George be my escort? It's high time he started looking for a wife."

"I'm sure he will be delighted," Billie said diplomatically. But in her head she was already painting Ghislaine's beautiful daughter with horns and a pitchfork.

"And you shall attend as well."

Billie looked up, alarmed. "Oh, I don't think—"

"We'll have to get you a dress."

"It's really not—"

"And shoes, I would imagine."

"But Lady Manston, I—"

"I wonder if we can get away without a wig. They can be difficult to manage if you're not used to wearing them."

"I really don't like wearing wigs," Billie said.

"Then you won't have to," Lady Manston declared, and it was only then that Billie realized just how deftly she'd been manipulated.

That had been two days earlier. Two days and five fittings. Six, counting this one.

"Billie, hold your breath for a moment," Lady Manston called out.

Billie squinted over at her. "What?" It was bloody difficult to focus on anything other than the two seamstresses currently yanking her about. She'd heard that most dressmakers faked their French accents so as to seem more sophisticated, but these two seemed to be genuine. Billie couldn't understand a word they were saying.

"She doesn't speak French," Lady Manston said to Crossy. "I'm not sure what her mother was thinking." She glanced back up at Billie. "Your breath, darling. They need to tighten your corset."

Billie looked at Crossy's two assistants, waiting patiently behind her, corset laces in hand. "It requires two people?"

"It's a very good corset," Lady Manston said.

"Ze best," Crossy confirmed.

Billie sighed.

"No, *in*," Lady Manston directed. "Breathe *in*."

Billie obeyed, sucking in her stomach so that the

two seamstresses could do some sort of choreographed crossways yank that resulted in Billie's spine curving in an entirely new manner. Her hips jutted forward, and her head seemed remarkably far back on her neck. She wasn't quite certain how she was meant to walk like this.

"This isn't terribly comfortable," she called out.

"No." Lady Manston sounded unconcerned. "It won't be."

One of the ladies said something in French and then pushed Billie's shoulders forward and her stomach back. "*Meilleur?*" she asked.

Billie cocked her head to the side, then twisted her spine a bit each way. It *was* better. Yet another aspect of genteel femininity she'd had no idea how to navigate: corset wearing. Or rather, "good" corset wearing. Apparently the ones she'd been wearing were far too permissive.

"Thank you," she said to the seamstress, then cleared her throat. "Er, *merci.*"

"For you, ze corset should not be too uncomfortable," Crossy said, coming over to inspect her handiwork. "Your stomach is lovely and flat. The problem we have is your breasts."

Billie looked up in alarm. "My—"

"Very little meat to them," Crossy said, shaking her head sadly.

It was embarrassing enough to have one's breasts discussed like chicken wings, but then Crossy actually *grabbed* her. She looked over at Lady Manston. "We need to push them up more, don't you think?"

She then demonstrated. Billie wanted to die on the spot.

"Hmmm?" Lady Manston's face screwed up as she considered the placement of Billie's breasts. "Oh yes, I think you're right. They look much better up there."

"I'm sure it's not necessary . . ." Billie began, but then she gave up. She had no power here.

Crossy said something in rapid-fire French to her assistants, and before Billie knew what was happening, she'd been unlaced and relaced, and when she looked down, her bosom was most definitely not where it had been just a few moments earlier.

"Much better," Crossy declared.

"Goodness," Billie murmured. If she nodded she could actually touch her chin to her chest.

"He won't be able to resist you," Crossy said, leaning in with a confidential wink.

"Who?"

"There's always a who," Crossy said with a chuckle.

Billie tried not to think of George. But she wasn't successful. Like it or not, he was her *who*.

WHILE BILLIE WAS trying not to think of George, he was trying not to think of fish. Kippers to be precise.

He'd spent the better part of the week at the War Office, trying to gain information about Edward. This had involved several meals with Lord Arbuthnot, who, before he had developed gout, had been a decorated general in His Majesty's army. The gout was a bloody nuisance (was the first thing he'd said) but it did mean he was back on English soil, where a man could have a proper breakfast every day.

Lord Arbuthnot was apparently still making up for his years of improper breakfasts, because when George joined him for supper, the table had been laid with what was normally morning fare. Eggs three ways, bacon, toast. And kippers. Lots and lots of kippers.

All things considered, Lord Arbuthnot put away a lot of kippers.

George had met the old soldier only once before, but Arbuthnot had attended Eton with George's father, and George with Arbuthnot's son, and if there was a more effective connection to press in the pursuit of truth, George couldn't imagine what it was.

"Well, I've been asking," Arbuthnot said, slicing up a piece of ham with the vigor of a red-faced man who'd rather be outside, "and I can't get much about your brother."

"Surely someone must know where he is."

"Connecticut Colony. That's as precise as it gets."

George clenched his fingers into a fist beneath the table. "He's not supposed to *be* in Connecticut Colony."

Arbuthnot chewed his food, then looked at George with a shrewd expression. "You've never been a soldier, have you?"

"Much to my regret."

Arbuthnot nodded, George's reply clearly meeting with his approval. "Soldiers are rarely where they're supposed to be," he said. "At least not ones like your brother."

George pressed his lips together, working to maintain an even expression. "I'm afraid I don't catch your meaning."

Arbuthnot sat back, tapping his steepled fingers as he regarded George with a thoughtful, eye-narrowed gaze. "Your brother is hardly an enlisted man, Lord Kennard."

"Surely a captain must still follow orders."

"And go where he's told?" Arbuthnot said. "Of course. But that doesn't mean he ends up where he's 'supposed' to be."

George took a moment to absorb this, then said incredulously, "Are you trying to tell me that Edward is a spy?"

It was unfathomable. Espionage was a dirty business. Men like Edward wore their red coats with pride.

Arbuthnot shook his head. "No. At least I don't think so. Damned unsavory, spying is. Your brother wouldn't have to do it."

He wouldn't do it, George thought. Period.

"It'd make no sense, at any rate," Arbuthnot said briskly. "Do you really think your brother could pass himself off as anything but a proper English gentleman? I hardly think a rebel is going to believe that the son of an earl is going to sympathize with their cause."

Arbuthnot wiped his mouth with his napkin and reached for the kippers. "I think your brother is a scout."

"A scout," George repeated.

Arbuthnot nodded, then offered the dish. "More?"

George shook his head and tried not to grimace. "No, thank you."

Arbuthnot gave a little grunt and slid the rest of the fish onto his plate. "God, I love kippers," he sighed. "You can't get them in the Caribbean. Not like this."

"A scout," George said again, trying to get the conversation back on topic. "Why do you think this?"

"Well, no one has told me as much, and to be quite frank, I don't know that anyone here has the entire story, but putting together the bits and pieces . . . it seems to fit." Arbuthnot popped a kipper in his mouth and chewed. "I'm not a betting man, but if I were, I'd say that your brother had been sent afield to get the lay of the land. There hasn't been much action in Connecticut, not since that thing with Whatshisname Arnold in Ridgefield back in seventy-seven."

George was not familiar with Whatshisname Arnold, nor did he have a clue where Ridgefield was.

There are some damned good ports on that coast," Arbuthnot continued, getting back to the serious business of cutting his meat. "I wouldn't be surprised if the rebels were putting them to use. And I wouldn't be surprised if Captain Rokesby had been sent out to investigate." He looked up, his bushy brows dipping toward his eyes as his forehead wrinkled. "Does your brother have any mapmaking skills?"

"Not that I'm aware."

Arbuthnot shrugged. "Doesn't mean anything if he doesn't, I suppose. They might not be looking for anything so precise."

"But then what happened?" George pressed.

The old general shook his head. "I'm afraid I don't know, m'dear boy. And I'd be lying if I said I'd found anyone who did."

George hadn't expected answers, not really, but still, it was disappointing.

"It's a damned long way to the Colonies, son," Lord Arbuthnot said in a surprisingly gentle voice. "News is never as swift as we'd like."

George accepted this with a slow nod. He was going to have to pursue some other avenue of investigation, although for the life of him, he did not know what that might be.

"By the way," Arbuthnot added, almost too casually, "you wouldn't happen to be planning to attend Lady Wintour's ball tomorrow night, would you?"

"I am," George confirmed. He didn't want to, but his mother had spun some convoluted story that had ended in his absolutely *having* to attend. And frankly, he hadn't the heart to disappoint her. Not while she was so worried about Edward.

And then there was Billie. She'd been roped into attending as well. He'd seen the look of panic on her face when his mother had dragged her from her breakfast to visit the *modiste*. A London ball was quite possibly Billie Bridgerton's personal hell, and there was no way he could abandon her when she needed him most.

"Are you acquainted with Robert Tallywhite?" Lord Arbuthnot inquired.

"A bit." Tallywhite was a couple of years ahead of him at Eton. Quiet fellow, George recalled. Sandy hair and a high forehead. Bookish.

"He is Lady Wintour's nephew and will most certainly be in attendance. You would be doing a great service to this office if you would pass along a message."

George raised his eyebrows in question.

"Is that a yes?" Lord Arbuthnot said in a dry voice.

George tipped his head in affirmation.

"Tell him . . . pease porridge pudding."

"Pease porridge pudding," George repeated dubiously.

Arbuthnot broke off a piece of his toast and dipped it into his egg yolk. "He'll understand."

"What does it mean?"

"Do you need to know?" Arbuthnot countered.

George sat back, regarding Arbuthnot with a level stare. "I do, rather."

Lord Arbuthnot let out a bark of laughter. "And that, my dear boy, is why you would make a terrible soldier. You've got to follow orders without question."

"Not if one is in command."

"Too true," Arbuthnot said with a smile. But he still did not explain the message. Instead he regarded George with a level stare and asked, "Can we rely on you?"

It was the War Office, George thought. If he was passing along messages, at least he'd know he was doing it for the right people.

At least he'd know he was doing *some*thing.

He looked Arbuthnot in the eye and said, "You may."

Chapter 19

Manston House was quiet when George returned later that evening. The hall was lit with two candelabras, but the rest of the rooms seemed to have been shut down for the night. He frowned. It wasn't that late; surely someone ought to be about.

"Ah, Temperley," George said when the butler stepped forward to take his hat and coat, "has my mother gone out for the evening?"

"Lady Manston had her dinner sent up to her room on a tray, my lord," Temperley said.

"And Miss Bridgerton?"

"I believe she did the same."

"Oh." George shouldn't have been disappointed. After all, he'd spent the better part of the past few days avoiding both of the aforementioned ladies. Now they seem to have done his work for him.

"Shall I have your dinner sent up as well, my lord?"

George thought for a moment, then said, "Why

not?" It seemed he wasn't to have company that night regardless, and he hadn't eaten much of Lord Arbuthnot's repast.

It had to have been the kippers. Honestly, the smell had put him off the entire meal.

"Will you have a brandy in the drawing room first?" Temperley inquired.

"No, I'll go straight up, I think. It's been a long day."

Temperley nodded in that butlerish way of his. "For us all, my lord."

George regarded him with a wry expression. "Has my mother been working you to the bone, Temperley?"

"Not at all," the butler replied, the barest hint of a smile cracking through his somber mien. "I speak of the ladies. If I may be so bold as to offer my observation, they seemed rather tired when they returned this afternoon. Miss Bridgerton especially."

"I'm afraid my mother has been working *her* to the bone," George said with a half-smile.

"Just so, my lord. Lady Manston is never as happy as when she has a young lady to marry off."

George froze, then covered his lapse by devoting an inordinate amount of attention to the removal of his gloves. "That would seem somewhat ambitious, given that Miss Bridgerton does not plan to remain in town for the Season."

Temperley cleared his throat. "A great many parcels have arrived."

Which was his way of saying that every item required for a young lady to successfully navigate the

London marriage mart had been purchased and delivered.

"I'm sure Miss Bridgerton will meet with every success," George said evenly.

"She is a very lively young lady," Temperley agreed.

George smiled tightly as he took his leave. It was difficult to imagine how Temperley had come to the conclusion that Billie was lively. The few times George had crossed her path at Manston House she had been uncharacteristically subdued.

He supposed he should have made more of an effort, taken her out for an ice or some such, but he'd been too busy hunting down information at the War Office. It felt so bloody good to *do* something for a change, even if the results were disappointing.

He took a step toward the stairs, then paused and turned back. Temperley had not moved.

"I always thought my mother hoped for a match between Miss Bridgerton and Edward," George said casually.

"She has not seen fit to confide in me," Temperley said.

"No, of course not," George said. He gave his head a little shake. How the mighty had fallen. He'd been reduced to dangling for gossip from the butler. "Good night, Temperley."

He made it to the stairs, his foot perched on the first step, when the butler called out, "They do speak of him."

George turned around.

Temperley cleared his throat. "I do not think it a breach of confidence to tell you that they speak of him at breakfast."

"No," George said. "Not at all."

There was a long beat of silence.

"We are keeping Master Edward in our prayers," Temperley finally said. "We all miss him."

It was true. Although what did it say about George that he missed Edward more now that he was missing than he ever had when he'd merely been an ocean away?

He walked slowly up the stairs. Manston House was much smaller than Crake, with all eight bedchambers clustered on one floor. Billie had been put in the second-best guest bedroom, which George thought was ludicrous, but his mother always insisted upon keeping the best guest bedroom free. *You never know who might unexpectedly visit*, she always said.

Has the King dropped by, he always parried. This generally earned him a scowl. And a smile. His mother was a good sport that way, even if the best room had gone empty these past twenty years.

He paused in the middle of the hall, not quite in front of Billie's door but closer to it than any other room. There was just enough of a crack under the door to show a faint flicker of candlelight. He wondered what she was doing in there. It really was much too early to go to sleep.

He missed her.

It came to him in a startling flash. He missed her. He was here, in the same house, sleeping just three doors down, and he missed her.

It was his own fault. He knew he'd been avoiding her. But what was he to do? He had kissed Billie, kissed her until he was nearly past the edge of reason, and now he was expected to make polite conversation with her at the breakfast table? In front of his *mother*?

George would never be as sophisticated as that.

He ought to marry her. He rather thought he'd like to, as mad as that might have seemed just a month earlier. He'd been quite warming to the idea back at Crake. Billie had said "you don't have to marry me," and all he could think was—

But I could.

He'd had just a moment with the idea. No time to think or analyze, only time to feel.

And it had felt lovely. Warm.

Like springtime.

But then his mother had arrived on the scene and started going on about how adorable Billie and Edward were together and what a perfect match they made and he couldn't remember what else but it was nauseatingly sweet and according to Temperley went very well over breakfast with toast and orange marmalade.

Toast and marmalade. He shook his head. He was an idiot.

And he had fallen in love with Billie Bridgerton.

There it was. Plain as day. He almost laughed. He *would* have laughed, if the joke weren't on him.

If he'd fallen in love with someone else—someone new, whose presence did not fill such a wealth of his memories—would it have been so clear? With Billie the emotion was such an about-face, such a complete departure from a lifetime of comparing her to a pebble in his shoe. He couldn't help but see it, shining in his mind like bright starry promise.

Was she in love with Edward? Maybe. His mother seemed to think so. She had not said as much, of course, but his mother had a remarkable talent for making sure her opinions were precisely known without ever actually stating them explicitly.

Still, it had been enough to render him insanely jealous.

In love with Billie. It was just the maddest thing.

He let out a long, pent-up breath and started walking again toward his room. He had to pass by her door, past that tantalizing flicker of light. He slowed, because he couldn't not.

And then the door opened.

"George?" Billie's face peered out. She was still in her day clothes but her hair was down, draped over her shoulder in a long, thick braid. "I thought I heard someone," she explained.

He managed a close-lipped smile as he bowed. "As you see."

"I was having supper," she said, motioning back into the room. "Your mother was tired." She gave a sheepish smile. "*I* was tired. I'm not very good at shopping. I had no idea it would involve quite so much standing still."

"Standing still is always more tiring than walking."

"Yes!" she said, quite animatedly. "I've always said that."

George started to speak, but then a memory sparked through his mind. It was when he'd been carrying her, after that debacle with the cat on the roof. He'd been trying to describe that odd feeling of when one's leg goes weak and bends for no reason.

Billie had understood perfectly.

The irony was that his leg hadn't gone weak. He'd been making it up to cover for something. He didn't even remember what.

But he remembered the moment. He remembered that she'd understood.

Mostly he'd remembered how she'd looked at him, with a little smile that said that she was happy to *be* understood.

He looked up. She was watching him with an expression of faint expectation. It was his turn to speak, he remembered. And since he couldn't very well say what he was thinking, he went for the obvious.

"You're still dressed," he said.

She glanced down briefly at her frock. It was the one she'd been wearing when he kissed her. Flowers. It suited her. She should always be in flowers.

"I thought I might go back down after I finish eating," she said. "Perhaps find something to read in the library."

He nodded.

"My mother always says that once you're in your dressing gown, you're in your room for the night."

He smiled. "Does she?"

"She says a great many things, actually. I'm sure I've forgotten whatever it is that I didn't ignore."

George stood like a statue, knowing he should bid her goodnight, but somehow unable to form the words. The moment was too intimate, too perfectly candlelit and lovely.

"Have you eaten?" she asked.

"Yes. Well, no." He thought of the kippers. "Not exactly."

Her brows rose. "*That* sounds intriguing."

"Hardly. I'm having a tray sent to my room, actually. I've always hated dining alone downstairs."

"I'm the same," she agreed. She stood for a moment, then said. "It's ham pie. Very good."

"Excellent." He cleared his throat. "Well, I . . . ought to go. Good night, Billie."

He turned. He didn't want to turn.

"George, wait!"

He hated that he was holding his breath.

"George, this is madness."

He turned back. She was still standing in the entrance to her room, one hand resting lightly on the edge of the door. Her face was so expressive. Had it always been so?

Yes, he thought. She'd never been one to hide her feelings beneath a mask of indifference. It was one of the things he'd found so annoying about her when they were growing up. She simply refused to be ignored.

But that was then. And this was . . .

Something else entirely.

"Madness?" he echoed. He wasn't sure what she meant. He didn't want to make assumptions.

Her lips trembled into a tentative smile. "Surely we can be friends."

Friends?

"I mean, I know . . ."

"That I kissed you?" he supplied.

She gasped, then practically hissed, "I wasn't going to say it quite so bluntly. For heaven's sake, George, your mother is still awake." And while she was frantically peering down the hall, George threw over a lifetime of gentlemanly behavior and stepped into her bedroom.

"George!"

"Apparently one *can* whisper and scream at the same time," he mused.

"You can't be in here," she said.

He grinned as she closed the door. "I didn't think you wished to conduct this sort of conversation in the hall."

The look she gave him was sarcasm in its purest form. "I believe there are two drawing rooms and a library downstairs."

"And look what happened last time we were in a drawing room together."

Her face flushed instantly. But Billie was a trouper, and after a moment of what appeared to be gnashing her teeth and telling herself to calm down, she asked, "Have you learned anything of Edward?"

Like that, his jaunty mood deflated. "Nothing of substance."

"But something?" she asked hopefully.

He didn't want to talk about Edward. For so many

reasons. But Billie deserved a reply, so he said, "Just the suppositions of a retired general."

"I'm sorry. That must be terribly frustrating. I wish there was something I could do to help." She leaned on the edge of her bed and looked over at him with an earnest frown. "It's so *hard* to do nothing. I hate it."

He closed his eyes. Breathed out through his nose. Once again, they were in perfect agreement.

"Sometimes I think I should have been born a boy."

"No." His response was immediate and emphatic.

She let out a little laugh. "That's very kind of you. I suppose you have to say that after, well, you know . . ."

He knew. But not nearly enough.

"I would love to own Aubrey," she said wistfully. "I know every corner. I can name every crop in every field, and every name of every tenant, and half of their birthdays, too."

He looked at her in wonderment. She was so much more than he'd ever allowed himself to see.

"I would have been an excellent Viscount Bridgerton."

"Your brother will learn his way," George said gently. He sat down in the chair by the desk. She wasn't sitting down, but she wasn't exactly standing, either, and as he was alone with her behind a closed door, he rather thought *this* would not be the critical breach of propriety.

"Oh, I know he will," Billie said. "Edmund is very clever, actually, when he's not being annoying."

"He's fifteen. He can't help being annoying."

She gave him a look. "If I recall correctly, you were already a god among men by the time you were his age."

He lifted a lazy brow. There were so many droll rejoinders to such a statement, but he decided to let them all pass and simply enjoy the easy camaraderie of the moment.

"How do you bear it?" she asked.

"Bear what?"

"This." She raised her hands in a gesture of defeat. "The helplessness."

He sat up a little straighter, blinking her into focus. "You do feel it, don't you?"

"I'm not sure I catch your meaning," he murmured. But he had a feeling he did.

"I know you wish you could have taken a commission. I see it in your face every time your brothers talk about it."

Was he that obvious? He'd hoped not. But at the same time . . .

"George?"

He looked up.

"You'd gone very silent," she said.

"I was just thinking . . ."

She smiled indulgently, allowing him to think aloud.

"I *don't* wish I'd taken a commission."

She drew back, her surprise evident in the way her chin tucked into her neck.

"My place is here," he said.

Her eyes lit with something that might have been pride. "You sound as if you're only just realizing it."

"No," he mused. "I've always known that."

"You hadn't accepted it?" she prodded.

He chuckled wryly. "No, I had definitely accepted it. I just think I hadn't let myself . . ." He looked up, straight into her lovely brown eyes and paused for a moment as he realized what he wanted to say. "I hadn't let myself *like* it."

"And now you do?"

His nod was quick and firm. "I do. If I don't—" He stopped, corrected himself. "If *we* don't care for the land and its people, what are Edward and Andrew even fighting for?"

"If they are going to risk their lives for King and Country," she said softly, "we should make it a *good* King and Country."

Their eyes met, and Billie smiled. Just a little. And they didn't speak. Because they didn't need to. Until finally she said, "They're going to be up with your food soon," she said.

He quirked a brow. "Are you trying to be rid of me?"

"I'm trying to protect my reputation," she retorted. "And yours."

"If you recall, I did ask you to marry me."

"No, you didn't," she scoffed. "You said, 'of course I'll marry you',"—this she said in a remarkable impression of a distempered crone—"which is not the same thing at all."

He eyed her thoughtfully. "I could get down on one knee."

"Stop teasing me, George. It's very unkind of you." Her voice wobbled, and he felt something tight, squeezing in his chest. His lips parted, but she pushed herself off the edge of her bed and walked over to her window, crossing her arms as she stared out into the night.

"It's not something you joke about," she said, but her words were oddly formed, round and wide, almost as if they were coming from somewhere deep in her throat.

He came quickly to his feet. "Billie, I'm sorry. You must know I would never—"

"You should go."

He paused.

"You should go," she said, more forcefully this time. "They'll be here with your dinner at any moment."

It was a dismissal, clear and sensible. It was a kindness, really. She was stopping him from making a fool of himself. If she wanted him to propose, wouldn't she have taken the bait he'd so casually dangled?

"As you wish," he said, executing a polite bow even though she was not facing him. He saw her nod, and then he left the room.

OH, DEAR GOD, what had she done?

He could have proposed to her. Right then and there. *George.*

And she had *stopped* him. Stopped him because— bloody hell, she didn't know why. Hadn't she spent the entire day in a blue haze, wondering why he was avoiding her and how she might get him to kiss her again?

Wouldn't marriage ensure future kisses? Wasn't it *precisely* what she needed to achieve her (admittedly unladylike) goals?

But he'd been sitting there, sprawled out in the desk chair like he owned the place (which she supposed he did, or rather, would), and she couldn't tell if he meant it. Was he teasing her? Having a spot of fun? George had never been cruel; he wouldn't purposefully hurt her feelings, but if he thought *she* regarded the whole thing as a joke, then he might feel permitted to treat it as such . . .

It was what Andrew would have done. Not that Andrew would ever have kissed her, or that she'd have wanted him to, but if for some reason they'd been joking about marriage, absolutely he'd have said something ridiculous about getting down on one knee.

But with George . . . she just hadn't known if he'd *meant* it. And then what if she'd said yes? What if she'd said that she'd *love* for him to get down on one knee and pledge his eternal devotion . . .

And then found out he was joking?

Her face flamed just thinking of it.

She didn't think he would tease about such a thing. But then again, this was George. He was the eldest son of the Earl of Manston, the noble and honorable Lord Kennard. If he were going to propose to a lady, he would never do it slapdash. He'd have the ring, and he'd have the poetic words, and he certainly wouldn't leave it up to her to decide if he ought to do it on bended knee.

Which meant he couldn't have meant it, right? George would never be so unsure of himself.

She flopped on her bed, pressing both hands against her chest, trying to quell her racing heart. She used to hate that about George—his unshakable confidence. When they were children he always knew better than the rest of them. About everything. It had been the *most* annoying thing, even if now she realized that at five years their senior, he probably *had* known better about everything. There was no way the rest of them were going to catch up until they reached adulthood.

And now . . . Now she loved his quiet confidence. He was never brash, never boastful. He was just . . . George.

And she loved him.

She loved him, and—*OH DEAR GOD, SHE HAD JUST STOPPED HIM FROM ASKING HER TO MARRY HIM.*

What had she done?

And more importantly, how could she undo it?

Chapter 20

—◆━►✦◄━◆—

George was always the first in his family to come down to breakfast, but when he stepped into the informal dining room the following morning, his mother was already at the table, sipping a cup of tea.

There was no way this was a coincidence.

"George," she said immediately upon seeing him, "we must speak."

"Mother," he murmured, stepping over to the sideboard to fix his plate. Whatever it was she was het up over, he was not in the mood. He was tired and he was cranky. He might have only *almost* proposed marriage the night before, but he had most definitely been rejected.

It was not the stuff dreams were made of. Nor a good night's sleep.

"As you know," she said, jumping right into it, "tonight is Lady Wintour's ball."

He spooned some coddled eggs onto his plate. "I assure you it has not slipped my mind."

Her lips tightened, but she did not take him to task for his sarcasm. Instead she waited with heavy patience until he joined her at the table.

"It is about Billie," she said.

Of course it was.

"I am very concerned about her."

So was he, but he doubted it was for the same reasons. He pasted a bland smile on his face. "What is the problem?"

"She is going to need all the help she can get tonight."

"Don't be ridiculous," he scoffed, but he knew what she meant. Billie was not meant for London. She was a country girl, through and through.

"She lacks confidence, George. The vultures will see this instantly."

"Do you ever wonder why we choose to socialize with these vultures?" he mused.

"Because half of them are really doves."

"Doves?" He stared at her in disbelief.

She waved a hand. "Perhaps carrier pigeons. But that is not the point."

"I would never be so lucky."

She gave him just enough of a look to make it clear that while she had heard this, she was graciously choosing to ignore it. "Her success is in your hands."

He knew he would regret encouraging her to expand upon this point, but he could not stop himself from saying, "I beg your pardon?"

"You know as well as I do that the surest way to ensure a debutante's success is for an eligible gentleman—such as yourself—to pay her attention."

For some reason, this irritated him greatly. "Since when is Billie a debutante?"

His mother stared at him as if he were an idiot. "Why else do you think I brought her to London?"

"I believe you said you wished for her company?" he countered.

His mother waved that away as the nonsense she clearly saw it to be. "The girl needed some polish."

No, George thought, *she didn't.* He jabbed his fork into his sausage with far too much force. "She's perfectly fine the way she is."

"That is very gracious of you, George," she replied, inspecting her muffin before deciding to add an additional dab of butter, "but I assure you, no lady wishes to be 'perfectly fine.'"

He fixed a patient expression on his face. "Your point, Mother?"

"Merely that I need you to do your part this evening. You *must* dance with her."

She made it sound as if he thought it a chore. "Of course I'll dance with her." It would be awkward as hell, all things considered, but even so, he could not help but look forward to it. He'd been longing to dance with Billie since that morning back at Aubrey Hall when she'd looked up at him, planted her hands on her hips, and demanded, "Have you ever danced with me?"

At the time, he couldn't believe that he'd never

done so. After all those years as neighbors, how could he not have danced with her? But now he couldn't believe that he'd ever thought he *had*. If he had danced with Billie, music washing over them as he placed his hand on her hip . . . It was not something he could forget.

And he wanted it. He wanted to take her hand in his and dance her down the line, to step and dip, and feel her innate grace. But more than that, he wanted *her* to feel it. He wanted her to know that she was every bit as womanly and elegant as the rest, that she was perfect in his eyes, not just 'perfectly fine,' and if he could only—

"George!"

He looked up.

"Kindly pay attention," his mother said.

"My apologies," he murmured. He had no idea how long he'd been lost in his own thoughts, although generally speaking, with his mother even a second or two of woolgathering was not to be tolerated.

"I was saying," she said somewhat peevishly, "that you must dance with Billie twice."

"Consider it done."

Her eyes narrowed; she was clearly suspicious at the ease at which she was getting her way. "You must also be sure to allow at least ninety minutes to elapse between dances."

He rolled his eyes and did not bother to hide it. "As you wish."

Lady Manston stirred a bit of sugar into her tea. "You must appear attentive."

"But not too attentive?"

"Don't mock me," she warned.

He set down his fork. "Mother, I assure you that I am every bit as eager for Billie's happiness as you are."

This seemed to appease her somewhat. "Very well," she said, "I am pleased that we are in agreement. I wish to arrive at the ball at half past nine. This will give us the opportunity to make a proper entrance, but it will still be early enough that it won't be so difficult to make introductions. It gets so loud at these things."

George nodded his agreement.

"I think we should depart at nine—there will surely be a line of carriages outside of Wintour House and you know how long *that* takes—so if you could be ready by three-quarters past eight—"

"Oh, no, I'm sorry," George interrupted, thinking of the ridiculous message he was meant to pass along to Robert Tallywhite. "I cannot accompany you. I'll need to make my own way to the ball."

"Don't be absurd," she said dismissively. "We need you to escort us."

"I wish I could," he said quite honestly. He would have liked nothing better than for Billie to make her entrance on his arm, but he'd already given a great deal of thought to this evening's schedule, and he had determined that it was imperative that he arrive on his own. If he came with the ladies, he would have to practically abandon them at the door. And heaven knew *that* would never happen without a full interrogation from his mother.

No, better to get there earlier so that he could find Tallywhite and take care of the whole thing before they even arrived.

"What can possibly be more important than accompanying Billie and me?" his mother demanded.

"I have a previous engagement," he replied, lifting his own cup of tea to his lips. "It cannot be avoided."

His mother's lips pressed into a firm line. "I am most displeased."

"I am sorry to disappoint."

She began stirring her tea with increasing vigor. "I could be completely wrong about this, you know. She could be an instant success. We could be surrounded by gentlemen from the moment we arrive."

"Your tone seems to imply that you think that would be a bad thing," George said.

"Of course not. But you won't be there to see it."

In truth, it was the last thing George wanted to see. Billie, surrounded by a pack of gentlemen astute enough to realize what a treasure she was? It was the stuff of nightmares.

And a moot point, as it happened. "Actually," he told his mother, "I will likely arrive at Wintour House before you do."

"Well, then I see no reason you cannot circle back 'round from your errand and pick us up on the way."

He fought the urge to pinch the bridge of his nose. "Mother, it won't work. Please leave it at that and know that I will see you at the ball, where I shall dance such attendance upon Billie that the gentlemen of London will be waiting in line just to fall at her feet."

"Good morning."

They both turned to see Billie standing in the doorway. George stood to greet her. He wasn't sure how much she had heard, beyond his obvious sarcasm, and he very much feared she would take it the wrong way.

"It is very kind of you to agree to attend to me tonight," she said, her tone so sweet and pleasant that he could not quite gauge its sincerity. She walked over to the sideboard and picked up a plate. "I do hope it will not be too much of a chore."

Ah, and *there* she was.

"On the contrary," he replied. "I am very much looking forward to being your escort."

"But not so much that you will actually accompany us in the carriage," his mother muttered.

"Stop," he said.

Billie turned around, her eyes darting from Rokesby to Rokesby with unconcealed curiosity.

"I regret to inform you that I have an unbreakable commitment this evening," he told her, "which means I will not be able to drive to Wintour House with you. But I will see you there. And I hope you will save me two dances."

"Of course," she murmured. But then again, she could hardly say anything else.

"Since you cannot escort us this evening . . ." Lady Manston began.

George nearly threw down his napkin.

". . . perhaps you may assist us in some other way."

"Please," he said, "inform me how I may be of service."

Billie made a sound that might have been a snort. He wasn't sure. But it was certainly in her nature to find amusement in his rapidly dwindling patience with his mother.

"You know all of the young gentlemen better than I do," Lady Manston continued. "Are there any we should avoid?"

All of them, George wanted to say.

"And are there any we should particularly look out for? That Billie may plan to set her cap for?"

"That I may—*what*?"

Billie must truly have been startled, George thought. She dropped three slices of bacon on the floor.

"Set your cap, darling," Lady Manston said. "It's an expression. Surely you've heard it."

"Of course I've heard it," Billie said, hurrying over to take her place at the table. "I don't, however, see how it applies to me. I did not come to London to look for a husband."

"You must always be looking for a husband, Billie," Lady Manston said, then turned right back to George. "What about Ashbourne's son? Not the oldest, of course. He's already married, and as delightful as you are,"—this, she said over her shoulder to the still-aghast Billie—"I don't think you could snag the heir to a dukedom."

"I'm fairly certain I don't want to," Billie said.

"Very practical of you, my dear. It's quite a lot of pomp."

"So says the wife of an earl," George remarked.

"It's not at all the same thing," his mother said. "And you didn't answer my question. What about Ashbourne's son?"

"No."

"No?" his mother echoed. "No, as in you don't have an opinion?"

"No, as in no. He is not for Billie."

Who, George could not help but note, was watching the mother-son exchange with an odd mix of curiosity and alarm.

"Any particular reason?" Lady Manston asked.

"He gambles," George lied. Well, maybe it wasn't a lie. All gentlemen gambled. He had no idea if the one in question did so to excess.

"What about the Billington heir? I think he—"

"Also no."

His mother regarded him with an impassive expression.

"He's too young," George said, hoping it was true.

"He is?" She frowned. "I suppose he might be. I can't remember precisely."

"I don't suppose *I* have any say in the matter," Billie put in.

"Of course you do," Lady Manston said, patting her hand. "Just not yet."

Billie's lips parted, but she appeared not to know what to say.

"How could you," Lady Manston continued, "when you don't know anyone but us?"

Billie put a piece of bacon in her mouth and began

to chew with impressive force. George suspected this was to stop herself from saying something she'd regret.

"Don't worry, my dear," Lady Manston said.

George took a sip of his tea. "She doesn't look worried to me."

Billie shot him a grateful look.

His mother ignored him completely. "You will get to know everyone soon enough, Billie. And then you can decide with whom you wish to pursue an acquaintance."

"I don't know that I plan to be here long enough to form opinions one way or another," Billie said, her voice—in George's opinion—remarkably even and calm.

"Nonsense," Lady Manston said. "Just leave everything to me."

"You're not her mother," George said quietly.

To which his mother raised her brows and said, "I could be."

To which both George and Billie stared at her in openmouthed shock.

"Oh, come now, you two," Lady Manston said, "surely it can be no surprise that I have long hoped for an alliance between the Rokesbys and Bridgertons."

"Alliance?" Billie echoed, and all George could think was that it was a terrible, clinical word, one that could never encompass all that he had come to feel for her.

"Match, marriage, whatever you wish to call it," Lady Manston said. "We are the dearest of friends. Of course I should like to be family."

"If it makes any difference," Billie said quietly, "I already think of you as family."

"Oh, I know that, dear. I feel the same way. I've just always thought it would be wonderful to make it official. But no matter. There is always Georgiana."

Billie cleared her throat. "She's very young yet."

Lady Manston smiled devilishly. "So is Nicholas."

The look on Billie's face came so close to horror George almost laughed. He probably would have done if he hadn't been fairly certain his own face held the same expression.

"I see that I have shocked you," his mother said. "But any mother will tell you—it's never too early to plan for the future."

"I would not recommend mentioning this to Nicholas," George murmured.

"Or Georgiana, I'm sure," his mother said, pouring herself yet another cup of tea. "Would you like a cup, Billie?"

"Ehrm . . . yes, thank you."

"Oh, and that's another thing," Lady Manston said as she put a splash of milk in Billie's teacup. "We need to stop calling you Billie."

Billie blinked. "I beg your pardon?"

In went the tea, and then Lady Manston held the cup out and said, "Starting today we will use your given name. Sybilla."

Billie's mouth hung open for a brief—but

noticeable—moment before she said, "That's what my mother calls me when she's cross."

"Then we shall begin a new, happier tradition."

"Is this really necessary?" George asked.

"I know it will be difficult to remember," Lady Manston said, finally setting the cup down near Billie's plate, "but I think it's for the best. As a name, Billie is so, well . . . I don't know that I would call it mannish, but I don't think it accurately represents how we wish to portray you."

"It accurately represents who she *is*," George practically growled.

"Goodness. I had no idea you would feel so strongly about this," his mother said, peering over at him with a flawlessly innocent expression. "But of course, it's not up to you."

"I would prefer to be called Billie," Billie said.

"I'm not sure it's up to you, either, dear."

George's fork came down heavily on his plate. "Who the devil is it up to, then?"

His mother regarded him as if he had asked *just* the stupidest question. "Me."

"You," he said.

"I know how these things work. I've done this before, you know."

"Didn't Mary find her husband in Kent?" George reminded her.

"Only after she gained her polish in London."

Good God. His mother had gone mad. It was the only explanation. She could be tenacious, and she could be exacting when it came to society and etiquette, but never had she managed to weave the two together with such complete irrationality.

"Surely it doesn't matter," Billie said. "Won't most everyone be calling me Miss Bridgerton, anyway?"

"Of course," Lady Manston conceded, "but they will hear us speaking with you. It's not as if they won't *know* your Christian name."

"This is the most asinine conversation," George grumbled.

His mother just flicked him A Look. "Sybilla," she said, turning to Billie, "I know you did not come to London with the intention of looking for a husband, but surely you see the convenience of it now that you're here. You'll never find so many eligible gentlemen in one place in Kent."

"I don't know," Billie murmured over her tea, "it's chock-full when all of the Rokesbys are home."

George looked up sharply just as his mother burst out in a trill of laughter. "Too true, Billie," she said with a warm smile (apparently forgetting that she meant to call her Sybilla), "but alas, I have only the one home right now."

"Two," George said incredulously. Apparently if one never went away, one wasn't counted as being home.

His mother's brows rose. "I was speaking of you, George."

Well, now he felt like a fool.

He stood. "I will call Billie what she wishes to be called. And I will see you at Wintour House as promised, when the ball is underway. If you will excuse me, I have much to attend to."

He didn't actually, but he didn't think he could listen to another word of his mother's on the topic of Billie's debut.

The sooner they all got this wretched day over with the better.

BILLIE WATCHED HIM walk away, and she wasn't going to say anything, honestly she wasn't, but even as she dipped her spoon into her porridge, she heard herself call out, "Wait!"

George paused at the door.

"Just a quick word," she said, hastily setting down her napkin. She had no idea what that quick word might be, but something was there inside of her, and it obviously needed to get out. She turned back to Lady Manston. "Pray excuse me. I'll be but a moment."

George stepped out of the small dining room and into the hall to afford them a spot of privacy.

Billie cleared her throat. "Sorry."

"For what?"

Good question. She wasn't sorry. "Actually," she said, "it's thank you."

"You're thanking me," he said softly.

"For standing up for me," she said. "Calling me Billie."

His mouth curved into a wry half-smile. "I don't think I could call you Sybilla if I tried."

She returned the expression in kind. "I'm not sure I would answer if it came from any voice other than my mother's."

He studied her face for a moment, then said, "Don't let my mother turn you into someone you're not."

"Oh, I don't think that's possible at this late stage. I'm far too set in my ways."

"At the grand age of three-and-twenty?"

"It's a very grand age when you're an unmarried female," she retorted. Maybe she shouldn't have said it; there were too many not-quite marriage proposals in their history. (*One*, Billie thought, was too many. Two practically marked her as a freak of nature.)

But she didn't regret saying it. She couldn't regret it. Not if she wanted to turn one of those almost-proposals into something real.

And she did. She'd been up half the night—well, twenty minutes at least—berating herself for her practically ensuring that he would not ask her to marry him. If she'd had a hair shirt (and any inclination for useless gestures), she'd have donned it.

George's brow furrowed, and of course her mind whipped into triple-speed. Was he wondering why she'd made a comment about her near-spinster status? Trying to decide how to respond? Debating her sanity?

"She did help me pick out a lovely gown for this evening," she blurted out.

"My mother?"

Billie nodded, then summoned a mischievous smile. "Although I did bring a pair of my breeches to town just in case I needed to shock her."

He let out a bark of laughter. "Did you really?"

"No," she admitted, her heart suddenly lighter

now that he'd laughed, "but just the fact that I pondered it means something, don't you think?"

"Absolutely." He looked down at her, his eyes so blue in the morning light, and his humor was replaced by something more serious. "Please allow me to apologize for my mother. I don't know what's come over her."

"I think perhaps she feels"—Billie frowned for a moment, choosing the best word—"guilty."

"Guilty?" George's face betrayed his surprise. "Whatever for?"

"That neither of your brothers ever offered for me." Another thing she probably should not have said. But as it happened, Billie *did* think that Lady Manston felt this way.

And when George's expression slid from curiosity to something that might have been jealousy . . . well, Billie could not help but feel a little pleased.

"So I think she's trying to make it up to me," she said gamely. "It's not as if I was waiting for one of them to ask me, but I think she thinks I was, so now she wants to introduce me—"

"Enough," George practically barked.

"I beg your pardon?"

He cleared his throat. "Enough," he said in a much more evenly tempered voice. "It's ridiculous."

"That your mother feels this way?"

"That she thinks introducing you to a pack of useless fops is a sensible idea."

Billie took a moment to enjoy this statement, then said, "She means well."

George scoffed audibly at this.

"She does," Billie insisted, unable to suppress a smile. "She just wants what she thinks is best for me."

"What *she* thinks."

"Well, yes. There's no convincing her otherwise. It's a Rokesby trait, I'm afraid."

"You may have just insulted me."

"No," she said, maintaining an impressively straight face.

"I'll let it pass."

"Very kind of you, sir."

He rolled his eyes at her impertinence, and once again, Billie felt more at ease. Perhaps this wasn't how the more refined ladies flirted, but it was all she knew how to do.

And it seemed to be working. Of *that* she was certain.

Maybe she did have a touch of feminine intuition after all.

Chapter 21

Ninety minutes in, and still he had not seen Tally-white.

George tugged at his cravat, which he was certain his valet had tied far more tightly than usual. There was nothing out of the ordinary about Lady Wintour's Spring Soirée; in fact, he'd have gone so far as to say that it was so ordinary as to be dull, but he could not shake the odd, prickly sensation that kept crawling up his neck. Everywhere he turned, it felt like someone was looking at him strangely, watching him with far more curiosity than his appearance should warrant.

Clearly, it was all in his imagination, which led to a most salient point—that clearly, he was not cut out for this sort of thing.

He'd timed his arrival carefully. Too early, and he would draw unwanted attention. Like most single men of his age, he usually spent a few hours at his club before fulfilling his social obligations. If he showed up at the ball on the dot of eight, it would look strange. (And he would have to spend the next two hours making conversation with his nearly deaf great-aunt, who was as legendary for her punctuality as she was for her fragrant breath.)

But he didn't want to follow his usual schedule, either, which involved arriving well after the party was underway. It would be too difficult to spot Tallywhite in such a crush, or worse, he could miss him altogether.

So after careful consideration, he stepped into the Wintour ballroom approximately one hour after the designated starting time. It was still unfashionably early, but there were enough people milling about for George to remain unobtrusive.

Not for the first time, he wondered if perhaps he was overthinking this whole thing. It seemed an awful lot of mental preparation for the task of uttering a line from a nursery rhyme.

A quick check of the time told him that it was nearly ten, which meant that if Billie had not already arrived, she would do so soon. His mother had been aiming for nine-thirty, but he'd heard numerous grumblings about the lengthy line of carriages queued up outside Wintour House. Billie and his mother were almost certainly stuck in the Manston coach and four, waiting for their turn to alight.

He didn't have much time if he wanted to get this taken care of before they arrived.

His expression carefully bored, he continued to move about the room, murmuring the appropriate greetings as he brushed past acquaintances. A footman was circulating with glasses of punch, so he took one, barely moistening his lips as he peered out at the ballroom over the rim of the glass. He did not see Tallywhite, but he did see—damn it, was that Lord Arbuthnot?

Why the hell was he asking George to deliver a message when he could bloody well have done it himself?

But maybe there were reasons why Arbuthnot could not be seen with Tallywhite. Maybe there was someone *else* here, someone who could not be permitted to know that the two men were working together. Or maybe Tallywhite was the one in the dark. Maybe he didn't know that Arbuthnot was the one with the message.

Or . . .

Maybe Tallywhite *did* know that Arbuthnot was his contact, and the whole thing was a plan to test George so that they could use him for future endeavors. Maybe George had just accidentally embarked upon a career in espionage.

He looked down at the punch in his hand. Maybe he needed . . . No, he *definitely* needed something with a higher degree of alcohol.

"What is this rot?" he muttered, setting the glass back down.

And then he saw her.

He stopped breathing. "Billie?"

She was a vision. Her gown was of the deepest crimson, the color an unexpectedly vibrant choice for an unmarried miss, but on Billie it was perfection. Her skin was like milk, her eyes sparkled, and her lips . . . He knew she did not color them—Billie would never have patience for that sort of thing—but somehow they looked richer, as if they'd absorbed some of the ruby brilliance of her gown.

He had kissed those lips. He had tasted her and adored her, and he wanted to worship her in ways she'd likely never dreamed possible.

It was odd, though; he had not heard her being announced. He was too far from the entrance, or maybe he had simply been too enmeshed in his own thoughts. But there she was, standing next to his mother, so beautiful, so radiant that he could not see anyone else.

Suddenly the rest of the world seemed like such a chore. He didn't want to be here at this dance, with people he didn't want to talk to and messages he didn't particularly wish to deliver. He didn't want to dance with young ladies he didn't know, and he didn't want to make polite conversation with people he did. He just wanted Billie, and he wanted her all to himself.

He forgot about Tallywhite. He forgot about pease, porridge, *and* pudding, and he stalked across the room with such single-minded purpose that the crowds seemed to melt from his path.

And somehow, amazingly, the rest of the world had not yet noticed her. She was so beautiful, so uncommonly alive and *real* in this room full of waxen dolls. She would not go undiscovered for long.

But not yet. Soon he would have to fight the throngs of eager young gentlemen, but for now, she was still his alone.

She was nervous, though. It wasn't obvious; he was sure he was the only one who could tell. With Billie, you had to *know* her. She was standing proud, back straight and head high, but her eyes were flitting about, glancing through the crowd.

Looking for him?

He stepped forward.

"George!" she said delightedly. "Er, I mean, Lord Kennard. How lovely and"—she gave him a hidden smile—"unsurprising to see you."

"Miss Bridgerton," he murmured, bowing over her hand.

"George," his mother said, nodding her head in greeting.

He leaned down to kiss her cheek. "Mother."

"Doesn't Billie look beautiful?"

He nodded slowly, unable to take his eyes from her. "Yes," he said, "she looks . . . beautiful." But it wasn't the right word. It was far too prosaic. Beauty wasn't the fierce intelligence that gave her eyes depth, and it wasn't the wit behind her smile. She was beautiful, but she wasn't *only* beautiful, and that was why he loved her.

"I hope that you have saved your first dance for me," he said.

Billie looked over at his mother for confirmation.

"Yes, you may dance your first with George," she said with an indulgent smile.

"There are so many rules," Billie said sheepishly. "I couldn't remember if for some reason I was meant to save you for later."

"Have you been here long?" Lady Manston asked.

"An hour or so," George replied. "My errand took less time than I'd anticipated."

"It was an errand?" she said. "I thought it was a meeting."

If George hadn't been so entranced with Billie, he might have had the wherewithal to muster irritation at this. His mother was clearly fishing for information, or at the very least, attempting to scold him retroactively. But he just couldn't bring himself to care. Not when Billie was looking up at him with shining eyes.

"You really do look beautiful," he said.

"Thank you." She smiled awkwardly, and his gaze fell to her hands, which were nervously riffling against the folds of her skirt. "You look very handsome as well."

Beside them, Lady Manston was beaming.

"Would you care to dance?" he blurted.

"Now?" She smiled adorably. "Is there music?"

There wasn't. It was some testament to how foolish in love he'd become that he did not even feel embarrassed. "Perhaps a turn about the room," he suggested. "The musicians will begin again shortly."

Billie looked to Lady Manston, who gave her approval with a wave. "Go," she said, "but stay well within sight."

George was jolted out of his dreamy haze for long enough to shoot his mother an icy look. "I would not dream of doing anything to compromise her reputation."

"Of course not," she said airily. "I want to make sure she's *seen*. There are many eligible gentlemen here tonight. More than I expected."

George grabbed Billie's arm.

"I saw the Billington heir," Lady Manston continued, "and you know, I *don't* think he's too young."

George gave her a look of mild disdain. "I don't think she wants to be Billie Billington, Mother."

Billie choked down a laugh. "Oh, my, I hadn't even thought."

"Good."

"She's Sybilla now, anyway," his mother said, demonstrating her talent for hearing only what she wished to. "And Sybilla Billington has rather a nice ring to it."

George looked at Billie and said, "It doesn't."

She pressed her lips together, looking highly amused.

"His surname is Wycombe," Lady Manston said. "Just so you know."

George rolled his eyes. His mother was a menace. He held out his arm. "Shall we, Billie?"

Billie nodded and turned so they were facing in the same direction.

"If you see Ashbourne's son . . ."

But George had already led Billie away.

"I don't know what Ashbourne's son looks like," Billie said. "Do you?"

"Bit of a paunch," George lied.

"Oh." Billie frowned. "I can't imagine why she'd think of him for me, then. She knows I'm very active."

George made a murmuring noise that was meant to convey his agreement and continued his slow promenade along the perimeter of the ballroom, enjoying the proprietary sensation of her hand on his arm.

"There was quite a line of carriages to get in," Billie said. "*I* told your mother we should just get out and walk, since the weather is so fine, but she was having none of it."

George chuckled. Only Billie would make such a suggestion.

"Honestly," she grumbled, "you would have thought I'd asked if we could stop off and see the King for a cup of tea on the way."

"Well, seeing as the palace is quite across town . . ." George teased.

She elbowed him in the ribs. But lightly, so no one would see.

"I am glad you did not wear a wig," he said to her. Her hair had been styled elaborately, as was the fashion, but it was her own, and only lightly powdered. He liked that the rich chestnut color shone through; it was Billie without artifice, and if there was one thing that defined her, it was that she *had* no artifice.

He wanted her to enjoy her time in London, but he did not want her to be changed by it.

"Dreadfully unfashionable, I know," she said, touching the long lock of hair that had been left to drape over her shoulder, "but I managed to convince your mother that there was a good chance I would step too close to a sconce and set myself on fire."

George turned sharply.

"Given my history being presented at court," she said, "it was not as unreasonable as it sounds."

He tried not to laugh. He really did.

"Oh, please do," she said. "It has taken me this long to be able to make a joke of it. We might as well be amused."

"What did happen?" he asked. "Or don't I want to know?"

"Oh, you want to know," she said with an impertinent sideways look. "Trust me. You definitely want to know."

He waited.

"But you won't find out now," she declared. "A woman must have her secrets, or so your mother keeps telling me."

"Somehow I don't think setting fire to the Court of St. James was the sort of secret she had in mind."

"Considering how fervently she wishes me to be seen as a young lady of grace and refinement, I think it might be exactly what she had in mind." She glanced over at him with an arch expression. "Lady Alexandra Fortescue-Endicott would never accidentally set someone on fire."

"No, if she did it, I imagine it would be purposeful."

Billie snorted back a laugh. "George Rokesby, that's a terrible thing to say. And probably not true."

"You don't think so?"

"Much as it pains me to admit it, no. She's not that evil. Or clever."

He paused for a moment, then asked, "It *was* an accident, wasn't it?"

She gave him a look.

"Of course it was," he said, but he didn't sound nearly as certain as he ought.

"Kennard!"

At the sound of his name, George looked reluctantly away from Billie. Two university friends of his—Sir John Willingham and Freddie Coventry—were making their way through the crowd. They were both perfectly pleasant, utterly respectable, and exactly the sort of gentlemen his mother would wish him to introduce to Billie.

George found that *he* rather wished to hit one of them. It didn't matter which. Either would do, so long as he could aim for the face.

"Kennard," Sir John said, approaching with a grin. "It's been an age. I wouldn't have thought you'd be in town yet."

"Family business," George said noncommittally.

Sir John and Freddie both nodded and said something along the lines of *just so*, and then they both looked over at Billie with clear expectation.

George forced a smile and turned to Billie. "May I present Sir John Willingham and Mr. Frederick Coventry." There were murmurs all around, and then he said, "Gentlemen, this is Miss Sybilla Bridgerton of Aubrey Hall in Kent."

"Kent, you say," Freddie exclaimed. "Are you neighbors, then?"

"We are indeed," Billie said prettily. "I have known Lord Kennard all of my life."

George fought a scowl. He knew she could not use his Christian name in such a milieu, but it still grated to be referred to so formally.

"You are a lucky man indeed," Freddie said, "to have such loveliness so close to home."

George stole a glance at Billie to see if she was as appalled by the sugary compliment as he was, but she was still smiling placidly, looking for all the world like a sweet-tempered, gentle debutante.

He snorted. Sweet-tempered and gentle? Billie? If they only knew.

"Did you say something?" she asked.

He matched her smile with one of his own, equally bland. "Just that I am indeed lucky."

Her brows rose. "How odd that I might have missed a sentence of such length."

He gave her a sideways look.

Which she returned with a secret smile.

He felt something settle within himself. All was right with the world again. Or at least all was right with this moment. The world was a bloody mess, but right here, right now, Billie was smiling secretly . . .

And he was content.

"May I claim a dance, Miss Bridgerton?" Sir John asked Billie.

"And me as well," Freddie immediately put in.

"Of course," she said, again so prettily that George wanted to gag. She didn't sound like herself.

"She has already promised her first to me," he cut in. "And the supper set."

Billie regarded him with some surprise, since she had not promised him the supper set, but she did not contradict.

"Nevertheless," Freddie said with smooth amusement, "there are more than two dances at a ball."

"I should be delighted to dance with both of you," Billie said. She looked about the room as if in search of something. "I don't believe there are dance cards this evening . . ."

"We can survive well enough without them," Freddie said. "All we must remember is that when you are done with Kennard here, you will dance with me."

Billie gave a friendly smile and a regal nod.

"And then you're on to Sir John," Freddie noted. "But I'll warn you, he's an atrocious dancer. You'll want to watch your toes."

Billie laughed at that, full and throaty, and once again she became so incandescently beautiful that George was half-tempted to throw a blanket over her, just to stop anyone else from wanting her.

He should not begrudge her this moment in the sun. He knew that. She deserved to be adored and fêted, to have her much-deserved moment as the belle of the ball. But by God, when she smiled at Sir John or Freddie, it looked as if she actually meant it.

Who smiled like that without actually meaning it? Did she have any idea what a smile like that could lead to? The two gentlemen were going to think she was interested. George had a sudden vision of bouquets filling the front hall of Manston House, of young gentlemen queuing up for the privilege of kissing her hand.

"Is something wrong?" Billie asked quietly. Sir John and Freddie had been distracted by another acquaintance and had turned slightly away, so her words were for George alone.

"Of course not," he said, but his voice was somewhat more clipped than usual.

Her brow pleated with concern. "Are you certain? You—"

"I'm fine," he snapped.

Her brows rose. "Clearly."

He scowled.

"If you don't want to dance with me . . ." she began.

"*That's* what you think this is?"

"So there *is* something!" Her expression was so triumphant; she really ought to have had a Pall Mall mallet in her hand to complete the look.

"For the love of God, Billie," he muttered, "it's not a competition."

"I don't even know what *it* is."

"You shouldn't be smiling like that at other gentlemen," he said in a hushed voice.

"*What*?" She drew back, and he wasn't sure if it was out of disbelief or outrage.

"It will give them the wrong impression."

"I thought the whole purpose was for me to attract gentlemen," she practically hissed.

Outrage, then. And quite a lot of it.

George had just enough presence of mind not to blurt out the spectacularly inane, "Yes, but not *too* much attention." Instead he warned, "Do not be surprised if they come calling tomorrow."

"Again, isn't that the point?"

George had no answer, because there *was* no answer. He was being an idiot, that much was clear to both of them.

Good God, how had the conversation deteriorated to *this*?

"Billie, look," he said, "I simply—"

He frowned. Arbuthnot was making his way over.

"You simply . . ." Billie prompted.

He shook his head, and she was smart enough to know that the motion had nothing to do with her. She followed his gaze over toward Arbuthnot, but the older gentleman had stopped to talk with someone else.

"Who are you looking at?" she asked.

He turned back and fixed his full attention on her. "No one."

She rolled her eyes at the obvious lie.

"Kennard," Freddie Coventry said, returning to their sides as Sir John wandered off, "I do believe the orchestra is retaking their positions. You had best lead Miss Bridgerton to the dance floor or I shall have to accuse you of shady dealings." He leaned toward Billie and said with faux confidentiality, "It will not do for him to claim your first dance and then keep you here among the wallflowers."

She laughed, but only a little, and to George's ears it did not sound quite true. "He would never do that," she said, "if for no other reason than his mother would have his head."

"Oh-ho!" Freddie chortled. "So *that's* how it is."

George smiled tightly. He wanted to throttle Billie for emasculating him so efficiently in front of his friends, but he was still very much aware of Arbuthnot, just a few feet away, presumably angling for a moment alone.

Freddie's voice dropped to a murmuring tease. "I don't think he's going to dance with you."

Billie looked over at George, and when his eyes met hers, he felt like he'd found his entire world. He bowed and held out his arm, because bloody hell, he'd been waiting for this moment for what felt like years.

But of course that was when Arbuthnot finally arrived. "Kennard," he said, his genial greeting exactly what one might expect from a man to the son of a friend. "Good to see you here. What brings you to town?"

"A dance with Miss Bridgerton," Freddie drawled, "but he doesn't seem quite able to lead her to the floor."

Arbuthnot chuckled. "Oh, I'm sure he's not as incapable as that."

George couldn't decide which of them he wanted to kill first.

"Perhaps I should dance with *you*," Billie said to Freddie.

Forget the gentlemen. He'd kill Billie first. What the hell was she thinking? This was forward, even for her. Ladies did not ask gentlemen to dance, especially when their acquaintance was of five minutes' duration.

"A lady who speaks her mind," Freddie said. "How perfectly refreshing. I see why Lord Kennard speaks so highly of you."

"He speaks of me?"

"Not to him," George bit off.

"Well, he should," Freddie said with a flirtatious waggle of his brows. "You would certainly be a more interesting topic than our last conversation, which I believe was about oatmeal."

George was fairly certain this was not true, but there seemed no way to protest without seeming childish.

"Ah, but I find oats fascinating," Billie said, and George almost laughed, because he was the only one who knew that she wasn't joking. Her father's recent successes at harvest was a testament to that.

"A truly singular female," Freddie applauded.

The orchestra began to make the groaning noises that always preceded the actual music, and Billie glanced over at George, waiting for him to repeat his bow and lead her into the dance.

But before he could do so, he heard Lord Arbuthnot clear his throat. George knew what he had to do.

"I give her over to you, Coventry," he said with a bit of a bow. "Since you are so eager for her company."

He tried not to meet Billie's eyes, but he couldn't quite manage it, and when his gaze passed over her face, he saw that she was shocked. And angry.

And hurt.

"Her next shall be yours," Freddie said with good cheer, and George's heart twisted just a bit as he watched him lead her off to dance.

"I am sorry to deprive you of the company of the lovely Miss Bridgerton," Lord Arbuthnot said after a moment, "but I am sure there was more purpose to your time in town than a dance."

There was no one else in their small circle of conversation now that Billie had trotted off with Freddie Coventry, but Arbuthnot clearly wished for circumspection, so George said, "This and that. Family business."

"Isn't that always the case?" He tilted his head toward George. "It's damned exhausting, it is, being the head of the family."

George thought of his father. "I am most fortunate that this particular privilege is not yet mine."

"True, true." Arbuthnot took a large swallow of the drink he was holding, a drink that looked considerably more substantial than the ridiculous punch George had been served earlier that evening. "But you will be soon enough, and we can't pick our families, can we?"

George wondered if Arbuthnot was employing double-speak. If so, it was another indication that he was not cut out for a life of mysterious messages and secret meetings. He decided to take Arbuthnot's words at face value and said, "If we could, I daresay I would have picked my own."

"Well, *that's* a lucky man for you."

"I think so."

"And how fares your evening? Successful?"

"I suppose it depends on how one measures success."

"Is that so?" Arbuthnot said, sounding slightly irritated.

George felt no sympathy. *He* was the one who had started this layered conversation. He could damn well let George have a little fun with it, too. He looked Arbuthnot in the eye and said, "Alas, we come to these events in search of something, do we not?"

"You are rather philosophical for a Tuesday."

"Normally I save my great thinking for Monday nights and Thursday afternoons," George snapped.

Lord Arbuthnot looked at him with sharp surprise.

"I haven't found what I'm looking for," George said. Good God, the double-speak was giving him vertigo.

Arbuthnot's eyes narrowed. "Are you certain?"

"As I can be. It's rather a crush in here."

"That is most disappointing."

"Indeed."

"Perhaps you should dance with Lady Weatherby," Lord Arbuthnot said softly.

George turned sharply. "I beg your pardon?"

"Have you been introduced? I assure you she is a woman without equal."

"We have met," George confirmed. He'd known Sally Weatherby back when she was Sally Sandwick, the older sister of one of his friends. She had married and buried a husband in the intervening years and only recently had moved from full mourning to half. Luckily for her, she wore lavender quite well.

"Weatherby was a good man," Arbuthnot said.

"I did not know him," George said. He'd been quite a bit older, and Sally was his second wife.

"I worked with him from time to time," Arbuthnot said. "A good man. A very good man."

"It has been years since I spoke with Lady Weatherby," George said. "I don't know if I'll have anything to say to her."

"Oh, I imagine you'll think of something."

"I imagine I will."

"Ah, I see my wife over there," Lord Arbuthnot said. "She's doing that thing with her head that either means she needs my assistance or she's about to die."

"You must go to her, then," George said. "Clearly."

"I suppose she'll need my assistance either way," Arbuthnot said with a shrug. "Godspeed to you, son. I hope your evening proves fruitful."

George watched as Lord Arbuthnot made his way across the room, then turned to carry out his mission.

It seemed it was time to dance with Sally Weatherby.

Chapter 22

◆—➤❋◀—◆

$\mathcal{M}$r. Coventry was an accomplished dancer, but Billie could give him no more than a fraction of her attention as he led her through the intricate steps of a cotillion. George had finished talking with the older gentleman, and now he was bowing before a lady of such staggering beauty it was a wonder all the people around her didn't need to shade their eyes from her miraculous glow.

Something seething and green churned within her, and the evening, once so magical, soured.

Billie knew that she shouldn't have asked Mr. Coventry to dance. Lady Manston would have had an apoplexy if she'd been there. She probably still would, once the gossip reached her. And it would. Billie might have avoided London for years, but she knew enough to realize that this would be all over the ballroom within minutes.

And all over town by the next morning.

She would be branded as overly forward. They would say she was chasing Mr. Coventry, that she was desperate for reasons no one quite knew, but she must have a wicked secret because why else would she throw over centuries of convention and ask a gentleman to dance?

And then someone would remember that unfortunate incident at court a few years earlier. Dreadful thing, really, they'd all cluck. Miss Philomena Wren's dress had caught on *fire* of all things, and by the time anyone knew what was happening, there was a pile of young ladies moored helplessly on the floor, unable to move against the awkward weight of their wide-hipped skirts. Wasn't Miss Bridgerton there? Hadn't she been on *top* of Miss Wren?

Billie had to clench her jaw just to keep from growling. If she had been on top of Philomena Wren, it had only been to put *out* the fire, but no one would ever mention that.

That Billie had also been the cause of the fire was still a closely held secret, thank heavens. But honestly, how could a lady be expected to *move* in full court dress? Court protocol demanded gowns with panniers far wider than anything women wore in day-to-day life. Billie normally had a wonderful sense of where her body stood in space—she was the least clumsy person she knew. But who wouldn't have had difficult maneuvering in a contraption that had her hips jutting out nearly three feet in either direction?

And more to the point, what idiot had thought it a good idea to leave a lit candle in a room populated with misshapen ladies?

The edge of her dress had been so far from her actual body that Billie hadn't even felt it when she'd knocked into the candle. Miss Wren hadn't felt it, either, when her dress began to smolder. And she never did, Billie thought with satisfaction, because _she'd_ been sensible enough to leap atop the other girl, smothering the flame before it reached her skin.

And yet when all was said and done, no one seemed to recall that Billie had saved Miss Wren from death and disfigurement. No, her mother was so horrified by the entire situation that they'd abandoned their plans for Billie's London Season. Which, Billie had tried to remind herself, was what she'd wanted all along. She'd been fighting against a Season for years.

But she hadn't wanted to win her point because her parents were _ashamed_ of her.

With a sigh, she forced her attention back to the cotillion she was apparently dancing with Mr. Coventry. She couldn't recall doing so, but she seemed to have taken the correct steps and not trod on any toes. Luckily she had not had to make too much conversation; it was the sort of dance that separated a lady from her partner as often as it brought them together.

"Lady Weatherby," Mr. Coventry said when he was near enough to speak.

Billie looked up with sharp surprise; she was quite certain Mr. Coventry knew her name. "I beg your pardon?"

They stepped apart, and then back together. "The woman Lord Kennard is dancing with," Mr. Coventry said. "Weatherby's widow."

"She's a widow?"

"Recently so," Mr. Coventry confirmed. "Just out of blacks."

Billie clenched her teeth, trying to keep her expression pleasant. The beautiful widow was very young, probably not more than five years Billie's senior. She was exquisitely dressed in what Billie now knew was the latest style, and her complexion was that perfect alabaster Billie could never achieve without arsenic cream.

If the sun had ever touched Lady Weatherby's perfect cheeks, Billie would eat her hat.

"She'll need to remarry," Mr. Coventry said. "Didn't give old Weatherby an heir, so she's living off the largesse of the new Lord Weatherby. Or more to the point . . ."

Again, the cotillion pulled them apart, and Billie nearly screamed with frustration. Why did people think it was a good idea to conduct important conversations while dancing? Did no one care about the timely impartation of information?

She stepped forward, back into Mr. Coventry's conversational sphere, and said, "More to the point . . . ?"

He smiled knowingly. "She must rely on the good graces of the new Lord Weatherby's wife."

"I am sure she will enjoy Lord Kennard's company," Billie said diplomatically. It wasn't going to fool Mr. Coventry; he knew perfectly well that Billie was jealous to the teeth. But she had to at least *try* to put on a show of indifference.

"I shouldn't worry," Mr. Coventry said.

"Worry?"

Once again, Billie had to wait for her answer. She stepped daintily around another lady, all the while cursing the cotillion. Wasn't there a new dance on the Continent that kept a lady and gentleman together for the entire song? It was being decried as scandalous, but honestly, could no one else see how very sensible it was?

"Kennard was not pleased to relinquish you to my care," Mr. Coventry said when he could. "If he has asked Lady Weatherby to dance, it is nothing more than tit for tat."

But that was not George's way. His humor might be sly, but his behavior never was. He would not ask one lady to dance for no purpose other than to make another jealous. He might have felt some pique, he might be furious with Billie for embarrassing him in front of his friends, but if he was dancing with Lady Weatherby, it was because he wanted to.

Billie felt suddenly sick. She shouldn't have tried to manipulate the situation earlier by saucily saying that she ought to dance with Mr. Coventry. But she had been so frustrated. The evening had all been going so well. When she had first seen George, resplendent in his evening clothes, she'd almost stopped breathing. She'd tried to tell herself that he was the same man she knew in Kent, wearing the same coat and shoes, but here in London, among the people who ran the country and quite possibly the world, he looked different.

He belonged.

There was an air of gravity around him, of quiet confidence and utter assurance of his place. He had this entire life that she knew nothing about, one with parties and balls and meetings at White's. Eventually he would take his seat in parliament, and she would still be the reckless Billie Bridgerton. Except that in a few years *reckless* would give way to *eccentric*. And after that it was all downhill to crazy.

No, she thought firmly. That was not what was going to happen. George liked her. He might even love her a little. She'd seen it in his eyes, and she'd felt it in his kiss. Lady Weatherby could never—

Billie's eyes widened. Where was Lady Weatherby?

And more to the point, where was George?

FIVE HOURS LATER George finally tiptoed through the front door of Manston House, tired, frustrated, and above all, ready to throttle Lord Arbuthnot.

When the general had asked him to deliver a message, George had thought—*How simple this will be*. He was already planning to attend the Wintour Ball, and Robert Tallywhite was precisely the sort of person with whom he might have an idle conversation. All in all, it would be ten minutes from his day, and he would be able to lay his head down that night knowing that he had done something for King and Country.

He had *not* anticipated that his evening would involve following Sally Weatherby to The Swan With No Neck, a somewhat unsavory pub halfway across town. It was there that he had finally found Robert Tallywhite, who appeared to be amusing himself by tossing darts at a tricorn hat pinned rather gruesomely to a wall.

Blindfolded.

George had delivered his message, the contents of which had not seemed to surprise Tallywhite in the least, but when he had attempted to take his leave, he had been compelled to stay for a pint of ale. And by compelled he actually meant *compelled*, as in shoved into a chair by two exceedingly large men, one of whom sported the most vivid black eye George had ever seen.

Such a bruise indicated a remarkable tolerance for pain, and George feared that this might correspond with a remarkable ability to *deliver* pain. So when old Violet Eye told him to sit down and drink up, George did as he was told.

He then spent the next two hours having a breathtakingly convoluted and inane conversation with Tallywhite and his henchmen. (Sally had disappeared immediately upon delivering him to the unfortunate neckless Swan.) They discussed the weather and the rules of cricket and relative merits of Trinity College versus Trinity Hall at Cambridge. They had then moved on to the health benefits of salt water, the difficulty of obtaining proper ice in summer, and whether the high cost of pineapples would affect the popularity of oranges and lemons.

By one in the morning, George suspected that Robert Tallywhite was not entirely sane, and by two he was certain of it. At three, he finally managed to take his leave, but not before "accidentally" taking an elbow to the ribs from one of Tallywhite's large friends. There was also a scrape on his left cheekbone, the provenance of which George could not quite recall.

Worst of all, he thought as he trudged up the stairs at Manston House, he had abandoned Billie. He knew this night had been important to her. Hell, it had been important to *him*. God only knew what she thought of his behavior.

"George."

He stumbled in surprise as he entered his room. Billie was standing dead center in her dressing gown.

Her dressing gown.

It was only loosely belted, and he could see the fine peach silk of her nightdress peeking out from underneath. It looked very thin, almost sheer. A man could run his hands over such silk and feel the heat of skin burning through. A man might think he had the right to do so, with her standing a mere six feet from his bed.

"What are you doing here?" he demanded.

Her lips tightened at the corners. She was angry. In fact, he might go so far as to say she was breathtakingly furious. "I've been waiting for you," she said.

"That much I'd surmised," he said, tugging at his cravat. If it bothered her that he was disrobing in front of her, that was her own problem, he decided.

She was the one who had taken up residence in his bedroom.

"What happened to you?" she demanded. "One moment you were foisting me off on poor Mr. Coventry—"

"I wouldn't pity him too much," George griped. "He did get my dance."

"You *gave* him your dance."

George kept working at his neckcloth, finally freeing it with one final yank. "I did not see that I had much choice," he said, tossing the now limp strip of linen on a chair.

"What do you mean by that?"

He paused, glad that he happened to be facing away from her. He had been thinking of Lord Arbuthnot, but of course Billie did not know—and could not know—of their dealings. "I could hardly do otherwise," he said, his eyes fixed on a random spot on the wall, "given that you'd asked him to dance."

"I did not precisely *ask* him."

He glanced over his shoulder. "Splitting hairs, Billie."

"Very well," she said, crossing her arms, "but I don't see that *I* had much choice, either. The music was starting and you were just *standing* there."

There was nothing to be gained by pointing out that he had been about to lead her to the dance floor when Lord Arbuthnot had arrived, so he held his tongue. They stared at each other for a long, heavy moment.

"You should not be here," George finally said. He sat down to pull off his boots.

"I didn't know where else to go."

He watched her intently, fiercely. What did she *mean* by that?

"I was worried about you," she said.

"I can take care of myself."

"So can I," she countered.

He nodded his *touché*, then turned his attention to his cuffs, pushing back the fine Belgian lace so that his fingers could work the buttons through their loops.

"What happened tonight?" he heard her say.

He closed his eyes, well aware that she could not see his expression. It was the only reason he allowed himself a weary sigh. "I wouldn't even know where to start."

"The beginning will do."

He looked over at her, unable to stop the wry smile that flitted across his lips. How very like her that statement was. But he just shook his head and said in a tired voice, "Not tonight."

She crossed her arms.

"For the love of God, Billie, I'm exhausted."

"I don't care."

That took him off guard, and for a moment he could only stare, blinking like some idiot owl.

"Where were you?" she demanded.

And because the truth was always best when possible, he told her, "At a pub."

Her head jerked back with surprise, but her voice was cool when she said, "You smell like it."

That earned her a grim chuckle. "I do, don't I?"

"Why were you at a pub? What could you possibly have been doing that was more important than—" She stopped herself with a horrified gasp, clasping her hand to her mouth.

He could not answer her, so he said nothing. There was nothing in the world that was more important than she was. But there *were* things more important than dancing with her, no matter how much he wished it were otherwise.

His brother was missing. Maybe tonight's absurd errand had nothing to do with Edward. Hell, George was certain it did not. How could it? Edward was lost in the wilds of Connecticut, and he was here in London, reciting nursery rhymes with a madman.

But he had been asked by his government to carry out this task, and more importantly, he had given his word that it would be done.

George would feel no compunction in refusing Lord Arbuthnot should he come with another fool's errand. He had not the temperament to follow orders blindly. But he had agreed this time, and he had followed through.

The silence in the room grew thick, and then Billie, who had turned away from him, hugging her arms to her body, said in a very small voice, "I should go to bed."

"Are you crying?" he asked, coming quickly to his feet.

"No," came her too-quick reply.

He could not bear it. He took a step forward without even realizing it. "Don't cry," he said.

"I'm not crying!" she choked out.

"No," he said gently. "Of course you're not."

She dragged the back of her hand inelegantly across her nose. "I don't cry," she protested, "and I certainly don't cry because of you."

"Billie," he said, and before he knew it, she was in his arms. He held her against his heart, and he stroked her back while her tears dropped one by one from her eyes.

She cried delicately, which seemed somehow unexpected. Billie had never done anything by half measure, and if she were going to cry, he would have thought she'd have done so with great big sobs.

And that was when he realized—she had been speaking true. She *didn't* cry. He had known her for twenty-three years, and he had never seen her shed a tear. Even when she'd hurt her ankle and had had to climb down that ladder on her own, she had not cried. For a moment she'd looked as if she might, but then she had steeled her shoulders, and swallowed her pain, and got on with it.

But she was crying now.

He had made her cry.

"I am so sorry," he murmured into her hair. He didn't know what he could have done differently, but that didn't seem to matter. She was crying, and every sniffle held the sound of his own heart breaking.

"Please don't cry," he said, because he didn't know

what else to say. "It will be all right. I promise, every-thing will be all right."

He felt her nod against his chest, a tiny little move-ment, but one that somehow was enough to tell him that she had turned a corner. "You see," he said, touching her chin and smiling when she finally raised her eyes to his, "I told you, it's all right."

She took a shaky breath. "I was worried about you."

"You were worried?" He hadn't meant to sound pleased, but he couldn't help it.

"And angry," she continued.

"I know."

"You left," she said baldly.

"I know." He wasn't going to make excuses. She deserved better.

"Why?" she asked him. And when he did not reply she stepped out of his embrace and said it again. "Why did you leave?"

"I can't tell you," he said regretfully.

"Were you with *her*?"

He did not pretend to misunderstand. "Only briefly."

There was but one three-pronged candelabra in the room, but there was light enough for George to see the pain flash across Billie's face. She swallowed, the motion trembling through her throat.

But the way she was standing, with her arms wrapped protectively around her waist . . . She might as well have donned a suit of armor.

"I will not lie to you," he said quietly. "I may not be able to answer your questions, but I will tell you no falsehoods." He stepped forward, his eyes boring into hers as he made his vow. "Do you understand? I will *never* lie to you."

She nodded, and he saw something change in her face. Her eyes grew softer, more concerned. "You're hurt," she said.

"Not very much."

"But still . . ." She reached toward his face, her hand stopping an inch short of its destination. "Did someone hit you?"

He shook his head. He'd probably acquired the abrasion when he'd been persuaded to have a pint with Tallywhite. "I don't remember, honestly," he told her. "It was a very strange evening."

Her lips parted, and he could tell she wanted to question him further, but instead she said, very softly, "You never danced with me."

His eyes met hers. "I regret that."

"I'd wanted . . . I'd hoped . . ." Her lips pressed together as she swallowed, and he realized he was holding his breath, waiting for her to continue. "I don't think . . ."

Whatever it was, she could not bring herself to say it, and he realized that he needed to be as brave as she was.

"It was agony," he whispered.

She looked up, startled.

He took her hand and kissed her palm. "Do you have any idea how hard it was to tell Freddie Coventry to go ahead and dance with you? What it felt like to watch him take your hand and whisper in your ear like he had a right to be near you?"

"Yes," she said softly. "I know it exactly."

And then, in that moment, it all became clear. There was only one thing he could do.

He did the only thing he *could* do.

He kissed her.

Chapter 23

Billie wasn't stupid. She had known, when she decided to wait for George in his bedroom, that this might happen. But it wasn't *why* she had done it. It wasn't why she had crept so silently into his room, turning the door handle with practiced ease so it slipped through the locking mechanism without a click. It wasn't why she'd sat in his chair, listening for sounds of his return, and it wasn't why she had stared at his bed the whole time, achingly aware that this was where he slept, where his body lay at his most vulnerable, where, should he take a wife, they would make love.

No, she told herself, she had come to his room because she needed to know where he'd gone, why he'd left her at Wintour House. And she was worried. She knew she would not sleep until he was home.

But she'd known this might happen.

And now that it was happening . . .

She could finally admit that she'd wanted it all along.

He pulled her against him, and she made no show of surprise, no feigned outrage. They were too honest with each other; they always had been, and she threw her arms around him, kissing him back with every fevered breath.

It was like the first time he'd kissed her, but it was so much *more*. His hands were everywhere, and her dressing gown was thin, the material far more silky and fine than her day dress. When he cupped her bottom, she felt every finger, squeezing her with a desperation that made her heart sing.

He wasn't treating her like a china doll. He was treating her like a woman, and she loved it.

His body pressed against hers, length to length, she felt his arousal, hard and insistent. *She* had done this to him. Her. Billie Bridgerton. She was driving George Rokesby wild with desire, and it was thrilling. And it made her bold.

She wanted to nibble at his ear, lick the salt from his skin. She wanted to listen to the way his breath quickened when she arched her body against his, and wanted to know the exact shape of his mouth, not by sight but by feel.

She wanted all of him, and she wanted him in every possible way.

"George," she moaned, loving the sound of his name on her lips. She said it again, and then again, using it to punctuate every kiss. How had she ever thought that this man was stiff and unyielding? The way he was kissing her was heat personified. It was as if he wanted to devour her, consume her.

Possess her.

And Billie, who had never much liked letting anyone take charge, found she rather wanted him to succeed.

"You are so. Unbelievably. Beautiful," he said, not quite managing to say it like a proper sentence. His mouth was far too busy with other pursuits to string the words together smoothly. "Your dress tonight . . . I can't believe you wore red."

She looked up at him, unable to halt the playful smile that spread across her lips. "I don't think white suits me." *And after tonight*, she thought naughtily, *it never would.*

"You looked like a goddess," he rasped. And then he stilled, just a little, and pulled back. "But do you know," he said, his eyes burning with wicked intent. "I think I still like you best in breeches."

"George!" She couldn't help but laugh.

"Shhhh . . ." he warned, nipping at her earlobe.

"It's hard to be quiet."

He gazed down at her like a pirate. "I know how to silence you."

"Oh, yes, pl—" But she couldn't finish the sentence, not when he was kissing her again, even more fiercely than before. She felt his fingers at her waist, sliding under the silky sash that held her dressing gown against her body. It came undone and then slipped entirely to the floor, the silky material shivering across her skin as it fell.

Goosebumps rose on her arms as they were bared to the night air, but she felt no chill, only awareness as he reached out reverently to stroke her, slowly, from shoulder to wrist.

"You have a freckle," he murmured. "Right"—he leaned down and dropped a light kiss near the inside of her elbow—"here."

"You've seen it before," she said softly. It wasn't in an immodest spot; she had plenty of frocks with short sleeves.

He chuckled. "But I've never given it it's proper due."

"Really."

"Mmm-hmm." He lifted her arm, twisting it just a bit so that he could pretend to be studying her freckle. "It is clearly the most delightful beauty mark in all of England."

A marvelous sense of warmth and contentment melted through her. Even as her body burned for his, she could not stop herself from encouraging his teasing conversation. "Only England?"

"Well, I haven't traveled very extensively abroad . . ."

"Oh, really?"

"And you know . . ." His voice dropped to a husky growl. "There may be other freckles right here in this room. You could have one here." He dipped a finger under the bodice of her nightgown, then moved his other hand to her hip. "Or here."

"I might," she agreed.

"The back of your knee," he said, the words hot against her ear. "You could have one there."

She nodded. She wasn't sure she was still capable of speech.

"One of your toes," he suggested. "Or your back."

"You should probably check," she managed to get out.

He took a deep, shuddering breath, and she suddenly realized just how much he was holding his passion in check. Where she was joyously setting herself free, he was waging a fierce battle against his own desire. And she knew—somehow she knew—that a lesser man would not have had the strength to treat her with such tenderness.

"Make me yours," she said. She had already given herself permission to let go. Now she was giving it to him, too.

She felt his muscles contract, and for a moment he looked as if he were in pain. "I shouldn't . . ."

"You should."

His fingers tightened against her skin. "I won't be able to stop."

"I don't want you to."

He drew back, his breath coming in shaky gasps as he put a few inches between their faces. His hands were at her cheeks, holding her absolutely still, and his eyes burned into hers.

"You *will* marry me," he commanded.

She nodded, her only thought to give her agreement as fast as she could.

"Say it," he said savagely. "Say the words."

"I will," she whispered. "I will marry you. I promise."

For about a second he stood frozen, and then before Billie could even think to whisper his name, he'd picked her up and practically thrown her onto the bed.

"You are mine," he growled.

She edged up onto her elbows and stared up at him as he stalked closer, his hands first tugging his shirt from his breeches and then moving to pull it over his head entirely. Her breath caught as his body was revealed. He was beautiful, as odd as that seemed to say about a man. Beautiful, and perfectly made. She knew he did not spend his days thatching roofs and plowing fields, but he must do some sort of regular physical activity because there was no softness to his form. He was lean and defined, and as the candlelight danced across his skin, she could see the muscles flex beneath.

She scooted up into a sitting position and reached out, her fingers itching to touch him, to see if his skin was as smooth and hot as it looked, but he was just beyond her grasp, watching her with hungry eyes.

"You are so beautiful," he whispered. He stepped closer, but before she could touch him he took her hand and brought it to his lips. "When I saw you tonight I think my heart stopped beating."

"And is it now?" she whispered.

He took her hand and laid it over his heart. She could feel it pounding beneath his skin, almost hear it reverberating through her own body. He was so strong, and so solid, and so wonderfully male.

"Do you know what I wanted to do?" he murmured.

She shook her head, too entranced by the low heat of his voice to make a noise of her own.

"I wanted to turn you around and push you right back through the door before anyone else saw you. I didn't want to share you." He traced her lips with his finger. "I still don't."

Heat flared within her, and she suddenly felt more daring, more womanly. "I don't want to share you, either."

He smiled slowly, and his fingers trailed down the length of her neck, across the delicate hollow of her collarbone, resting only when he reached the ribbon that tightened the neckline of her nightgown. Without ever taking his eyes from hers, he gave one of the strands a tug, sliding it slowly from the knot, its corresponding loop getting smaller and smaller until it finally popped through, and she was undone.

Billie watched his fingers, mesmerized, as they whispered across her skin, the edge of the now loosened bodice catching between his thumb and forefinger. The silk slipped from her shoulder, then slowly slid down her arm. She was so close to being revealed to him, but she could feel no modesty, summon no fear. All she had was passion, and the unrelenting need to follow it through.

She looked up, and so did he, almost as if they'd planned it. He caught her eyes with a questioning gaze, and she nodded, knowing exactly what he was asking. He drew a breath, its ragged sound speaking of desire, and then he nudged her nightdress over the rise of her breasts before allowing gravity to do the rest. The pale peach silk pooled luxuriously around her waist, but Billie didn't notice. George was staring at her with a reverence that took her breath away.

With a trembling hand, he reached out and cupped her breast, her nipple grazing lightly against his palm. Sensation shot through her, and she gasped, wondering how such a touch could make her abdomen clench. She felt hungry, but not for food, and the secret place between her legs tightened with what she could only assume was desire.

Was this how it was supposed to feel? As if she were incomplete without him?

She watched his hand as he caressed her. It was so big, so powerful, and so thrillingly male against her pale skin. He moved slowly, a stark contrast to the feverish kissing of just a few minutes earlier. He made her feel like a priceless work of art, and he was studying every curve.

She caught her bottom lip beneath her teeth, a little moan of pleasure slipping through her lips as his hand drew slowly away, teasing her skin until their only connection was his fingertips at her nipple.

"You like that," he said.

She nodded.

Their eyes met. "You'll like this even better," he growled, and then, as she gasped in surprise, he leaned down and took her into his mouth. His tongue rolled across her, and she felt herself tighten into a hard little bud—the sort she normally only felt in the chill of winter.

But she was the farthest thing from cold.

His touch was electric. Her entire body tightened, arching until she had to plant her hands on the bed behind her just to keep from falling over.

"George!" she practically squealed, and once again he shushed her.

"You never learn, do you?" he murmured against her skin.

"You're the one who's making me scream."

"That wasn't a scream," he said with a cocky smile.

She eyed him with alarm. "I didn't mean it as a dare."

He laughed aloud—although more quietly than she'd done—at that. "Merely planning for the future, when volume is not an issue."

"George, there are servants!"

"Who work for me."

"George!"

"When we are married," he said, lacing his fingers through hers, "we shall make as much or as little noise as we wish."

Billie felt her face go crimson.

He dropped a teasing kiss on her cheek. "Did I make you blush?"

"You know you did," she grumbled.

He looked down at her with a cocky smile. "I probably shouldn't take quite so much pride in that."

"But you do."

He brought her hand to his lips. "I do."

She lifted her gaze to his face, finding that despite the urgency in her body, she was content to take a moment just to look at him. She caressed his cheek, tickling her fingertips with the light growth of his beard. She traced his eyebrow, marveling at how such a straight, firm line could arch so imperiously when he wished. And she touched his lips, which were so improbably soft. How many times had she watched his mouth when he was speaking, never knowing that those lips could bring such pleasure?

"What are you doing?" he asked, his voice a husky smile.

Her lashes swept up as her eyes met his, and it was only when she spoke that she knew the answer. "Memorizing you."

George's breath caught, and then he was kissing her again, the levity of the moment giving way once again to desire. His mouth moved to her neck, teasing along the side, trailing fire in its wake. She felt herself descending, lying back against the bed, and then suddenly he was on top of her, skin to heated skin. Her nightgown slid past her legs, and then it was off completely. She was nude beneath him, without a stitch, and yet somehow it didn't feel awkward. This was George, and she trusted him.

This was George, and she loved him.

She felt his hands move to the fastening of his breeches, and then he swore under his breath as he was forced to roll off her in order to (in his words), "get the bloody things off." She couldn't help but chuckle at his profanity; he seemed to be having a much rougher time of it than she imagined was usual.

"You're laughing?" he asked, his brows rising into a daring arch.

"You should be glad I was already out of my gown," she told him. "Thirty-six cloth-covered buttons down the back."

He gave her a fearsome look. "It would not have survived."

As Billie laughed, one of George's buttons finally went flying, and his clothing fell to the floor.

Billie's jaw dropped.

George's smile was almost feral as he climbed back onto the bed, and she had a feeling he was taking her amazement as a compliment.

Which she supposed it was. With a healthy dose of alarm.

"George," she said cautiously, "I know that this *will* work, because, goodness, it *has* worked for centuries, but I have to say, this does not look comfortable." She swallowed. "For me."

He kissed the corner of his mouth. "Trust me."

"I do," she assured him. "I just don't trust *that*." She thought of what she had seen in the stables over the years. None of the mares ever seemed to be having a good time.

He laughed as his body slid over hers. "Trust me," he said again. "We just need to be sure you're ready."

Billie was not sure what *that* meant, but she was having a difficult time even thinking about it because he was doing very distracting things with his fingers. "You've done this before," she said.

"A few times," he murmured, "but this is different."

She looked at him, letting her eyes ask her question.

"It just is," he said. He kissed her again as his hand squeezed its way up the length of her thigh. "You're so strong," he said softly. "I love that about you."

Billie took a shaky breath. His hand was at the top of her leg now, spanning the whole width of it, and his thumb was very near to her center.

"Trust me," he whispered.

"You keep saying that."

His forehead rested against hers, and she had a feeling he was trying not to laugh. "I keep meaning it." He kissed his way back down her neck. "Relax."

Billie wasn't sure how *that* was possible, but then, just before he took her nipple in his mouth again, he said, "Stop thinking," and that was an order she had no trouble following.

It was the same as before. When he teased her this way she lost her mind. Her body took over, and she forgot whatever it was she'd thought she feared. Her legs parted, and he settled between them, and then *oh God*, he was touching her. He was touching her and it felt so wicked and so divine, and it just made her want more.

It made her hungry in a way she'd never been before. She wanted to draw him closer; she wanted to devour him. She grabbed his shoulders, pulling him down. "George," she gasped, "I want—"

"What do you want?" he murmured, sliding a finger within her.

She nearly bucked off the bed. "I want—I want—I just *want*."

"So do I," he growled, and then he was opening

her with his fingers, spreading her lips, and she felt him pressing at her entrance.

"I'm told it will hurt," he said regretfully, "but not for long."

She nodded, and she must have tensed up, because he once again crooned, "Relax."

And somehow she did. Slowly he pushed inside. The pressure was stranger than it was great, and even when she felt a light stab of pain, that was overshadowed by her need to keep him close, then closer.

"Are you all right?" he asked.

She nodded.

"Are you sure?"

She nodded again.

"Thank God," he groaned, and he moved forward, entering her more deeply.

But she knew he was holding back.

He was gritting his teeth and holding hard, and she would swear he looked like he was in pain. But at the same time he was moaning her name as if she were a goddess, and the things he was doing to her—with his member and his fingers, with his lips and his words—were stoking a fire that consumed her.

"George," she gasped, when the tightness within seemed to grab her from the inside out. "*Please.*"

His movements grew more frenzied, and she pushed back, the need to move against him too overwhelming to ignore. "Billie," he groaned. "My God, what you do to me."

And then, just when she was certain she could take no more, the strangest thing happened. She grew stiff, and she shook, and then the moment she realized could no longer so much as draw a breath, she shattered.

It was indescribable. It was perfect.

George's movements grew more frenzied, and then he buried his face in the crook of her neck, muffling his hoarse cry against her skin as he plunged forward one last time within her.

"I'm home," he said against her skin, and she realized it was the truth.

"I'm home, too."

Chapter 24

When George went down to breakfast the following morning, he was not surprised to learn that Billie was still abed.

She had not, he thought with some satisfaction, had a restful evening.

They had made love three times, and already he could not help but wonder if his seed was taking root within her. It was odd, but he'd never given much thought to having children before. He'd known he must, of course. He would one day inherit Manston and Crake, and he had a sacred duty to provide the earldom with an heir.

But even with all that, he had never *imagined* his children. He had never pictured himself holding a child in his arms, watching him learn to read and write, or teaching him to ride and hunt.

Or teaching *her* to ride and hunt. With Billie as their mother, his daughters would surely insist upon learning all the same skills as their brothers. And while he'd spent his childhood thoroughly annoyed by Billie's insistence upon keeping up with the boys, when it came to his daughters . . .

If they wanted to hunt and fish and shoot a pistol like a marksman . . .

They would hit the bull's-eye every time.

Although he might draw the line at jumping hedges at the age of six. Surely even Billie would now accept that that had been absurd.

Billie would be the *best* mother, he thought as he walked down the hall to the small dining room. Her children would not be trotted out once a day for her inspection. She would love them the way her own mother loved her, and she would laugh and tease and teach and scold, and they would be happy.

They would *all* be happy.

George grinned. He was already happy. And it was only going to get better.

His mother was already at the breakfast table when he entered the room, glancing at a recently ironed newspaper as she buttered her toast.

"Good morning, George."

He leaned down and kissed her proffered cheek. "Mother."

She looked at him over the rim of her teacup, one of her elegant brows set into a perfect arch. "You seem in an exceptional mood this morning."

He gave her a questioning glance.

"You were smiling when you entered the room," she explained.

"Oh." He shrugged, trying quell the bubbles of joy

that had had him nearly hopping down the stairs. "Can't explain, I'm afraid."

Which was the truth. He certainly couldn't explain it to *her*.

She regarded him for a moment. "I don't suppose it would have something to do with your untimely departure last evening."

George paused briefly in the act of spooning eggs onto his plate. He had forgotten that his mother would surely require an explanation for his disappearance. His presence at the Wintour Ball was the one thing she'd asked of him . . .

"Your presence at the Wintour Ball was the one thing I asked of you," she said, her voice sharpening with each word.

"I beg your forgiveness, Mother," he said. He was in far too good a mood to spoil it by quibbling. "It won't happen again."

"It is not *my* forgiveness you must obtain."

"Nevertheless," he said, "I would like to have it."

"Well," she said, momentarily flustered by his unexpected contrition, "it is up to Billie. I insist that you apologize to her."

"Already done," George said unthinkingly.

She looked up sharply. "*When?*"

Damn.

He took a breath, then returned to fixing his plate. "I saw her last night."

"Last night?"

He shrugged, feigning disinterest. "She was up when I came in."

"And when, pray tell, did you come in?"

"I'm not entirely certain," George said, subtracting a few hours. "Midnight?"

"*We* did not get home until one."

"Then it must have been later," he said equably. It was amazing what an excellent mood could do for one's patience. "I was not paying attention."

"Why was Billie up and about?"

He plopped four pieces of bacon onto his plate and sat down. "That I do not know."

Lady Manston's mouth clamped into a frown. "I do not like this, George. She must take more care for her reputation."

"I'm sure it's fine, Mother."

"At the very least," she continued, "*you* should know better."

Time to tread carefully. "I beg your pardon?"

"The instant you saw her, you should have gone to your room."

"I thought it behooved me to use the time to apologize."

"Hmmph." His mother did not have a ready response to that. "Still."

George smiled blandly and got down to the work of cutting his meat. A few moments later he heard footsteps coming toward them, but they sounded far too heavy to be Billie's.

Indeed, when a body filled the doorway a moment later, it belonged to the butler. "Lord Arbuthnot is here to see you, Lord Kennard."

"This time in the morning?" Lady Manston said with surprise.

George set his napkin down with a tight-jawed frown. He had anticipated that he would need to speak with Arbuthnot about the events of the previous night, but *now*?

George knew just enough about Lord Arbuthnot's dealings to know that they were inherently flavored with secrets and danger. It was unacceptable that he would bring his business to Manston House, and George would have no compunction telling him so.

"He is a friend of Father's," George said as he stood. "I will see what he needs."

"Shall I accompany you?"

"No, no. I'm sure that will be unnecessary."

George made his way to the drawing room, his mood growing blacker with every step. Arbuthnot's appearance this morning could mean only one of two things. First, that something had gone wrong after George had departed the Swan the night before and now he was in danger. Or worse, held responsible.

The more likely possibility, George thought grimly, was that Arbuthnot wanted something from him. Another message relayed, probably.

"Kennard!" Lord Arbuthnot said jovially. "Excellent work last night."

"Why are you here?" George demanded.

Arbuthnot blinked at his bluntness. "I needed to speak with you. Is that not why a gentleman usually calls upon another?"

"This is my home," George hissed.

"Are you saying I am not welcome?"

"Not if you wish to discuss the events of last night. This is not the time or the place."

"Ah. Well, I don't, actually. Nothing to discuss. It all came off brilliantly."

This was not how George would have described it. He crossed his arms, and stared Arbuthnot down, waiting for him to state his intentions.

The general cleared his throat. "I've come to thank you," he said. "And to request your help with another matter."

"No," George said. He did not need to hear anything more.

Arbuthnot chuckled. "You haven't even—"

"No," George said again, his fury cutting his words like glass. "Do you have any idea what I ended up doing last night?"

"I do, as it happens."

"You—What?" This was unexpected. When the hell had Arbuthnot learned of the farce at The Swan With No Neck?

"It was a test, m'boy." Arbuthnot slapped him on the shoulder. "You passed with flying colors."

"A test," George repeated, and if Arbuthnot knew him better, he'd have realized that the utter lack of inflection in George's voice was not a good sign.

But Arbuthnot didn't know him very well, and so he was chuckling as he said, "You don't think we'd trust just anyone with sensitive information."

"I think you'd trust me," George growled.

"No," Arbuthnot said with an odd, owlish solemnity. "Not even you. Besides," he added, his mien perking back up, " 'Pease, porridge, and pudding?' A bit of credit, if you will. We've more creativity than *that*."

George sucked in his lips as he pondered his next action. Tossing Arbuthnot out on his ear was tempting, but so was a well-thrown punch to the jaw.

"All in the past now," Arbuthnot said. "Now we need you to deliver a package."

"I think it's time you left," George said.

Arbuthnot drew back in surprise. "It's essential."

"So was pease, porridge, and pudding," George reminded him.

"Yes, yes," the general said condescendingly, "you have every right to feel abused, but now that we know we can trust you, we need your help."

George crossed his arms.

"Do it for your brother, Kennard."

"Don't you dare bring him into this," George hissed.

"It's a little late to be so high and mighty," Arbuthnot shot back, his friendly demeanor beginning to slip. "Do not forget that you were the one who came to me."

"And you could have declined my request for help."

"How do you think we go about defeating the enemy?" Arbuthnot demanded. "Do you think it's all shiny uniforms and marching in formation? The real war is won behind the scenes, and if you're too much of a coward—"

In an instant, George had him pinned against the

wall. "Do not," he spat, "make the mistake of thinking you can shame me into becoming your errand boy." His hand tightened on the older man's shoulder, and then abruptly, he let go.

"I thought you wished to do your part for your country," Arbuthnot said, tugging on the hem of his jacket to smooth it out.

George nearly bit his tongue, stopping himself from making an untempered retort. He almost said something about how he had spent three years wishing he was with his brothers, serving with his rifle and sword, prepared to give his life for the good of England.

He almost said that it had made him feel useless, ashamed that he was somehow judged to be more valuable than his brothers by virtue of his birth.

But then he thought of Billie, and of Crake and Aubrey Hall, and all the people there who depended upon them. He thought of the harvest, and of the village, and of his sister, who would soon bring the first of a new generation into this world.

And he remembered what Billie had said, just two nights earlier.

He looked Lord Arbuthnot in the eye and said, "If my brothers are going to risk their lives for King and Country, then by God, I am going to make sure it's a *good* King and Country. And that does not include carrying messages I do not know the meaning of to people I do not trust."

Arbuthnot regarded him soberly. "Do you not trust me?"

"I am furious that you came to my home."

"I am a friend of your father's, Lord Kennard. My presence here is hardly suspect. And that wasn't what I asked you. Do you not trust me?"

"Do you know, Lord Arbuthnot, I don't think it matters."

And it didn't. George had no doubt that Arbuthnot had fought—and continued to fight, in his own way—for his country. For all that George was furious that he'd been subjected to the War Office's version of an initiation rite, he knew that if Arbuthnot asked him to do something, it would be a legitimate request.

But he also knew—*now*, at last, he knew—that he was not the right man for the job. He would have made a fine soldier. But he was a better steward of the land. And with Billie by his side, he would be excellent.

He would be getting married soon. Very soon, if he had anything to do with it. He had no business running around like some sort of spy, risking his life without fully knowing why.

"I will serve in my own way," he said to Arbuthnot.

Arbuthnot sighed, his mouth twisting with resignation. "Very well. I thank you for your assistance last night. I do realize that it disrupted your evening."

George thought that he might have finally got through to him, but then Arbuthnot said, "I have just one more request, Lord Kennard."

"No," George tried to say.

"Hear me out," Arbuthnot interrupted. "I swear

to you, I would not ask if the situation were not so critical. I have a packet that needs to go to a posting inn in Kent. On the coast. Not far from your home, I should think."

"Stop," George began.

"No, please, allow me to finish. If you do this, I promise I shall not bother you again. I will be honest, there is some danger involved. There are men who know it is coming, and they will wish to stop it. But these are documents of vital importance." And then Arbuthnot went in for the kill. "It could even save your brother."

Arbuthnot was good, George would give him that. He did not believe for a second that this Kent-bound packet had anything to do with Edward, and he still almost blurted his assent the moment the general had stopped talking.

"I'm not your man," he said quietly.

That should have been the end of it.

It *would* have been the end of it, but then the door slammed open and there, standing in the doorway, eyes shining with reckless purpose, was Billie.

BILLIE HAD NOT meant to eavesdrop. She had been on her way down to breakfast, her hair perhaps too-hastily pinned due to her eagerness to see George again, when she'd heard his voice in the drawing room. She'd assumed he was with his mother—who else would be at Manston House this time in the morning?—but then she heard the voice of another gentleman, and he was saying something about the night before.

The night that George had said he could not tell her about.

She shouldn't have listened, but honestly, what woman could have pulled herself away? And then the man asked George to deliver a package, and he said it might help *Edward*?

She could not stop herself. All she could think was—*this was Edward*. Her dearest childhood friend. If she was prepared to fall out of a tree to save an ungrateful cat, she could certainly take a package to some inn on the coast. How difficult could it be? And if it was dangerous, if it was something that required discretion, surely she was an excellent decoy. No one would expect a woman to be making the delivery.

She didn't think. She didn't need to think. She just ran into the room and declared, "*I'll* do it!"

GEORGE DIDN'T THINK. He didn't need to think. "The hell you will," he roared.

Billie froze for a moment, clearly not expecting this sort of reaction. Then she girded her shoulders and hurried in. "George," she said entreatingly, "we're talking about Edward. How can we not do everything—"

He grabbed her by the arm and yanked her aside. "You do not have all of the facts," he hissed.

"I don't need all the facts."

"You never do," he muttered.

Her eyes narrowed dangerously. "I can do this," she insisted.

Good God, she was going to be the death of him. "I'm sure you can, but you won't."

"But—"

"I forbid it."

Billie drew back. "You *forbid*—"

That was the moment Arbuthnot sidled over. "I don't think we were properly introduced last night," he said with an avuncular smile. "I am Lord Arbuthnot. I—"

"Get out of my house," George bit off.

"George!" Billie exclaimed, her face betraying her shock at his rudeness.

Arbuthnot turned to him with a thoughtful expression. "The lady appears to be quite resourceful. I think we could—"

"*Get out!*"

"George?" Now his *mother* appeared in the doorway. "What is all the yelling about? Oh, I'm sorry, Lord Arbuthnot. I did not see you there."

"Lady Manston." He bowed properly. "Forgive my early visit. I had business with your son."

"He was just leaving," George said, tightening his grip on Billie's arm when she started to squirm.

"Let me go," she ground out. "I might be able to help."

"Or you might not."

"Stop it," she hissed, now pulling furiously. "You cannot order me about."

"I assure you I can," he shot back, his eyes burning down into hers. He was going to be her husband, for God's sake. Did that not count for anything?

"But I want to help," she said, lowering her voice as she turned her back on the rest of the room.

"So do I, but this is not the way."

"It may be the *only* way."

For a moment he could do nothing but close his eyes. Was this a taste of the rest of his life as Billie Bridgerton's husband? Was he destined to live in terror, wondering what sort of danger she'd thrown herself into *that* day?

Was it worth it?

"George?" she whispered. She sounded uneasy. Had she seen something in his expression? A sign of doubt?

He touched her cheek, and he looked into her eyes.

He saw his whole world there.

"I love you," he said.

Someone gasped. It might have been his mother.

"I cannot live without you," he said, "and in fact, I refuse to do so. So no, you will not be going on some ill-advised mission to the coast to hand off a potentially dangerous package to people you don't know. Because if anything happened to you . . ." His voice broke, but he didn't care. "If anything happened to you, it would *kill* me. And I'd like to think you love me too much to let that happen."

Billie stared at him in wonder, her softly parted lips trembling as she blinked back tears. "You love me?" she whispered.

He nearly rolled his eyes. "Of course I do."

"You never said."

"I must have done."

"You didn't. I would have remembered."

"I would remember, too," he said softly, "if you'd ever said it to me."

"I love you," she said immediately. "I do. I love you so much. I—"

"Thank *God*," Lady Manston exclaimed.

George and Billie both turned. He didn't know about Billie, but he'd quite forgotten they had an audience.

"Do you know how *hard* I've been working toward this? My *word*, I thought I was going to have to beat you with a stick."

"You planned this?" George asked in disbelief.

She turned to Billie. "Sybilla? Really? When have I ever called you Sybilla?"

George looked over at Billie. She couldn't seem to stop blinking.

"I have waited a long time to call you daughter," Lady Manston said, tucking a lock of Billie's hair behind her ear.

Billie frowned, her head moving from side to side as she tried to puzzle it all out. "But I always thought . . . you wanted Edward. Or Andrew."

Lady Manston shook her head with a smile. "It was always George, my dear. In my mind, at least." She looked over at her son with a considerably more focused expression. "You *have* asked her to marry you, I hope."

"I might have demanded it," he admitted.

"Even better."

George suddenly straightened, glancing about the room. "What happened to Lord Arbuthnot?"

"He excused himself when the two of you started declaring your love," his mother said.

Well, George thought. Maybe the old man had more discretion than he'd thought.

"Why was he here, anyway?" Lady Manston asked.

"It doesn't matter," George said. Then he looked at his fiancée.

"It doesn't matter," she agreed.

"Well," Lady Manston declared with a beaming smile, "I can hardly wait to tell everyone. The Billingtons are hosting a ball next week and—"

"Can we just go home?" Billie interrupted.

"But you had such a wonderful time last night," Lady Manston replied. She looked over at George. "She danced every dance. Everyone loved her."

He smiled indulgently. "I am not surprised in the least."

She turned back to Billie. "We can make the announcement at the Billington ball. It will be a triumph."

Billie reached over and squeezed George's hand. "It already is."

"Are you sure?" he asked her. She had been so apprehensive about making her London debut. He would like nothing more than to go home to Kent, but Billie deserved to revel in her success.

"I am," she said. "It was a heady thing. And it's

lovely to know that when I have to attend such functions that I can do it well and have a good time. But it's not what I love. I would rather be home."

"In breeches?" he teased.

"Only if I'm out in the fields." She looked over at Lady Manston. "A future countess must behave with some propriety."

Lady Manston chuckled at that. "You will be an excellent countess, although not too soon, I hope."

"Not for years and years," Billie said warmly.

"And you," Lady Manston said, looking at George with watery eyes, "my son. You look happier than I have seen you in a very long time."

"I am," he said. "I only wish . . ."

"You can say his name," his mother said softly.

"I know." He leaned down and kissed her cheek. "Edward is going to have to resign himself to missing the wedding, because I'm not waiting for him to get home."

"No, I expect you ought not," Lady Manston said, in just the right tone to make Billie blush ferociously.

"We will find him, though," George said. He was still holding Billie's hand, so he brought it to his lips and kissed his vow to her skin. "I promise."

"I suppose we're off to Kent, then," his mother said. "We could even leave today if that is your wish."

"Oh, that would be brilliant!" Billie exclaimed. "Do you think my mother will be surprised?"

"Not even a little bit."

"What?" Billie's mouth fell open. "But I hated him!"

"No, you didn't," George said.

She gave him a look. "You vexed me immensely."

"*You* were like a boulder in my shoe."

"Well, you—"

"Is this a competition?" Lady Manston asked in disbelief.

George looked at Billie, and when she smiled, it filled his soul. "No," he said softly, drawing her into his arms, "we're a team."

Billie looked up at him with such love it nearly stole his breath. "Mother," he said, never taking his eyes off his fiancée, "you might want to leave the room now."

"I beg your pardon?"

"I'm going to kiss her now."

His mother let out a little shriek. "You can't do that."

"I'm fairly certain I can."

"George, you're not married yet!"

He studied Billie's lips with the hot gaze of a connoisseur. "All the more reason to hurry things up," he murmured.

"Billie," his mother said firmly, transferring her attention to what she clearly considered to be the weaker link, "let's go."

But Billie just shook her head. "I'm sorry, but it's as he says. We're a team."

And then, because she was Billie Bridgerton and she'd never minded taking charge, she sank her fingers into his hair and pulled his mouth down to hers.

And because he was George Rokesby, and he was going to love her for the rest of his days, he kissed her right back.

Epilogue

Several months later
Crake House

"The results are final," Billie said, adding up the last column with a flourish. "I win."

George glanced up at her from his position on their bed—a large, lovely, four-posted piece that Billie had redressed in green a few weeks into their marriage. He was reading a book; Billie hadn't caught the title. He always read before they went to bed. She loved that about him. He was such a creature of habit. Another reason they were a perfect match.

"What is it this time?" he murmured.

She knew he was being indulgent, but she was so pleased by the numbers in front of her that she decided she didn't care. "The barley harvest," she said. "Aubrey Hall outdid Crake by a factor of . . . hold on one moment . . ." She chewed on her lower lip as she worked out another computation. "One point one!"

"Such a triumph."

She pursed her lips, trying for an unamused expression.

"Did you factor in Aubrey's greater barley acreage?"

"Of course!" She rolled her eyes. "Honestly, George."

His lips curved ever-so-slightly. "Might I remind you that you live at Crake?"

Billie felt herself smile in return.

"And that your name is Billie Rokesby now?"

"I'll always be a Bridgerton at heart. Well," she added, not liking George's frown, "a Bridgerton *and* a Rokesby."

He sighed. Just a little. "I don't suppose you've any plans to turn your formidable skills to the running of Crake."

Not for the first time Billie felt a rush of gratitude that George had not objected when she'd told him that she wanted to continue her work at Aubrey Hall. He was an uncommon man, her husband. He understood her. Sometimes she thought he might be the only person who did.

"My father still needs me," she said. "At least until Edmund is ready to take over."

George rose from the bed and walked over. "Your father's steward would be thrilled to finally earn his wages."

She glanced up. "I'm better than he is."

"Well, *that* goes without saying."

She batted him on the arm, then sighed when he leaned down and kissed her neck. "I should thank you," she said.

His lips stilled, and she felt him smile against her skin. "For what?"

"Everything, really. But mostly for being you."

"Then you're most welcome, Lady Kennard."

"I'll try to cut back a little," she said. George was right. She probably didn't need to do *quite* so much at Aubrey Hall. And the way they were going, she'd be pregnant sooner rather than later. She was going to have to learn to let go of her life at Aubrey, or at least loosen her grip.

She pulled back so that she could look at his face. "You wouldn't mind if I took a more active role here at Crake? With the lands, not just the house?"

"Of course not! We'd be lucky to—" He stopped, his words interrupted by a knock at the door. "Enter!"

The door opened to reveal a visibly agitated footman. "A messenger, my lord," he said.

Billie blinked in surprise. "This time of night?"

The footman held out a folded missive. "It's addressed to Lord Manston, but he's—"

"In London," George finished for him. "I'll take it."

"He said it was urgent," the footman said. "Otherwise, I'd never give over your father's private correspondence."

"It's all right, Thomas," Billie said gently. "If it's urgent, it's more important that it is attended to quickly than it is to deliver it to Lord Manston."

George slid a finger under the wax but did not break the seal. "Does the messenger wait for a reply?"

"No, sir. But I directed him belowstairs for a hot meal."

"Very good, Thomas. That will be all."

The footman left, and Billie fought the urge to go to her husband's side to read over his shoulder. Whatever was in the missive, he'd tell her soon enough.

She watched as his eyes scanned left to right, quickly reading the words. About four lines down his lips parted and he looked up. Her heart stopped, and she knew what he was going to say even before the words left his lips.

"Edward's alive . . ."